Introd the Apocrypha

Jewish Books in Christian Bibles

Lawrence M. Wills

Yale

UNIVERSITY PRESS

New Haven & London

Published with assistance from the foundation established in memory
of Henry Weldon Barnes of the Class of 1882, Yale College.

Yale University Press books may be purchased in quantity for educational, business, or
promotional use. For information, please e-mail sales.press@yale.edu (U.S. office) or
sales@yaleup.co.uk (U.K. office).

Set in Bulmer type by Integrated Publishing Solutions, Grand Rapids, Michigan.
Printed in the United States of America.

Library of Congress Control Number: 2020946416
ISBN 978-0-300-24879-1 (paper : alk. paper)

A catalogue record for this book is available from the British Library.

This paper meets the requirements of ANSI/NISO Z39.48-1992 (Permanence of Paper).

10 9 8 7 6 5 4 3 2 1

Contents

Acknowledgments   vii

Note on Abbreviations   ix

INTRODUCTION   1

ONE
Novellas   21

TWO
Historical Texts   88

THREE
Wisdom Texts   124

FOUR
Apocalypses and Visionary Literature   172

FIVE
Psalms, Prayers, and Odes   217

CONCLUSION   227

Notes   233

Bibliography   273

Index of Subjects   293

Index of Modern Authors   297

Index of Ancient Sources   302

Acknowledgments

WHEN I LOOK BACK ON THE PAST TWENTY years or so, I realize that the greatest influences on my studies of the Apocrypha and related literature arose from the sessions of the Wisdom and Apocalypticism group of the Society of Biblical Literature. I want to thank the other members of the Steering Committee, the composition of which, like the Apocrypha, has changed over the years. Their combination of creativity and high scholarly standards has been an inspiration. Another important influence has been my coeditor of the *Jewish Annotated Apocrypha*, Jonathan Klawans. I express my gratitude as well to the contributors to that volume. The *Jewish Annotated Apocrypha* exceeded the hopes of the two coeditors, in that the contributors managed to say something new about the texts on every page. I have many fond memories of teaching at Episcopal Divinity School in Cambridge, Massachusetts, and since then have felt welcomed and supported as the Croghan Bicentennial visiting professor at Williams College and visiting professor in the Program in Judaic Studies and Department of Religious Studies at Brown University. The collegiality that I experienced with faculty, staff, and students in each of those institutions will remain with me. Other scholars have influenced me as well on the issues of the Apocrypha, and I thank them: Joan Branham, John Collins, Sidnie White Crawford, Nathaniel DesRosiers, Angela Kim Harkins, Richard Horsley, Mary Joan Leith, Gregory Mobley, George Nickelsburg, Saul Olyan, Christine Thomas, Annewies van den Hoek, Benjamin Wright, and Gale Yee. Two scholars passed from our field far too early and are truly missed: Ellen Aitken and Daniel Harrington. I recall all of our time together with warmth and gratitude. Heather Gold, Jessie Dolch, and Joyce Ippolito of Yale University Press along with the outside reviewers and others on the editorial staff have been a joy to work with, and this book has been greatly improved as a result of their involvement. Finally, my family has been a constant support and has recognized the value in studying ancient texts: Shelley, Jessica, Daniel, Heloisa, and Emma.

Note on Abbreviations

IN THE TEXT AND NOTES THE ABBREVIATIONS for journal titles, series, and primary sources are found in *The SBL Handbook of Style* (2nd ed.; Atlanta: SBL, 2014). All other journal titles and series names are provided in full. Translations of passages from the books of the Western Apocrypha are from the NRSV unless otherwise stated. Translations from other works are noted.

Introduction to the Apocrypha

Introduction

THE GREEK TERM *APOCRYPHA* LITERALLY meant "things hidden" and often carried a negative connotation. In the West, Apocrypha has referred to those texts that were included in the Christian Old Testaments but were not part of the Jewish Bible and were as a result not included in the Protestant Old Testaments. Yet the inclusion of these texts in the Bible was unsettled and even hotly debated for the entire history of Christianity, and ambiguity about both the term "Apocrypha" and the texts to be included in this category has never disappeared. In the sixteenth century, when Protestants removed these texts from their Old Testament, they sometimes took up the term Apocrypha to fuel polemics against alleged Catholic error. How then do we refer to these texts? Should we avoid the embattled term and use instead the official one coined in the Catholic and some other churches, "deuterocanonical texts," meaning "second canon"? Deuterocanonical, however, was not a term used in the earliest Christian churches, introduced only in 1566 by the Catholic theologian Sixtus of Siena in response to Protestant challenges. And today, since the term Apocrypha is generally used in a neutral way, avoiding it does not seem so pressing. Even Catholic books on the topic use it; the Catholic scholar Daniel Harrington chose "Apocrypha" for the title of his book on these texts and used "deuterocanonical" only sparingly.[1] In this book, therefore, as in most others, I use Apocrypha as a neutral term. I note as well that although the term "Old Testament" in some contexts came to be viewed as referring to a lesser sacred text when compared with the "New Testament," this does not seem to reflect the view of the early church at the time when the texts of the Apocrypha were coming into the Christian Bible and the *only* "Bible" was the Old Testament.

1

The term Old Testament, in fact, *Palaia Diathēkē*, should perhaps be translated Ancient and Venerable Covenant. In this book I use the term Old
Testament to describe the first part of the Christian Bibles, with no judgment as to its relation to the New Testament. I make these observations as a
historian, not as a theologian.

Standing behind our discussion is the observation that "canon" and
"apocrypha" are ambiguous terms, much more so than most students or
even scholars realize. There has been a move in biblical studies away from
the traditional canonical views of ancient Jewish and Christian texts. Canons arose slowly and were not as fixed as later believers assumed. I am fully
in agreement with this trend to challenge the notion of canons, and I see this
book as an extension of that trend. I treat interesting Jewish texts that were
included in various Christian Bibles, but this book is also a discussion
about canon. In speaking of "Apocrypha," the varied, conflicted, and cul-
turally defined nature of the category becomes a critical topic. This book
is therefore a meta-canonical discussion of the Jewish texts that have been
added to and subtracted from Christian Bibles. Apocrypha is therefore in
some ways an artificial grouping of Jewish texts. In the ancient period, these
texts were spread throughout the other Old Testament texts, and there was
no sense that they belonged *together* until they were discussed as problem
texts. Of course, one could simply treat them as a second tier of the Old
Testament. The Apocrypha have indeed often been seen as less worthy, a
sort of "Bible Lite." Even Harrington, a highly regarded Catholic scholar
and priest, could say, "The wider canon was accepted. But the additional
books made little doctrinal or practical difference."[2] The Apocrypha were
often considered less important, both in the ancient period and today, and
it is striking to read Harrington's plea to readers to take the Apocrypha seriously, as also that of the Protestant scholar David deSilva. Why should
their pleas be seen as necessary? Other historians have also balked at ana-
lyzing the texts of the Apocrypha as a group, as if to caution us against the
canonizing of the canonizers. That is, one should analyze these texts individually in their historical contexts and not consciously or unconsciously
assume that the Apocrypha constituted a group of texts, were less theologically valid than the canonical texts, or were more theologically valid than

other Jewish texts outside the canon, often referred to as pseudepigrapha, or "false writings."[3] For this introduction, however, it is assumed that the Apocrypha are important historically and theologically and are compelling and entertaining both as individual texts and as part of an evolving canon.

The texts of the Apocrypha indeed have double or even multiple identities, in that they were Jewish texts preserved in Christian Bibles. This is a significant point—hence the subtitle of this book. The authors were Jewish, as were the first audiences. However, although some of the individual texts were known to later Jews, there is no evidence that they were well preserved by Jews or ever considered a part of the Jewish canon. The texts were most often interpreted by Christian scholars and authors as part of the Old Testament, and often in relation to the New Testament and later Christian tradition. Readers and scholars alike have brought Christian theological beliefs to them and have asked Christian questions of them. More secular historians have studied the texts of the Apocrypha in the context of ancient Jewish literature in general, but there has also been a growing sense among some scholars that the texts could be analyzed with an eye toward how they relate to Jewish, not Christian tradition. An attempt to accomplish this is now also found in the *Jewish Annotated Apocrypha*.[4] The attention to the Jewish origin, and in some cases continuing Jewish tradition, can be presented in tandem with the explicitly Christian interpretive framework of Harrington and deSilva. Yet although we may imagine three different groups of scholars—Christian, Jewish, or emphatically secular, in addition to Muslim, Buddhist, or other—the approaches may ultimately be mutually illuminating.

Despite a common assumption today that "Apocrypha" is a clear category—the books that are included in the Catholic Bible but not in the Jewish Bible or Protestant Old Testament—when we turn to the ancient period, we find that the Christian canon of the Old Testament was unsettled, and the Jewish canon of scripture as well. The notion of a clear canon was very slow to develop. By the turn of the Common Era Jews were perhaps closer to arriving at an agreed-upon canon, but some of the books now included in the Jewish Bible were almost excluded. The rabbis at times debated the inclusion of Esther, Song of Songs, and Ecclesiastes (*m. Yadayim*

4:5, *b. Megillah* 7b). Ben Sira was specifically discussed as a book that was not canonical, which in itself suggests that some Jews were reading it as authoritative (*t. Yadayim* 2:13). "In Jewish, Christian, and other religious traditions," says Annette Yoshiko Reed, "one typically finds a concept of Scripture, as well as a shared core of authoritative writings, long before efforts to enumerate its exact contents or police its precise boundaries."[5] What she suggests is that there existed a notion of an idealized, authoritative text even though there was as yet no clear demarcation of its contents. Tessa Rajak proposes that a better term than canonicity is centrality. This suggests a constellation with a center, but no clear outside boundary.[6] Canon is then a set of concentric circles. Also relevant here is the growing consensus that Jews did not perceive all the books of the Bible as equally authoritative. The five books of Moses were at the center, with histories and prophets and general writings in successively broader circles. The texts of the Apocrypha or other Jewish texts were sometimes read as circles beyond that but were often viewed with skepticism or even condemned.

We have seen, then, that not only is the term Apocrypha ambiguous, but the specific books that were included in that category varied as well. The extra texts included in the Old Testament varied enormously in the different Christian Bibles. This ambiguity becomes especially pressing when we note that most scholarly works on the Apocrypha arose in the West. Scholars often grant the varying extra texts of the Catholic and Greek and Eastern Orthodox Old Testaments, yet the important Christian Bibles from the East are ignored. The Ethiopic, Syriac (Peshitta), Armenian, and Coptic Bibles contain other additional texts that should also be considered when discussing Apocrypha. (There are other Eastern and Oriental Orthodox churches as well, but their canons are similar to those listed here.) It is striking that the most commonly used scholarly ecumenical Bibles, the *New Oxford Annotated Bible* and the *HarperCollins Study Bible,* treat the Apocrypha of only the Catholic and Greek/Eastern Orthodox Bibles. Texts such as 1 Enoch and Jubilees are found in the Ethiopian canon and 2 Baruch in the Syriac Bible. Scholars today sometimes simplify discussion by referring to the "Apocrypha of the Catholic Bible," but this implies that the other Old Testaments do not exist. A statement of John Barton reveals much about the Western scholarly tradition. He begins with an accurate characterization of the Ethiopic Bible: "In addition to including the deuterocanonical books of the Greek tradition, the Ethiopic Bible also recognizes Enoch and Jubilees, and the medieval *History of the Jews* attributed (wrongly) to Joseph ben Gorion [= Josippon]: taken together these works give the Ethiopic Old Testament a quite different character from the other canons." Yet he notes only the extra Ethiopian texts that have been deemed important to Western scholars, and interestingly continues: "In what follows we shall not deal further with this Bible, different as it is from those familiar in the rest of the world, but it is worth noting how differently the other canons might have developed given different circumstances: there is nothing predetermined about the contents of the Old Testament."[7] Barton registers the intriguing challenge of the Ethiopian Orthodox Bible, at the same time that it is expressly excluded from discussion.

Can the Eastern canons find a place in discussions of Christian Bibles? The groups that produced the Eastern Bibles were early, large, and important, today representing millions of members. There are about 40 million Ethiopian Orthodox Christians, 12 million Coptic Orthodox Christians, 9 million Armenian Christians, and 1.4 million Syrian Christians.[8] Including these texts from the Eastern canons reflects the growing interest in the global nature of religions, including Christianity. Limiting the consideration of Apocrypha to the Catholic and Orthodox Bibles resulted from a Western bias. The *Global Bible Commentary,* despite its title, surprisingly does not treat the Apocrypha at all.[9] There is also a racial aspect to this exclusion. The earlier discussions focused on European canons while ignoring Near Eastern, Eastern, and African canons. The discussion must be consciously expanded to become truly global and multiracial. Even the very concept of canon differs among Christians around the world. What does "Bible" mean in the narrow canon of, say, the Presbyterian Church, and in the broadest of the canons, the Ethiopian Orthodox Tewahedo Church? A similar question could be engaged concerning the Bible of the Samaritans— who, contrary to the assumptions of many, still exist—which includes only the five books of Moses; or the practice of Karaite Jews, who deny the oral traditions of Moses; or in other religions as well, such as Islam, Buddhism, and Indian religion.

This comparison of the Western and Eastern Christian churches also brings to light an important difference in the way that the extra texts were discussed. The debates about the texts of the Apocrypha—that is, the "problem" of the Apocrypha, and even the term Apocrypha—are really a Western concern. The issue of extra texts was rarely raised in the Syrian, Armenian, Ethiopian, or Coptic churches until the twentieth century. This distinction between Western and Eastern attitudes arose partly because the Catholic Church debated the theological value of the Apocrypha: Could these texts be used to settle questions of doctrine? In the Eastern churches, the Apocryphal texts were encountered more in liturgy; they were widely read aloud in services, hardly distinguished from the other Old Testament texts.[10] Given all of these ambiguities concerning the category Apocrypha, it is clear that writing a book on this topic generates all sorts of problems. But this book is *about* the problems. No problems, no book.

Jews in the Greek and Roman Periods: A Historical Summary

The books of the Hebrew Bible were likely composed in the ninth through second centuries BCE, under a range of very different political conditions. Israel was established as a kingdom by David in about the year 1000 BCE, and his son, Solomon, ruled successfully for about forty years. After that, however, the nation was split by two of his sons, and the north, often called simply Israel, and the south, centered in Judah (where Jerusalem was located), struggled against each other. Both halves were threatened by the surrounding great empires, Egypt and Assyria, and the northern half of Israel was defeated by the Assyrians in 721 BCE. The south, Judah, survived this incursion, but at the turn of the sixth century BCE it was defeated by the new empire on the horizon, the Neo-Babylonians. Responding to further rebellions in Judah, the Babylonians in 589 BCE destroyed the temple and exiled more of Jerusalem's leaders to Babylon and elsewhere. This was the beginning of the Babylonian Exile. In 539 BCE this empire was in turn defeated by Cyrus of Persia, who created an empire much larger than the previous ancient Near Eastern kingdoms. As Cyrus presented to the world the persona of a benevolent dictator, allowing more local autonomy, Judah found some measure of peace; it was allowed to rebuild the temple. But in

332 BCE a young Alexander the Great led a Greek and Macedonian force that swept through the eastern Mediterranean and Egypt and extended east to include Persia and part of India. He died in the process, and as a result his empire splintered into successor kingdoms. Judah, now called Judea, lay at the boundary between two of these Greek successor kingdoms, the Seleucids in Asia Minor and the Ptolemies in Egypt. Fortune favored first one and then the other, and Judea remained a buffer state between them.

How Judea ceased to be the pawn in this imperial struggle and achieve independence is a compelling story, treated in 1, 2, and 4 Maccabees and texts of the Ethiopian Bible, and that kingdom was "comparable in Jewish history only with the kingdom of David."[11] Under the Persians, religious worship had remained a matter of local custom, generally protected by the benign paternalism of the imperial rulers. But the form of Hellenization in Syrian-ruled areas imposed a new kind of local administration. Greek colonization, coupled with the philosophical ideals of a universal world order, called for a more thorough transformation of local customs. Greek cities founded colonies or reconstituted older cities by imposing the *nomima,* laws and customs, of the parent city. These included laws and a constitution, rituals, and a religious calendar. A *dēmos,* or roll of citizens, was established; a *boulē* or city council of aristocratic leaders was appointed; and a *gymnasium* and *ephēbeum* were constructed for the education of elite boys. A universal Greek education would ensure the inculcation of Greek values, and even native texts became increasingly modeled on Greek literature.

Hellenization proceeded quickly and successfully as a policy because it required changes on the public and constitutional levels, while allowing native customs to be observed on a private level. Some cities willingly embraced such a reconstitution, for instance, Samaria (the heirs of the northern half of Israel) to the north of Jerusalem. But whereas Samarians and Phoenicians in general were more willing to allow a mixing of religious symbols with Greek culture, Jews retained tighter boundary markers and did not bifurcate public and private practices to the same extent. The Maccabean Revolt (167–160 BCE) established the independence of Judea from the Seleucids, and the leaders of this revolt, the Hasmonean family—sometimes nicknamed "Maccabee"—established their positions first as high priests and then as kings. Many of the Jewish texts of this period either supported this new power structure in Jerusalem or opposed it. In Egypt, however, the large Jewish community remained under Ptolemaic control; some of the important texts of the period were composed there. There are thus two geographical zones for the texts (or three, if some of them were composed farther east) and three different languages: Hebrew, Aramaic, and Greek. In the first century BCE, the Greek successor states were pushed aside as Rome began its rise to dominance. When the Romans expanded their control over the eastern Mediterranean, they focused their sights on Judea as well. In 63 BCE, the Roman general Pompey easily defeated the Judean defenses of Jerusalem. True Hasmonean independence came to an end, although Jewish puppet kings and high priests were allowed to serve at the pleasure of Rome.

This short survey makes it clear that Israel continued to live out a boundary consciousness as a buffer state or province among the great empires—Egypt, Assyria, Babylonia, Persia—and on the boundary between the Greek successor states of the Seleucids and Ptolemies. Under Rome Judea was at times a vassal kingdom and at times a province; either way it stood once again at the boundary between the Roman Empire and the non-Roman East. A continuous history at the boundaries, or as a separate people within an empire, thus characterized Jewish consciousness, and this is reflected in the Apocrypha.

The Rise of the Greek Old Testament

Jews in Alexandria had long used a Greek Bible, but it is not clear how it arose or when. We begin with a legendary account, although it was accepted as factual by both Jews and Christians. The Hellenistic Jewish *Letter of Aristeas,* written in third- to second-century BCE Egypt, told the story of how the Greek translation of the five books of Moses came about. In the Egypt ruled by the Greek successors to Alexander the Great, one of the kings, Ptolemy II Philadelphus, was persuaded by the director of the famous library at Alexandria to invite seventy-two learned elders from Jerusalem to translate the five books of Moses into Greek. In this legendary retelling, they divided into teams to prepare translations, and after conferring and comparing, they arrived at a single translation. The legend contained in the *Letter of Aristeas* was bound to grow. "The role and purpose of [*Aristeas*]," says Sylvie Honigman, "was to turn the story of the origins of [the Septuagint] into a myth."[12] The Jewish philosopher Philo, writing in Egypt in the first century CE, considered the translation of the biblical books a perfect unveiling of God's mysteries (*Life of Moses* 2.37–40). This intellectual process in Alexandria did not spring up in a vacuum; there was a Hellenistic and Roman context. In a situation of ethnic competition among the ruled peoples, authors from the various ethnic groups often claimed a superiority for their histories. A genre of universal world history had arisen, often composed by intellectuals from the ruled ethnic groups, an attempt by the colonized to write a longer and truer history. The careful, simple translation of the Hebrew texts into Greek reads as both a triumph of Hellenism in Jewish life and a respectful preservation of the Hebrew text underlying it, a navigation between the colonizer and the colonized, creating what Rajak refers to as "a degree of sly subversion."[13]

The Septuagint very quickly supplanted the Hebrew text in Egypt and became a source for the Christians in the East who translated it into Syriac, Ethiopic, Armenian, Coptic, and other languages. Christians soon expanded the significance of the translation recounted in *Aristeas:* not only were the five books of Moses translated, but the entire Jewish Bible. The seventy-two elders were sometimes numbered as seventy, *septuaginta* in Latin, and the translation of the Bible came to be referred to as the Septuagint, abbreviated LXX. Scholars sometimes speak of "the Septuagint" as if it were a single text, but when the large codex versions were created, there was great variation, especially in the order of the books. It is important, then, to acknowledge that the common order in modern study Bibles is actually arbitrary, based on Alfred Rahlfs's 1935 edition of the Septuagint.[14] Further, the originally Jewish texts of the Apocrypha did not enter the Christian Bibles as part of a separate "deuterocanonical" group but were interspersed in various places among the other texts, considered by most Christian leaders as simply books of the Old Testament. (The placement of the Apocryphal books in the various early Christian Bibles can be observed in Table 1 below.) As a result, the present book is intentionally not organized by Rahlfs's arrangement or by the order of any one early Old Testament, but the texts are instead grouped by genre.

What then remains of the legendary account in *Aristeas?* The text romanticized the origin of the Septuagint, but it accurately communicates two things. First, the five books of Moses were probably translated into Greek before the other books and were held in greater honor. Second, Alexandria in Egypt was the center of Jewish study of the Bible in Greek. Yet scholars often disagree about the next developments. Robert Hanhart revived an older theory that the fervent scribal activity in Alexandria indicates that the Septuagint, *with the Apocrypha,* was created there first for a *Jewish* audience. Christians, he argues, took over this fuller Old Testament that was already in Jewish use.[15] Yet Hanhart likely exaggerates the *biblical* identity of the additional texts, and he does not allow for the possibility that some—actually, all—of the books of the Apocrypha were known at first as separate, independent texts. The few texts that are discussed by the rabbis are treated individually, not as part of a disputed group of texts, or as part of a Bible. Although the authors of the Apocrypha may have treated their texts as related to earlier Israelite texts (see, for instance, Judith or 1 Maccabees), they may have done so seeing their texts as independent and not as "biblical" texts. Neither the authors nor the first Jewish audiences likely thought of the new texts as biblical, yet because of their popularity, they may have been accepted by many Christians before bishops began to debate the issue. A similar dynamic occurred among Jews: Esther likely became a popular text before the rabbis deliberated its status. Still, the texts that became the Apocrypha were enjoyed by Jews and were readily available when the early Christians began to expand their Bible.

We must also take note of the physical form of the text itself. At first, there was no Christian *book* of the entire Bible, Old and New Testaments. The individual books of the Bible existed as scrolls, sometimes grouped, for instance, as the "five books of Moses." This changed with the invention of the codex format, the shape of modern books—that is, the texts of the Bible written on pages and bound on the left side. In the fourth century the Greek versions of the Bible known as Sinaiticus and Vaticanus appeared in this new codex format. These large Bibles included the Old Testament, with Apocrypha interspersed, and the New Testament, also a mixed canon. Another large version, Alexandrinus, and the comprehensive Latin version known as the Vulgate appeared in the fifth century. Both Jews and Christians continued to transmit scrolls, but the modern notion of "Bible," collected into one book, arose only with these versions. Regardless of the reservations harbored by some church leaders, these texts were now all visibly present in one big Bible and in church usage. A number of reasons might be offered for why the church now felt the need for the large codices, but one is especially suggestive. In the so-called Great Persecution of the church in 303–304 CE, Roman authorities collected and burned Christian books. Far from reducing the Christian focus on scriptures, this likely encouraged the notion of one big book as the embodiment of scripture and the banner of a persecuted church.[16] These large Bibles thus represented in one book the very notion of canon—even though they did not contain exactly the same texts. Be that as it may, Apocryphal texts were comfortably included in all of the fourth- to fifth-century Christian Bibles, interspersed among the texts of the Old Testament.

Debates on the Apocryphal Texts

The Apocrypha were not considered secondary simply because they were written after the Hebrew Bible. They are mainly later texts, but there is some overlap in dating. Daniel 7–12 (or at least 8–12), the latest part of the Jewish Bible, was likely written in the middle of the Maccabean Revolt, about 165 BCE, and some of the Apocrypha may have been composed before that: Tobit, the original version of Ben Sira, and parts of 1 Enoch. Nor were the Apocrypha considered secondary simply because they were written in Greek; Ben Sira, Tobit, 1 Maccabees, and perhaps other Apocryphal books were likely composed in Hebrew or Aramaic. In some cases, it is not clear why these texts were excluded from the Jewish canon. They were indeed Jewish texts, most of them were quite middle-of-the-road, and most were composed before the rise of Christianity.

Almost all of the ancient churches accepted the Jewish Bible as the basis of their Old Testament, but they included other texts as well. (An exception was the Marcionite Church, which rejected the Old Testament entirely.) Although the Jewish canon was still in a formative stage until the second to third centuries CE, there are several references that indicate a general agreement on the books. In 4 Ezra (2 Esd) 14:45–46, God tells Ezra to present to Israel twenty-four public books, to be used by both the worthy and the unworthy, but to "keep the seventy that were written last for the wise among your people." Twenty-four books is the same as modern Jewish and Protestant Bibles. The seventy books for the wise, however, is an ideal number of secret or revelatory texts, perhaps texts like 1 Enoch and Jubilees, popular in the Qumran community. Josephus probably knows a canon like the public canon in 4 Ezra, although he seems to join some books together and counts them as twenty-two. Among Jews, he says, "there are not thousands of books in disagreement and conflict with each other, but only twenty-two books, containing the record of all time, which are rightly trusted" (*Against Apion* 1.37). We must also note that in some cases, as here, the *number* of total books may have been considered more important to define the whole than the names of the texts so included; twenty-two is, after all, the number of letters in the Hebrew alphabet.[17] A similar focus on the number of books occurs in the Ethiopian canon. Be that as it may, not all Jews restricted the number of inspired texts, as 4 Ezra implies. Among the Dead Sea Scrolls at Qumran were found fragments of Ben Sira, Letter of Jeremiah, Psalm 151, and Tobit, but there is no indication how much authority they commanded. First Enoch and Jubilees were highly regarded at Qumran, perhaps even being authoritative "scripture" for the community. The rabbis later also introduced a negative term for "outside books," *sefarim ḥitzonim* (*m. Sanhedrin* 10:1), but this refers to *all* outside books, what have long been referred to as Apocrypha *and* Pseudepigrapha.

The New Testament never explicitly quotes a text from the Western Apocrypha, although Jude 14–15 does quote 1 En. 1:9. Some scholars have questioned whether Jude quotes 1 Enoch as fully scriptural, but for Jude, 1 Enoch is evidently as authoritative, prophetic, and canonical as any prophecy from the Old Testament.[18] There is also some evidence in New Testament texts of awareness of the theological themes of the Apocrypha. Romans

1:20–29 may reflect knowledge of Wisdom of Solomon (Wis 13:5, 8; 14:24, 27), and other parallels have been suggested. But these are vague and could be simply resonances of teachings that were gaining in popularity. Soon, however, early Christian authors began quoting the Apocrypha explicitly. First Clement 3:4, 27:5 quotes Wis 2:24 and 12:12, and at 55:4–6 it puts Judith forward as a positive example. Epistle of Barnabas 12:1 quotes 2 Esdras (4 Ezra) as "another of the prophets." Others followed in an increasingly rapid flow, yet it is possible that the texts we now know from the Apocrypha were being referred to as separate scrolls and not as part of the canon. In addition, the Muratorian fragment, composed in the third century, lists the books of the New Testament, surprisingly including the Wisdom of Solomon among them. This confirms the importance of the text, but as part of the New Testament, not the Old.

When the Western church fathers turned to a discussion of these texts, they could not come to a consensus. The term apocrypha itself was generally negative, often referring to what were since called Apocrypha and Pseudepigrapha, yet some ancient authors also referred to the extra texts as "ecclesiastical," that is, worthy to be used in instruction.[19] A negative view was expressed by Origen, but again, he may have been referring to *all* outside books, not just the Apocrypha. Melito of Sardis preferred the Hebrew canon from Palestine, which incidentally lacked Esther.[20] The fourth-century bishop Epiphanius saw these texts not as biblical, but as part of the more general history of Judaism and thus the pre-history of Christianity: "The Jews have two other books of disputed canonicity, the Wisdom of Sirach and the Wisdom of Solomon, apart from certain other apocrypha [*enapokryphōn*]. All these sacred books taught them Judaism and the observances of law till the coming of our Lord Jesus Christ" (*Panarion* 8.6.1–4).

Many aspects of the canon, then, were not rigidly fixed. Cyril of Jerusalem, also negative about the inclusion of the Apocrypha, introduced the notion of a second circle of texts, in Greek *deuteros,* although the exact term deuterocanonical came much later. When confronted with interpretations they considered heretical, some Christian leaders responded by imposing distinctions among the books. Athanasius, like Melito, limited the Old Testament to the twenty-two books of the Jewish Bible, equivalent to the present twenty-four, although he added Baruch and excluded Esther.[21] He also seems to have allowed some role for useful books beyond the Hebrew canon ("the others besides these"), but for him the term Apocrypha referred to the wholly external books that were potentially dangerous; Apocrypha were the creation of heretics. He and others also referred to *anaginōskom-ena*, "things read out," the texts that may be read in church settings (compare "ecclesiastical" texts). It also became common to distinguish books that were considered appropriate for theological doctrine and those that were acceptable for edification. The latter, it was assumed, could not be referred to in order to settle a theological dispute. Other church figures were more positive about the Apocrypha. Tertullian, who affirmed the idea that Christian prophecy was not closed as many believed but continued into his day, valued 1 Enoch; though popular among more radical and prophetic groups, it was not associated with the canon in the West. Clement of Alexandria, responding to the philosophical themes, was enthusiastic about Wisdom of Solomon, and Augustine expressed a broader view still, including the Western Apocrypha in general as scripture.[22]

When the councils of Hippo (393 CE) and Carthage (397 CE) affirmed the texts of the Apocrypha as part of the Bible, the question would seem to have been settled, but it was not. At the end of the fourth century, the Roman church moved to create a new, authoritative translation of the Bible into Latin, the Vulgate or "popular" Bible. Jerome was charged with this task, yet he himself had rejected the inspiration of the Apocryphal texts, revering rather the *hebraica veritas*, Hebraic truth. He opposed the inclusion of texts for which there was no known Hebrew text, and even though Hebrew texts of some of the books of the Apocrypha have since come to light, at the time Jerome was unaware of any Hebrew texts for most of the books. His reservations about the Apocrypha can be found in his introductions to Judith and Tobit in the Vulgate; he still valued these texts, but not as canonical. His remarks about Judith as a model for both men and women is telling. Jerome's use of terms also highlights their ambiguity. In his introduction to Samuel and Kings (called the "Helmeted Preface," *Prologus Galeatus*), he referred to the third section of Jewish scriptures, the *Ketuvim* or "Writings," as *agiografa* (Greek *hagiographa*), sacred writings, but *apocri-*

pha is used for the books not included in the Hebrew canon. In the introduction to Judith, however, *agiografa* evidently means what we call Apocrypha. His preface to Tobit also refers to Tobit as one of the "agiografa,"
that is, Apocrypha. Still, despite his strong reservations, the bishops pre-
vailed upon Jerome, and by about 400 CE he completed the translation that
would become authoritative in the Catholic Church, and this included the
Western Apocrypha.[23] But in summary we note that, although throughout
these debates the term Apocrypha was not used often—whether negative,
positive, or neutral—it was somewhat more common in Augustine (twenty-
one times) and Jerome (thirty-nine times). And while Augustine was positive about including these texts, he actually reserved the term Apocrypha
for books that in his mind were favored by heretics, what today would be
counted among the Pseudepigrapha.

By the Middle Ages some Catholic theologians still wanted to restrict
the Old Testament to the Jewish canon. The most famous example was the
fourteenth-century biblical scholar Nicholas of Lyra, who distinguished between the books of the Hebrew canon and the others. His efforts were satirized in a later Catholic play on words: *Si Lyra non lyrasset, Luther non
saltesset* ("If Lyra had not played the lyre, Luther would not have danced").[24]
At the end of the fourteenth century John Wycliffe published the first English Bible, which, though it included the Apocrypha, also contained a
notation that they were not canonical.[25]

At the time of the Protestant Reformation in the sixteenth century, the
issue of canon came to a head. While Luther downgraded the Apocrypha
because they were not part of the Jewish canon, he nevertheless retained
them in an appendix, establishing a pattern in Protestant Bibles. He continued to speak highly of the Apocryphal texts, and Paul Rebhun, whom he
had ordained, composed a drama of Susanna and asserted, probably accurately, that Luther recognized the authoritative nature of the text.[26] The
Presbyterian tradition was less welcoming of the Apocrypha than were the
Lutheran Church and the Church of England. Calvin accepted the Apocrypha as edifying reading material, but not as scripture. The Presbyterian
Westminster Confession in 1646 rejected the Apocrypha as sacred writings.

The Catholic Church responded to the Reformation challenges, and the Council of Trent (1546) settled the issue for Catholics by affirming the larger canon: "Anyone who does not receive these entire books as sacred and canonical" would be anathematized. The books of the Apocrypha had long been used in worship and would continue to be. Just as liturgical use had effectively canonized these texts in the Eastern churches with very little debate, so now in the Catholic Church. Passages from the Apocrypha were recited in relation to Mary (Sir 24:9–11, Jdt 13:18–20, 15:9) and in other liturgical contexts as well (2 Macc 12:43–44, Wis 3:1). Further, as noted above, Sixtus of Siena in 1566 coined terms to distinguish "protocanonical" and "deuterocanonical." Says John J. Collins, "The tendency to inclusiveness and to blurring the line between canon and tradition, remain typical of a Catholic as distinct from a Protestant sensibility."[27] Church figures in the East found less occasion to debate the inclusion of these texts. Patriarch Photios, in the ninth century, did not distinguish the Jewish canon from other texts. In general, one finds in all Orthodox churches "theologians both lay and clergy who consider the deuterocanonical books divinely inspired and of equal value to other Old Testament books."[28] But the Protestant challenge also had an effect even in the East, and pronouncements from the synods of Jerusalem and Constantinople (1672) were necessary to affirm the Apocryphal texts. The Russian church, for whom the challenges to the Apocrypha were less pressing, was not definitive.

It generally comes as a surprise that Protestant Bibles continued to include the Apocrypha in a separate section. Even the King James Version, which would become the most accepted English translation among evangelical Protestants, included them. It was not until the nineteenth century that the Foreign Mission Society of Britain began to omit the contested texts. From that point on, the Apocrypha were excluded from most Protestant Bibles. Conservative and evangelical churches continue to omit the Apocrypha, but even here there has been some interest in the Apocrypha as part of the Jewish background of Jesus.[29] An ecumenical trend of the late twentieth century also resulted in the creation of the *Revised Common Lectionary,* an ecumenical listing of biblical texts to be read in worship on particular days. Here the Apocrypha are included as Old Testament readings, although protocanonical readings are also listed as alternatives.

From this survey we see that the Apocrypha have remained boundary texts, met with ambivalence. Yet in every period, for every instance in which the Apocrypha were considered secondary to the main canon of scripture, cases can be found where they continued to resonate in people's lives. From literary references to art and music, the Apocrypha were treated with a sense of importance, as "scriptural family." For some theologians the Apocrypha were not equal to the main canon, but Christians in general did not insist on maintaining their secondary status.

Texts in the Different Bibles and Their Genres

The early versions of the Greek Bible already differed on the texts included and, just as important, on their order. To be sure, the seven extra books that were accepted in the Catholic canon—Judith, Tobit, 1 and 2 Maccabees, Baruch, Ben Sira, and Wisdom of Solomon[30]—were a sort of de facto secondary canon of Apocrypha, since they are common to most of the Bibles. But beyond that, there were variations. In addition to the seven texts, the Greek and Eastern Orthodox Bibles also included the following:

Greek Orthodox	**Eastern Orthodox**
Prayer of Manasseh	Prayer of Manasseh
Psalm 151	Psalm 151
1 Esdras	2 Esdras (= 1 Esdras)
	3 Esdras (= 2 Esdras or 4 Ezra)
3 Maccabees	3 Maccabees
4 Maccabees (in appendix)	

The Syriac Bible (Peshitta) generally contains all of the books of the Maccabees, 2 Baruch, 1 (3) Esdras, 2 Esdras (4 Ezra), Psalms 151–155, and Josephus *Jewish War* Book 6 (as an appendix to 4 Maccabees).[31] The Ethiopian Orthodox Tewahedo Bible includes, in addition to the Catholic Apocrypha, the Prayer of Manasseh, 2 and 3 Esdras, 4 Baruch (Paralipomena of Jeremiah), Jubilees, 1 Enoch, and the three books of the Meqabyan. It should be noted, however, that the Ethiopian Bible is quite fluid; there is no strict concept of which books are included in the canon. Some lists, for example, include Josippon, but there is no evidence that it was ever included as part of a Bible.[32] The name of the Meqabyan sounds like Maccabees, and indeed the content, though imaginative history, is superficially like 1 and 2 Maccabees. They are sometimes referred to as the Ethiopian Books of Maccabees. One might say that the Ethiopian Orthodox Church honestly embraced the idea of an ever-changing Bible while other Christian churches struggled to declare a strict canon that was, in reality, also changing. What we may conclude from these differences is that the Christian Bible, and the Jewish Bible to a lesser extent, had an accordion-like quality, moving in and out in various collections to include or exclude first one text and then another. Throughout we will also note the reintroduction of the narratives of 1 and 2 Maccabees, Judith, Esther, Daniel, Susanna, Josippon, and Jerahmeel into European Jewish culture in the medieval period and after. Even in Jewish tradition, midrash becomes a kind of Apocryphal addition to scripture, and Josippon became so popular among Jews that the version of Esther from Josippon, taken from the Apocryphal Additions to Esther, was inserted into some Hebrew Bible manuscripts as a supplement to Esther.[33]

The texts of the Apocrypha fall into the genres that had already been represented in the Hebrew Bible. It is noteworthy that there are no prophetic books among the Apocrypha, although 2 Baruch and Letter of Jeremiah are sometimes similar. Despite the fact that the Apocrypha can be matched with biblical genres, however, they exhibit some developments as well under the influence of Hellenistic and Roman culture:

Novellas: Greek Esther, Tobit, Judith, Bel and the Dragon, Susanna, Prayer of Azariah and Song of the Three (included here as part of the expanded Daniel novella), 3 Maccabees

History: 1 and 2 Maccabees; 1 Esdras; 1, 2, and 3 Meqabyan; Josephus *Jewish War* Book 6; Josippon (appears in some Ethiopian canon lists)

Wisdom texts: Ben Sira, Wisdom of Solomon, 4 Maccabees, Baruch, Letter of Jeremiah, 4 Baruch or Paralipomena of Jeremiah

Apocalypses and visionary texts: 1 Enoch, Jubilees, 4 Ezra or
2 Esdras, 2 Baruch
Psalms, prayers, and odes: Psalms 151–155, Prayer of Manasseh,
Odes, Psalms of Solomon

Table 1. Order of Books in the Three Earliest Greek Bibles

Vaticanus	Sinaiticus	Alexandrinus
Genesis	Genesis	Genesis
Exodus	Exodus	Exodus
Leviticus	Leviticus	Leviticus
Numbers	Numbers	Numbers
Deuteronomy	Deuteronomy	Deuteronomy
Joshua	Joshua	Joshua
Judges	Judges	Judges
Ruth	Ruth	Ruth
1, 2 Kingdoms	1, 2 Kingdoms	1, 2 Kingdoms
3, 4 Kingdoms	3, 4 Kingdoms	3, 4 Kingdoms
1, 2 Chronicles	1, 2 Chronicles	1, 2 Chronicles
1 Esdras		
Ezra-Nehemiah	Ezra-Nehemiah	
	Esther	
	Tobit	
	Judith	
	1, 4 Maccabees	
Psalms		
Proverbs		
Ecclesiastes		
Song of Solomon		
Job		
Wisdom of Solomon		
Sirach		
		Twelve Minor Prophets
	Isaiah	Isaiah
	Jeremiah	Jeremiah + Baruch
	Lamentations	Lamentations + Letter of
	Letter of Jeremiah	Jeremiah
	Ezekiel	Ezekiel

Vaticanus	Sinaiticus	Alexandrinus
	Daniel, Susanna, Bel Twelve Minor Prophets	Daniel, Susanna, Bel
		Ezra-Nehemiah
Esther		Esther
Judith		Tobit
Tobit		Judith
		1 Esdras
		1–4 Maccabees
Twelve Minor Prophets		
Isaiah		
Jeremiah + Baruch		
Lamentations + Letter of Jeremiah		
Ezekiel		
Daniel, Susanna, Bel		
	Psalms + Psalm 151	Psalms + Psalm 151
		Odes
		Job
	Proverbs	Proverbs
	Ecclesiastes	Ecclesiastes
	Song of Solomon	Song of Solomon
	Wisdom of Solomon	Wisdom of Solomon
	Sirach	Sirach
	Job	
		Psalms of Solomon

Table based on Greg Goswell, "The Order of the Books in the Greek Old Testament," *JETS* 52 (2009): 449–66.

ONE

Novellas

AFTER THE BABYLONIAN EXILE, A GROUP of entertaining texts arose among Jews characterized by courtly settings, women characters, humor and irony, and happy endings: Esther, Daniel, Tobit, Judith, and *Joseph and Aseneth,* most of these in multiple versions. Discovered at Qumran were also fragments of Tobit and a narrative similar to Esther called by scholars *Tales of the Persian Court.* We may also compare *Prayer of Nabonidus* from Qumran and the later and possibly Christian *Testament of Abraham* and *Testament of Job.* Comparable to these are also the historical novellas *Tobiad Romance* and *Royal Family of Adiabene* (from Josephus, *Antiquities,* Books 12 and 20), Artapanus, and in the present volume 3 Maccabees and the court narrative contained at 1 Esd 3:1–5:6. By genre, the Jewish novellas are similar to the ancient Greek and Roman novels, but we refer to them as novellas simply to emphasize that they are shorter than the novels and more informally constructed. The Jewish historical novellas are also similar to the *Alexander Romance* and the Assyrian/Aramaean *Story of Ahikar.* Some of the Jewish texts are preserved in multiple versions, and the order and even the dates of the various texts are known more precisely than is the case with many other texts. As a result, the progressive development of this genre can be reconstructed in more detail than is typically the case.

The grouping of these texts together is not solely a result of modern scholarly studies. There is some evidence that the Jewish novellas were viewed as similar in the ancient world. At Qumran, novelistic texts were written on smaller scrolls, what one scholar referred to as the "paperbacks of antiquity."[1] The ancient Greek Bibles placed Esther, Tobit, and Judith together. There are also reasons to assume that the first audiences viewed them as fictitious entertainments, not history. First, there are patently false kings and queens—"Darius the Mede" in Daniel (Darius was a famous Persian king), "Nebuchadnezzar king of the Assyrians" in Judith (Nebuchadnezzar was a famous Babylonian king), and "Esther queen of Persia" (there was no Jewish queen of Persia). Second, the novellas feature whimsical plot devices and outrageous resolutions of threats and dangers. Third, the happily-ever-after endings of novellas provide a closure that differs from the histories (see the introduction to Chapter 2). One might argue, of course, that as there was no word for novel, nor clear discourse on fiction, the genre could scarcely have been recognized as a separate or clear entity. However, the same can be said for almost all popular genres: they are difficult to define clearly and often lack a common genre name until well after their golden age. Ancient novels, and Jewish novellas as well, present no greater problems in definition than do other genres.

History and novels look similar in that they both consist of a prose narrative about events. In the case of history, it is assumed that the events really occurred, and in the case of novellas, that they did not. But how did the ancients understand the difference between history and fiction? Greek rhetoricians and grammarians, influenced by Plato and Aristotle, divided narrative into three types: (1) *historia,* a true account of events that actually occurred; (2) *plasma* or *argumentum,* an account narrating events that did not occur but are like real events; and (3) *mythos* or *fabula,* an account that narrates events that are not true and not similar to real events. *Plasma* would then come closest to what we would call novel, and *mythos* to myth or fantasy.[2] Yet if the novellas were enjoyed as fictions, how did they come so quickly to be considered "Bible" and also history? It is not clear how this happened, but it may have occurred because the protagonists became models of virtue. Already in about 100 CE Judith and Esther were recommended as models for their courage (1 Clem. 55:4-6), and Jonah, Daniel, his three companions, and Susanna were soon treated in Christian art as heroes and heroines of the faith. By the third century CE Esther and Mordecai adorned the synagogue at Dura Europos. Their personal stories were so powerful—thanks to the novellas—that the texts provided models for a new, more independent moral agent. In addition, as soon as Jewish authors began to write a connected, universal world history (see especially *Seder Olam Rabbah*

28–29), they found that the books of Daniel and Esther were necessary to fill in the gaps left by other biblical books.

The background of some of the Jewish novellas lies in the stories of the ancient Near East, especially the wisdom court narratives. There are Persian and Egyptian precedents, and especially close is the Aramaic *Story of Ahikar*. Among Jews, the Joseph story of Genesis 37–50 was set in a royal court, and Esther, Daniel 1–6, Bel and the Dragon, and 1 Esdras 3:1–5:6 were as well, while Susanna was set in a local Jewish court.[3] Tobit also begins in a way similar to the court narratives. The moral structure of some of these court narratives—the narrative of the persecuted righteous person—can be represented in this way:

1. The protagonist begins among equals in the court of the king; there is a false sense of stability.
2. *Either* the protagonist *or* the antagonist ascends within the court, causing instability.
3. An edict or demand is announced putting the protagonist in danger.
4. The protagonist defies the edict in an act of courage and virtue.
5. Other courtiers conspire against the protagonist.
6. The execution of the protagonist is announced and attempted.
7. The protagonist escapes death and is vindicated.
8. The antagonist is punished by his own device.
9. The protagonist is promoted in court, resulting in true stability.

A similar moral theme can be found in Wisdom of Solomon 2–5, and it surfaces as well in the structure of the Christian gospels.[4] Daniel, Esther, and Tobit likely grew by stages and indicate that the novelistic growth can occur by the assembling of shorter pieces of story tradition to form a lengthening novella.

The Jewish novellas must also be compared to the somewhat later, fully developed Greek and Roman novels. Well studied now are the "canon" of five Greek and two Roman novels: Chariton, *Chaereas and Callirhoe;*

Xenophon of Ephesus, *An Ephesian Story;* Achilles Tatius, *Leucippe and Clitophon;* Heliodorus, *An Ethiopian Story;* Longus, *Daphnis and Chloe;* Apuleius, *Golden Ass;* and Petronius, *Satyricon.* In addition, a vast constellation of near-novels has also been compared with these.[5] They cannot be treated here, but it should be noted that among the earlier near-novels there are perhaps closer points of similarity to the Jewish novellas. *Alexander Romance, Ninus Romance,* and *Life of Aesop* can be considered along with the Jewish novellas as part of an eastern Hellenistic exploration of the possibilities of entertaining narrative, arising *before* the Greek novels proper.

The Jewish novellas should be analyzed as "popular literature." There was no mass production of texts in the ancient world, and literacy was limited to the elite and to certain professions, yet we nevertheless witness the proliferation and transmission of some entertaining texts across national and linguistic barriers. This is partly indicated by the wide variety of textual versions of, say, *Story of Ahikar, Alexander Romance, Aesop,* Esther, Daniel, and others. Entertaining texts were likely performed as well as read and may have had a social function in festivals and dinner entertainments for the wealthy. In the ancient world, "popular literature" does not refer to the number of readers, but to the text's function.[6] Popular literature is text that no one *has* to read. These texts were transmitted without official sponsorship, even if some of them later become "biblical." The novel cross-culturally exhibits certain characteristics that are related to its origins in popular as opposed to official literature: the exploration of emotions, interior reflection, immediacy of impact, an indifference to elite conventions, repetition of common *topoi* and clichés, unequivocally happy endings, women characters, a lack of elite restraint, and theatricality. Indeed, Judith, Esther, 3 Maccabees, and Tobit all may have been associated with *actual* theatricality and performativity, if the first three were performance pieces for festivals and Tobit for a wedding celebration in the Tobiad family. But be that as it may, the frivolity of the texts also speaks to the experiences of pious Jews living in the dominant empires. The audiences likely felt threatened as Jews who wanted to maintain their commitment to God's law.

Jewish novellas are often compared to Greek novels, but this raises a recurring problem of interpretation. The Greek novels came to be perceived by modern scholars as the "Platonic form" of ancient novelistic literature because they were longer and fully developed, with an overarching plotline: a surpassingly beautiful young male and female protagonist from wealthy families fall in love, are separated by plot entanglements and exposed to every danger and degradation, and are reunited in their home city to begin an ideal family life. The Jewish novellas lack this romantic coupling that provides the foundation of a new family, but perhaps the difference is not so great. The Jewish novellas feature a pious woman who is connected to an extended family and often to an elder male relative. As in the Greek novels, she is forced out of her domestic protection but in the end often becomes actively involved in saving the larger body of Jews. The role of young women, and the protection of young women, is a theme of novels cross-culturally—not only in ancient Greek novels and Jewish novellas, but in the earliest English and French novels. The novel genre cross-culturally may arise out of the anxiety of the father for the family and the protection of the family's women (see Ben Sira). But the problem of interpretation noted above is this: the Jewish novellas are often considered derivative versions of the Greek novels, even poor imitations of their more sophisticated cousins, even though they predate the Greek novels by several centuries. It is very difficult, even for scholars, to imagine the Jewish texts as creative and imaginative if the "Platonic form" of the novel lies in the future. Any comparison between them, then, requires a conscious effort to keep the order of the two in view.

Yet compare we must. The Jewish novellas and the Greek novels both emphasize inner thoughts and emotions, reflections and doubts, tensions and resolutions, often presented through the eyes of the female protagonist. The later Greek novels would take the point of view of both the female and male protagonists, but the Jewish novellas favor that of the woman. We could pause at almost any point in the Jewish novellas to find examples of this—even Haman's wife Zeresh at Esth 6:13—but we notice especially the highly charged woman's prayer scene, centrally placed in Judith 9, Greek Esth 14:1–15:5, and *Aseneth* 10:9–17, 14:14–15. Here a woman does not simply pray to God—men also pray in Israelite narrative—but she engages in an undressing-and-redressing scene, accompanied by a full prayer that in Greek

Esther and *Aseneth* signals, first, a personal transformation and, second, an acceptance of God's mission for her. Long ago Arnold van Gennep and Victor Turner spoke of "rites of initiation" that consisted of three parts: separation from society, a liminal period that might include openness or communion with the divine, and reintegration into society with a new status.[7] The woman's prayer scenes in Judith, Greek Esther, and *Aseneth* all partake of the rite of initiation and exhibit a balanced V pattern. At the center, in the liminal stage, is the female protagonist's prayer, presented as a spontaneous, heartfelt communication:

Rends self *	* Emerges for mission
Takes off beautiful garments *	* Puts on beautiful garments
Puts on mourning garments *	* Takes off mourning garments
Puts ashes on head *	* Bathes
	*
	Prays

This observation calls to mind two other themes of the Jewish novellas. First, the novellas contribute to the stronger emphasis during this period on an ideal moral agent. The Hebrew Bible had included very powerful ideal figures: the patriarchs, Moses, David, Solomon. But in the novellas we find morally righteous figures who were not raised so far above the audience: Daniel, Susanna, Judith, Esther, Tobit, and Sarah. Second, corresponding to this turn to a more down-to-earth moral agent is the use of the term "Jew" or "Judean." A surprising aspect of the Israelite literature of this period is that the word translated as "Jew" or "Judean"—masculine *Yehudi* and feminine *Yehudiyah,* and their equivalents in Aramaic, Greek, Latin, and other languages—is relatively rare until after the turn of the Common Era, when the New Testament, Josephus, and Philo use them often, likely because of Roman usage. It is a question still in need of an adequate explanation: Why were the terms for "Jew" and "Judaism" so rare in ancient Judaism? But although the word for Jew was rare before the turn of the era, it did occur in very interesting passages. It appears often in 2 Maccabees, where it is invested with a stronger rhetorical power (see Chapter 2).[8] This is an interesting observation by itself, but just as important is the fact that

Yehudi/Ioudaios occurs in every single novelistic text except for Tobit. In these texts the term is generally emphasized as a strong identity marker. Other short narratives related to the novellas also use the term: 3 Maccabees, *Tales of the Persian Court* and *Prayer of Nabonidus* from Qumran, the court narrative interlude in 1 Esd 3:1–5:6, and the story of Mosollamus the Jewish archer in Josephus, *Against Apion* 1.201–3. The freer nature of the novellas allowed them to become the vehicle for asserting "Jewish" identity in the Hellenistic empires.

Greek Esther

The book of Esther in the Hebrew Bible, long associated with the Jewish festival of Purim, was a court narrative similar to the Joseph story in Genesis 37–50, Daniel 1–6, Bel and the Dragon, Susanna, and the Assyrian *Story of Ahikar*. It exhibits a number of developments in the direction of the novella: it is focused on a female protagonist in the interior world of the palace, with more humor and greater emphasis on the psychological states of that protagonist. The version of Esther in the Apocrypha, which we will call Greek Esther, has moved even farther in this novelistic direction, with the addition of six significant supplements labeled A–F below. They exhibit a roughly chiastic structure, that is, an arrangement in which each motif is matched by a similar motif, but in reverse order:

A. A pseudo-apocalyptic dream scene foreshadowing the drama to come
    B. Wording of Haman's edict announcing destruction of the Jews
        C. Prayers by Mordecai and Esther
        D. Details of Esther's audience before the king
    E. Wording of Mordecai's edict canceling Haman's earlier edict
F. The final interpretation of Mordecai's earlier dream

For the Vulgate edition, Jerome removed these additions and gathered them at the end, where they received the chapter numbers 11–16. In modern Bibles, then, where the additions are once again placed in the story, the chapter numbers are out of order.

These Additions to Esther, says Sidnie White Crawford, "add drama, plumb the emotional depths of the characters, add information to fill in the gaps of the [Hebrew text], and, most important, supply an overt religious element that is lacking." Perhaps most remarkable is this God-centered focus. The book of Esther in the Hebrew Bible is notable in never mentioning the name or role of God, nor any distinct religious activity such as prayer, presumably because it functioned as a text for the raucous party atmosphere of Purim. From the beginning of Greek Esther, however, God's role dominates. Mordecai's dream-vision is a prediction of the events that are about to come, and God's role is explicit. The "apocalyptic" aspect, unreal as it is, adds a romanticized sense of the revelation of God's will. Crawford continues, "The effect of all these changes is that God becomes the hero of the Greek story, and the importance of human action is greatly lessened."[9] And while Esther and Mordecai shared the stage in Hebrew Esther, in Greek Esther Mordecai is introduced first and figures much more prominently at the end as well. There are in addition other changes that at first seem minor but reflect an attempt to tie up the many loose ends of Hebrew Esther. Addition A, for instance, tells us that Mordecai's promotion *prompted* the conspiracy against the king; these two plot points were not actually related in Hebrew Esther. Addition C specifies that Mordecai refused to bow to Haman *because it is idolatrous.* Although this does not accord with known Jewish law, it at least provides a recognizable motive for Mordecai.

The approximate date and place of origin of Greek Esther is provided in the notation added at the end. This colophon was perhaps affixed to the text by an official librarian in Alexandria.[10] The book, it says, was brought to Egypt "in the fourth year of the reign of Ptolemy and Cleopatra." All of the Egyptian kings at this time were named Ptolemy, and many of the queens were named Cleopatra. Depending upon which Ptolemy and Cleopatra this refers to, that would date the translation to either 114 BCE (Ptolemy VIII), 77 BCE (Ptolemy XII), or 48 BCE (Ptolemy XIV). There is little to argue for one over the other, but we are still provided with a date between 114 and 48 BCE. It is important to note, however, that there were two quite different versions of Greek Esther. The version from the Greek Bible—the canonical

Greek version—is called the B text, while the A text (or Lucianic) contains the same Additions but is much shorter at the end. David J. A. Clines, probably correctly, takes 8:33–42 in Greek A (corresponding to 8:2 in the Hebrew) to be the ending of an Esther story that is actually earlier than the present Hebrew Bible version.[11]

Possible influences on Esther can be found in the earlier novelistic histories of the Greek author Ctesias and the *Cyropaedia* of Xenophon of Athens, and even Herodotus's *Histories* as well. These historians were familiar with the Persian East and the story traditions found there, especially those that concerned the harem intrigues at the king's court. Even at Qumran, where no fragment of Esther has been found, there are remnants of an Esther-like narrative that is also similar to these Greek histories, the so-called *Tales of the Persian Court.* Michael V. Fox, to be sure, had insisted that Hebrew Esther was not a romance for the following reasons: "It lacks the romance's favorite themes and motifs: sudden and overpowering passions, heavy sentimentality, swooning, separation and reunion, chastity under temptation, and religion (cults, prayers, oracles and divine interventions)." Yet these are precisely what Greek Esther adds, and so by Fox's definition, Greek Esther is a romance. Cameron Boyd-Taylor concurs: "Esther has stepped through the looking-glass of Greek sentimental romance, and she will never be the same."[12] It would be incorrect, of course, to suggest that Hebrew Esther lacked literary qualities—its literary achievement may be greater—but the expansions in the Greek version played up the newer literary techniques of novels.

The changes toward the novelistic in Greek Esther are subtle yet significant. Mordecai's and Esther's prayers, for instance, like the prayers of the later Greek novels, reveal traits of the characters who utter them and in this case are strictly gendered. First, Esther's preparation for prayer is different. She is "seized with deadly anxiety," and "instead of costly perfumes she covered her head with ashes and dung, and she utterly humbled her body; every part that she loved to adorn she covered with her tangled hair." Compare here the woman's scene of transformation in Judith, as well as that in the Jewish novella *Joseph and Aseneth.* The scene is actually a mourning and redressing scene but is applied in the novelistic setting to the theme of personal transformation and mission. To be sure, Mordecai has also demonstrated his grief in wearing mourning garments, but there is far greater and more intimate detail in the description of Esther. Mordecai expresses his concerns on a more abstract level, turning to classic motifs of Israelite confessions and praising the God of creation, who is all-powerful and omniscient (compare Psalms 8, 19, 21). Esther's prayer is twice the length of Mordecai's and emphasizes her interior state—her fear and sense of personal danger. Stating that she has humbly subjected herself as a slave of God, she reports her emotions from within; she confesses Israel's sin of idolatry, but also her own sexual impurity. Abhorring the bed of the king, her crown sits on her head like a "menstruous rag."[13] If Mordecai's prayer is gendered as masculine, hers is feminine.

Following the prayers, Esther appears before the king, yet there are differences here as well. There is a palpable erotic theme in the relation of Esther and Ahasuerus. In the Hebrew version, when Esther comes before the king, she bravely stands and makes her petition, but in the Greek version, the act initiates a crisis:

> Thus clothed in splendor, she called upon the all-seeing God and savior, and chose two maids to accompany her. On one she leaned gracefully for support, while the other trailed behind her, carrying her train. Blushing and in the full bloom of her beauty, her face seemed bright and cheerful, as though she were basking in her love's affection; within, however, her heart was frozen with fear. Making her way through each of the doors, she came before the presence of the king, as he sat upon his royal throne, dressed in the awesome radiance of his majesty and covered with gold and precious jewels—a formidable sight! He lifted his face, flushed with the power of his bearing, and glared at her in anger. The queen suddenly swooned, turned pale and faint, and collapsed upon the maid at her side. (15:1–7)

In this addition the audience witnesses the powerful king through Esther's eyes—very unlike the king in Hebrew Esther. Her perception of the king has the elements of a theophany, an appearance of a deity, but suggests as well an erotic vision of the love partner. Linda Day entertained the possibility of erotic overtones in this scene, and André LaCocque emphasized it more strongly, even condemning Esther as a weak heroine.[14] The passive heroine must be seen in context, however, and is somewhat more complex. The quaking hero or heroine became common in the Greek novels and was already developing in Jewish novellas. Versions of this Jewish protagonist are seen in Susanna and *Testament of Joseph,* and a very close parallel can be adduced in a fragment of the *Ninus Romance* (A.IV.20–V.4), probably concerning the future queen Semiramis:[15]

> Asking for a chance to speak to her aunt, she burst into tears and had something ready to say; but before she could begin she would cut herself short. For whenever she spontaneously signaled her desire to speak, she would open her lips and look up as if about to say something, but no complete word came out. Tears burst out and a blush spread over her cheeks as she shrunk from what she wanted to say. When of a sudden she began again to try to speak, her cheeks grew pale with fear. For she was between fear and desire and hope and shame; so while her emotions were being strengthened, the conviction to express them was wanting.

Esther's inability to speak is also accompanied by a report of her conflicting interior emotions. And for the later European artists, her fainting became the iconic moment that represented her essence. To be sure, the depiction is indeed passive, but the characterization of the ideal agent, either male or female, was shifting, now being deeply introspective and stricken. The passive protagonist became the medium through which the audience could experience threat and vulnerability. Joseph and Daniel had also been passive and reflective, even feminized, and the Greek novels would emphasize that the male protagonist could be passive as well.[16] The king's response also plays into romantic themes: "God changed the spirit of the king to gentleness, and in alarm he sprang from his throne and took her into his arms until she came to herself. He comforted her with soothing words, and said to her, 'What is it, Esther? I am your husband'" (15:8–9).[17] The king is no longer like a god, but a novelistic, romantic partner. Has God arranged, as in the Greek novels, a special union?

We turn to another issue raised above: Hebrew Esther, though it lacks any reference to God, contains more uses of the word for Jew or Judean than any other text in the ancient period. The references to Jews may indeed act as a compensation for the lack of references to God—the story omits references to God to speak about "Jews." Both Maimonides and Adolf Hitler recognized a special role for Hebrew Esther in the assertion of Jewish identity. For Maimonides, "All the prophetic books and all the holy writings will be nullified in the messianic era except for the Book of Esther. It will continue to exist just like the five books of the Torah and the *halakhot* of the Oral Law, which will never be nullified" (*Mishneh Torah, Megillah veHanukkah* 2:18). Even if his judgment were expressed as hyperbole, he would still recognize that a brash celebration of Jewish victory would be an apt text for the messianic age. As for Hitler, the excess of revenge in the text was read as a final threat by Jews; he outlawed the reading of Esther at Purim.[18]

But as Greek Esther places references to God back into the text, is the emphasis on Jewish identity lessened? Evidently not. There are even more appearances of the word for Jew or Judean—more than forty—and one odd reference in Hebrew Esther is clarified. In both the Hebrew and the Greek versions, many come to Judaism in some sense, but exactly how remains unclear. The Hebrew term *mityahadim* and the Greek term *Ioudaizō* mean something like "took up the practices of the Judeans"—but in the Greek it is further specified: they were circumcised (8:17). In the Hebrew text, Esther also eats all of the king's food without reservation, while in Greek she "has not eaten at the king's table nor drunk the wine of libation" (14:17). This means of remaining observant of food laws in a foreign land is similar to that in Dan 1:8 and Jdt 12:1–4. Further, at Greek Esth 8:11 there is now an explicit reference to Jewish laws.[19] The wording of the two edicts in Greek Esther also increases the theme of Jewish distinctiveness and gentile hostility. In Hebrew Esther, before delivering the edict Haman states that Jews have separate practices, but the wording of the edict is not included; in Greek the edict is included, spelling out what Haman perceives as an objectionable separatism of the Jews: they are a "hostile people who have laws contrary to those of every nation" (13:4–5). The second edict, which annuls the first, is also spelled out in Greek Esther and includes an affirmation by the king that the "Jews are governed by most righteous laws and are children of the living God" (16:15–16). By means of these edicts, lacking in Hebrew Esther, the author can project both anti-Jewish prejudice as Jews assumed it would be expressed by those who hated them and also a fantasy of how they wished the great kings would support the Jewish people.

Esther is the only biblical text that does not appear among the biblical fragments at Qumran. The inclusion of Hebrew Esther in the Jewish Bible was debated by the rabbis, and so it is remarkable that a text so canon-challenged should attract—even within what became official Judaism—so many versions, additions, targums, midrashic expansions, and rabbinic commentaries. Josephus, and later Josippon, included aspects of the Apocryphal Additions in their histories.[20] This section of Josippon was evidently reinserted into Jewish texts of the Hebrew Bible (see Chapter 2). Although Esther was not as variegated a subject in painting as Judith and Susanna, she could at times be depicted as triumphant (Dura Europos synagogue, third century BCE), or as crowned by Ahasuerus (Joen François de Troy, ca. 1764), or as participating in the writing of the new decree (Aert de Gelder, late seventeenth century). However, as noted above, the most popular moment of her story in art—Esther fainting before Ahasuerus—is not found in the Hebrew version but only in the Greek; note Tintoretto (1548, fig. 1), Antoine Coypel (1704), and Julia Margaret Cameron's photograph (1865, fig. 2) richly reenacting the scene of Esther fainting. This frozen moment raised up the masculinity of Ahasuerus while increasing the passive femininity of Esther. The satirical vision of Artemisia Gentileschi (1628–1630) caricatured Esther's pose as theatrical, thoroughly undercutting Ahasuerus's masculinity. Modern viewers may have difficulty appreciating the power or humor of Artemisia's satire precisely because they cannot imagine that the earnest version of the fainting scene was taken so seriously. In 1575 Palestrina also composed a motet, *Quid habes Hester,* that, like most of

Figure 1. Jacopo Robusti Tintoretto, *Esther before King Ahasuerus,* 1548. Real Monastero de San Lorenzo, Madrid. Erich Lessing/Art Resource, NY

the paintings, focused on the interaction of Esther and the king from the Additions.

Tobit

The book of Tobit is a fanciful story that combines warm depictions of a Jewish extended family with comedy, magical cures, demons bound and cast into Egypt, and happy weddings. Beneath this diverting surface we also perceive biblical themes and righteous affirmations of Jewish values, reinforced by the very names of the characters: Tobit is a shortened form of Tobi-yah, "Yahweh is my good," or perhaps "Yahweh is good."[21] His wife is named Anna, or Hannah, "Grace," and the angel Raphael, "El has healed," in his human guise is also named Azariah, "Yahweh has helped." Sarah bears the name of the matriarch.

The entertainment aspects of this novella are undeniable, yet significant disagreements remain as to precisely how they would have been understood by the first audience. Is the story a warm evocation of a respectable

Figure 2. Julia Margaret Cameron, *Queen Esther before King Ahasuerus*, 1865. © Victoria and Albert Museum, London

Jewish patriarch and his family, a comedy of manners that gently parodies the main protagonist, or a full-on satire that undermines the protagonist? Is the text fully engaged with the theological issues that are present, or are they simply the language of everyday life, Jewish "local color"? These interpretive questions are directly related to the problem of the three narrative arcs of the text, each marked with its own literary tone and perhaps even by its own genre.

FIRST NARRATIVE ARC (1:1–22)

The opening arc is set in the eighth century BCE. An actual historical situation provides the backdrop: the ten tribes of northern Israel have been defeated by the Assyrians, and many Israelites have been deported to Nineveh, the Assyrian capital. Tobit introduces himself in first-person narration as a pious member of the northern tribe of Naphtali. Although his family and tribe had participated in the "false worship" of the north in the vicinity of Dan, Tobit all alone made pilgrimages to worship in Jerusalem. The first-person introduction evokes the tone of royal autobiographical inscriptions, as well as the characterization of Abraham as righteous (Gen 15:6, 18:9). While in exile, Tobit becomes a courtier for the Assyrian kings and is threatened with death when, in violation of the king's edict, he buries the bodies of dead Israelites. A new king arises, however, and with the intervention of Tobit's nephew Ahikar, he is allowed to resume his role as courtier. This very eventful first arc has some of the same narrative structure of the biblical court narratives of Daniel 1–6 and Esther and is tied to the international *Story of Ahikar* by more than plot: Ahikar and Nadab from that popular Aramaean court narrative appear here as Israelites and relatives of Tobit (compare Achior in Judith).

SECOND NARRATIVE ARC (2:1–14:2)

Although much occurred in the short first arc of Tobit, the core story is actually the long second arc; chapter 1 was in fact only the backstory for the main tale. Tobit is now safe from Assyrian persecution but somehow much poorer than before. He interrupts his Shavuot feast to bury another fallen Israelite. The pious burial of the dead is a motif that connects the first and second arc, although now there is no danger from the authorities. Instead, the narrative problem is of a fantastic order. Impure from contact with the corpse he has buried, Tobit is forced to sleep outdoors. Birds above his head drop feces into his eyes, rendering him blind. The realism of the first arc has given way to the magical quality of the second, which will continue. Tobit becomes depressed by his poverty and his affliction and wrongly accuses his wife of stealing; she reproaches him strongly, and he prays for death. But simultaneously, far away to the east in Rages of Media, his relative Sarah is also beset with problems. She has had seven grooms—a giveaway of a folk-tale origin?—but on each of her wedding nights the evil demon Asmodeus has entered her bedchamber and killed her betrothed. (Asmodeus is the name of the Zoroastrian demon Aeshma Deva.) She is also reproached strongly by her female slaves, who wish she were dead. Like Tobit, she prays for death, and it is ironically the two prayers for death that cause God to send the angel Raphael to take a solution to both of them.

The situations of Tobit and Sarah are recounted using simultaneous, interrelated narration:

Tobit's piety	Sarah's innocence
His blindness	Her demon
He is reproached	She is reproached
He prays for death	She prays for death

The intertwining of narrative threads continues. "Each problem," says George W. E. Nickelsburg, "contains the germ of a solution for the other. . . . The combination of these plots for the common alleviation of everyone's suffering . . . is a literary device by which [the author] creates a portrait of a God who carefully orchestrates the events of history, working them to his own gracious ends."[22] This section is a romantic comedy and fantasy, a fairy tale, in which no tension is created about whether events will turn out for the good. We are even told in 3:16 that all will end well: "At that very moment, the prayers of both Tobit and Sarah were heard in the glorious presence of God." The audience never experiences any threat or danger, such as we would expect even in the absurd moments of the other novellas, or even in the first narrative arc. Is the author inept, or reaching for some other effect? What is narrated is *how* God will respond to the needs of both Tobit and Sarah. The text thus engages the reader: God's providence, already announced, will save the main characters. Tobit sends his son Tobias, accompanied by Raphael in a human disguise, to Rages in the East to recover money lent many years before. On the way, Raphael has Tobias catch a fish whose organs can be used for magical cures. He also persuades Tobias to wed his relative, Sarah, and the organs now serve to bind and exile the demon Asmodeus to Egypt. Tobias weds Sarah, and they return to Nineveh, where the fish organs are also used to restore Tobit's sight. All celebrate the marriage and their good fortune together.

A distinction can be made between biblicist and historicist approaches to our narratives: the biblicist finds influences from the biblical tradition, while the historicist looks to broadly comparative and folkloristic influences. This second arc has been likened to the journeys of Isaac and Abraham in Genesis 22 and Eliezer's search for a bride for Isaac in Genesis 24. Indeed, many phrases from these biblical stories find parallels in Tobit. At the same time, the second arc can be seen as a version of a common folktale, the Grateful Dead Man, which often runs something like this: A traveler comes upon men who are abusing the corpse of one who owed them money. Though the man is already dead, the traveler pays the debt in order to give him a proper burial. After proceeding on his way, the man encounters a mysterious figure who, the audience recognizes, is the ghost of the dead man. The mysterious stranger urges the traveler to become betrothed to a princess, even though her previous grooms have been killed on their wedding nights, in many versions by a serpent that comes out of her mouth. The stranger's only condition is that he receive half of whatever the protagonist may gain. He accepts, and when the serpent appears in the bedchamber, the stranger appears and slays it. The man then bestows half of his new kingdom on him. The similarities are obvious, although the novelistic elements in Tobit render the folktale, ironically, a bit more "realistic." The ghost is now an angel, and the evil spirit is easily chased away; in short, the categories of night and dread, even the phallic nature of the serpent, are removed. Further, the single protagonist of the folktale is divided into two in the novella: Tobit buries a man, while it is his son Tobias, young and marriageable, who travels with the mysterious stranger and wins the lady. Yet in folktales cross-culturally a single role may be divided in some tellings between two characters who operate in tandem.[23]

The second arc concludes with chapter 13, Tobit's hymn of praise for God's greatness, justice, and mercy; the hymn is quite general but appropriate for a hymn at the end of the story. It may have been composed for another setting and inserted here, but it does connect with certain motifs in Tobit. The original coda may also have been 12:22, which celebrates God's actions, not Tobit's (compare also the heroic coda for Tobias at 14:12–14). This chapter speaks of being in the land of exile (v. 6) and predicts a restored Jerusalem (vv. 8–9). At the end of the hymn a heroic conclusion summarizes the honor that was accorded Tobit. It is similar to the heroic coda at the end of Judith, and both are influenced by the heroic codas about the judges (Judg 3:11, 30; 5:31; 8:28).

THIRD NARRATIVE ARC (14:3–15)

The third arc is Tobit's last testament, a prophecy of eschatological developments; in tone it is very different from arcs one and two. It predicts the fall of Nineveh and Assyria—which, of course, the audience knows did happen when the Babylonians came to power. This arc looks forward to a period of the restoration of Jerusalem and the temple, but also to a more eschatological point in the future: the in-gathering of the nations to worship at Jerusalem (14:6–7).[24] In addition, the last half of chapter 14 expresses issues found in arc one (burial, Ahikar) and also arc two (almsgiving). As noted, like arc two, chapter 14 concludes with a heroic coda for Tobias and his family.

A SEPARATE ORIGIN FOR THE THREE ARCS?

The discrepancies among the three arcs have long been noted. The problem of the exile, says John J. Collins, is present only in arcs one and three and not at all in the second, main arc. Arcs one and three are also more concerned with Jewish law, while in the second arc burying the dead is a more universal human law. Indeed, here the "law of Moses" refers only to marrying within the extended family. More specifically, Tobit's advice to his son in chapter 4 does not refer to Mosaic law—which is very odd, if it was originally composed by the same author as chapter 1. Says Collins, "The problems ... that generate the core story of Tobit, are neither exile nor guilt, but the arbitrary suffering of innocent people, a phenomenon seldom acknowledged in the Hebrew Bible, with the notable exception of Job." We may add: it is a very "international" and not a "Jewish" theme. For Collins, the first and third arcs also "impose a Judean, Deuteronomistic theology upon it."[25] Although some occasionally object to the ease with which scholars resort to theories of cobbled parts, Karel van der Toorn reminds us that cobbling is in fact the most common process of composition in ancient Near Eastern literature.[26] This is what we find in the case of Daniel, which grows by a succession of cobbling exercises in both the Hebrew Bible version and the Greek Additions, and Greek Esther provides a marvelous laboratory example, since here we know precisely where the cobbling seams are (see Greek Esther, but contrast Judith). The changes introduced by 1 Esdras are interesting in this regard, as well as the construction of Matthew and Luke from Mark. We should be surprised, then, when narratives of this period are not cobbled.

To be sure, it is possible to read the three separate sections together as a three-part narrative. The earliest fragments from Qumran include all three sections, and indeed the book has functioned with three parts for more than two millennia. Overlapping motifs can be found: an *inclusio* in 1:3, and 14:9 names the three charter virtues of the text: truthfulness, righteousness, and mercy or almsgiving, repeated also in Tobit's admonitions to his son at 4:5–7.[27] This lends a structure to the three-part story, and an exhortation to the audience's generation. A chiastic structure can then be observed in this larger text:[28]

A. Exposition: Israel in exile; Tobit's and Sarah's problems (1:2–3:17)
    B. Tobit's speech (4:1–21)
        C. Quest for Tobias's guide (5:1–6:1)
            D. Travel to Ecbatana (6:2–7:9a)
                E. Wedding at Ecbatana (7:9b–10:13)
            D'. Travel back to Nineveh (11:1–18)
        C'. Parting from Tobias's guide (12:1–22)
    B'. Tobit's speech of praise (13:1–14:1)
A'. Epilogue: Exile resolved (14:1b–15)

The question then remains whether the three-part structure is compelling enough to render a theory of sources unnecessary, or results only from the editing of the sources, as Greek Esther or Matthew and Luke constitute coherent narratives edited from sources.

As in the case of many ancient Jewish texts, there are multiple versions of this novella. The three most important for our purposes are the long version (found in Sinaiticus, sometimes labeled G^{II}), the short version (found in Alexandrinus, Vaticanus, and Venetus, sometimes labeled G^{I}), and the Vulgate version. (A further late, mixed recension is labeled G^{III}.) Although scholars once questioned which of these was closer to the original—if we can say in the case of popular texts that there is one clear original version—the Aramaic and Hebrew fragments discovered at Qumran now indicate clearly that the longer Sinaiticus version is prior to the others. A consensus has now also formed around the dating to the period before the Maccabean Revolt, since the political struggles of the revolt are not evident. There is no way to specify the date further, and so scholars now generally posit a date around the third century BCE. The genre of the text as it stands—that is, aside from any prior folktale version—is also often agreed upon: words like "didactic story," "wisdom narrative," or "novelistic wisdom story" are used.[29]

The two main disagreements noted above, the unity of the text and its precise genre or even subgenre, are often treated as related issues. The second arc, the core story, can be understood quite differently if it was originally separate from the first and third arcs. First, it could be entirely unrelated to the theme of arc one (Jewish righteousness in the court of the foreign kings) or to the theme of arc three (an eschatological consideration of Israel and the nations). Benedikt Otzen sums up well the nature of this middle arc taken by itself. It is "a fairy-tale about a young man, Tobias, who goes out into the wide world, encounters many dangers, but is under the protection of the Heavenly Powers and returns with great riches and with Sarah, his wife, with whom he lives happily ever after." In Otzen's view, the addition of the prior narrative about Tobit risking his life to bury dead Jews (arc one) is understood earnestly, not as part of the humor of arc two concerning Tobit's prickly personality. Arc one creates a "story about divine reward bestowed upon those that are faithful to the Law of Moses and who never fail in their trust in Providence." The book is now "not just an entertaining fairy-tale, but is a legend, an edifying and didactic narrative, told among the Jews in the eastern Diaspora."[30] The mode of the story is no longer "once upon a time," but "in the history of ancient Israel." Other scholars have agreed. Collins distinguished the different tones in the three arcs.[31] By genre, the first arc is a court narrative, much like Daniel 1–6 or the *Story of Ahikar*. The third arc, 14:3–15, is even more difficult to reconcile with the core story. Tobit's vision and testamentary warning to Tobias is infelicitously inserted *after* Tobit's happy death—happy death being an oxymoron possible only in novellas. The focus also returns to Assyria and predictions of its just fall, a moral issue prepared to some extent by arc one but not expressed in the core story of arc two.

Those who have found more commonality in the three arcs point to its expression of biblical themes; indeed, it can be argued that the looseness of the relation of the three parts was possible *because* biblical paradigms provided some overarching connections. Like Judith, it is a palimpsest in Gérard Genette's sense of the word: the hypotext (biblical tradition) is refracted in the hypertext (Tobit). The book is part of an interpretive tradition of biblical texts that "refictionalize" them for an audience that already knows biblical texts.[32] In the book of Tobit we recognize the Joseph story (separation of family members, burial as a family concern, many tears) and also the drama of betrothal and travel of the patriarchs and matriarchs (Genesis 24, 29, 34). Genesis 24, the travel and betrothal of Isaac, even may have served as the inspiration for Tobit.[33] The proverbial wisdom of Tobit's words to Tobias evokes Proverbs and the wisdom tradition of the contemporary Ben Sira. In addition, Deuteronomic theology—the doctrine that when Israelites remain faithful to God's law they flourish, and when they fall away from the law they are punished—can be detected in the treatment of actions and God's rewards. Steven Weitzman sums up this literary adventure of Tobit: "Tobit's progressive echoing of Genesis and then Deuteronomy evokes the entirety of pentateuchal history . . . almost as if to enclose the experiences of Tobit within pentateuchal bookends."[34] Yet it has also been argued that the misfortunes of exile introduced in chapter 1 cannot be resolved in the fairy-tale manner of chapters 1–13. They are, as William Soll says, "a misfortune of greater magnitude and more lingering duration than the fairy tale can deal with."[35] The problems of exile require the eschatological resolution of chapter 14.

The scholarly debate, then, often revolves around the question, Which are stronger—the parallels among the sections, or the differences? Hans J. Lundager Jensen finds a satirical edge in the core story of arc two that does not allow room for any earnest biblical theology. Here the notion that "God cares for those who abide in the law" becomes an almost trivial theme. Does arc two truly engage this theology, or is the message merely present as a conventional scaffolding, even a foil? To be sure, the book of Tobit exhibits parallels to Genesis 24, but "the family narratives in Genesis make room also for internal conflict, while in the book of Tobit only exemplary piety is needed in order to survive and succeed." Why bother with the story, he asks, if the point is so self-evident? Rather, the main attraction according to Jensen is "bird droppings, fish galls and fettered demons in Egypt."[36] Tobit, like Ruth, is a family idyll, but where Ruth is touching and realistic, Tobit is comical and satirical. Jensen then presses a difference with Judith as well: "While Judith the woman-warrior cuts off Holofernes's head with his own sword, Tobias would not hurt a fly. But the contrast between heroism and peaceful passivity is also the contrast between sterility and fertility: the beautiful, seductive Judith remains a sterile widow, while the young, unmarried Tobias becomes a husband and a father." Key here is the phrase "would not hurt a fly." Is Tobit, like Daniel, part of the construction of a new moral agent in Judaism, a moral agent that in the case of Daniel has been called "feminized" because he is passive? If so, does the book of Tobit satirize it?

Others have similarly questioned the author's commitment to Deuteronomic theology. Deuteronomic theology may not be a central concern of the book but simply background theology that one can trace with academic effort. Stuart Weeks distinguishes Deuteronomic theology in a precise sense and the older and more general Israelite tribal history and identity, which also posited a loyalty requirement and a belief in God's providence. The older Israelite theology was "unconcerned with the systematic presentation of any specific religious ideology. If there is a Deuteronomic heritage in Tobit, visible at least in the book's presentation of the past, it jostles for space amongst many other concerns."[37] Further, in the second arc there is no mention of covenant, God and nation, or the drama of the whole nation going astray. There is, rather, family and tribal history; it is, continues Weeks, "more dependent on concepts of election and exceptionalism than on the conditional, covenantal ideas of Deuteronomy, and the book places more weight on individual support of the community than on the fidelity of the community itself."[38] Weeks traces an important aspect of the worldview of Tobit that is only tangentially "Deuteronomic": tribe, family history, and inheritance.

To be sure, if Deuteronomic theology is a "deep assumption" of a text, part of the story world, this is not a minor thing. It is as important as, say, the Elizabethan political ideas that played out in Shakespeare's plays. As many contemporary theorists have asserted, the deeper assumptions of a work, especially at the popular level, are often more powerful than the views argued on the surface—the "strong propaganda" of unexpressed assumptions, as opposed to the "weak propaganda" of explicit politics. As a result of such considerations, we return to Otzen's dismissal of any higher-order meaning in the core story. The message of this section may hold more import for the audience than he allows. He and others point to examples of bad writing in Tobit. There is, first, the shift from first-person to third-person narration, but more important, the characters of Tobias and Sarah are not as well drawn as that of Tobit.[39] To some extent, this is true, but romantic youths in novels and novellas generally fulfill a role more than exist as real characters. Are they less filled in as characters because of the author's lack of talent or because they play a role in a bigger plan? The same charge is laid against the young hero and heroine in the later Greek novels, although here as well complexity is sometimes seen behind the apparent simplicity.

It is also argued that the early announcement of a happy ending, eliminating any narrative tension, presents an artistic problem, but this too may have been a typical element in the enjoyment of light novellas. A similar oracle of a happy ending occurs in the *Ephesian Story* of Xenophon of Ephesus (1.6). Tobit, unlike Esther, Judith, and Susanna, is also similar to Greek novels in that it turns on a love match and the exotic appeal of travel. In the Greek novels the love match is invested with far more romantic significance,

and there is indeed a great deal of lovesickness as well, but both Jewish novellas and Greek novels are entertainments that address social conditions of
the Hellenistic East. *Testament of Abraham* works with the same dramatic
problem of the inevitable ending: Abraham avoids death, while the audience knows that he will in fact come to his end, and he does. If we look to a
modern comparison, say, *It's a Wonderful Life,* does the heavenly narration
in that film render it mawkish and pedestrian or charmingly uplifting? In
both cases, Tobit and the Frank Capra film, are we really arguing whether it
is "great art" or whether it channels important social issues by propping up
a moral order? *It's a Wonderful Life,* then, actually becomes a very relevant
comparison. Postmodern theory often affirms the significance of comedy,
especially light-hearted comedy, and its codification of social roles; comedy
reveals and even constructs who we are.

Most commentators agree that there is an intentional whimsical tone
in the text.[40] Tobit's gruff interview of an angel who, as the audience knows,
will solve all of the problems seems humorous enough, but are the characters Tobit and Sarah to be understood as positive models of faithfulness to
God, or as individuals who are whiny and petulant, saved in spite of themselves when they are supported by the safety net of extended family? Irene
Nowell has recently advocated the more earnest interpretation. Tobit is
described with a series of "charter virtues" that presumably correspond to
those of the author. Like Job, Tobit suffers unfairly yet rises to a higher
faithfulness and bequeaths to his son a set of maxims which affirm that the
one who abides in God will be rewarded.[41] However, a number of scholars
follow Jensen in pushing farther in the direction of satire and find Tobit and
Sarah to be petulant and self-centered.[42] Their egocentrism is lampooned.
The more positive interpretation of Nowell, then, identifies the author's
point of view with that of Tobit, while the satirical interpretation would
differentiate them in a way more similar to Oscar Wilde. Is it a romantic
comedy that embraces Tobit as an old, old-world Tevye from *Fiddler on the
Roof* (whose name is a variant of Tobiah), or does the comedy go so far as to
satirize the misplaced idealism? There may be a middle ground in this debate. Irony and satire can be mixed. Most grant that there is much irony and
humor in this second arc, but do Tobit and Sarah "survive" their humorous

treatment? To return to *It's a Wonderful Life,* this film presents a bungling but likable middle American family man who "wouldn't hurt a fly," is unable to fight in World War II because of a disability, is unable to defend himself against the aggression of the owner of a larger bank, yet finds support in the community of townspeople he has helped. The film parodies this everyday family man at the same time that it reaffirms his importance as the very foundation of American town life. He is ultimately admired and emulated.

While Deuteronomic or other biblical themes, then, can be detected in Tobit, other scholars have pointed instead to motifs that are explicit, prominent, and repeated often: brother/sister (or kinsperson), food, blessing, death/burial, wedding, inheritance. The repetition of these motifs creates a comic performance.[43] Marriage is strongly emphasized, but it is *always* marriage to a close relative; at 4:12, marriage outside of the family is fornication! Tobit is concerned that his son Tobias should marry a close relative within their clan, yet this seems inevitable: almost every single person mentioned in the story is a close relative of Tobit—even the angel Raphael in his human guise. The terms *adelphos* and *adelphē,* brother and sister, are used often, but not just for siblings. Tobit and his wife refer to each other with this term, and to nonsibling relatives as well, in keeping with the meaning of the term in Hebrew and Aramaic. And in regard to death and burial, Carey Moore notes that 22 percent of the verses treat these topics.[44] The characters are enveloped in a birth-to-death extended family identity that includes marriage to a member of the *mishpachah* and a proper burial by the same. Burial is not opposition to marriage, death over life, but part of the blessings of the extended family.[45] János Bolyki charts the importance of burial for extended families during this period: lack of a burial would deprive one's ancestors of honor, and provisioning the dead ensures honor and memory.[46] But above the ground, it also marks inheritance and family territory. Inheritance is treated centrally at 6:12 and invokes the special biblical inheritance law of the "daughters of Zelophehad" (Numbers 27, Josh 17:3–6). In these passages the passing of wealth through daughters is allowed in order to keep it in the larger male lineage of the family.[47] Just as Greek novels reintegrated an elite nuclear couple to start a family in an eastern Roman city, the book of Tobit may restore the marriage and inheritance of an elite eastern Jewish family.

An intriguing possibility is that our story began as a romanticized text for a wedding celebration for the Tobiads, a wealthy Jewish family of international merchants who operated in the very zone described in the main arc of the book of Tobit.[48] The most romanticized of the Jewish novellas has the greatest chance of being connected to actual archaeological evidence. The Tobiad family traded between Jerusalem, Samaria, Ammon (in modern-day Jordan), and Egypt. Their family estate in Ammon has now been discovered and excavated.[49] It is likely the Ammonite connection that was in Nehemiah's mind when he insulted a certain Tobiah as an "Ammonite" despite the fact that his name includes "Yah" for Yahweh (Neh 2:10). The Tobiad family are met again as wealthy international traders in the Zenon papyri, and the *Tobiad Romance* (from Josephus, *Antiquities* 12.4.154–236) heroizes this family of entrepreneurs. The book of Tobit's fictional historical setting in the Assyrian period may provide a charter myth for the Tobiad family, even if it is told as a family comedy. Outside of the book of Tobit, the various names related to Tobiah are encountered often, but all as members of the Tobiad family. The international sensibilities of the novella would match well this family's identity. The book of Tobit would in that case express the kinder and gentler side of an aristocratic family. Almsgiving is the value that the family members would want to demonstrate before God and is the activity that would reflect their patronage of the poor and the poor's indebtedness to them. If aspects of the patriarchal family are satirized, it is not necessarily to challenge them; it may be to reaffirm them. That is what comedy generally does. But in that case, why would the middle arc have been preserved outside the original extended family wedding context? First, artistic works are often created for one occasion before they find a larger and more continuous audience. Second, when the first and third arcs were added, the text became a didactic novella, a teaching vehicle for a wider audience. Indeed, we may see that the marriage/family/burial motifs—appropriate for an original wedding entertainment—are diminished somewhat when the first and third arcs are added.[50]

A consensus has coalesced around the date of Tobit—third to second

century BCE—but the location of the writing remains controverted. Tobit
and his son Tobias both have names composed with Yah for Yahweh, usually associated with Judah and the south, but the setting of the second arc is
in the East, and the rosy notion of Jewish life away from Jerusalem in that
arc has led many to consider the Eastern diaspora as the place of composition.[51] Richard Bauckham, however, has taken seriously the premise of chapter 1—the northern, exiled status of the tribe of Naphtali—and argued that
the text is a parable for living addressed to Israelites in the north.[52] This
argument, though interesting, applies only to arc one and is not compelling. The author of Tobit was well aware of the history of struggle between
northern Israel and southern Judah and easily could have followed the
habit of Judeans who remake "Israel" as the idealized, united entity now
under the control of Judah. The book of Judith reflects such a political vision, and Susanna plays on this as well. More compelling is the alternative
proposed by Devorah Dimant. Opposed to both an Eastern diaspora and
a northern Israelite origin, she notes that the Aramaic fragments of Tobit
found at Qumran suggest that it should be grouped with the other Aramaic
texts found there: *Genesis Apocryphon, Aramaic Levi Document, Visions of
Amram,* and *Testament of Qahat.*[53] The province of Judah, in that case, is
a more likely place of origin. Marriage within the family figures as a theme
in these texts, so one should not assume that the extended family issues are
"Eastern" or "diaspora" concerns. One notes, however, that if arcs one and
three were added onto the core story of arc two, it is possible that an originally Eastern story was brought west and reframed in Judah. As a result of
all these considerations, the location of the author is still undetermined.

Tobit, Judith, and Greek Esther, then, were likely composed and interpreted as fictitious texts and only later adopted in Christian Bibles and
treated as historical. Tobit was valued at Qumran—multiple copies have
been found, in both Aramaic and Hebrew—but there is no indication that
it was ever considered biblical or historical by Jews. Other novelistic texts
were found at Qumran (*Tales of the Persian Court*), and in general they are
written on smaller scrolls, what one scholar calls, as we have seen, the "paperbacks of antiquity." From our earliest evidence the Septuagint included
the texts of the Apocrypha. Many of the church's theologians assumed this,

but when Jerome was commissioned to translate the Bible into Latin (Vulgate), he objected to including Tobit and Judith because Jews did not include them as scripture. The texts that he was familiar with were also quite varied (see the Introduction and "Judith" below). Still, Jerome acquiesced and translated Tobit, and as noted above, elements of a heroic Tobit are increased in the Vulgate: Tobit's boyhood virtue is stated (1:4, 8), the plaints and negativity of Tobit are reduced (5:13), the ending heroic coda—where Tobit is acclaimed as a hero—is stronger (14:17). As in the case of Judith, the Vulgate establishes Tobit as a hero of the faith. In rabbinic literature, there is more interest in the demon Asmodeus than in Tobit. In a long and complex narrative, Asmodeus begins as king of the demons dwelling on a mountain. Solomon's captain Benaiah ben Jehoiadah captures him so that he may be forced to assist in the construction of the temple, but Asmodeus manages to escape. This story indicates that there was a rich tradition of Asmodeus stories in Judaism.[54] In the medieval period Jews rediscovered Tobit, composing new versions, as they did also in the cases of Judith and Susanna. This continued into the early modern period.[55]

The book of Tobit also contained motifs that were highlighted as significant in later Christian tradition. Raphael's affirmation (12:6–10) of the three righteous practices of prayer, fasting, and almsgiving with righteousness is similar to Matthew 6.[56] As the fish was identified as the symbol of Christ, so the fish in Tobit became iconic among Christians, and Catholics later developed the practice of "Tobiah Nights," that is, abstention from sex on the first three nights of marriage (as in the Vulgate version). Characters from the book of Tobit were well known in Christian art. Images can be seen in the Catacomb of Domitilla and in illustrated Bibles. In church architecture Raphael subduing Asmodeus was sometimes featured, and at Chartres we find Tobias and Sarah. The emphasis on a personal angel, as opposed to angels for Israel as a whole, was influential. In Florence we note especially Andrea del Verrocchio, *Tobias and the Angel* (1470–1480, fig. 3). In other cases, some freedom was displayed in that Tobias is portrayed with three angels. Anxieties concerning the sending off of young sons on business journeys may have prompted this tripling of the angels.[57] In Naples during the seventeenth century, Andrea Vaccaro painted a number of mov-

Figure 3. Andrea del Verrocchio, *Tobias and the Angel*, 1470–1480. © National Gallery, London/Art Resource, NY

ing, fairly "realistic" depictions of Tobias and the angel. In the Netherlands, Rembrandt seemed inspired by many aspects of the narrative and painted or etched more than twenty *Tobits*. The most notable is *Tobit and Anna with the Goat* (1626), where the great humanity of Tobit and Anna are explored.

Figure 4. Anonymous, *Sarah and Tobias,* fifteenth century. Sainte-Chapelle, Paris. Musée National du Moyen Âge–Thermes de Cluny. © RMN–Grand Palais/Art Resource, NY

Returning to the heavenly motifs was Jan Havicksz Steen, *Tobias' and Sara's Wedding Night* (ca. 1650–1660) (also see the anonymous fifteenth-century church window of fig. 4). Throughout Europe, Tobit represented a genial heroism, and Raphael an angelic protector of the extended family.

It would be a mistake to assume that the Apocrypha ceased to have an influence among Protestants, but the interpretation of the Tobit story moved from biblical history to illustrative story. Just as Martin Luther was the first to consider Judith fictitious, he also allowed that Tobit might not be history: "If the events really happened, then it is a fine and holy history. But if they are all made up, then it is indeed a very beautiful, wholesome, and useful fiction or drama by a gifted poet."[58] Yet this indicates that neither Luther nor later Protestants had tossed these Apocryphal works aside (see the Introduction). Samuel Taylor Coleridge, influenced by an Anglican view of the Apocrypha as edifying reading, was strongly influenced by Sarah and the demon-lover motif.[59] Søren Kierkegaard also took a special interest in the role of Sarah, devoting four pages of *Fear and Trembling* and *Repetition* to her. For him, she was the true hero of the text, as a result of her difficult experiences. Kierkegaard perhaps saw in her a spirit kin to that of his former fiancée, Regine Olsen. Tobit has not been set to music as often as Judith, but an oratorio of Tobit was reconstructed from the works of George Frideric Handel after his death in 1764, and as recently as 1999 a new opera was composed by Jonathan Dove (libretto by David Ian) to some acclaim. It takes advantage of the operatic setting to have first Tobit and Sarah sing their plaint in harmony, then Anna and Edna singing together concerning their children.

Judith

The book of Judith was most likely a fictitious, humorous text that played on multiple levels.[60] It is first of all a parody of foreign imperial rulers, probably written in the wake of the Maccabean Revolt at the end of the second or beginning of the first century BCE. On another level, it is an outrageous comedy, featuring a pious Jewish woman who brazenly risks her virtue to save her people. Judith is a woman who violates every rule of decorum assumed for wealthy widows: she chides and overrules the village elders; she lies and deceives constantly; she makes suggestive advances to a foreign general, skirting very close to having sex with him, and enters his intimate quarters to coolly chop off his head. She places the severed head in her slave's food bag, and back at her village, she draws it out to show her people. She oversees her people's charge against the Assyrians and at the end is memorialized as a hero. Before it became "Bible," the text was likely perceived as an entertaining fantasy of a woman hero, a common cross-cultural folk motif. In some ways Judith is like the historical figure Joan of Arc, but because of the text's fictitious nature, perhaps she is more similar to Wonder Woman. Like much popular art cross-culturally, the text contains erotic and adventurous elements with no concern for realism. The evil villain, "Nebuchadnezzar, king of the Assyrians"—Nebuchadnezzar was king of the Babylonians—destroys first one enemy and then another, growing in power as the nations sue for peace and beg to become his allies. He sends his general Holofernes to the west to subjugate the nations that had refused to ally with him. Soon Israel stands alone, and the only access to Jerusalem is the mountain pass guarded by the village of Bethulia—also a geographical fiction. Among the Assyrian general's other tasks, he destroys the local cults in his path, establishing a principle of one world, one king, one god.[61] This, of course, reads as a challenge to the Jewish ideal of one temple, one king, and one God.

By genre the text is a novella, placed with Esther and Tobit in most ancient Bibles, but unlike these Jewish novellas (and Daniel and *Joseph and Aseneth* as well), it did not expand over time by the accumulation of parts. It was likely written at one point in time by one author, and as a result it has the clearest single arc of all the Jewish novellas. To be sure, this single arc is divided into two movements, chapters 1–7 and chapters 8–16, and this has presented a problem for the literary appreciation of Judith. While the iconic central image of the narrative, Judith's beheading of the general Holofernes—now often referred to as the "acteme"[62]—is quick and even bloodless (13:1–10), scholars have bemoaned the literary qualities of the first half. It consists of military campaigns, alliances, and speeches. For modern readers it only seems to delay Judith's heroic act. Ancient audiences, however, were probably strongly affected by this part of the narrative. The foreign king was looming as a threat over Israel. His army grows larger and larger, as one nation after another effectively abandons the resistance and surrenders to his power, begging for mercy and magnifying the Assyrian forces even further.

An important digression also figures prominently in the first half, providing some relief from the growing threat. Support arises from an unlikely source, Achior the Ammonite general. Although Ammonites were an ancient enemy of Israel, as they are in this text as well, Achior knows Israel well:

"If the Israelites have not sinned," he says to Holofernes, "their god will protect them. Pass them by." For this advice, Achior is bound and deposited below the Israelite village, and this becomes the key action in the first half of the book. The audience, probably familiar with the storyline, recognize this as the beginning of the arc that will ultimately rescue the Israelites from the mighty Assyrians. We are also introduced here to the mountain village of Bethulia, which stands at the narrow pass through which the Assyrian army must march to take Jerusalem. This is where the first act will end (chapter 7): the courageous Ammonite Achior is welcomed in the "doomed" Israelite village that stands in the path of the Assyrian army.

Chapter 7 ends at a dramatic pause, and in chapter 8 Judith is finally introduced. She is given the longest genealogy of any woman in the Bible; it is *her* lineage, not her dead husband's, that defines her. She is both wise and beautiful and has a commanding presence, but we are told that since the death of her husband she has actually been in seclusion, spending her time in a tent on the roof of her house. She is described with a number of traits typical of heroes cross-culturally: the hero is in seclusion, unable to integrate into society, and is called upon by his or her people to rise up to defend them. Judith, then, is not only like the Israelite heroes of Judges, or the more contemporary Daniel and Esther, but also like Beowulf, Deerslayer, or countless heroes of film. (This is not a far-fetched comparison; our only early copy of Beowulf was bound with an epic poem of Judith.) Such a hero is not like other people but is stronger, smarter, and better, able to cross boundaries between peoples and, more important, to pass into the valley of danger in order to slay the beast. The hero can save his or her people by being untethered to society and not subject to typical moral scruples.

Judith's function as more of a "male" hero provides the key to the entertainment value of the text. It is an outrageous farce, depicting the transgression of the typical rules of women's roles. (Ben Sira will outline those rules, without allowing for any variation.) As if her deeds were not transgressive enough, her words also serve to shock. While she is among the Assyrians, she will lie, dissemble, misrepresent, and seduce, her words dripping with sexual innuendo. This comic irony—and lying—becomes the typical discourse of Judith. Sex and deceit are the tools of her trade, before she graduates to physical violence. She is protected from dishonor by two factors: she is devoted to God, and she places herself in this situation only to save her people and God's temple in Jerusalem. In comparing the Jewish novellas, Jensen notes that while Tobit and his son Tobias are rather unassertive, Judith is extremely assertive, and indeed is a trickster.[63] The righteous agent in Israel is often passive (see the Introduction), but Judith will have none of that.

The story of Judith seems totally self-contained, yet in terms of biblicist versus historicist approaches, scholars have identified a very large number of biblical motifs that may inform it, and many Greek and ancient Near Eastern parallels as well. Some biblical connections are explicit, such as her affirmation of Simeon's revenge on Shechem in Genesis 34. Judith also acts as an alternative Moses in many ways: she responds to the testing of God and the murmuring over the lack of water, her hand similar to the hand of Moses. Judith's prayer to God in 9:7 and her song in 16:2 resonate with the Song of the Sea in Exod 15:3.[64] Judith is also presented like one of the judges who delivered Israel; the final verse is an almost verbatim copy of the conclusion of each judge's story.[65] Ehud the trickster (Judges 3) is similar, but a closer parallel—of a woman defeating an enemy general by an attack to the head—is found in the story of Deborah (Judges 4–5). There the woman Jael slays the Canaanite general Sisera by driving a tent peg through his temple. The negative portrayal of "Nebuchadnezzar, king of the Assyrians," is similar to that of Nebuchadnezzar of the Babylonians in Daniel 1–4. "Assyrian" was considered an older name for "Syrian" or Seleucid, so "Nebuchadnezzar the Assyrian" combines both the Babylonian tyrant and the Seleucid enemies of the Maccabees. Indeed, the ancient Ammonites and Moabites, Assyrians, Babylonians, and contemporary Seleucids are all merged in this story into one threat of the "nations roundabout." In addition, the hubris of Nebuchadnezzar, king of the Assyrians, in Judith—"Who is god except Nebuchadnezzar?" (Jdt 6:2)—also plays as the opposite of God in Isa 45:21.

Even among the other Apocrypha we find possible influences. The display of Holofernes's head at the end of the story is similar to the treatment of the Seleucid general Nicanor in 2 Macc 15:28–36. This is significant because in many ways Judith, whose name is the feminine form of Judah and means "Jewish woman," is perhaps an idealized equivalent of Judah the Maccabee.[66] Intriguing similarities to 1 and 2 Maccabees include:

1. The hero or heroine prays to God.
2. The arrogant foreign king sends a field commander to destroy Israel.
3. Judith and Judah first pose as friends of their archenemy.
4. The field commander is killed.
5. The enemy army is thrown into panic and retreats.
6. The surrounding Israelites attack.
7. They kill and plunder.
8. The enemy commander's head (and arm) is chopped off.
9. The Israelites celebrate.
10. There is peace over the land.

But together with these biblical influences, we find many international and folk influences as well. The Greek histories of Herodotus, Ctesias, and Xenophon of Athens provide a number of such motifs.[67] Just as the Assyrian figures can remind one of the excesses of Nebuchadnezzar in Daniel, they may also be composed on the basis of the descriptions of Eastern potentates in Greek sources. Achior's wise advice to the unwise general Holofernes about Israel is very similar to that of Demaratus before Xerxes in Herodotus 7.101-4. Mark Stephen Caponigro speaks of a "Xerxizing" of Nebuchadnezzar in Judith. This extends to Holofernes's eunuch Bagoas, who is depicted negatively, as was the case in Greek sources (see also Chapter 3 on eunuchs in Ben Sira). The ancient Near East was also full of stories of warrior women, such as Tomyris, Artemisia, Zarinaea, Panthea, Semiramis, Zenobia, and Jalila, whose stories were known through Greek sources.[68] And not all of the influences need be literary. One must also consider the role of the well-known depictions of Seleucid kings beheading enemies with a Persian *akinakēs,* the same kind of sword that Judith uses, or the female divinities Athena and Nike slaying the giant Alkyoneus from the great battle scene on the Pergamon Altar (early second century BCE).[69] Such visual images may not have directly influenced the text of Judith, but they do indicate how a tradition of images might have been viewed.

For all the simplicity and brash popular appeal of Judith, there are

five ways in which the text also enacts themes found in ancient Greek
philosophy:

1. Her strength and control suggest the Greek virtue of *enk-rateia*, self-mastery.
2. In contrast to this, the depiction of the blustery tyrants Neb-uchadnezzar and Holofernes illustrates the opposite disposi-tion, *akrasia* or lack of self-mastery.
3. Judith exhibits *parrhēsia,* the bold speech that the true phi-losopher uses before superiors.
4. Judith divides time into past, present, and future (9:5), sur-prisingly absent in Israel and many other cultures but present in Greek.[70]
5. Judith condemns her townspeople's prayer as self-interested and testing God by imposing a deadline, traits not con-demned in Israel, though they were among Stoics.

Greek philosophical themes are also sometimes perceptible in Greek nov-els, but the author of Judith, whether consciously or unconsciously, is more
aggressive in presenting a Jewish protagonist as truly superior to the figures
of the great empires. It is a postcolonial novella.

Although often considered a lesser literary work by nineteenth- and
twentieth-century scholars, the book of Judith early on held a commanding
role in Christian art and letters, inspiring a vast number of European paint-ings; and with the rise of feminist analysis the text experienced a rediscovery.
The central scene—the beautiful Judith insinuating herself into the sleeping
chamber of the enemy king, getting him drunk, and slicing off his head with
his own sword—proved to be an irresistible concoction of sex and violence.
The text is sometimes seen as a parable of traditional Israelite theology.[71]
Nebuchadnezzar has defined himself as a god on earth, and Holofernes rep-resents him. Opposing them are God and *his* general, Judith. Holofernes
and Judith engage in a heroic struggle, and Judith must slay the beast. The
worldwide dimension is also part of the adventurous tone. We may date the
recent scholarly appreciation of Judith to the literary studies of Luis Alonso-Schökel and Toni Craven in the 1970s and 1980s.[72] The bombastic surface
level of Judith—the intentional tawdriness of this "pop art"—had blinded

scholars to the bold literary effects, which were now coming into view. Another decisive step came when feminist scholars looked seriously at the reversal of male and female roles and Judith's transgression of every rule of feminine decorum. This was brought to the fore not by biblical scholars or literary scholars—who were perhaps affected by the book's "biblical" cast—but by those who investigated the representations of Judith in painting. Mary Jacobus traced the visual tradition and noted that Judith was depicted as a virtuous heroine until about 1600, when Holofernes came to be treated more sympathetically and Judith as a mad woman out of control.[73] Was it the Renaissance realism that led people to now see her as a real woman and not as an icon, a type of Mary? The influence of the art historians brought biblical scholars as well to raise deeper questions about the original text.

Judith is a narrative of one arc, divided evenly into two acts. It is not episodic, as Daniel is and the Greek and Roman novels are. Several structuring principles make this single-arc narrative possible. In addition to the parallel contrasts of Nebuchadnezzar/Holofernes and God/Judith, Toni Craven discerned a clear chiastic pattern. An identifiable chiastic structure (with slight variation) is found in both the first and second halves:[74]

First half

A. Campaign against disobedient nations; the people surrender.
    B. Israel is "greatly terrified."
        C. Joakim prepares for war.
            D. Holofernes talks with Achior.
                E. Achior is expelled.
                E'. Achior is received in the village of Bethulia.
            D'. Achior talks with the people.
        C'. Holofernes prepares for war.
    B'. Israel is "greatly terrified."
A'. Campaign against Bethulia; the people want to surrender.

Second half

A. Introduction of Judith.
    B. Judith plans to save Israel.

   C. Judith and her maid leave Bethulia.
    D. Judith beheads Holofernes.
   C'. Judith and her maid return to Bethulia.
  B'. Judith plans the destruction of Israel's enemy.
A'. Conclusion about Judith.

  The delay of the climax, which is often cited as a literary problem in the text, is partially justified by this structural chart: the long first half has an important function for the development of the story. Such a delay is also just as common in popular art of the modern world as in the ancient. The issues that are built up in the first half—the threat of the nations roundabout against the fledgling Judean state—would have seemed very pressing as a means of building suspense. The sweep of peoples of the first half will ultimately bear down on one Jewish village, where one woman will stand up both to her leaders and to the Assyrian bully. And there is some artistry in how this rising threat alternates with periods of rest, as in 1:16: "Nebuchadnezzar returned to Nineveh with all his combined forces, a vast body of troops; and there he and his forces rested and feasted for one hundred and twenty days." Other such pauses occur at regular intervals in the first half:

Action	Action	Action	Action	Dialogue	Action
Pause	Pause	Pause	Pause	Pause	Pause
1:16	2:28	3:10	4:13–15	6:21	7:32

  Above it was suggested that Judith follows the pattern of the cross-cultural hero narrative: the call of the reclusive hero to step forward to save the people, the sojourn of the hero, with a companion, into the area of chaos and danger to slay the beast, and then the return of the heroic pair. Within this overarching pattern our novella also engages other smaller narrative moments that enrich the text. Judith's preparation for her mission consists of an elaborate undressing and redressing scene, with her prayer at the center of it (chapter 9). The dressing of the hero is a common part of the heroic tradition, and Judith's scene involves the pattern of the rite of initiation: separation from society, a liminal period that can include openness or communion with the divine, and reintegration into society with a new mission and status. A very similar scene occurs in Greek Esther and *Joseph and Aseneth*. Another fascinating literary pattern is found in the movements of the characters in the middle third of the book: at Judith 6 Achior the Ammonite, the sympathetic opponent, is bound and deposited at the site of the Jewish village, where he is taken in, hosted by the leaders, and ultimately converts to Judaism; he has moved from the Assyrian camp to the Jewish village. When Judith leaves her village to go to the Assyrian camp, she will pass over this same path in reverse, moving from Jewish village to Assyrian camp. They are coordinated characters, in that only Judith and Achior display courage before the Assyrian general, and both express a positive devotion to God. The main difference—and this is played ironically—is that Achior the Ammonite is exceedingly earnest and honest (an Ammonite!?), and Judith, from the moment that she arrives in the Assyrian camp, will lie and manipulate in every sentence.

This last observation leads us to the discourse that will mark Judith's persona: lying and irony. Irony, of course, is an honored literary form in the ancient world; in different cultural contexts we note the book of Jonah, Plato's portraits of Socrates, and the Gospel of John. If Judith does not match the theological and dramatic heights of those texts, she does compete well in terms of the number of ironic statements and her use of irony to affect others. Not only can we perceive larger instances of irony, such as a great Assyrian general felled by the hand of a woman, or the Ammonite Achior converting and joining Israel, but the pleasure of irony is found in Judith's countless little lies. Judith plays with Holofernes by flattering him, making statements about her "lord" that he understands as referring to him, while the audience understands them as referring to God: "I will say nothing false to my lord tonight! And if you follow closely the advice of your servant, God will accomplish a great deed through you, and my lord [Holofernes or God?] will not fail to achieve what he has prepared [sex with Judith or killing Holofernes?]" (11:5–6). Corresponding to Judith's lies and irony is Holofernes's own unwitting irony: he makes statements that can equally be taken in two different ways, but he is oblivious to this fact. The blustery general, for instance, had bellowed at Achior, "You will not see my face again until I take revenge on this people!" The audience, who doubtless know the story, are aware that the next time Achior will see the general's face it will indeed be in the Jewish village, but separated from the rest of his body. If he were in fact capable of understanding Judith's lies and his own comical mis-statements, he would not fall into her trap. But he is without any wisdom or insight, doomed to be beheaded by Judith.

Massimo Fusillo has commented on the constant shifting of perspec-tive in Greek novels; this dramatizes the threats bearing down on the pro-tagonists, one after another.[75] In Judith as well, a similar effect is achieved by two dynamics occurring simultaneously. On one hand, there is a constant voyeurism as every male figure sees Judith and is swept away by her beauty (compare Susanna). This would seem to place Judith in a passive position, but occurring at the same time, she does all the talking and commands peo-ple, even Holofernes, at every turn—a very active depiction. Both dynamics occur in the same scene when she *tells* the Jewish elders what she will do and *commands* them to have the servants open the gates. They then *watch* Judith as she and her maid descend the hill toward the enemy camp, in a passage that has rightly been called "cinematographic":[76] "So they ordered the young men to open the gate for her as she requested. . . . Judith went out, accompanied by her maid. The men of the town watched her until she had gone down the mountain and passed through the valley, where they lost sight of her" (10:9–10). "Popular literature" often works with types rather than with fully three-dimensional characters. Judith is a powerful figure in this novella, but not a complex character like those encountered in modern novels. She does not exhibit any ambivalence, momentary weakness, tragic flaws—or indeed any flaws at all—or character change. But even if the *char-acter* is not complex, the *text* may be complex by using the simple types present here to challenge conventions. Freudian undertones may even be perceived in the questions raised. Is the decapitation a symbolic castration? Is Judith's dead husband, Manasseh, depicted as impotent? Is Judith a "phallic woman"? Indeed, the *audience* may have a complex reaction to these actions of a two-dimensional heroine. But Judith is not a complex character in the sense usually emphasized in the modern analysis of novels.

The book of Judith is generally dated to about 100 BCE, but it is difficult to pin down the original performance setting for it. The text was a brash, provocative novella and seems to have attained its first popularity by telling the story of a trickster heroine who was dedicated to God. She transgressed the usual restrictions placed upon women, but did so to save her people. As in the case of Esther, the seemingly unreal story may have been accepted as biblical and historical because the heroine could inspire others; Clement of Rome, writing in about 100 CE, raises up Esther and Judith as models of courage, *andreia* (1 Clem. 55:4–6). With that, her story could become exemplary.

Although Judith is less well known in modern, especially Protestant culture, for two thousand years the text was very important for art and letters.[77] From her role as a model of courage, Judith was also seen in Christian culture as a type for Mary, Church, or Chastity, and Holofernes could be seen as Satan or Lust. Judith was treated often by church figures, though this book was not the subject of commentaries. Paintings came to portray her as a gleeful assassin, triumphantly displaying the head of Holofernes. During the Renaissance, Judith was central to political theology and iconography. In Florence she was displayed as a consort of David, and in decapitating a tyrant, she became a symbol of civic liberty. She was a constant subject for Renaissance and Baroque artists—many of the most famous artists produced multiple Judiths—and the subject of epic poems, oratorios, operas, and dramas. Paintings generally continued to present her as a heroine of virtue (Guido Reni's version became iconic), but many artists also found threatening or sadistic aspects in her actions (Caravaggio, Trophime Bigot, Johann Liss). Artemisia Gentileschi presented Judith's gruesome deed realistically, but without the moral reservations of some of her contemporaries (fig. 5; compare Giulia Lama's more pious Judith, fig. 6). Among Jews Judith played no role for centuries, but she reentered Jewish tradition from the Middle Ages on. A rich story tradition developed, in which she became associated with Hanukkah, appearing on some Hanukkah menorahs. Nachmanides also quoted a snippet of Jdt 1:7–11, mistakenly attributing the passage to Susanna, and her story was included in the fourteenth-century *Sefer Hazikhronot*. The Ethiopian and Samaritan versions of Susanna also include parallels to Judith.[78] Though her popularity faded somewhat

Figure 5. Artemisia Gentileschi, *Judith and Holofernes,* ca. 1620. Uffizi Gallery, Florence. Alinari/Art Resource, NY

in the nineteenth and twentieth centuries, she remained a potent subject for many artists and intellectuals. Sigmund Freud understood her decapitation of Holofernes as penis envy. In the twentieth and twenty-first centuries she still appeared in art, drama, opera, and even the new medium of cinema: D. W. Griffith chose this book as the subject for the first feature-length

Figure 6. Giulia Lama, *Judith and Holofernes,* 1730. Galleria dell'Accademia, Florence. Cameraphoto Arte/Art Resource, NY

movie ever created, *Judith of Bethulia.* Recognizing the unfamiliarity of Protestant audiences, however, he was forced to insert into the opening subtitles an explanation of the origin of the story. Judith is still sometimes depicted in paintings, a homage to the rich artistic tradition as much as to the notion of a "biblical book." Feminist interest has also given her more currency, making room for many new interpretations of her deed.[79]

Additions to the Book of Daniel

The book of Daniel in the Hebrew Bible consists of two different kinds of writings. Daniel 1–6 are court narratives of Daniel and his three associates in the courts of Babylon, Media, and Persia (told in the third person), and Daniel 7–12 are apocalyptic visions concerning the events leading up to the Maccabean Revolt (told in the first person). The visions can be dated to the middle of the revolt, 165 BCE, making it likely that Daniel 1–12 was the latest writing of the Hebrew Bible. However, since the court narratives of Daniel 1–6 do not refer to the turmoil of the revolt, they were likely written earlier. A number of other short narratives and prayers became associated with Daniel and his three friends: Susanna, Prayer of Azariah and Song of the Three, and Bel and the Dragon. They are included in the book of Daniel in the early versions of the Greek Bible, albeit in different positions. Also relevant is the fact that there are two Greek versions of Daniel 1–12 and the Additions to Daniel, the Old Greek (OG) and the Theodotionic (Th), with significant differences between them. At many points—especially in Daniel 4–6, Susanna, and Bel—the differences are so great as to justify the assumption of two early story traditions in circulation.[80] And for Lorenzo DiTommaso, "Even the terms 'biblical' and 'apocryphal' are in some ways inappropriate with respect to the Hellenistic-era Daniel cycle of material, since we do not know the extent to which all or some of these texts were granted a measure of authority."[81] However, the shifting position of the Additions in the Greek Bibles relative to Daniel 1–12 indicates that the latter was already a "core" text, around which the other texts could be arranged.

SUSANNA

The simple little story of Susanna is spun with deceptive skill, creating in a short space enduring, even iconic images. The name Susanna is the Greek form of Hebrew Shoshana, lily. Strongly emphasized is that she is both the daughter and wife of leading citizens, and it is also noted that she is beautiful and that her parents educated her in the law of Moses (v. 3). Because she is married to the wealthy Joakim, she is mistress of a large estate, the gathering place of the leading Jewish citizens of Babylon. While walking in her garden after the guests have left, she decides to bathe. Two elders have each independently lingered behind to watch her bathe, and when they discover each other they confess their secret sin. Now in league, they step forward and accost Susanna: "Have sex with us, or we will denounce you and say that you were dallying with a young man." An element of novelistic development can be seen here in the communication of a woman's thoughts. Her reflection on her ethical dilemma, though brief, is compelling and memorable: "Susanna groaned aloud and said, 'I am trapped either way! If I do what they ask, it would be worse than death to me, yet if I do not, I will never escape their clutches! Yet it is better for me to refuse and fall into your hands than to sin against the Lord'" (vv. 22–23). As a result of this moment of reflection, Susanna became a model of chastity, female courage, and righteousness.

The trial that follows is as stirring as the previous confrontation. The elders, in the presence of the assembled people, accuse her of having lain with a young man who ran away. On the basis of this testimony, the people quickly condemn her to death. Susanna prays to God for deliverance, and God raises up the spirit of the young man Daniel. This brash young man surprisingly assumes the authority to cross-examine the elders. Separating them, he asks each under what tree the couple had lain. His use of puns in Greek to denounce them, here replaced with English substitutes, demonstrates his cleverness. The first elder says they lay under a clove tree, to which Daniel responds, "You have lied, and under a *clove* tree the angel of God will *cleave* you in two!" The second states that they lay under a yew tree, and Daniel responds, "You have also lied, and under a *yew* tree the angel of God will *hew* you in two!" The Greek play on words is: *schinos* mastic tree/*schizō* to split, and *prinos* oak/*prizō* to cut. Julius Africanus noted that the play on words depended on Greek, which suggested a Greek original, but Origen refuted his arguments, and the English puns prove that the wordplay does not require a Greek medium. The two elders are thus exposed and are themselves punished with death according to Jewish law.

Each of the two episodes of this narrative, the predicament and its resolution, has folktale parallels. The predicament is similar to the "falsely accused chaste wife," and the resolution to the "wise child who prevents an unjust action by the elders."[82] We have noted the distinction between biblicist and historicist approaches—those that emphasize the reworking of biblical tradition on one hand and those that emphasize contemporary, international, popular, and folkloristic influences on the other. The folklore parallels contribute to a historicist approach, but Lawrence Lahey also argues that Jer 29:21–23 provided inspiration for motifs in Susanna.[83] Both Jeremiah the figure and the book of Jeremiah were popular in this era (see Letter of Jeremiah, Baruch, and 2 and 4 Baruch), and Origen (*Letter to Africanus* 7) makes the connection between Susanna and Jeremiah.

The story of Susanna is also like the court conflict narratives in many ways (Daniel 3, 6; Bel; Esther; and the Assyrian *Story of Ahikar*), yet these are generally set in the highest courts in the land, while in Susanna the entire drama is given a lower, more everyday "novelistic" setting: an aristocratic home and the local Jewish court. The geographical setting of Babylon may have been added to provide the proper origin for Daniel, but it communicates the drama of living among the exiles as well. The story of Susanna was likely inserted at the beginning of the book of Daniel to introduce the protagonist as a young man, although in the OG version and Vulgate it appears after Daniel. In either position, the narrative serves as the backstory of the Daniel tradition, introducing a brave and pious young woman and the youthful Daniel who saves her from disgrace and execution. As such, it often has a very modern ring. The author Dorothy Sayers considered Susanna and Bel to be the first "detective stories," although they are more precisely "courtroom dramas." Like the John Ford film *Young Mr. Lincoln*, it also provides a picture of the virtue of the hero as a young man. Issues of honor and shame, central to the power of the story, are also emphasized in both the Th and OG versions. Susanna's parents are wealthy, as is her husband, Joakim. He maintains a rich estate in Babylon, because he is "more honorable than all the others" (v. 4). In the Th version, the story begins with Joakim and ends with him as his family honor is restored. (The father's anxiety over the sexual reputation of his daughter was featured in Ben Sira.)

Much discussion of the text also concerns its voyeurism: in art or literature, the audience may intrude, even participate in viewing a private or sexual act, as in Judith. This story, though brief, engages the voyeurism of the audience through a careful manipulation of a short narrative: Susanna is from the first described as beautiful, and the elders' obsession with her is the means by which the audience sees her. The later artistic tradition focused on the bathing scene, but that is only in the Th version, and in fact we are told only of Susanna's intention to bathe—she never actually bathes. Her tryst with the young man is also only reported by the elders. The culmination of the voyeurism comes near the end as her veils are removed at the trial.[84] The guilt incurred from this descent into sexual voyeurism may be purged, however. The forbidden desires of the elders—and of part of the audience as well—are exposed, condemned, punished, and eliminated when the elders are executed. The text, then, indulges an experience of lust in order to reestablish virtue, and Susanna remains a heroine of virtue. Yet the erotic elements are not precisely the same in the two versions and may indeed be increased in the Th version. *Apokalyptein,* to uncover, is used in both versions, but in Th it is specified as unveiled, while in OG it is not clear that she is exposed. The bath scene occurs only in Th, where there is a lively description of running and shouting, characterization, and indirect dialogue. In Th, Susanna is unveiled "to see her beauty," an erotic aspect, but in OG she is stripped in the course of her trial to shame her. The court ordeal mirrors the trial of the Sotah or suspected adulteress in *Mishnah Sotah* 1:5, based on Numbers 5 (also compare Lev 20:10).[85]

An unexpected contrast is also introduced in v. 57: Susanna, as a "daughter of Judah," rejected the wicked demands of the elders, unlike the "daughters of Israel," who had previously agreed to their demands. This contrast can be viewed in several ways. First, it may simply represent a sort of dramatic parallelism, so similar to poetic parallelism in Israelite poetry: this one said no, but those had acquiesced. A rather more pointed interpretation is offered by Jennifer Grillo: the contrast does not refer to the political situation at the time of the writing of Susanna but is a re-creation of the situation in the days before the Babylonian Exile. It replays the animosity between southern Judah and northern Israel or Samaria.[86] The elders are like the wicked sinners of the preexilic period who caused the exile as punishment. But in the Introduction and the opening of this chapter, we also noted the increased use in the novellas of the word for Jew or Judean, *Ioudaios* (feminine *Ioudaia*). Though the emphasis on Judah here may call to mind the traditional criticism of northern Israel, like the other novellas this text may be emphasizing the identity associated with the term Judah.

We turn now to the endings of the OG and Th versions and raise again the question of how the two texts were formed. The OG probably arose before the Th version. The Th is more assimilated to the Daniel corpus, and in fact, in the OG the name Daniel appears to be awkwardly inserted into a story about a "young man" (*neōteros,* OG vv. 44–45). The ending of OG does not mention Daniel at all, but only *neōteroi,* young men (v. 63).[87]

And if the OG story was not originally about Daniel, what was its genre and function? Susanna's moment of moral choice is still central, but the story moves at the end toward an exciting resolution regarding an *anonymous* young man who saves the innocent damsel:

OG ending	Th ending
For this reason young men are beloved of Jacob on account of their sincerity [*haplotēs*].[88] And as for us, let us watch over young men so that they may become men of worth; they will be God-fearing, and there shall be in them a spirit of knowledge and discernment forever and ever.	Hilkiah and his wife praised God for their daughter Susanna, with Joakim her husband, and all her kinfolk, because there was no dishonesty in her. And from that day forth, Daniel was held in great honor by the people.

The Th text concludes by returning Susanna, now vindicated, to her husband Joakim and her family. Here the young Daniel is established as a great figure in Israel. But more significant, the ending defines the story as a prequel for the growing Daniel tradition. It is an effective introduction for the hero of Daniel 1–12. The OG ending has none of that. Unrelated to the Daniel corpus, it appears to be an address on the theme of watching over young men (*neōteroi*) so that they grow up to be men of worth; that is, it expresses the theme of *paideia,* education, and wisdom. We will see in Letter of Jeremiah that the "word of exhortation" (*logos paraklēseōs*) was a common rhetorical form, also related to the formation of the new moral agent. It is a three-part presentation that consists of worthy examples or important information to be considered, a conclusion based on that information, and an exhortation. The OG version of Susanna loosely fits this pattern, as it consists of the example-story of the *neōteros,* continues to a conclusion ("For this reason"), and ends with an exhortation ("Let us watch over").

The date of Susanna is unclear. The Th version was added to Daniel 1–12 sometime after 165 BCE, but as noted, the OG version may not have originally been related to the Daniel cycle and may have been composed earlier than Th. The fact that the issues of the Maccabean Revolt are not reflected in the text might suggest that it is pre-Maccabean, but this is not clear, since the setting is so fanciful. It is possible that the surprisingly stern stand against elders and their legal procedures may reflect a Pharisaic critique of Sadducees, who were in power and running the courts.[89] However, as plausible as this may seem, it goes beyond the meager evidence of the story.

The story of Susanna had an impact in later culture far greater than most people realize. Although the text was not quoted in the New Testament and does not appear in the Dead Sea Scrolls, she was referred to in the early church, and Hippolytus wrote a commentary in about 200 CE. She could appear as a type of Church, Mary, Chastity, or Christ handing over a scroll to the viewer; she is practically the only female figure to be a type of Christ.[90] For Hippolytus and Ambrose, the garden symbolizes Church, Eden, the society of saints; Joakim symbolizes Christ; Susanna's bath symbolizes baptism. For Hippolytus the elders represent the enemies of the church, both Jewish and non-Jewish, and for Gregory of Nazianzus simply the Jews.[91] The story provided the narrative for understanding the boundary between Christians and Jews, and a sharper definition of Jews as Other. During the Reformation, Martin Luther took up her story as a *schöne geistliche Gedicht,* a "beautiful spiritual poem."[92] A Lutheran author, Sixt Birck, wrote poems about Susanna and Judith, and George Frideric Handel composed an oratorio of Susanna. She was taken up again by Jews in medieval midrashic works, in Josippon, and in *Chronicles of Jerahmeel.* An Ethiopian Jewish version (ca. fifteenth century) retells the story, as does a medieval Samaritan telling.[93] An Armenian Susanna tradition also developed.[94]

As a favorite biblical figure in European art, Susanna was a subject in paintings by Tintoretto, Rembrandt, Alessandro Allori, Artemisia Gentileschi, Massimo Stanzione, Peter Paul Rubens, Guido Reni, and many others, as well as a sculpture by Francis van Bossuit. Scholars have debated whether the original story took the voyeuristic perspective of the elders or balanced Susanna's perspective as well,[95] but in the visual medium of paintings and sculpture, male voyeurism is more the norm. Many artists depicted a fully exposed, nude Susanna, with the elders peering in at her or accosting her to make their demands. She is often grappling with them, trying to fend off their hands, or recoiling as they fondle her—although neither her nudity nor the physical attack occurs in the ancient texts (figs. 7 and 8). Still, it

Figure 7. Alessandro Allori, *Susanna and the Elders,* 1561. Musée Magnin, Dijon.
© RMN–Grand Palais/Art Resource, NY

Figure 8. Artemisia Gentileschi, *Susanna and the Elders,* ca. 1610. Schloss Weissenstein of Counts of Schönborn, Pommersfelden, Germany. © Bildarchiv Foto Marburg/Art Resource, NY

should be noted that European artists depicted her in different ways.[96] Rembrandt, Artemisia Gentileschi, Massimo Stanzione, and Guido Reni granted her more strength and dignity in her resistance to the elders' advances.

PRAYER OF AZARIAH AND SONG OF THE THREE

Daniel 3 in the Hebrew Bible tells the stirring account of Daniel's three companions refusing to worship a golden statue in Babylon. They are punished by being thrown into a fiery furnace but emerge unharmed. King Nebuchadnezzar is astounded and reverses his decree and confesses the power of the companions' God. Though the story is part of the book of Daniel, Daniel himself is not mentioned; we may see here an independent story of three Jewish courtiers assimilated to the Daniel tradition. It is also likely that the story of Daniel 3 was originally read as humorous. The three young men have jaw-breaker names typical of comic folktales—Shadrach, Meshach, and Abednego—and the repetitious lists of officials and musical instruments, along with the exaggerated actions of the king and court, communicate a sense of slapstick. Most of the story is told from the visual perspective of the blustery king, as he first peers into the furnace and then witnesses the Jews' miraculous escape from the fire unharmed.

Yet even if the original story was humorous and understood as fictitious, the tone was altered, first by the inclusion of the text in Daniel 1–12, and second by the addition in the Greek versions of a long prayer and song uttered by the three while inside the furnace. The dramatic center of the chapter is no longer the rousing story elements but the long poetic confessions of the prayer and song.[97] Short prayers and confessions of God's work are found elsewhere in Daniel 3, as well as in Daniel 2, 4, and 6, so they are already a Danielic motif, yet none of those are more than a verse or two. Here the prayer experience becomes an end in itself, not a mere ornament in an entertaining narrative. More important, the humor of Daniel 3 is turned to a more serious theme by these Additions. The Babylonian names are not used in the Addition, but rather the Hebrew names Hananiah, Mishael, and Azariah (compare Dan 1:6–7). The visual point of view of the story is shifted from the king's perspective, on the outside looking into the furnace, to the righteous Jews' perspective, on the inside speaking to God. The threat to the protagonists is now experienced from the inside, part of the internal psychological perspective of novellas. Finally, a short transition (vv. 23–27) is added between the two parts of the Addition that explicitly identifies the fourth person mentioned in Daniel 3 as an angel, increasing the heavenly presence. Through the insertion of the prayer and song, then, the psychological states of the idealized, righteous Jews become central. This is a narrative detail appropriate for the novelistic development of the Daniel collection. In the biblical version of Daniel 1–6, neither Daniel nor his associates betray any sense of having sinned, and so the confession here brings with it a different spiritual experience. A confession of sin also suggests that the covenant between Jews and God is being reestablished (compare Prayer of Manasseh). Since other issues of the book of Daniel are not mentioned in this Addition, it is possible that it was composed independently and inserted at this point.

The Prayer of Azariah and Song of the Three are not quite the same, however, and may reflect separate origins. Prayer of Azariah begins as a national lament, similar in form to Psalms 44, 74, 79, and 80 and similar in content to confessions of sin such as Daniel 9, Ezra 9, Nehemiah 9, and Bar 1:15–3:8 (compare Greek Esther 14 as well). In broad strokes, we may say that these confessions consist of threat to Israel/prayer/redemption/praise of God; more specifically, we note a succession of the following motifs: confession of God's justice, confession of sin, present humiliation, reminder of covenantal promises, expression of contrition, prayer for deliverance, and divine vindication. One particular aspect of the prayer has caught scholars' attention as more distinctive at this early stage: once it is granted that there is no prince, prophet, or place of sacrifice, Azariah prays that it is the experience of the three that may serve as sacrifice: "Yet with a contrite heart and a humble spirit may we be accepted, as though it were with burnt offerings of rams and bulls . . . such may our sacrifice be in your sight today" (vv. 16–17).[98] The prayer itself may then be seen as the sacrifice. Though these three do not die, their willingness to become martyrs also became a model for later martyrdom accounts (compare 2 Maccabees 7). The prayer, then, contributes to the new reflections on the ideal Jewish moral agent (see the Introduction).

After the prayer there is a short prose interlude, serving as a narrative connector (vv. 23–27): extra materials are added to the flames to make them burn hotter, and the fourth figure within the furnace is explicitly identified as an angel. This prose interlude makes no sense after the prayer, since it introduces the miracle. Collins thus argues that the prose interlude and song may have been inserted first, after which the prayer was added.[99] We also note in passing that the motif of being saved from a fiery execution by an act of the gods is not necessarily simply "biblical"; the scene is similar to the intervention of Isis at Xenophon of Ephesus 4.2. The song follows after the prose interlude. Although it is often called Song of the Three Jews, the word "Jews" does not appear in the Greek and is supplied in translations; they are simply called "the three" (*hoi treis,* v. 51 in Greek, v. 28 in English). In its present location, they are the three young associates of Daniel, but this identification may have been added to a text not originally related to them. The Song of the Three is a hymn of praise, divisible into two parts. Verses 28–34 constitute a royal enthronement psalm: God rules the heavens like a king (compare Psalms 96, 97). The second part, vv. 35–41, calls upon all creation to bless God. In terms of content, it is similar to Psalm 148, but the use of a repeated, antiphonal refrain recalls the same pattern as in Psalm 136.[100] All of the orders of creation are called upon to praise God, from the highest heavenly bodies and angels (vv. 36–41), to the elements of the atmosphere (vv. 42–51), to the earth and its creatures (vv. 52–59), culminating with the human worshippers of God (vv. 60–68). Each verse concludes with the refrain, "Sing praise to him and highly exalt him forever," likely sung as an antiphonal communal response. The names Hananiah, Azariah, and Mishael are added at the end of the song to connect it to the story as a whole, with the earnest confession, "He has rescued us from Hades and saved us from the hand of death." This concludes the Addition and clearly expresses the change in tone from the humorous original.

The prayer and song are typically dated to the second to first centuries BCE. The "unjust king" who ruled while the temple was not in use (v. 15) at first suggests the period between 167 and 164 BCE, and v. 32 may also refer to Antiochus IV Epiphanes. These verses are quite general, however, and could refer to the period of the exile, when Daniel is set. Verse 31 also appears to assume that the temple is standing—"Blessed are you in the

temple of your holy glory"—but this more likely refers to the heavenly temple. It has also been suggested that several passages assume aspects of the
narrative of Daniel 3, yet these too are very vague, and as a result Collins
argues that the prayer and song were composed independently and adapted
for the present context.[101] Although the poetic qualities of the prayer and
song have not been lauded, some scholars now defend them in terms of
their probable communal function. These were not psalms and prayers limited to the priests and temple worship but were democratized and would
have had meaning for a broader audience.[102] The song affirms that neither
the heavenly elements nor the natural beings are gods, but they sing praises
to God, and that the ideal Jewish agent should witness to this truth to the
point of death.

The prayer and song had more effect on the interpretation of Daniel
than is usually realized. First, they became part of the church's liturgy. They
appear as Odes 7 and 8 among the Odes, a collection of Old Testament and
New Testament prayers and songs that were gathered together as a liturgical book and printed separately in Codex Alexandrinus. The Odes were
also canonized as a separate book in the Eastern Orthodox Church. The
prayer also influenced Tertullian (*On Prayer* 29), and the song was taken up
in Latin liturgy as *Benedicite*. Second, they provided an iconic image of
those who endeavored to remain righteous in the face of hostile govern-
ments; the prayer and song are probably responsible for raising the profile
of the three youths in this regard. As early as the second century Justin
could include the three with Abraham and Elijah as those who were "Christian" before the coming of Christ (*Apology* 1.46). The three youths in the
fiery furnace have been depicted in artwork through the ages (fig. 9), including the early catacomb of Priscilla (third–fourth century CE), and often
appeared with Daniel, Noah, Jonah, and Susanna. Christian theologians
also linked martyrdom and asceticism, and the fiery furnace was likened to
the inner passions of the mind (Origen, *Exhortation to Martyrdom*). Azariah's prayer became a martyr's confession in Theodoret of Cyrus, but because the three youths did not die, the question was sometimes raised as to
whether they should be considered merely confessors and not martyrs. Yet
over time the three were transformed from Jewish confessors into Christian
martyrs. At times this was also expressed as martyrdom-as-sacrifice, even

Figure 9. *Shadrach, Meshach, and Abednego, the Three Youths in the Fiery Furnace of Nebuchadnezzar*, eleventh-century Byzantine mosaic, Hosios Loukas, Greece. Erich Lessing/Art Resource, NY

more so in the Peshitta: "so will be the sacrifice of our soul today." The three became the new "center" of the book of Daniel as a whole.[103] Although 4 Macc 13:9 refers to the three youths in the fire, the prayer and song do not appear often in Jewish tradition. There may still be some influence on the rabbinic narrative of Abraham thrown into a furnace and emerging unharmed (*Genesis Rabbah* 38:13). The Daniel Additions, however, did reenter Jewish tradition in Josippon. The fiery furnace—minus the prayer and song—also became a potent symbol for Jews in modern times, especially after World War II.[104]

BEL AND THE DRAGON

Bel and the Dragon is included in the book of Daniel in all of the ancient Christian Old Testaments. In both Bel and Daniel 6, Daniel is thrown into a lions' den and emerges unharmed, and so the texts are clearly related. In addition to the lions' den, there is another important similarity: in both, Daniel has a warm relation with the post-Babylonian king. But which reflects the earlier tradition? The canonical status of Daniel 6 has perhaps influenced scholars to treat it as the prior version, but long ago James A. Montgomery suggested, probably correctly, that Bel was the "earlier, popular form of the story."[105] Some of the differences in Daniel 6 probably entered in when an earlier text similar to Bel was incorporated into Daniel 1–6. As with Susanna and Daniel 4–6, there are interesting differences between the Th and OG versions. The court narratives of Daniel 1–6 are generally dated to the period before the Maccabean Revolt, since they do not reflect any awareness of that pivotal conflict. The same argument applies to Bel, which is tentatively dated to the early second century BCE.

Bel can be divided into two separate episodes, each humorous and entertaining. In the first, the king is in awe of the idol of Bel in the temple. This setting for the story would have made sense in the Hellenistic East. Bel is an alternative form of the Babylonian god Ba'al, meaning Lord, and was a name for Marduk (see Isa 46:1). As was common in ancient Near Eastern polytheism, Cyrus of Persia adopted the worship of the Babylonian Bel and claimed to have been chosen by him to liberate the Babylonians from their king—in much the same way that Isa 45:1–7 declares Cyrus to be God's "messiah." Herodotus (*History* 1.183) also describes a statue of Bel in Babylon eighteen feet tall made of gold, to which Nebuchadnezzar offered provisions of food and drink. All of the elements of the story, then, comport with historical circumstances. In our humorous version, however, when food is placed inside and the doors are sealed shut, the provisions disappear, presumably consumed by the great idol of Bel. "Great is Bel," the king exclaims to Daniel, "and there is no guile in him!" (v. 18). Daniel, however, enlists the king—who seems always ready for a boys' club adventure—and sprinkles fine flour around the temple before closing the door. There is even a bit of magician's patter: "Priests, look at your seals to make sure they are intact, and King, note well whether anything has happened of which you have disapproved" (v. 16, OG version). On the next day, when the doors are opened, Daniel stops the king from entering and points out that in the flour one can see footprints of men, women, and children. The guilty priests and their families are then executed.

The irony and humor continue into the second episode. Although the inanimate statue in the first part made an unconvincing "living god," here it is a dragon that is worshipped. Although *drakōn* can mean dragon or large snake, the story likely concerns a dragon. The story seems to demand that the beast be a dragon and not a snake, for it must be marvelous enough to command worship. Certainly, snakes or other animals could be involved in divine iconography, but a snake would not seem to *require* worship as a "living god." The dragon would also call to mind mythological tales from Babylonia and elsewhere. At any rate, the beast moves and clearly eats on its own. "Surely," says the king, "you cannot say that this is not a living god!" (v. 25). Daniel responds, however, by feeding the dragon a concoction of pitch, fat, and hair. These ingredients are not likely perceived as magical, although that is possible. A more sensible version in *Genesis Rabbah* 68:14, and in Josippon as well, states that Daniel concealed nails in the food. The story, rather, seems to make use of a plot device in which natural ingredients swell up in the dragon's stomach and burst it open—that is, the "worldly" dragon is destroyed by natural items. Just as the Prayer of Azariah and Song of the Three emphasize that the heavens are not gods but under God's control, Bel and the Dragon emphasizes that "living god" does not apply to idols and animals but to the God who lives in heaven. Bel is also a narrated version of the parody of idols common in the Jewish texts of this period. Probably inspired by Jeremiah 51, both Wisdom of Solomon and Letter of Jeremiah create multilayered accounts of the irrationality of worshipping idols made with hands.[106] The parody of idols is more philosophical in Wisdom of Solomon and Letter of Jeremiah and more physical in Bel; the latter is perhaps closer to the account of the idol of Dagon falling over and breaking in 1 Sam 5:5 or Elijah's contest with the priests of Ba'al in 1 Kings 18. The parody of idols often proceeds by simply *exposing* idols; the reductionist critique seems so philosophical that there is little room for the actions of God. The story of Bel, however, keeps the God of Israel in focus by naming him as the cause of Daniel's rescue, and at the conclusion of the story God will directly intervene.[107] The OG and Th versions also exhibit slight differences in the details of the critique. In OG Daniel says he worships the creator God, as opposed to the created elements, while in Th Daniel says he worships the living God, as opposed to a god made with hands. The difference is slight, but the latter allows for an extra dose of irony and humor: the king says, "Surely Bel is a living god if he eats all this food!" (v. 6).

The court narratives in Daniel 1–6 already showed signs of humor, psychological interest, and the role of the Jewish courtier in a potentially threatening world. Bel continues these narrative interests with two trickster tales. Jacob and Judith are also tricksters, and we note as well the example of Mosollamus the Jewish archer in Josephus, *Against Apion* 1.201–3. The trickster is very common in folklore cross-culturally, and similar to Bel is the story in Herodotus 2.121 of the chamber of Rhampsinitis. Literary effects also enliven our narrative. In both episodes, the humor plays out especially in regard to the motif of food: the priests of Bel have gorged themselves on the food set out for Bel; the dragon gorges on various substances, swells up, and bursts; and the lions gorge on the punished priests. In addition, the Th version surprisingly takes the viewpoint of the deceptive priests of Bel, as they themselves urge the king to place the food and mix the wine, and lock and seal the temple doors. Their plan, and the story's "reveal," is also explained from their point of view: "They were not concerned, for beneath the table they had made a secret entrance, through which they would enter and consume the food" (v. 13). Susanna and the two stories in Bel are indeed very primitive specimens of the detective novel, in which the brash protagonist sees through appearances to uncover the truth.

These humorous trickster stories, however, give way at the end to a more serious message, similar to that of the court conflicts of Daniel 3, Daniel 6, and Susanna. The destruction of the dragon has become too much for the Babylonian priests, and they force Darius—who is surprisingly sympathetic to Daniel—to cast him into the lions' den. The two stories in Bel are thus different from Daniel 6 in an important way: whereas in Daniel 6—and Daniel 3 as well—the persecution of the righteous Jews is initiated *for little apparent reason* by the other courtiers, in the two stories of Bel Daniel is quite provocative, attacking the religious beliefs of the other courtiers. In

Daniel 3 and 6 the Jews *maintain* their observances; in Bel Daniel *destroys* others' observances. Corresponding to this heightening of conflict, we also find a stronger statement of identity. The Babylonian courtiers now respond to the attacks on their idols by rising up against the king and shouting, "The king has become a Jew [*Ioudaios*]!" (v. 28). (See the Introduction and the opening of this chapter for the use in the novellas of "Judean" or "Jew" as an identity marker.)

The punishment in the lions' den, found in both Bel and Daniel 6, was otherwise unknown in ancient sources, although a pit of dogs serves this purpose in Xenophon of Ephesus 4.6. Still, confinement of a person in a pit is not unusual—compare Joseph or Ahikar. The descent into a pit can mark a transformation for the protagonist.[108] A surprise extra in Bel, however, when compared with Daniel 6, is the miraculous appearance of the prophet Habakkuk. Far away in Judea, he is instructed by an angel to take his pot of food to Daniel. Like many a good prophet, Habakkuk begins by insisting that he cannot, but the angel whisks him by the hair to Babylon to deliver the food to Daniel. Habakkuk's presence does not save Daniel from the lions, but it does provide divine aid in the form of a good meal. Once Habakkuk is returned to Judea, the story concludes as a Daniel story, but the two figures are now intertwined. The OG even labels the story as a Habakkuk legend. The king, mourning for Daniel, comes to the den expecting to find that he has been devoured. Seeing him alive with the lions, he exclaims—in words very similar to his earlier false declarations about a living god—"Great are you, O Lord, God of Daniel, and there is no other god beside you!" The king's confession of the God of Israel is also similar to the endings of Daniel 2, 3, 4, and 6. The final consummation of the story is very brief: the king draws Daniel out of the lions' den and throws in those who persecuted him; they are devoured immediately.

The story of Bel was not recounted as often in Christian tradition as the Prayer of Azariah and Song of the Three, but the angel's abduction of Habakkuk was featured in a wooden panel in the door of the Basilica of Santa Sabina in Rome (ca. 430 CE), in a sculpture by Gian Lorenzo Bernini (1655), and in paintings by artists such as Jacopo Guarana (ca. 1750). Although not found among the Dead Sea Scrolls or in Josephus, Philo, or the

earliest rabbinic sources, the Daniel Additions were added late in the text
history of Josippon and appeared in *Chronicles of Jerahmeel*.[109] They appeared also in other later medieval Hebrew collections, including *Sefer
Hazikhronot*. Many of the Apocrypha have a role in European culture that
is more emotive or iconic than strictly theological. Despite the fact that
Daniel 11–12 introduced the idea of resurrection of the body, judgment, and
eternal life, it was often more valued for Susanna's heroic rejection of the
elders, the prayer and song of the three in the fiery furnace, and the prophet
Habakkuk being dragged by the hair to minister to Daniel in the lions' den.
The three Additions to Daniel each compellingly presents the themes of
courage and piety, and each is very visual.

Third Maccabees

Despite its name, 3 Maccabees does not describe the Maccabee brothers
and their battles. It was a work of historical fiction that was grouped with
1 and 2 Maccabees in some ancient manuscripts, and the similarities to
2 Maccabees were probably intentional.[110] It begins by recounting the campaigns of one of the Hellenistic kings of Egypt, Ptolemy IV Philopator.
(Josephus, *Against Apion* 2.51–55, recounts a similar story involving Ptolemy VIII Physcon and Cleopatra II.) After scoring a victory against the
Seleucids at the Battle of Raphia in 217 BCE, he arrives at Jerusalem and,
against priestly objections, tries to enter the temple, but he is rebuffed by
the miraculous intervention of God (1:6–2:24). Returning to Egypt, he trans-
fers his fury to the Jews there. He forces a decision on them: they must be
initiated into the mysteries of Dionysus or be registered for a poll tax and
reduced to slavery (2:28–29). In addition, they will be branded with the
ivy-leaf symbol of Dionysus; if they object to this punishment, they are to
be rounded up and executed. Some Jews agree to be initiated, but the majority refuse. When the king learns that most of the Jews have not com-
plied, he drives them into the hippodrome, where, on the next day, they are
to be trampled by inebriated elephants, a motif that seems absurd, although
it is stated in 1 Macc 6:34 that thirty-two elephants are given "the juice of
grapes and mulberries to arouse them for battle." On three different occa-

sions, however, the plan is foiled in comical ways. On the first attempt, the king, who had drunk too much the night before, oversleeps. On the second attempt, drunk again, the king forgets his decree. On the third attempt, a Jewish priest Eleazar prays for God's help, and an appearance of angels frightens the elephants, who turn and kill their handlers (6:18–21). The repetition of the attempts, in addition to building tension, allows the horrific threat to be viewed three times, with much pathos. After the third failure, the king finally relents, and the Jews are saved from destruction. A different but equally absurd effect is observed in *Acts of Paul and Thecla* 32–35, where four times beasts are thwarted from killing the condemned Thecla; in one, women sympathetic to Thecla throw perfumes that calm the wild beasts.

Some of the motifs in this text will sound like those in Esther, Judith, 2 Maccabees, Daniel 5, and the Egyptian Jewish text by Artapanus *On Moses.* The edicts of Ptolemy, for instance, are similar to the first edict in Greek Esther, giving voice to the views of the anti-Jewish adversaries. Daniel 5 also presents the revelry of the foreign king and his friends as they worship idols. There are also in 3 Maccabees clear references to aspects of Greek rites, specifically, initiation into the cult of Dionysus (2:29), including inebriation and madness; the text can even be viewed as an anti-Dionysian satire. The highly honored, exclusive Dionysiac mysteries are being forced as a punishment upon the masses. In J. R. C. Cousland's reading, the theme of reversal, developed in histories such as Herodotus, is carried out precisely.[111] Each threat to the Jews at the beginning is matched by a reward and blessing at the end. For instance, when the edict arrives in each town at the beginning, the gentiles join in a great celebration at public expense. At the end a Jewish festival is inaugurated that recalls the gentile feasts. And while the king organized some of the royal feasts, at 6:30 the Jewish feast is lavishly prepared by the reformed Ptolemy.

When we turn to genre, however, the situation is complicated by the fact that some aspects connect 3 Maccabees to histories, but many others call to mind the novellas. In terms of history, there are so many close similarities to 2 Maccabees that it is clear that 3 Maccabees is rewriting the drama of 2 Maccabees for a mixed Jerusalem–Egyptian Jewish context.[112]

Motif	3 Macc	2 Macc 3:1–10:9
Gentile leader tries to violate temple	1:1–29	3:1–21
High priest offers prayers	2:1–20	3:31–34
God chastens the insolent leader	2:21–24	3:22–30
Hellenization crisis follows; some Jews fall away	2:25–33	chs. 4, 6
Faithful Jews are persecuted	3:1–5:51	6:12–7:42
God intervenes in response to prayers	6:1–21	chs. 6–8
God saves people, accompanied by angels	6:18–21	chs. 8–9 (see also 11, 15)
Festival established in perpetuity	6:30–40	10:1–8

Third Maccabees intentionally copies the pattern of 2 Maccabees, probably to emphasize that Egyptian Jews share a strong connection to the Jerusalem temple and also to reaffirm that Jews are protected by God even in the diaspora, and with their own festival. As 2 Maccabees pressed for the celebration of Hanukkah and Greek Esther the celebration of Purim, 3 Maccabees may have responded by advocating a different, unnamed festival (6:36). More specifically, it may have been written to assure Jews in Judea that those in Egypt are living a truly Jewish life in diaspora.

Although this text was modeled on 2 Maccabees, it was likely written in a fictitious register and is thus grouped here with the novellas—even if it is considered a historical novel. All of the actions are played out in an exaggerated, even outrageous mode. In addition to the drunk elephants (was there enough wine and frankincense in all of Egypt to inebriate five hundred elephants?), we note as well the writing utensils that gave out, causing a delay in enrolling the Jews (4:17–21). Story structuring elements also fall into the novella category. There are similarities in structure to the court conflicts of Daniel 3 and 6 and Esther; and like Judith, where the main action is delayed for seven chapters in order to build suspense, 3 Maccabees includes a long prayer by Simon, a full rendition of Ptolemy's edict, and a detailed description of the gathering of the Jews from every region—taking up two-thirds of the text—all before turning to the climactic actions. The high comedy of the text also is exhibited in the second attempt to kill the Jews. God places in Ptolemy a sort of unconscious prophecy; he shouts at the servant in charge of the elephants, "I should make your entire family a rich feast for the animals, instead of the Jews, who give me no ground for complaint and have exhibited a full and firm loyalty to my ancestors" (5:31). Ptolemy may express a more positive perspective on the Jews—but only for one day. Scholars often remark on the pretension of the author in choosing many rare words; more than one hundred words are not found in the Greek Bible, fourteen not found in Greek literature. The stilted style has been called verbose, florid, and bombastic. N. Clayton Croy has insisted, however, that the choice of unusual words is typical of the educated authors of the day.[113] In addition, this trait can be described as a novelistic effect. After the third attempt, in which God turns the elephants against their handlers, Ptolemy's mind is finally altered and he praises the Jews' loyalty (5:30–35). The Jews must be provided, he says, "both wines and everything else needed for a festival of seven days" (6:30). The ending is a festive celebration of escape from persecution, like the end of Esther and Judith. One can imagine the text of 3 Maccabees performed at such a festival, as Esther was likely already a "Purim text." In addition to the festivities, the Egyptians who wished them ill were "overcome by disgrace," and more surprising: the Jews were allowed to execute those other Jews who had agreed to be initiated (7:10–12).

The novellas in general create a strong sense of Jewish identity. Third Maccabees surpasses them all in concentrating so many affirmations of Jewish identity in such a short text. (Like the other novellas, the term *Ioudaios* is used often, for example, at 2:28; 4:2, 21.) From the beginning, the text constructs contrasting sets of good and evil characters that continue through the story. Ptolemy and his friends are characterized as the worst sort of self-willed, foolish leaders, "strangers to everything just" (2:25). They exemplify not moderation and control, but the *lack* of control. The king is a victim of every conceivable extreme emotion—madness, rage, cruelty—and is likened here to the famous tyrant Phalaris of Akragas. Although some critique of arrogant kingship can be found in Herodotus, Plato, and the biblical tradition (Deuteronomy 17), a new genre of philosophical literature arose in the Hellenistic period called *peri basileias,* on kingship. Benjamin Wright characterizes the Hellenistic belief in the ideal king: "The king should rule without passion, because that is how God rules."[114] The "Greek" values of a rational king were contrasted to the irrational, divine pretentions of the Eastern kings (see Judith). In contrast to the blustery Egyptian king, the Jewish authorities, including Simon II "the Great," exhibit the high-minded values typical of the Greek philosopher: "The calm, rational, and serenely dignified way in which both the high priest Simon in Jerusalem and the Egyptian Jewish priest Eleazar face extreme peril, and quietly pray to God, is surely offered as a contrast to the wild, irrational, and erratic behavior of the king and his sister."[115] In the midst of this stirring account of persecution and escape are a host of social issues that should not be overlooked. The book is quite focused on the relations of native Egyptians, Greek overlords, and Jews, both those who are devoted to the law of God in the face of all threats and those who are not. From the very beginning it is recognized that Jewish identity is a problematic category: Dositheus is described as "a Jew by birth who later changed his manner of life [*nomima*] and apostasized from the ancestral traditions" (1:3). The Jews who agreed to be initiated into the cult of Dionysus will be mentioned later as well. The negative attitudes of native Egyptians are also treated transparently and realistically: at 3:4 the Jews' "separateness with respect to foods" is acknowledged, as is the fact that "they appeared hateful to some."

A complex colonial situation is at play in this text. Both Jews and gentiles are divisible into two groups. The Jews are divided into those who remain faithful to God's laws in the face of mortal threats, and those who do not. The insecurity and anxiety of Jewish life communicated here has been likened to that in Esther, with one important difference. In Esther Jews killed thousands of non-Jews who meant to do them harm, but in 3 Maccabees the loyal Jews kill only apostate Jews.[116] The gentiles are divided into those sympathetic to the Jews and those who foment persecution against them. The former are evidently identified as "Greeks," and those who harbor anti-Jewish prejudices appear to be native Egyptians. The Jews residing in Egypt, then, are identified more with the Greek colonizers than with the Egyptian colonized. It is in general the native Egyptians who are depicted as responding with anti-Judaism, although at 3:3-7 the author wants to have it both ways, indeed many ways. As deSilva notes, "That the Jews were held in good repute by 'all' while also being maligned on all sides on account of their peculiar customs—a paradox that is simply impossible for the author to resolve—reflects the cognitive dissonance of the Jewish author and, no doubt, his audience."[117]

It has long been noted that Daniel 1–6, Bel, and Esther conclude with a reconciliation between Jews and empire; the texts are not *anti*-empire as much as *negotiated*-empire. The core of 3 Maccabees presents a very negative vision of the surrounding peoples who want to destroy the Jews, but does it also express a more positive hope? The two possibilities are summed up well by Sara Raup Johnson: "Those who see the text as Roman stress the elements in the story which depict the Jews as a persecuted minority, tormented by the cruel king, hated by their enemies, bitterly hostile toward apostates in their own community. Those who view the text as Hellenistic stress the possibilities for peaceful compromise found in the story, wherein the Jews prove themselves faithful, their enemies are confounded, the king is reformed, and the Jews are restored to favor."[118] In terms of dating, it was formerly assumed that the use of the word *laographia,* poll or census tax (2:28), indicated that the text must have been written after 27 BCE, when that term was introduced in Egypt. However, it is now known that the term was used earlier. Does the deep sense of persecution and the erratic nature of the king indicate the period of Caligula? Perhaps, but this is not certain. A date of about 100 BCE is argued by Philip Alexander and Loveday Alexander, but not necessarily in Alexandria; the regions of Egypt are mentioned often. It is possible that the text is from an earlier period, about second–first century BCE. This text was evidently not known to Jews, except possibly by the author of Greek Esther, and was not referred to by Christians in the West. It was, however, used in the Eastern churches and translated into Syriac and Armenian.

Historical Texts

AMONG THE APOCRYPHA ARE A NUMBER of texts that can be categorized as history: 1 and 2 Maccabees; 1 Esdras; and in the Syriac Bible (Peshitta), Josephus *Jewish War* Book 6 (as an appendix to 4 Maccabees); while in the Ethiopian Bible, 1, 2, and 3 Meqabyan. Josippon will be treated as an important text in the Ethiopian Orthodox Church that may have been considered part of the canon, although this is not clear. While the genre terms novella and apocalypse are sometimes challenged in regard to Apocryphal texts, this is rarely the case for history, yet this term is as ambiguous as novella or apocalypse. However, because it is a more "canonical" category in Western intellectual culture, the ambiguity of history is not generally perceived. The term is more muddled than many realize even in the context of Greek history, and Martin Goodman rightly registers some of the problems in regard to the Jewish histories of this period:

> We often speak of Hellenistic Jewish historiography without taking note of its extraordinary diversity. Let us consider Eupolemus, Artapanus, 3 Maccabees, and 2 Maccabees. Eupolemus provides us a midrashic commentary on the Bible, Artapanus a historical or etiological novel, 3 Maccabees contains the legend of the elephants, while 2 Maccabees represents contemporary political history. . . . They do not constitute what one could call a school of "Judeo-Hellenistic historiography." . . . School, no, to be sure, but different and related sub-genres in a cultural constellation, yes.[1]

Goodman makes an excellent point, yet he includes some texts that should not be considered history (Artapanus, 3 Maccabees) and does not include other texts gathered in this chapter.[2] We may agree with Goodman, however, that some of these texts have a common literary character.

All modern discussions of history are dependent upon ancient Greek authors and their reflections on the genre. We consider here the Greek discussion before turning to Israel. Herodotus is appropriately called the father of history for his connected account of the war between the Greek cities and Persia. He reflected often in his work on the value of his various sources and introduced the term *historia* as reasoned inquiry. Still, one should note well that Herodotus never used *historia* to refer *to the genre;* he used it to refer to only the reasoned discernment of sources. Some years later, Euripides could still use *historia* to mean inquiry (*Antiope* F 910). Thucydides improved upon Herodotus's project, but the term *historia* was not used for the genre of writing until Aristotle (*Poetics* 1450a–51b, 1459a). And if, with the careful discernment of sources, history in Greece asserted a higher claim of truthfulness in representing what "really happened," we may still ask, how is the depiction of events shaped? All scholars grant that the novel invents a narrative world and affirms particular values within that world, but history is no less "constructed" and value laden. Michel de Certeau goes so far as to argue that history is a propagandistic account of a society's own story of itself, yet the author of history hides this assertion by claiming simply to report past events. History thus shapes a society by recounting its story of the origins of common symbols and values; it is the account of earlier constitutional moments.[3]

Even with the introduction of the term history, it was noted in Chapter 1 that the distinction between history and fiction was not often explicitly stated. In fact, the category of "historical novel" is sometimes now used for texts such as Xenophon's *Cyropaedia* or Ctesias's *Persica,* which fall between the two genres. Some classicists also distinguish between the "first-register historians," such as Thucydides and Polybius and Xenophon's other major works, *Anabasis* and *Hellanica,* and "second-register historians," who mixed temple lists, miraculous stories, and dubious sources, creating entertaining accounts that lacked the discipline of true *historia.*[4] Yet here we must pose a challenge: What if the *hybrid* between history and novel was the more common and more recognized text-type in the ancient world, and what we would refer to as "true history" and "true novel" were aberrations, outliers? Still, we find that in the Apocrypha *historia* and related words are occasionally used, and in a very reflective way, as a reasoned narrative of past events—a very "Greek" discourse of the genre of history (1 Esd 1:33, 42; 2 Macc 2:24, 30, 32; 4 Macc 3:19, 17:7).

Concerning Israel, we may set aside the question of whether the early biblical books—the five books of Moses and Joshua and Judges—were "history" or epic and focus on the texts that followed, 1 and 2 Samuel and 1 and 2 Kings. These texts recorded the events of the foundation of Israel and the kings and queens down to the fall of Judah and the exile. The genius of this history, says John Van Seters, "is that it attempted such a wide-ranging integration of forms in order to set forth within one work the whole foundation of Israelite society."[5] This historical narrative, connected over a number of books, is part of the "Primal Narrative" and the "Deuteronomistic History," so called because it everywhere narrates one of the powerful theological beliefs of Deuteronomy: when Israel or Judah remained committed to God's laws they prospered, and when they did not, they were conquered. Whether this historical record is accurate is an important question, but in terms of genre, our judgment of accuracy is not the sole criterion. The connected narrative is still a kind of history, accurate or not. Granted, the biblical authors did not explore some aspects of Greek reasoned inquiry—the explicit questioning of the truthfulness of sources.[6] This is what constituted *historia* for Herodotus. But the overall achievement of "biblical history" was remarkable and served as a model for the texts of the Apocrypha.

We also make comparison here to that group of texts referred to as "rewritten scripture": Jubilees; Pseudo-Philo, *Biblical Antiquities;* and from Qumran, *Temple Scroll, Genesis Apocryphon,* and *Reworked Pentateuch.* Hindy Najman has referred to these as Mosaic discourse, because they channel and extend Moses, yet surprisingly, none of these, except for Jubilees in the Ethiopian canon, became part of the canon or the Apocrypha.[7] Casting an earlier net, however, some scholars also include as rewritten scripture Deuteronomy, 1 and 2 Chronicles, and 1 Esdras. Yet Chronicles and 1 Esdras are not focused on the five books of Moses as are the others; they are thus not rewritten scripture so much as rewritten history. Interestingly, although rewritten scripture was not generally found among the Western Apocrypha, rewritten history was.

Goodman was correct that histories in Israel varied enormously, as they did in Greece. And so we cannot here provide a full description of the genre. However, as a means of raising some insights into the nature of these works, we note two key characteristics of history that also aid in differentiating them from novellas. In Israel as in Greece, histories presented events that were thought to have actually occurred. In Greece the author of history chose a starting point and an ending point, a specified subsection of the timeline that had actually begun earlier and continued beyond the ending point of the history to the author's present.[8] This explicit *selection* of a starting point and ending point, and their connection to the longer timeline of the audience's past, was an important aspect of the history genre. We consider first the choice of an ending point. Artistic texts like poetry, epic, and novels, in contrast to history, concluded with a clear sense of closure. The satisfaction of a well-wrought artistic text was that it had a neat ending. Histories, however, remained open-ended, as if to say, "I am ending our narrative here by choice, but the events of history continued to the present day, and will continue into the future." Jewish histories were similar in this regard. We note the reference to the *chosen* end of the account, combined with the assurance that other events of the timeline would continue, as in 2 Maccabees: "This, then, is how matters turned out with Nicanor, and from that time the city has been in possession of the Hebrews. So I will here end my story. If it is well told and to the point, that is what I myself desired; if it is poorly done and mediocre, that was the best I could do. . . . And here will be the end" (15:37–39). When we turn to the beginnings of Jewish histories we find that, like their Greek counterparts, they also stated clearly that a point in time had been *chosen* as the starting point of the history, the *archē*, and that it could conceivably have begun earlier or later. Just as Herodotus strove to trace the *aitiai* or causes of the Persian War back to the *archē* or primal cause, so also 1 and 2 Maccabees attempt to do the same for the Maccabean Revolt.

If Greek and Israelite histories were similar in positing a beginning point and an ending point on the timeline, and related events that supposedly really occurred, then what were the differences? A significant difference is that Israelite history often lacked a named author. In Greece, the named author of history claimed responsibility for the truth of the account, while in Israelite history there is rather an assumption that history recounts "God's truth" and is not affected by the role of the human author. But as Jewish history moved into the broader Hellenistic world, this attitude changed. Jewish histories came to be penned by named authors—or at least names were associated with the texts: Nicolaus of Damascus, Demetrius the Chronographer, Eupolemus, Cleodemus Malchus, Theophilus, Thallus, and Justus of Tiberias. Second Maccabees, interestingly, was written by an unnamed author but based on the history by a named author, Jason of Cyrene. Thus the histories of the Apocrypha fall into both the Israelite and the Greek model: 1 Maccabees, 1 Esdras, and Meqabyan lack a named author, while 2 Maccabees, Josephus *Jewish War* Book 6, and Josippon all assume a named author—even if the last of these was written centuries after the time of its supposed author.

First Maccabees

When Seleucid officers came to Modein, north of Jerusalem, in 167 BCE and required the sacrifice of a pig to the Greek gods, a Jew stepped forward and agreed to conduct the sacrifice. (For the historical background, see the Introduction.) A local priest, Mattathias, whose family name was Hasmon, was outraged and slew the sacrificing Jew and a Greek officer. This ignited the rebellion that resulted some years later in an independent Judea. The Maccabean Revolt was a family affair; Mattathias had five sons who carried the rebellion to completion, and although the dynasty is referred to as Hasmonean, one son, Judah or Judas, acquired the nickname Maccabee, from the Hebrew or Aramaic word for hammer. The nickname was then applied to the other brothers. The books 1 and 2 Maccabees are twin accounts of the revolt, typical minor histories in many ways. As noted above, history cross-culturally defines the character of a people; it is not objective or disinterested. The heroism of the ruling family is here foremost in the author's plan, reflected in the speeches and prayers. The Hasmonean family instill bravery and devotion to God, and God guides their campaigns and brings them to victory. The two books present slightly different views of God and history. It may seem that 2 Maccabees is presenting a more theological notion of history and 1 Maccabees a more restrained account, but the latter is theological on a traditional model of biblical histories.

After the preamble concerning Alexander, which provides the historical context, the core of the book covers forty years from the accession of Antiochus IV Epiphanes (175 BCE) to the death of Simon, brother of Judah Maccabee (134 BCE). In the process the author justifies both the founding of the Hasmonean dynasty and the adoption of the title high priest by the last brothers, Jonathan and Simon. While Judah Maccabee will be the focus of 2 Maccabees, here it is Simon who finally reestablishes an independent Israel (13:41–51). Simon is thus the main star of this Maccabean history, with Judah the star of 2 Maccabees. John R. Bartlett argues that 1 Maccabees reflects an attempt to bring Chronicles-Ezra-Nehemiah down to the author's own day, but there is little indication of that in the text.[9] The modern reader may perceive in 1 Maccabees a text too obvious in its support of the Hasmonean rulers, too transparent in its methods, and heavy-handed in wrapping the brothers in the mantle of biblical heroes. Yet though 1 Maccabees will never be confused with great literature, its overall rhetorical effect is not to be dismissed. Every ancient Near Eastern king indulged in dynastic propaganda, and this text manages this through an updated version of history writing. Proceeding through the book, we are met with one broad rhetorical effect after another. Traditional biblical elements are combined with Greek-era political concerns in a way that was probably quite effective in establishing the authority of the ruling dynasty.

The biblical references tend to be explicit and the Hellenistic political themes more submerged. Concerning biblical references, Robert Doran points out that the text begins in a way similar to Joshua, Judges, Ruth, and 2 Samuel.[10] The opening can also be compared to that of Judith, and Judah's speech at 3:16–22 is similar to Achior's speech in Judith 5. The text likens the Hasmoneans' violent resistance to that of the heroes of the past.

Mattathias is compared to Phinehas (Pinchas), whose violent actions earned him an eternal priestly covenant (Num 25:1–9), and Jonathan is likened to the judges (1 Macc 9:73). The struggle between Israel and the "nations roundabout" often takes up traditional biblical language:

> In those days certain renegades came out from Israel and misled many, saying, "Let us go and make a covenant with the Gentiles around us, for since we separated from them many disasters have come upon us." This proposal pleased them, and some of the people eagerly went to the king, who authorized them to observe the ordinances of the Gentiles. So they built a gymnasium in Jerusalem, according to Gentile custom, and removed the marks of circumcision, and abandoned the holy covenant. They joined with the Gentiles and sold themselves to do evil. (1:11–15)

This is especially close to Deut 13:12–15, while 1 Macc 1:36–40 echoes the style of biblical prophets. Ancient-sounding heroic poetry, similar to the celebrations of heroes in Judges, is also sung in passages such as this one about Judah:

> Then his son Judah, who was called Maccabeus, took command in his place. All his brothers and all who had joined his father helped him; they gladly fought for Israel.
>> He extended the glory of his people.
>>> Like a giant he put on his breastplate;
>> he bound on his armor of war and waged battles,
>>> protecting the camp by his sword.
>> He was like a lion in his deeds,
>>> like a lion's cub roaring for prey.
>> He searched out and pursued those who broke the law;
>>> he burned those who troubled his people.
>> Lawbreakers shrank back for fear of him;
>>> all the evildoers were confounded;
>>> and deliverance prospered by his hand.

> He embittered many kings,
>> but he made Jacob glad by his deeds,
>> and his memory is blessed forever.
> He went through the cities of Judah;
>> he destroyed the ungodly out of the land;
>> thus he turned away wrath from Israel.
> He was renowned to the ends of the earth;
> he gathered in those who were perishing. (3:1–9)

The resonances to biblical language seem to appear at every turn. The family's own history reminds one of the freeing of Israel: "In the one hundred seventieth year [of the Seleucid Empire] the yoke of the Gentiles was removed from Israel, and the people began to write in their documents and contracts, 'In the first year of Simon the great high priest and commander and leader of the Jews'" (13:41–42). It is lines such as these that prompted George Nickelsburg to refer to 1 Maccabees as "the gospel according to the Hasmoneans."[11] The Hasmoneans are thus clothed throughout in biblical authority, and indeed a passing historical note undermines the authority of their Jewish rivals: when Jews who are not associated with the Hasmonean family launch a campaign without the brothers, it fails utterly: "They did not belong to the family of those men through whom deliverance was given to Israel" (5:62).[12] The Maccabees' forces at 3:55–56 follow the protocols of the holy war of Israel (Exod 18:21, 25; Deut 20:1–9), and the military engagement at chapter 5 is described as the present-day struggle between the descendants of Jacob and the descendants of Esau. Judas, Jonathan, and Simon are portrayed as deliverers and benefactors, and when Judah dies, all Israel cries out, "How is the mighty fallen, the savior of Israel" (9:21), repeating David's lament over Saul and Jonathan (2 Sam 1:19). A final hymn is attached to the text that suggests that the golden age of Davidic and Solomonic rule has been reinstated, and Daniel R. Schwartz calls our attention to some of the details: "It is only when Simon is replaced by his son John [Hyrcanus]—that is, when the dynasty is firmly established because a son succeeds 'after his father' (the book's last words)—that the book can, in fact, end."[13]

Despite the fact that 1 Maccabees often mimics biblical history, Greek aspects of writing history are also found. We may even wonder whether 1 Maccabees is a Hellenistic Jewish text that has merely clothed itself in biblical garb. In chapter 3 the style shifts to a description of military engagements that is typical of Greek history writing. Ezra-Nehemiah had already moved down this road to some extent in regard to Persian connections, but 1 Maccabees now more closely approximates "Greek history." For instance, the author chooses an appropriate *archē* or starting point for the account. The history begins with a preamble on the death of Alexander the Great—who had inaugurated the "Hellenistic world"—and then focuses on three of the five Maccabee brothers, Judah (3:1–9:22), Jonathan (9:23–12:53), and Simon (13:1–14:15). As in Greek histories, an ending point is also explicitly chosen: Simon's successes and the installation of Jonathan as high priest, and the complete independence of Judea from the outside kingdoms. (An addendum is attached that refers to the rise of Simon's son John Hyrcanus.) Rousing speeches also abound in 1 Maccabees (for example, 3:18–22), which owe more to Thucydides's "military harangues" than to Samuel and Kings. In the Greek translation of 1 Maccabees a new Greek term for such speeches, *logoi paraklēseōs,* words of exhortation, may be in evidence (10:24), although it is unclear whether the original Hebrew reflected this.[14] Reference is also made to a large number of archival documents, and the author focuses strongly on diplomatic history, including not only Jewish sources, but also Greek—Seleucid, Ptolemaic, and even Spartan—along with Roman archives. Relations with surrounding Semitic peoples are recounted as well. In addition, there is a careful chronology of events with dates numbered according to the Seleucid calendar, which was no small adjustment: the Seleucid Empire was the first to adopt a continuous calendar that would provide a single timeline for all nations, a universal history.[15]

Observing the structure of a text is important for determining what the author wanted to communicate, and also what the audience may have perceived. But as is the case with many texts, different structuring patterns can seem equally plausible. For Bartlett, the text breaks down into three sections: (1) 1:1–2:70: historical context; (2) 3:1–9:22: Judah; and (3) 9:23–16:24: Jonathan, Simon, and John Hyrcanus.[16] The second and third sections both end with "biblical" historical epilogues: "Now the rest of the acts of Judah, and his wars and the brave deeds that he did, and his greatness, have not been recorded, but they were very many" (9:22); "The rest of the acts of John [Hyrcanus] and his ward and the brave deeds that he did, and the building of the walls that he completed, and his achievements, are written in the annals of his high priesthood, from the time that he became high priest after his father" (16:23–24). This is a simple division, but certainly compelling. However, a more complex literary structure is proposed by David S. Williams.[17] The main body of 1 Maccabees can be divided into two parts, each of which reflects a chiastic structure; Judah is at the center of one and Jonathan of the other, although, as noted, the second chiasm concludes with Simon:

Section One

A. 1:1–10   Alexander the Great dies; Antiochus IV is introduced.
 B. 1:11–15   Renegade Jews seek to join with gentiles around them.
  C. 1:16–64   Temple is desecrated by the Greeks.
   D. 2:1–70   Mattathias urges his sons to rebel.
    E. 3:1–26   Judah leads Jewish revolt.
   D'. 3:27–4:35   Antiochus IV seeks to quell Jewish revolt.
  C'. 4:36–61   Temple is liberated and rededicated by Jews.
 B'. 5:1–68   Righteous Jews defeat gentiles around them.
A'. 6:1–17   Antiochus IV dies.

Section Two

A. 6:18–7:50   Jews obtain freedom of religion.
 B. 8:1–32   Jews make a treaty with Rome.
  C. 9:1–10:66   Jonathan rises in power.
  C'. 10:67–11:74 Jonathan maintains his power.
 B'. 12:1–23   Jews renew their treaty with Rome.
A'. 12:24–14:15   Simon liberates the citadel and obtains independence.

We found above that the book of Judith, a pro-Hasmonean novella written at about the same time as 1 Maccabees, exhibits a very similar two-

part chiastic structure. Indeed, as history and novella, they explore two perspectives on a similar postwar celebration. Williams equates this precise
structuring with literary artistry, but as in the case of Judith, is literary structuring proof of artistry—or rhetoric? Williams's structure also assumes that
chapters 15–16 were added—Josephus did not include these chapters though
he had been following 1 Maccabees closely—but others are not convinced,
and Bartlett's structure takes into account all sixteen chapters. The inclusion of chapters 15–16 has remained controversial. At one point it was also
debated whether some of the many letters and archival materials were inserted into the history, but the scholarly consensus has moved toward the
acceptance of these as part of the original history.[18] It is quite possible, however, that though the texts may preserve some memory of genuine letters
and documents, they may have been heavily edited for their present rhetorical purpose.

In 1 Maccabees Judaism is sometimes described in political terms,
with the law of Moses as a constitution, *politeia,* but the text also relies on
more theological, Deuteronomic language.[19] The author contrasts the conceptions of Hellenistic rule—and their attraction for the Jews of Jerusalem—
with biblical covenant language of separation and distinctness. Greek tyr-
anny is described in terms of Greek universalism: "Antiochus Epiphanes
wrote to his whole kingdom that all should be one people, and that all
should give up their particular customs [*nomima*]" (1:41–42). First Maccabees thus paints a portrait of Antiochus Epiphanes as a mad despot with a
goal of imposing his religious reform on all parts of his empire (compare
Judith). But in reality, his policies in Judea may have been a limited response
to a local rebellion. Antiochus, indeed, was elsewhere considered a reasoned
leader who was right to suppress Judean local rule—although this judgment too may reflect anti-Jewish sentiment.

At any rate, when various Jewish groups are being described, biblical
language is stressed, as here in regard to the turncoat, assimilationist Jews:
"In those days lawless men came forth from Israel and misled many, saying,
'Let us go and make a covenant with the gentiles around us, for since we
separated from them many disasters have come upon us'" (1:11). Also biblical in style are the interspersed poetic fragments. Unlike 2 Maccabees, this

author is restrained in the use of emotion, but as in the books of Samuel, emotional outbursts are included in the poetic passages.[20] The net effect is a sober account of the divinely approved foundation of the Hasmonean dynasty, more biblical in tone than 2 Maccabees. Still, this text never refers to God or Lord, and after the first few chapters—perhaps a different source?—there are few references to prayer or heaven. First Maccabees expresses heartfelt affirmations of God's power to save the people Israel while at the same time communicating the confident belief that the Hasmoneans had, by their own heroism, defeated all enemies. The victory ode of Simon (14:4–15), for instance, makes no mention of God's help. In this respect, 1 Maccabees is somewhat like the roughly contemporary Judith. "The Hasmoneans," says Schwartz, "seem to have been convinced that they won the wars by themselves."[21] It becomes more a biblical *history* than a biblical *theology*. We note as well that by mimicking the "ancient" style of the biblical texts, 1 Maccabees is clearly a Hellenistic-era text that is *looking backwards* to include so many biblical examples of courage and fidelity—Abraham, Joseph, Phinehas, Joshua, Caleb, David, Elijah, and the three companions of Daniel. The text also refers often and explicitly to law, books of the law, and lawbreakers, and so on. At 3:48 the book of law is used as a divinatory guide. These are "late" aspects of a learned Judean style.

Although 1 Maccabees may at first appear to oppose gentiles as a policy, much as Jubilees is anti-gentile, this would be a misreading of the text. The author begins by strongly opposing those Seleucid rulers who reduced Israel to servitude (and this by virtue of their genealogy, 1:1–10!), but alliances develop with other gentiles. Although the nations roundabout threaten Judea, the Nabataeans ally with them (5:25–27, albeit with one group opposing them later, 9:35–42). The distant Spartans had supposedly also joined Israel in alliance and were descended from the same people (ch. 12)! Indeed, when read closely, biblical texts had always distinguished between "eternal enemies" and those gentiles with whom alliances were possible. The alliance with some gentiles in 1 Maccabees (Spartans and Romans) and consistent hatred of others (Seleucids) is not surprising. Yet it is in fact surprising to witness such glowing praise of the Roman constitution, based as it is not on Eastern-style kings but on the votes of a senate (8:14–16). One wonders whether a similarity is seen here with the Jewish assemblies convened at key points in the text (e.g., 5:16). This is another indication that despite strong evidence of what sociologists would call nativist or revitalization-movement tendencies, beneath the surface the text also takes on many of the trappings of Hellenistic culture.[22]

The author's familiarity with the topography of Israel suggests that 1 Maccabees was written there. Origen (in Eusebius, *Church History* 6.25) even knew a more Semitic title, *Sarbēth Sabanaiel,* which in Hebrew or Aramaic was perhaps *spr byt srbny 'l, Book of the House of God's Resisters;* but the original version has unfortunately now been lost, and the text exists only in the Greek translation and the biblical translations derived from that.[23] The author, who had knowledge of Judean archival material and demonstrated ability in Greek and Roman diplomacy, may have been the state historian of the Hasmoneans. The date of 1 Maccabees is not clear. Because 1 Maccabees 8 is pro-Roman, it must have been written before the Roman conquest of Judea in 63 BCE.[24] The conclusion speaks of John Hyrcanus as if his reign is in the past, but since the chiastic structure noted above ends at 14:15, as does the anti-gentile rhetoric, it is sometimes argued that what follows that point was added later. We note here as well that Josephus borrowed material only up to this point; he perhaps knew only a shorter version. Schwartz then prefers to date the core text at 130 BCE, before the ending sections were added, and the final text in the last decade of the second century. DeSilva, however, choosing to include the last two chapters as part of the original composition, argues that the whole must be dated closer to 100 BCE.[25]

Finally, we raise another issue about the modern interpretation of the Maccabean literature. There is a danger in thinking of Jewish identity and the Christian identity that followed as unique in the ancient world, and it is often assumed that Jews were the only native group to resist Hellenization. This, indeed, is what 1 and 2 Maccabees and Judith would have the audience believe. However, native groups other than Jews also rebelled against Hellenistic rulers, both in the Seleucid East and in Egypt. In Egypt, the rebellions also formed around the temples of Egyptian deities. If they had succeeded, they might have been remembered in much the same way as the Maccabees.[26]

Second Maccabees

Two of the most important Jewish histories of our period have been lost:
the books of Nicolaus of Damascus and Jason of Cyrene. Fortunately, the
gist of Jason's five-volume history is preserved in 2 Maccabees, though now
only a fraction of its original length. Second Maccabees is nevertheless a
powerful evocation of Jewish identity in a turbulent world, and its importance is often underestimated. Scholars may suggest other goals of the text,
but "Jewish identity" is always central. While 1 Maccabees is self-consciously
modeled on biblical histories and does not speak in the voice of a particular
"I," the author-editor of 2 Maccabees speaks in a personal, if self-deprecating
voice: "Considering the flood of numbers involved and the difficulty there
is for those who wish to enter upon the narratives of history because of the
mass of material, we have aimed to provide amusement [*psychagōgia*] to those
who wish to read, to provide ease [*eukopia*] for those who are inclined to
memorize, and profit [*ōpheleia*] for all readers" (2:24–25). Further, at the
end the author states (quoted partially above): "If it is well told and to the
point, that is what I myself desired; if it is poorly done and mediocre, that
was the best I could do. For just as it is harmful to drink wine alone, or, again,
to drink water alone, while wine mixed with water is sweet and delicious
and enhances one's enjoyment, so also the style of the story delights the ears
of those who read the work." (15:38–39). And yet, although this author describes carefully the editing of the source written by the named author Jason
of Cyrene, the so-called epitomist does not provide his own name.

Despite its title, 2 Maccabees is in no way a sequel to 1 Maccabees.
The two texts treat some of the same events, but in very different ways. The
author of 2 Maccabees was probably unaware of 1 Maccabees, and indeed
may have written his volume earlier.[27] Among the differences, 2 Maccabees
holds up only Judah of the five brothers for close consideration and includes other heroes not found in 1 Maccabees: the high priest Onias III and
the brave Jewish martyrs of 2 Maccabees 6–7, all of whom have special roles
as intermediaries with God. The failure to include the other brothers or
even Mattathias is surprising, yet this may not reflect a demotion of the rest
of the family. The genre of this text is an encomium, or praise, of one figure,
and this is consistently carried through; no negative treatment of the other

Hasmoneans need be inferred.[28] Second, the sanctity and centrality of the temple, though assumed in 1 Maccabees, is strongly emphasized in 2 Maccabees.[29] Further, while 1 Maccabees presents the courageous deed and death of Mattathias as the turning point in the resistance to oppression, 2 Maccabees joins a number of other texts (Jubilees 23, 4 Maccabees, *Testament of Moses* 9) in assigning the crucial turning point to the death of the Jewish martyrs as a ransom or expiation for the sins of Israel. And finally, a series of miraculous divine interventions are described in 2 Maccabees, along with affirmations of immortality and heavenly reward for the pious (2 Maccabees 7). First Maccabees, on the other hand, in accordance with Sadducean theology, made no allowance for an afterlife, angels, or providence. We may, then, distinguish 1 and 2 Maccabees on the basis of the role of God. First Maccabees features a notion of luck and the correct moment, with no miraculous intervention by God, while 2 Maccabees emphasizes God's providence and miracles.[30]

While 1 Maccabees made no explicit attempt to be taken as "Greek" history, 2 Maccabees exhibits clear traits of popular Greek history, complete with a Greek historical preface and terminology, miracles, studied wordplay, and an appeal to enjoyment.[31] Should the text, then, be considered "history" or grouped instead with the novelistic literature, specifically with Jewish historical novels (see the introduction to Chapter 1)? To be sure, there was some ambiguity concerning histories; historical and novelistic texts lay on a spectrum, some occupying an ambiguous middle area. Non-Jewish texts such as *Story of Ahikar* or *Alexander Romance* might be compared at this point. We cannot, for instance, impose modern standards of truthfulness on ancient histories. It was considered acceptable for even the best historians to compose speeches as they might have been uttered or to mix various sources. Miracles are not unknown in Greek histories, and for lesser histories, there is even more room for marvel and entertainment. Histories were also considered rhetorical, likely read aloud to audiences, and not mere written tomes. The emotional scenes of the suffering Israelites, for instance, comport with the established standards of the reporting of battles and sieges. Second Maccabees, then, can be considered quite typical of popular Greek histories. In terms of the shorter compass of the history—it covers only about

twenty years, ending before the death of Judah Maccabee in 160 BCE—
there would have been models in Greek for the writing of local histories and
so-called historical monographs.[32] At one time scholars also spoke of "tragic
history" or "pathetic (that is, emotional) historiography" and would have
likened 2 Maccabees to this literature, but it is not likely that such a category
was recognized in the ancient world. Yet there was a sense that there were
greater and lesser sorts of histories, and 2 Maccabees would have been associated with "second-register history."[33]

Other differences between 1 and 2 Maccabees that may at first appear to
be minor are actually quite significant. At the beginning of 2 Maccabees, for
instance, we find two letters. The first (1:1–9), dated 124–123 BCE, repeats an
earlier letter of 143 BCE in urging the Jews of Egypt to observe the "Feast of
Booths in the month of Chislev," that is, Hanukkah. The prayer for the recipients in Egypt first invokes the covenant of Abraham, Isaac, and Jacob but
then takes up very interesting imagery: "May God give you all a heart to worship him and to do his will with a strong heart and a willing spirit. May he
open your heart to his law and his commandments, and may he bring peace"
(1:3–4). This language is similar to expressions of the heart in Pr Man 3:5, Ps
51:10, or Deut 6:4–7, but by repeating "heart" three times, it also seems to turn
inward. This may reflect the continuing development in this time period of
a focus on the interior life of the ideal Jewish agent (see the Introduction).

The second letter (1:10–2:18) pursues a different theme. It also urges
the Egyptian Jews to celebrate Hanukkah but turns as well to the fire at the
altar in the temple. This fire, supposedly first ignited by God (2 Chr 7:1–3),
was to remain an eternal flame; the continuity of this fire was crucial. When
the temple was destroyed, pious priests had hidden some of the fire of the
altar in an unknown place. As part of God's plan, Nehemiah was sent to
retrieve the fire, but by then it had been transformed into a thick liquid.
Nevertheless, under Nehemiah's orders it was placed on the wood of the
sacrificial altar. The sun caused it to blaze up, and the sacrifices were carried out. This care for maintaining and transferring the continuous fire of
the earlier temple shows some similarities to non-Jewish stories of the transfer of a sacred cult from one city to another, although here the fire follows a
path away from the temple to a hiding place and then back to Jerusalem.[34]

The "constitutional" language in the two texts also differs. The author of 1 Maccabees takes up very ancient, biblical images, as quoted just above: lawless men came forth from Israel and misled many, saying, "Let us go and make a covenant with the gentiles round about us, for since we separated from them many evils have come upon us" (1 Macc 1:11). Second Maccabees, however, un-self-consciously turns to Greek political language:[35] Antiochus sent an Athenian senator to compel the Jews to forsake their ancestral laws (*patrioi nomoi*) and cease to live (*politeuesthai*) in accordance with the laws of God (2 Macc 6:1). We may also compare 1 and 2 Maccabees in terms of how they view the nations roundabout. In 1 Maccabees, the external enemy is not Hellenism or Greeks in general, as some have supposed, but only the bad kings like Antiochus Epiphanes and also the Jewish "lawless men" who embraced his reform. The bad kings and lawless men, in fact, are not identified with the *Greek* as Other, but with the older biblical nations, the Canaanites, Ammonites, Moabites, and so on.[36] Indeed, 1 Maccabees emphasizes that Israel and Sparta descended from a common ancestor, and Rome is viewed positively. Second Maccabees, however, moves to a more generalized opposition between Judaism and Hellenism. Indeed, the two terms, Judaism (*Ioudaismos*) and Hellenism (*Hellēnismos*), both appear in 2 Maccabees for the first time, invented for precisely this distinction. Elsewhere the author characterizes the construction of the Greek gymnasium as the "height of Hellenism [*Hellēnismos*] and a means of increasing 'foreignism' [*allophylismos*]" (2 Macc 4:13). Erich Gruen has argued that the words do not appear in the same passage and are not contrasted with each other, but they both occur a number of times in the central section of the text (*Ioudaismos* 2:21, 8:1, 14:38; *Hellēnismos* 4:13), and their novelty—both are created for this context—speaks to an intentional philosophical contrast that is lacking in 1 Maccabees.[37] The use of "foreignism" only strengthens the contrast. Although the opposition between Judaism and Hellenism may not be as sharp as in, say, Jubilees, it is still understood as a philosophical or even religious difference.

In connection with this last point, we also note that 2 Maccabees emphasizes the word *Ioudaios* more strongly than does 1 Maccabees (see the Introduction and the introduction to Chapter 1). It has been suggested, though with some controversy, that 2 Maccabees even attaches a new sense to this word. The Greek term *Ioudaios* translated the Hebrew *Yehudi,* one from Judah. In English, *Ioudaios* could be translated as either "Judean" or "Jew." It is surprisingly rare in Hellenistic Judaism, and although it occurs forty-one times in 1 Maccabees, it is found sixty-five times in the much shorter 2 Maccabees. Shaye J. D. Cohen highlighted some of the *Ioudaios* passages for close analysis:[38]

2 Macc 6:6
After the new laws of Antiochus, people could neither keep the Sabbath, nor observe the festivals of their ancestors, nor so much as confess to being a Jew [*Ioudaion*].

2 Macc 9:13–17
On his deathbed, Antiochus IV Epiphanes repented of his evil deeds in suppressing Jewish practices, and promised that if he lived he would become a Jew [*Ioudaion esesthai*] and proclaim the power of God.

In these passages, *Ioudaios* becomes something other than a standard ethnic designation of "one from Judea." Cohen argues that here it first comes to have a sense of a heightened identity: a member of a category into which one could convert or convert away from. Corroborating his theory, the word *Ioudaios* is invested with a stronger sense of identity in the Jewish novellas.[39] Other Jewish identity terms also are invoked somewhat differently in 1 and 2 Maccabees. "Israel" is an important identity term in 1 Maccabees, appearing sixty-five times, while in 2 Maccabees it appears only five times, restricted to stereotyped formulas. "Hebrews," on the other hand, absent from 1 Maccabees, occurs three times in 2 Maccabees, and always with a strong affirmation of identity (7:31, 11:13, 15:37).

Still, this sense of a noble Jewish identity that is superior to Greek should not be interpreted as a deep chasm. The tone is often fairly restrained concerning Hellenism *in general,* as opposed to particular Hellenistic tyrants like Antiochus Epiphanes. The cataloguing of peoples in the

Hellenistic world, and especially the sense that some were "good" and some "bad," was more complex than at first appears. For instance, whereas Greeks had long looked down on "barbarians" (*barbaroi*), we are surprised to find 2 Maccabees stating that the Jewish loyalists repulsed the "barbarian hordes," that is, Greeks![40] These puzzling examples can perhaps be explained as "colonial universalism," the strong affirmation by the colonized that their conceptions are in fact superior to and more universal than those of the colonizer (see the Conclusion).

Second Maccabees finally achieves resolution by establishing Nicanor's Day (15:36), a festival celebrating the Maccabees' defeat of the Seleucid general. It has been plausibly suggested that this history, like Greek Esther and 3 Maccabees, served as the reading for a celebration. The festival, however, may have been a narrative motif only, meant to provide a resolution to the action.[41] In favor of this judgment, we note that *two* festivals are promulgated in 2 Maccabees, Nicanor's Day and Hanukkah (10:6–7), each of which serves as the resolution of one of the two major parts of the work. However, even if the festivals were originally only literary motifs, when the two letters from another hand are placed at the beginning, the resulting work undoubtedly becomes a festal text. It is now more like Greek Esther and 3 Maccabees in serving as a festal document, a narrative of God's miraculous intervention that is to be celebrated at a particular festival.[42]

The most enduring part of 2 Maccabees is the detailed account of the deaths of the Jewish martyrs: the elderly scribe Eleazar, and the mother and her seven sons, all unnamed. The origins of the concept of martyrdom were thus already present in Judaism before the Christian developments. What is significant here, however, is that it is not *one* hero who is featured, but nine, of different ages and genders. The ideal moral agent is now not limited to the Maccabee warriors, but can be anyone—male or female, old or young— who remains loyal to Jewish law to the point of death. Says Daniel R. Schwartz, "Martyrs, rather than soldiers, are the real heroes of the book, and the long central section of the book, Chapters 6–7, dedicated to martyrs, provides the turning point; after those scenes, and because of the blood of those martyrs (7:38; 8:3–4), everything changes."[43] A *philosophical* understanding of the persecution is also developed before the reader: "These

punishments were designed not to destroy but to discipline our people"
(6:12). In fact, God shows mercy to Israel by punishing *now* as opposed to
waiting for a later judgment that will be more harsh (6:13–16). The seven
sons and their mother also enter into a philosophical dialogue with the king
as they are tortured and executed. This achieves two rhetorical goals: it allows the martyrs to express noble Jewish philosophical ideals—the Greek
tradition of the "noble death"—and it characterizes the king as a "blustery
tyrant," a common foil in Greek philosophy. The tortured sons with their
last breath speak in the language of virtue: "You accursed wretch, you dis-
miss us from this present life, but the king of the universe will raise us up
to an everlasting renewal of life, because we have died for his laws" (7:9).
When it comes the mother's turn, she also displays a philosopher's forti-
tude in the face of death: "Although she saw her seven sons perish within a
single day, she bore it with good courage because of her hope in the Lord.
She encouraged each of them in the language of their ancestors. Filled with
a noble spirit, she reinforced her woman's reasoning with a male spirit"
(7:20–21). She finally places the list of sufferings in a different perspective,
that of an eternal reward: "Accept death, so that in God's mercy I may get
you back again" (7:29). The youngest brother is last and speaks longest. He
also sees in their deaths an expiation for the sins of the nation: "through me
and my brothers bring to an end the wrath of the Almighty that has justly
fallen on our whole nation" (7:38).

Second Maccabees was composed sometime after 160 BCE, the years
just after the Maccabean Revolt. It was not likely composed after 63 BCE,
when the Roman general Pompey conquered Jerusalem, because it is positive toward Rome (4:11; 8:10, 36; 11:34–36). On the basis of the letters at the
beginning, we can limit the date further to between 143 BCE and the time of
John Hyrcanus or his successors, 125–63 BCE. It was probably epitomized
in Judea, although some have argued for the diaspora.[44] The books 1 and
2 Maccabees exercised a broad but intermittent influence on both Jews
and Christians. That the Maccabee brothers were imbued with great authority is seen in the fact that memorial tombs were constructed for them
near Jerusalem (Josephus, *Antiquities* 12.412; Tertullian, *Adversus Iudaeos*
4.10). Although Jews did not at first adopt the texts of 1 and 2 Maccabees,

the story of the Maccabees resonated in rabbinic texts (*Lamentations Rabbah* 1:16, 50; *b. Gittin* 57b; *Pesikta Rabbati* 43:180). Just as Jews would later transpose the Judith story to the Maccabean period, after the Bar Kokhba revolt the Maccabean incident was "updated" to the Roman period.[45] Josippon and Meqabyan demonstrate that its influence was felt in the medieval period, and the narrative would become popular with Muslims as well. The sixteenth-century *Sefer Hazikhronot* includes 1 and 2 Maccabees.

Of the early versions of the Christian Bible, only Alexandrinus and Venetus included 2 Maccabees; however, the segment on the martyrs in 2 Maccabees 6–7 created a paradigm of martyrdom that was very influential. Fourth Maccabees depends directly on 2 Maccabees 6–7, and the martyrs serve as examples in Heb 11:35–36. This was commented on by Origen, Cyprian, John Chrysostom, and Gregory of Nazianzus.[46] The stirring Maccabean story would find a place in later European culture, as well. Judah Maccabee was included with other Old Testament figures, including Judith, in the magnificent floor mosaic in the Siena Duomo Cathedral. Raphael was commissioned by Julius II to paint a large fresco in the Vatican, *The Expulsion of Heliodorus from the Temple* (1511–1512; fig. 10). At the time of the Protestant Reformation, Catholics quoted Judas's prayer for the dead (2 Macc 12:45–46) to justify intercession for the dead. In the seventeenth and eighteenth centuries, when a sense of nationalism gave rise to group and civic scenes for group portraits, the Maccabees and Judith were enlisted. In music, George Frideric Handel composed *Judas Maccabaeus,* second only to his *Messiah* in popularity, and Antonio Ciseri captured both the civic space and high emotions of the mother's sacrifice (fig. 11).

Jewish songs and prayers arose in the medieval period concerning Hanukkah, and among Jews today there are three slightly different understandings of the Maccabean Revolt:

1. It is a warning story about assimilation.
2. In Israel, it is a story of nationalist founding and independence of the Seleucids.
3. In very religious Jewish circles, it is a miracle of God's intervention, with less emphasis on history.

Figure 10. Raphael (Raffaello Sanzio), *The Expulsion of Heliodorus from the Temple*, 1511–1512. Stanze di Raffaello, Apostolic Palace, Vatican City. Scala/Art Resource, NY

Each of these depends on a different ancient narrative: the first follows the story line of 2 Maccabees, the second follows the nationalist story of 1 Maccabees, and the third is based on a rabbinic version. Modern Zionism, especially the strain more oriented to the foundation of a Jewish state than to religious Judaism, regarded 1 Maccabees highly. For Daniel R. Schwartz, "To the extent that Zionism, especially since the Holocaust, is based on a lack of trust both in gentiles and in God, 1 Maccabees fit right in."[47]

First Esdras

First Esdras is a historical narrative that closely parallels parts of 2 Chronicles, Ezra, and Nehemiah, with an inserted court story not found elsewhere.

Figure 11. Antonio Ciseri, *Saint Felicity and the Maccabean Martyrs,* 1863. Santa
Felicità, Florence. Scala/Art Resource, NY

The blocks of material in 1 Esdras and their relation to proto-canonical texts are as follows:

1 Esdras	Parallel Biblical Section
1:1–55	2 Chr 35:1–36:21
2:1–14	Ezra 1
2:15–25	Ezra 4
3:1–5:6	Three bodyguards story (not known elsewhere)
5:7–70	Ezra 2:1–4:5
6:1–9:36	Ezra 5–10
9:37–55	Neh 7–8

First Esdras may have been woven from these biblical texts, but it is also possible that it derives from an earlier historical narrative and that Chronicles-Ezra-Nehemiah constitute parts of later, secondary editions. Depending, then, upon where it comes in this editorial process, the date of this text could range over several centuries, from the fifth century to the second century BCE. Although included in the appendix to the Vulgate, it was not accepted as one of the deuterocanonical texts by the Council of Trent in 1545–1563. It was, however, treated as deuterocanonical in the Anglican Church and fully canonical in the churches of the East.

First Esdras arises out of a rich tradition of texts that took the name of Ezra or Esdras (Esdras is the Greek and Latin form of Ezra).[48] First, it should be noted that 1 and 2 Chronicles and Ezra and Nehemiah from the Hebrew Bible share much in the way of language and editorial perspective. This led some scholars to suggest that they were edited by one figure or school, termed the "Chronicler." The similarities among the texts are undeniable, although fewer scholars today attribute the texts to one school. Yet even if there was no clear Chronicler, many of the texts in the name of Ezra or Esdras are indirectly related to this tradition. Among these texts we find a strong tendency to combine and rewrite previous texts. The books 1 and 2 Chronicles, for example, were rewritten versions of Samuel and Kings, and Ezra-Nehemiah in the Hebrew Bible was likely assembled from several sources. One can compare rewritten scripture, but the present texts do not treat the Moses segment of Israel's history; they are, rather, rewritten history. They narrate the transition from the preexilic period to the exile and restoration. The larger Bible, then, contained quite a number of texts that covered this transition.

If 1 Esdras was a rewritten version of parts of Chronicles, Ezra, and Nehemiah, its purpose was not likely to improve the chronological problems in those texts; it often makes things worse. What we can suggest is that the purpose of 1 Esdras was to provide an idealized account of a segment of Israelite history. As we have seen, Greek historians carefully marked a beginning and end to their narratives, an *archē* and a *telos*. First Esdras begins with the "good" king Josiah's celebration of Passover in 622 BCE, then narrates the decline in Israelite history through the disaster of the exile under Zedekiah, and follows with a positive upswing: the beginning of restoration under Ezra in the fifth century BCE. First Esdras thus begins with a constitutional festival enacted before the temple while it was still standing—a symbol of a time of peace and strength—and concludes with the restoration of the temple and a new constitutional festival in its presence. At this latter festival, the law is read aloud. First Esdras probably presupposes that the audience knows much of the history of Israel and Judah; this selective narrative may have been composed as a festival reading. In this narrative account the exile does not create a fundamental break in history, but it is a temporary setback only, which God has indeed overcome.[49] In addition, the Prayer of Manasseh (also in the Apocrypha) may be an extension of this same tradition. Granting the plausibility of this rationale for the arc of the narrative, it still must be noted that it is not clear how 1 Esdras began and ended. The opening is unusually abrupt, and the ending even more so. The snippet at the end, an incomplete sentence, may have been added as a way of indicating where the narrative would connect with the longer version of Ezra-Nehemiah.

The fact that 1 Esdras concludes specifically with Ezra's heroic role in the restoration of the temple cult, and not Nehemiah's, may also be significant. The verses from the book of Nehemiah that are found in 1 Esdras (1 Esd 9:37–55 are taken from Nehemiah 7–8) derive from the section that many scholars believe was originally part of an Ezra section that was later interlarded with the Nehemiah Memoir. First Esdras in its present form thus lacks any treatment of Nehemiah's activity. The two figures not only had their separate memoirs in Ezra-Nehemiah, but they were often revered independently of each other in later Judaism. Thus it is possible that Ezra is either intentionally separated from Nehemiah and promoted to an independent, authoritative position, or was only joined to Nehemiah by the editor of Ezra-Nehemiah. Zipora Talshir presses further: the intent here is to establish Ezra-Zerubbabel, not Ezra-Nehemiah; Zerubbabel even may have been demoted in Ezra-Nehemiah.[50] If Ezra was separated off and promoted, it is interesting that a preference for him continued in rabbinic tradition as well. He was associated with the teaching of the law and considered a second Moses. Says *b. Sanhedrin* 21b: "Ezra would be worthy for the Torah to have been given to Israel through him had Moses not preceded him." One would also like to know more precisely how 1 Esdras originally began and ended. Interestingly, however, the Greek is superior to the Greek translation of Chronicles and Ezra-Nehemiah in the Greek Old Testament.[51] The translation was evidently not governed by the same need to preserve a literal reading. This may reflect another possible reason for its composition: it was perhaps viewed as an improved edition, fit for more educated Greek-speaking Jews. Certainly Josephus and Clement of Alexandria, who used 1 Esdras, may have preferred it for that reason. It was thus a well-accepted history by the first century CE.

An entertaining court narrative is inserted at 1 Esd 3:1–5:6 that is not found elsewhere in ancient Judaism; it concerns Zerubbabel in the court of Darius of Persia. Zerubbabel is introduced in Ezra-Nehemiah as well, but he is the warm-up act to Ezra and Nehemiah and not a main character as he is here.[52] The opening of this court narrative is similar to Esther, and the rewards proposed are like those conferred upon Mordecai (Esther 6). The ending focuses on written edicts and letters, common motifs in both Jewish novelistic and historical texts.[53] This "court contest" is similar to Daniel 2, 4, and 5 and is perhaps even more structured for entertainment. At the court of Darius three royal bodyguards propose a contest: "Let each of us state what is strongest. To the one whose statement seems wisest, Darius will give rich gifts . . . and he will sit next to Darius and shall be called kinsman of

Darius" (3:4–7). Their responses are written down and placed under Darius's pillow. The first wrote "Wine is strongest," the second "The king is strongest," and the third—who is only later identified as Zerubbabel (4:13)—wrote "Women are strongest, but above all things truth is victor."

When the king awakes and reads the statements, he summons the bodyguards to explain their reasoning. They speak in turn, and the speeches are humorous, clever, and satirical, each superior to the one before. The first two are restrained and "conservative"—they assume the value of moderation in wine and respect for the power of the king—while the third, by Zerubbabel, pushes the boundaries of what is permissible. Darius, he says, is prisoner of his concubine Apame (4:29–31). Zerubbabel is thus more a trickster, and the exposé of the treacherous woman at court would resonate with stories of the Persian court found in Herodotus, Xenophon of Athens, and Ctesias.[54] The speech at first depicts women as a danger, leading to their husbands' lapse of self-control, though it is also stated that men bear responsibility for falling as well. Even so, says William Loader, "it probably assumes that women's sexuality is so out of control and dangerous that men must be especially careful to control their responses (and by implication to control women's sexuality)." Nickelsburg adds, "If wine *leads* men's minds astray, women cause men to *lose* their minds."[55] Like many ancient discussions about the relations of the sexes, the point of view of men is the one that is presented (compare Ben Sira). At any rate, the literary device of a round of speeches, the first of which are on a humorous or more mundane level and the last transcending them to propose an eternal truth, is found also in Job and Plato's *Symposium*.

A common question is the origin and nature of the final speech on truth. Truth will rightly sound like a Greek value of independent reason, but it also held an important place in Persian affirmations of eternal truth, and in Egyptian tradition as well. Verses 37–40 do add righteousness and unrighteousness (*dikaios, adikia*) to the debate about truth, a congenial marriage of Western and Persian ethical language, but the speech is perhaps not supposed to sound "typically" biblical. Israelite tradition speaks often of wisdom, but truth, *'emet,* is used in a practical sense of honesty or faithfulness, and rarely of abstract "truth."[56] A number of scholars have proposed that this section grew in stages. An older entertaining folk riddle about

"What is the strongest?" formed the basis and probably originally featured a courtier so clever that he could insult the king and get away with it—a common folk motif. Since Zerubbabel's name appears to have been artificially inserted late in the story, it is conceivable that the third and most clever courtier was not originally Zerubbabel, and perhaps not even Jewish. At any rate, this figure is now given the name of an important Jewish figure from the past, Zerubbabel, just as the name of Daniel was perhaps inserted into the story of Susanna and an anonymous youth. It is also noteworthy that in this story there is no mention of Jews, Israel, covenant, Torah, prophets, priests, temple, exile, Jerusalem, or David. The third speech, originally on women, was also fitted with an additional and more serious hymn to truth, although even this may not have been originally Jewish. As the court narrative now stands, it affirms that Zerubbabel was indeed the most clever of courtiers and that Jews can speak to the international, universal value of truth better than anyone—another example of colonial universalism. This story is placed here to create a transitional point in the historical narrative, as the process of rebuilding would have been a major constitutional moment for Israel.

Finally, then, how does 1 Esdras differ from the parallel sections in the biblical texts? The temple and the law are mentioned more often in 1 Esdras, and Ezra is not just a priest but a high priest (9:40). Several other figures are given greater prominence here. Josiah, the king loyal to God who instituted a massive reform, begins the narrative and is depicted even more heroically here (1:33). Jeremiah is introduced at various points as the principal prophet of the exile (1:28, 58). Most remarkable, however, is the increased role of Zerubbabel, the governor of Judea responsible for rebuilding the temple (Ezra 1–6). Here he is the main hero of the Judean restoration (chs. 3–6). He was in the lineage of David and would have been viewed by the Persians as a potential threat. A conservative view of Israelite intermarriage is also assumed in 1 Esdras, although this is found in the biblical book of Ezra as well. Says Jonathan Klawans, "First Esdras, with its retelling of Ezra's opposition to intermarriage, is certainly among the more exclusive approaches to be found (1 Esd. 8.68–9.36), speaking even of the people's 'holy seed' (8.70; cf. Ezra 9.3). First Esdras is seconded here only by Jubilees, which is similarly vehement in its opposition to intermarriage (22.16–23)."[57]

   The final construction of the story, therefore, emphasizes Jewish identity and not just the humor of the situation. As we have noted, the term for
"Jew" or "Judean," *Ioudaios,* is found as a strong identity term mainly in the
novellas (see Chapter 1). In this novelistic little story it appears as well:
"Cyrus wrote in behalf of all the Jews who were going up from his kingdom
to Judea, in the interest of their freedom, that no officer or satrap or governor or treasurer should forcibly enter their doors; that all the country that
they would occupy should be theirs without tribute; that the Idumeans
should give up the villages of the Jews that they held" (4:49–50). Although
it was noted that Josephus (*Antiquities* 10.70–83, 11.1–157) and Clement of
Alexandria preferred 1 Esdras over Ezra-Nehemiah as their historical source,
it has not exercised much influence in Jewish or Christian culture. Many
early Christian theologians cited it in passing but did not treat it extensively.
The story of Zerubbabel and the two bodyguards was included in Josippon
6 and from there was taken up in *Chronicles of Jerahmeel.*

Josippon

For most Western scholars, the engagement with Ethiopic as an ancient language begins and ends with 1 Enoch and Jubilees. Indeed, these are very
important ancient texts, preserved, for instance, with great interest at Qumran as well as in the Ethiopian Bible. Still, there are other texts in the Ethiopian canon that demand attention, some hardly studied at all in the West.
Among these are Josippon and 1, 2, and 3 Meqabyan. Sefer Yosippon, or the
book of Josippon, is known in Ethiopian tradition as Zena Ayhud, *History
of the Jews.* Written in Italy in 953 CE, but wrongly attributed to Joseph ben
Gorion, it is a Jewish history covering the period of the late stages of the
Second Temple period down to the destruction of the temple.[58] Since Josephus mentions in the introduction to *Jewish War* that he had first written
his history in Aramaic for his fellow Jews, it was only natural that scholars
saw in Josippon the earlier Aramaic account. This theory, however, has now
been discounted. The text was translated into Arabic and in the fourteenth
century into Ethiopic. Although Yosef Yerushalmi, in *Zakhor: Jewish History and Jewish Memory,* had argued that there was no Jewish history writing

from the classical rabbinic period through the Renaissance, Reuben Bonfil counters that there were a number of historical texts, including Josippon.[59] Our unknown author made use of the Hebrew Bible, the Christian Latin Bible (including the texts of the Apocrypha), the New Testament, and Latin versions of Josephus transmitted by Rufinus and Pseudo-Hegesippus. The author follows 1 Maccabees fairly closely at times and utilized Virgil's *Aeneid* and Livy's *History* as well. Although the many editions vary, the text can also include an account of Alexander the Great, Bel and the Dragon, and 1 Esdras 3–4 on the three courtiers.

Josippon was originally written to counter polemics of Christian authors, telling the story of the fall of Jerusalem from a Jewish view of God and covenant, interrupted but not canceled or transferred to Christians. Very popular with Jews, it was translated and transmitted widely and received as well by Christian and Muslim readers. To this day, Josippon is read by orthodox Jews in Hebrew as the "original Josephus." It is also interesting that Josippon was influenced by the Christian Latin Bible at about the same time that Jews adapted versions of Judith, Tobit, and Susanna, reflecting a new Jewish interest in the Christian Old Testament. Josippon is surprisingly "modern" and rationalistic in that it is intended as a record of the past that is not treated principally for its theological references.[60] As Saskia Dönitz says, "*Sefer Yosippon* represents a unique Jewish literary work possibly written in a complex environment where Jews, Christians, and Muslims met. Moreover, it belongs in a region and time in which Greek and Latin (and maybe Arabic) existed side by side." Steven Bowman also bemoans the fact that the text is not fully appreciated in this regard:

> [*Yosippon*] is occasionally glanced at by contemporary historians who read it, not through [David] Flusser's insightful commentary but through their biased attitude towards legend and mythology. But then that has been the fate of *Yosippon* since its appearance to be misread, misidentified, misappropriated. Despite, indeed perhaps because of, this tradition, *Yosippon* is one of the most important books produced by Italian-Byzantine-Ashkenazi Jewry and has been a central influence for the past mil-

lennium on Jewish perceptions of the past as well as in the nineteenth and twentieth centuries a popular guide for the future.[61]

Bowman himself characterizes Josippon as a combination of history and
midrash that strongly influenced both Jewish conceptions of their historical
origins and later Jewish nationalism. Still uncertain is the status of Josippon
within the Ethiopian Orthodox Tewahedo Church. Although it held an
important place in the Ethiopian tradition, sometimes mentioned in canon
lists, sometimes supplanting Meqabyan, there is no evidence that it was
ever published in Ethiopic Bibles. It was also mentioned as part of the Coptic canon and sometimes was published with other biblical books. We must
recognize the ambiguity of canon in this context; there was simply no clearly
demarcated canon. The same is true of all scriptural traditions at one time
or another, and we should perhaps view the idea of a fixed canon as a Greek
and Western idea.

Meqabyan

The Ethiopian Orthodox Bible lacks 1, 2, 3, and 4 Maccabees but includes
a text generally divided into three parts, 1, 2, and 3 Meqabyan, sometimes
referred to as Ethiopian Maccabees. Practically unread in the West even by
scholars, the texts were perhaps written in the late fourteenth to early fifteenth century.[62] Since they are not Jewish texts, but an Ethiopian Christian
compendium of ancient Jewish history with a light sprinkling of Christian
references, they are included in this book as further examples, like 5 and
6 Ezra, of Christian composition of "Old Testament"–like texts. Still, it
should be noted that these are the only distinctively Ethiopian texts in the
Old Testament of the Ethiopian Orthodox Tewahedo Church. The name
Meqabyan is clearly related to Maccabees; the Ethiopian texts are influenced by that tradition, and Alessandro Bausi refers to them as the Ethiopic
Books of Maccabees.[63] The connection is evident in some passages, but the
Meqabyan texts are a series of sermons utilizing many biblical examples to
draw moral and theological conclusions. A strong, explicit exhortation is
often intoned: do not worship idols, do not deny resurrection, do not be

like those biblical figures who abandoned the law of God, and so on. There are consequences for one's theology and mode of life. Wicked people, in the Bible and after, worshipped idols and denied the hope of immortality; they will be confined in Gehenna. The righteous refused to worship idols, placed their faith instead in resurrection, and will be rewarded with immortality. The Old Testament stories, including Tobit, are retold repetitively in their many permutations, although no explicit examples are taken from the New Testament. The occasion for the texts was probably a religious reform intended to present a stronger profile to Muslim and other surrounding peoples. The campaign against idolatry was also likely aimed at non-Christian practices within the Ethiopian kingdom.[64]

First Meqabyan begins by retelling the events of the Maccabean Revolt, but in a very different fashion. It treats two revolts, the first against Tsirutsaydan, king of Media and Midian, who worshipped idols. The name Tsirutsaydan is likely derived from Tyre and Sidon (*Tsyr u Tsaydon* in Punic/Phoenician). Antiochus IV Epiphanes had stamped this on coins in those Phoenician cities, and so Tsirutsaydan may have originally suggested the Seleucid rulers against whom the Maccabees rebelled. Just as the Maccabees were a family of warriors, a father and five sons, so here a Benjaminite named Maccabeus, with sons Abya, Seela, and Pantos, refused to worship idols. (Two other unnamed sons will be mentioned in chapter 3, bringing the number of sons to five). In chapter 15 a new narrative arc begins that is also related to the stories of the Maccabees: Yihuda (= Yehuda or Judah), Mebikyas, and Meqabees revolted against King Akrandis of Midian. Akrandis is standard Ge'ez for Alexander, so here perhaps Alexander I Balas is meant, who succeeded Antiochus IV Epiphanes and ruled from 150 to 145 BCE.[65] The stories thus evoke the Maccabean narratives at points but are also so different that they are not simply retellings. Here, for instance, "Maccabeus" is of the tribe of Benjamin—as was Paul, but not the Maccabees—and the names of the sons in the first arc are not like those of the historical Maccabees. The three names added in chapter 15 also evoke the Maccabees, but the story is more similar to Daniel 3 and the non-Maccabean martyrs at 2 Maccabees 7, in addition to Christian martyr stories.

More explicit Christian references are found at 1 Meqabyan 8:21 (com-

pare 8:35), 21:1–2, and 3 Meqabyan 1. Throughout, God's just punishment
of Israel is assumed (compare Josippon and 5 Ezra, and see Josephus *Jewish War* Book 6). Yet the texts also reflect the strong emphasis in the Ethiopian Orthodox Tewahedo Church on aspects that have been associated
with a positive incorporation of "Judaizing" tendencies, or "Jewish Christianity": strict Sabbath observance, circumcision, and veneration for the ark
of the covenant. Old Testament law retained a very strong hold. At 1 Meqabyan 24:16, the dietary laws are treated in what seems a "Jewish" way. As
Edward Ullendorff notes, "Early Jewish influences, deep-rooted Old Testament practices, and a widespread *imitatio Veteris Testamenti* [imitation of
the Old Testament] have combined to bring about a syncretistic nature
of Ethiopian civilization."[66] Yet it is important that these impressions not
be misinterpreted through a Western lens. All Christian churches have retained some aspects of Old Testament law and life and rejected others; the
Ethiopian choice may appear remarkable, or even more "Jewish," only when
the European tradition is taken as the norm.

Aside from the Maccabee family related arcs, the other episodes are
similar to the stories in Daniel 1–6, Bel and the Dragon, and 2 Maccabees 7.
Josippon also may have provided inspiration for Meqabyan, and indeed
some canon lists substitute Josippon for Meqabyan. The constant theme of
the parody of idols and the reward of immortality is also similar to Wisdom
of Solomon. At one point the text calls to mind 3 Maccabees, in that the
blustery wicked king tries time and again to destroy the dead bodies of the
martyrs, yet they remain intact. Here we perhaps see influences of the Christian martyr tradition, where relics are valued and retain divine power. The
exact nature of resurrection is not always clear, perhaps suggesting a distance from Western theological discussions. At one point, "Angels received
and took their souls to the garden where Isaac and Abraham and Jacob are,
where joy and happiness are found" (1 Meqabyan 3). In the central section,
1 Meqabyan also treats the sins of Israel, emphasizing God's decision to
transfer the glory of Israel over to Christians: Jerusalem fell into sin, killing
the prophets in her delight. She did not abide in the nine commandments
and proper worship. When the dead arise, the sins of Jerusalem will be revealed, and God will judge her. He will take revenge and extinguish her for
all the sins that she had committed (11:3–4).

First Meqabyan is in prose, but 2 and 3 Meqabyan are poetic. They cover much of the same material as the first book, albeit in a reflective manner. The error of Samaritans, Jews, Sadducees, and Pharisees is recounted in turn. The first three groups deny resurrection. "We will die tomorrow," Jews say. "Let us eat and drink. There is no joyful bliss we will see in the grave." This is a brief sounding of a theme found in Wisdom of Solomon 2, but in this Christian text most Jews are identified with the position of the wicked in Wisdom 2. The Pharisees alone express a vague notion of resurrection (2 Meqabyan 14). An interesting digression provides arguments from nature regarding resurrection: fingernails and hair grow when cut, and plants grow from seeds. A poetic reflection is also expressed on how death entered into our world:

> By Adam's infringement of God's command,
>> we received hardship as a result.
> Our flesh melted in the grave
>> and our beautiful words were buried in the earth.
> Worms proceeded from our shining eyes,
>> and our features perished in the grave and became
>>> dust. (2 Meqabyan 18–19)

Third Meqabyan is similar, although here Christ is explicitly mentioned. Christ will come to Egypt in a later era (in the form of the Ethiopian Church) and destroy Diabolos, who has led people astray (ch. 1). Yet even in passages where one might have expected a reference to Christ, especially regarding resurrection, it is lacking:

> You blind of reasoning, who say "Persons who died won't arise,"
>> if you have knowledge or wisdom,
>> how will you say persons who died won't arise
>> by their Creator God's word? (3 Meqabyan 10)

In some ways, 1 Meqabyan is similar to the eleventh-century Jewish version of Judith, also seasoned with new stories about the Maccabees, as well as Catholic legends of saints.

Josephus *Jewish War* Book 6

As noted above, Josippon is influenced by Josephus, and now we note that
Josephus's *Jewish War* Book 6 was included in the Syriac Bible as an appendix to 4 Maccabees. Both texts are Jewish, telling the story of the Jewish
War in a way that is sympathetic to Jewish sensibilities, but they may have
been included in their respective Christian Bibles to narrate the fall of the
temple, that historical moment when God supposedly punished the Jews
for rejecting Christ. The emotional detail found in Josephus may have contributed to a Christian theological narrative. We note, for instance, how Josephus begins Book 6: "The sufferings of Jerusalem thus daily grew worse,
the fury of the rebels being intensified by the calamities in which they were
involved, and the famine now extending its ravages from the people to
themselves."[67] The sufferings of the Jewish people are treated often in *Jewish War* as a way of communicating the tragedy of the fall of Jerusalem and
the blow to Israel. Book 6 thus represents a crescendo. Also like Josippon,
and perhaps like earlier Greek histories as well, *Jewish War* presents the
struggle in a way surprisingly fair to both sides. Although Josephus had
essentially changed sides, from rebel general of the Jews to field historian of
the Romans, he brings to life the experiences of war of both parties. Here,
for instance, the Romans breach the main wall of the fortress in Jerusalem
only to discover that behind it lies a second wall:

> The effect of this incident [the destruction by the Romans of
> the main wall] on the spirits of the belligerents was surprising.
> For the Jews, who might reasonably have been disheartened by
> it, were, in consequence of their being prepared for this ca-
> tastrophe, and having taken precaution to meet it, quite confi-
> dent, as [the fortress] still remained; whereas the unlooked-for
> joy of the Romans at the downfall was extinguished by the ap-
> pearance of a second wall which [the rebel leader] John and his
> party had built within. (6.29–31)

Book 6 also describes the grim end of the second temple, focusing as well
on the cessation of sacrifices (6.93–99).

In his history Josephus often included his own speeches—with a generous dose of self-promotion—one of which was addressed to the rebel leader John of Gischala. Here Josephus gives voice to the belief that God had willed the fall of Jerusalem because of the sins of its inhabitants:

> Who knows not the records of the ancient prophets and that oracle which threatens this poor city and is even now coming true? For they foretold that it would then be taken whensoever one should begin to slaughter his own countrymen.[68] And is not the city, aye and the whole temple, filled with your corpses? God it is then, God Himself, who with the Romans is bringing the fire to purge His temple and exterminating a city so laden with pollutions. (6.109–10)

We may perceive, then, what the Syrian Christians saw in Josephus's history: something similar to what the Ethiopian Christians saw in Josippon and Meqabyan. Josephus provided an eloquent theology of God's abandonment of Israel on account of its sins. In addition, the pathos of war, told vibrantly by the historian, served to dramatize all the more powerfully the divine effect: how the mighty are fallen!

THREE

Wisdom Texts

THROUGHOUT THE ANCIENT NEAR EAST, wisdom was asso-
ciated with courtly instruction and the profession of the scribe. This can
still be seen in Prov 16:1–22:16, an early wisdom collection that may have
been the original core of the book. The book of Proverbs grew and likely
became a textbook for the education of elite males, especially scribes. For
centuries the individual proverb remained the unit of instruction, at first
with indicative verbs, as if to say, "this is the way things are," while later
scribal wisdom was expressed in imperatives and motive clauses, uttered in
the voice of a watchful father: "son, do this, and you will be happy." After the
exile, wisdom speculation became more varied. It was applied to more than
just the highest courts in the land and the major temple establishments;
scribes were now both elite courtly functionaries and local administrators.
Some biblical figures are associated with wisdom in the court and are called
wise: Joseph (Gen 41:39), Daniel (Dan 1:20), Zerubbabel (1 Esdras 3:1–5:6),
and also Judith (Jdt 8:29), who lacks a court but creates one for herself.
While Ben Sira and Wisdom of Solomon stand firmly in the tradition of
Proverbs, the somewhat less clear category of wisdom narratives may be
considered in regard to some of the novellas: Additions to Daniel, Greek
Esther, Judith, and Tobit.[1] In addition, Baruch and Letter of Jeremiah contain wisdom content and are included in this chapter.

Because the word for wisdom in both Hebrew and Greek is feminine
(*hokmah* and *sophia,* respectively), the figure is personified as a woman.
When this personified figure is meant, rather than the general concept of
wisdom, it is generally capitalized as Wisdom, and when the gender of the
figure is emphasized, we often find Woman Wisdom or even Sophia. (He-

brew *Hokmah* is less often used.) But was this figure ever conceived of as more than a personification, an actual heavenly figure, a consort of God? This is unclear. Responding to the question, scholars introduced the term "hypostatization" of Wisdom, meaning more than a personification, perhaps an enduring personification, but not quite an independent heavenly figure. With the discovery that many Israelites considered Asherah—elsewhere an ancient Near Eastern goddess—to be a female consort of Yahweh, Bernhard Lang argued that Wisdom was an independent figure, even as early as Proverbs 8. To be sure, some scholars, such as Maurice Gilbert, objected to conceiving of Wisdom as independent; this violates God's direct action in creating and maintaining the world and saving those in it.[2] However, his argument seems theological and not historical in orientation, designed to protect the Jewish God from surrounding influences. These developments even may have arisen within Judah at the same time that they can be found elsewhere. The female figure is more fully developed in Ben Sira and Wisdom of Solomon. She is appealed to as a savior figure and is the object of desire (Ben Sira 14). She functions, therefore, as an independent heavenly figure.

During the Hellenistic era, as the high gods became more elevated and transcendent, cosmic savior figures evolved who took on greater significance as intermediators: Hekate (in the *Chaldean Oracles*), Hermes/Thoth (in *Hermetica*), Wisdom, Christ, Barbelo (in Sethian Gnosticism), and Isis, especially as she was worshipped outside of Egypt.[3] These cosmic saviors are generally active in the creation of the world, demonstrate compassion, and provide access for their followers to the more transcendent gods. Isis, for instance, though originally one deity among many in Egypt, spread throughout the Greek and Roman world as a more independent cosmic savior figure; her attributes influenced Wisdom of Solomon and the Gospel of John. Among Jews, Wisdom was raised up as a more accessible figure.

The nature of Wisdom thus evolved. Different stages can be observed, summarized here. (Note that each stage may assume aspects of the preceding ones.)

Experiential wisdom (preexilic period and ancient Near East)
Wisdom is an international, elite learned discourse; collections

are used for scribal instruction; there is little or no appeal to God.

Examples: Proverbs 10–30, Egyptian collections of proverbs
Characteristics: Sayings are pithy and often rhyming or humorous.
Themes: Collective experience is emphasized; there is a conservative worldview and a limit on human knowledge of the divine.

Theological wisdom (sixth to fourth centuries BCE)

As above, wisdom is an educational program for scribes.

Examples: Proverbs 1–9, the opponents in Job
Characteristics: Wisdom is personified as a divine figure, but not as a separate goddess (?).
Themes: Strong wisdom piety, related to God; the doctrine of the limits of knowledge is overcome.

Critique of theological wisdom (sixth to third centuries BCE)

Examples: Job, Ecclesiastes
Characteristics: There is a radical protest against the dogmas of theological wisdom.
Themes: The doctrine of the limits of human knowledge of God is a tragic problem.

Mantic wisdom (third to first centuries BCE)

Examples: Daniel 1–6, Babylonian astrological wisdom
Characteristics: Divine wisdom is revealed to gifted sages, who can prophesy events.

Wisdom revealed to Israel as law (second century BCE to fifth century CE)

Examples: Ben Sira 24, Baruch 3–4, *Genesis Rabbah* 1:1
Characteristics: Wisdom is not international but identified with

Jewish law; the limits of knowing God become a comforting boundary; new prophecy is dangerous.

Apocalyptic wisdom (third century BCE to second century CE)

Examples: Daniel 7–12, 1 Enoch, 4 Ezra, 2 Baruch, some Qumran texts

Characteristics: Wisdom is not generally available but is revealed to the sectarian seer and those who are initiated into the text; cosmic insight "sees through" history to its consummation (see introduction to Chapter 4); the scribes who are revered by the texts achieved a kind of immortality that is available to those who read the texts with insight.

Speculative, mystical, or philosophical wisdom (second century BCE to first century CE)

Examples: Wisdom of Solomon, *Prayer of Joseph,* Gospel of John

Characteristics: Inward-turning of individual wise person leads to "de-ethnicizing" of wisdom.[4]

Certain enduring questions about wisdom in Israel are still engaged by scholars, and a consensus concerning them does not appear to be forthcoming. Among them: (1) Should wisdom be defined narrowly as proverbial collections (Proverbs, Ben Sira, Wisdom of Solomon) or more broadly to include rebellions against conservative wisdom (Job, Ecclesiastes), wisdom Psalms (Psalms 1, 34, 37, 112), and even wisdom narratives about paradigmatic wise figures (Joseph, Daniel, Esther)? (2) Is wisdom more of a genre (Proverbs, Ben Sira) or more of a theme (Job, Ecclesiastes)? (3) Is wisdom to be defined by motifs or by the discourse of education and the focus on the transmission of knowledge from one generation to the next?[5] In addition, certain topics may cut across the different phases of wisdom above, for instance, the rise of a proto-ascetic "discipline of the self" that is expressed in terms of devotion to wisdom.

Ben Sira

The book here referred to as Ben Sira went by a number of names. In Jewish tradition it was called Book of Ben Sira—which means son of Sira—or Book of Instruction, and in the early Christian Bibles it is titled Wisdom of Jesus Son of Sira, or simply Sirach for Sirachides (son of Sira). In the Vulgate it was also given the title Ecclesiasticus, or Church Book. The book is very similar to the book of Proverbs and was popular among both Christians and Jews, yet although it stands firmly within the biblical tradition in some ways, it is unusual in others. On one hand, it was a mainstream Jewish text in supporting the theology of the Jerusalem leadership, but on the other it was popular in Alexandria as well. It is one of the longest of all ancient Jewish texts—nearly twice as long as Proverbs—and is one of the earliest Jewish texts to be labeled both with the name of the actual author and with information about the place and date of composition and translation. Yet despite the specificity of the author's and translator's information, the text itself was surprisingly unfixed, in both its Hebrew and Greek forms.[6] Further, for all of its conservative mainstream views, it innovates in important ways. The Wisdom of Jesus Ben Sira was written in about 180 BCE in Jerusalem and taken to Egypt by the author's grandson, who translated it into Greek in about 132 BCE. Ben Sira includes many sayings that are similar to those in Proverbs, utilizing many of the same sayings patterns as well: numerical sayings, parallelism, instructions, "better than" sayings, "do not say" sayings. Ben Sira is less structured than Proverbs, but some structure can be discerned: it is clearly divided into two parts, each of which begins with a poem about Wisdom (chs. 1-2, 24). The second half culminates in a long poem about the Israelite ancestors, with the opening "Let us now sing the praises of famous men" (chs. 44-50). The book ends with the author's subscript, a thanksgiving for being delivered from death, and a final paean to Wisdom (50:27-51:30). The author's advertisement for his school of wisdom concludes the text, although it is not clear whether this describes an actual school or is merely metaphorical.

Ben Sira is self-consciously the heir of a proud tradition of Jewish wisdom. At first it reads as simply a longer version of Proverbs, even a pedantic or long-winded one. The author retains two important theological

themes of that earlier wisdom collection: the fear of God is the beginning of
wisdom (Sir 1:18), and Wisdom, personified as a figure, was present with
God at the creation of the world (ch. 24). There are international influences
as well; David deSilva notes parallels to the Egyptian *Satire on the Trades*
and *Papyrus Insinger* and to the Greek *Sayings of the Seven Sages*. For Ben
Sira, say Patrick Skehan and Alexander Di Lella, "The best of Gentile
thought is no danger to the life of the faith but can even be incorporated
into an authentically Jewish work."[7] Ben Sira continues the practice of Proverbs of streaming proverbs together that are sometimes related by catch-
words, sometimes not. Yet Ben Sira also gathers proverbs into topics much
more often than does his predecessor, and they sometimes cohere into a
lesson plan. There are a number of examples of "addressed wisdom teaching" in Ben Sira, suggesting that this form became central in the educational
process.[8] Clear addresses to "my child" occur at 2:1; 6:18, 23; 11:10; 37:27;
and 41:14, followed by a series of imperatives and motive clauses with sum-
marizing conclusions. The length is usually six two-line stanzas. This particular form indicates a more rhetorical bent in Jewish education, and yet,
although some of the author's innovations might be attributed to Greek influence, this addressed wisdom teaching cannot. Ben Sira was clearly from
the Jerusalem aristocracy. The text, as Michael Satlow notes, "is directed at
a moneyed class with ties to royalty and the priesthood."[9] When the grandson translated the Jerusalem Hebrew text for his Alexandrian Jewish audience, he composed the prologue in the educated Greek associated with
Alexandria. The translator aimed for an aesthetically satisfying composition and yet is self-effacing—a typical trait of the well-written Greek preface
(see 2 Macc 2:24–32). The grandson was a member of the guild of sages
himself, and twice he mentions the motive for studying this book of wisdom:
"progress in living according to the law" (prologue).

Ben Sira blends the notion of divine instruction (*torah*) as wisdom,
from Deuteronomy 4 and 32, with the notion of the Torah as a book, from
Deuteronomy 30 (Sir 17:11–14; 45:3, 5). The word *torah* in Proverbs meant
instruction, not law, but in Ben Sira and Baruch it comes to be identified
with Israel's law. Says Greg Schmidt Goering, "Most famously, Sirach associates the Torah with a divine revelation of knowledge, asserting that the

wisdom given to Israel is 'the book of the covenant of the Most High God, the Torah that Moses commanded us'" (Sir 24:23). Compared with Proverbs, there is now a much stronger emphasis on the acquiring of wisdom as an advanced religious state. Gerhard von Rad noted that in Ben Sira wisdom is a "charisma bestowed by God." Training in wisdom gives rise to a deeply emotional experience of humility that von Rad likened to pietism and a psychological focus on the reverence of God.[10] This is related to the exploration of the moral agent in the Jewish texts of this period (see the Conclusion).

Wisdom as a female figure, found already in Proverbs 8–9, is explored further in Ben Sira. Apocalyptic texts like 1 Enoch would argue that the world in general is blind to Wisdom (1 Enoch 42), although the small number of those initiated into the text of 1 Enoch would have a full understanding. Ben Sira, however, opposes this sectarian view by taking the more mainstream, conservative Israelite position: Wisdom is available to all, though none can fully understand it (1:3, 24:28). As noted, Ben Sira argues and Baruch argued that wisdom is available in the form of the law of God; it can be embraced in that form by all Jews. It is often noted that Proverbs rarely mentioned any aspects of Israelite history, covenant, or law; it focused, rather, on an appreciation of the order that is found in God's creation. By the time of Ben Sira, however, wisdom and law had merged—which assumes a covenant theology—and Israelite history is now replayed in the praise of its famous heroes (44–50). Perhaps the most impressive passage of Ben Sira is the hymn to Wisdom in chapter 24. Here Wisdom, originating in God's presence, sings a hymn to herself. And here we see another important development in Ben Sira: Wisdom is a "cosmic savior" figure. She is involved in creation, she orders the cosmos and has dominion over the earth, she established law for humanity, and she is sent forth from the mouth of God, as in Egyptian creation accounts, saving those who receive her. Wisdom praises herself, just as does the Egyptian goddess Isis, and seeks a resting place like that of Isis. The Isis parallels in Ben Sira are nearly as strong and vibrant as those in Wisdom of Solomon.[11] Since Wisdom is now more fully personified as a female figure, the relation between the young sage and Wisdom also becomes highly charged, even eroticized: "Those

who eat of me," says Wisdom, "will hunger for more, and those who drink
of me will thirst for more" (24:21). At 14:20–24, the author's voice now suggests one who is stalking a woman:

> Happy is the person . . .
> who reflects in his heart on her ways
>   and ponders her secrets,
> pursuing her like a hunter,
>   and lying in wait on her paths;
> who peers through her windows
>   and listens at her doors;
> who camps near her house
>   and fastens his tent peg to her walls.

Ben Sira not only brought wisdom and law together, but he brought wisdom and the history of Israel together as well—a connection lacking in
Proverbs. As John J. Collins says, "Ben Sira had taken the revolutionary
step of using examples from Israelite history to illustrate the workings of
wisdom." This will be developed further in Wisdom of Solomon, although
with some ambiguity. Ben Sira also takes positions on a number of important theological issues of the day. He affirms many views that would be central to Jewish scribal life in Jerusalem and Alexandria, and later by the rabbis as well. Says Jonathan Klawans, he is "aristocratic, cosmopolitan, and
conservative—all the while believing in freedom of choice, earthly justice,
and the finality of death."[12] As in Proverbs, he assumed that the righteousness of God is reflected in the rewards that people receive in this world. The
wise and deserving will have long life, wealth, and children. The deserving
need not look outside of this life for a reward. Unlike Wisdom of Solomon,
here the only immortality to be found is a hope of children and a heroic
memory. As a result, Ben Sira opposes the depositing of food offerings at
the graves of the dead, as advocated in Tob 4:17. Also, what may at first seem
a minor issue should not be overlooked: Sir 43:6–7 shows approval of the
lunar calendar used by the Jerusalem authorities, as opposed to the solar
calendar advocated in 1 Enoch, in Jubilees, and at Qumran.[13]

Scholars have questioned whether Ben Sira exhibits significant influences of Greek philosophy. The Greeks often focused on four cardinal virtues, with slight variations, and Sir 36:23–38:23 clearly refers to this tradition in affirming judgment, wisdom, moderation, and courage. Martin Hengel argued for other evidences of Stoic philosophy. Wisdom is like the Stoic *logos*, "a kind of 'world reason' emanating from God, which filled and permeated the whole creation." The identification of Wisdom and *torah* (24:23) would then seem similar to the Stoic identification of universal law and universal *logos*. However, others have disagreed. Sharon Lea Mattila finds the parallels weak and unconvincing. The divine order that Ben Sira affirms is typical of other ancient Near Eastern religions and does not imply an identification of *torah* or Wisdom with a universal ordering principle. Ben Sira also fails to affirm a *universal* ethical principle; the hymn to Wisdom in chapter 24 states that the law dwells *in Israel* (24:6–8).[14]

The issues of gender in Ben Sira are much more thoroughly addressed, and more complex, than at first appears. In addition to the depiction of an idealized Woman Wisdom, many other passages—far more than in Proverbs—treat wives, other women, and daughters in a way that has drawn scholarly attention. As with many texts of this period, social ethics is often based on the notion of public honor and public shame, here stated explicitly (10:19–24). Ben Sira's advice is addressed only to the wealthy, free, male head-of-household. As common as this is throughout Mediterranean culture, deSilva also helpfully ties this specifically to the value constructions of a minority culture.[15] Even in Judea, where Jews were in the majority, their existence as a colonized people—which would continue *after* the Maccabean Revolt as well and would certainly be the case in Egypt—would accentuate the desire to acquire public honor and avoid public shame.

In Ben Sira as in Proverbs, the father is the voice who speaks, addressing his son. His son must learn how to control those people within his future household: his wife, his daughters, his slaves. The theme of threats to women is found in novels cross-culturally and in the Jewish novellas as well (see Chapter 1). We would expect this to be reflected in teaching books, and Ben Sira does not disappoint.[16] We sense here the anxiety of the male head-of-household; the author is more revealing on this score than he realizes. What stands out in Ben Sira, in comparison with Proverbs, is the greater attention focused on the control of sexuality, a theme common in Stoicism. Of all wisdom books, Ben Sira devotes most space to women, and his misogyny is well documented. A man must exercise self-mastery in regard to wanton women and in regard to controlling the sexuality of his wife and daughters. Jon L. Berquist notes that in Ben Sira the daughter "is not the subject of her own sexuality. She possesses no possibility for self-control." "Daughters," says Ibolya Balla, "attract especially negative, at times obscene, comments from the sage, as persons who can cause the most problems to a father regardless of their marital status, but in the end it is from married women that they learn to do harm to their father (42:12–13)."[17] How, then, may we make sense of the many female images in Ben Sira? Claudia V. Camp correlates the emphasis on honor and shame and the male head-of-household's control of women's sexuality. A free male head-of-household in ancient Israel was perceived to have more honor if he had a model wife and dutiful children who in turn married well and produced children. Slaves are also treated as members of the household who must be corrected, even beaten; they must be obedient and reflect well on the master. Honor is associated with a man's ability to control how he is viewed, especially in response to the challenges of others; one's wives, daughters, and slaves are one's honor. Any violation of this—public criticism of the wife or children— resulted in palpable, public shame to the head-of-household. The bad wife is treated in detail, revealing the author's anxiety. "The possibility of having an *evil wife*," says Camp, "is not just raised, but given rather extensive treatment."[18] Anxiety about real women and lack of control is also sublimated into a more authoritative rendering of law, teaching, and canon as a controlled field. Although it is unclear to what extent Ben Sira or his audience would have perceived a biblical canon, it is Ben Sira's grandson who in the prologue first provides a three-part description of the authoritative texts— "law, the prophecies, and the rest of the books." Control in these areas is a compensation for the lack of control over real women. Anxiety over relations with real women may also lie behind Ben Sira's creation of an idealized but eroticized Woman Wisdom. This idealized woman can protect the young man from out-of-control real women. The out-of-control Judith was perhaps a novelistic exploration of Ben Sira's dangerous women.

Yet also featured in Ben Sira is another gender category, the eunuch.

As people with ambiguous gender or ambiguous genitalia were discussed by Jewish, Greek, and Roman authors, we must think of the category of eunuchs as part of a larger gender discussion. Eunuchs were castrated males, often slaves, sometimes castrated as boys and sometimes when older. The eunuch was a common figure in the highest courts of the ancient Near East, Hellenistic kingdoms, and Rome. As Ben Sira is very dualistic about gender categories (33:14–15, 42:23–25), the eunuch violates his rigid distinction of male and female. As a result of being ambiguous, the eunuch is scorned (20:4, 30:20). In addition, since Ben Sira himself was a highly placed scribe, his comments about eunuchs perhaps reflect his contact and even competition with eunuchs as fellow courtiers. He shames eunuchs by finding humor in their attempt at sex (20:4, 30:20; a similar motif can be found in a Greek novel, Chariton, *Chaereas and Callirhoe* 5.2–4). The eunuch is perhaps a lightning rod for Ben Sira's anxiety about gender in general.

Ben Sira was one of the most popular of the texts of the Apocrypha among both Christians and Jews. The scholarly edition of the Greek New Testament, which lists quotations and allusions, provides ninety-nine occurrences of possible allusions to Ben Sira, although this might indicate more the common cultural matrix than direct literary influence. Among later Christians it was perhaps second in popularity to Wisdom of Solomon, but it was still important enough in the West to receive the title Ecclesiasticus, or Church Book. It has been used in Catholic and Orthodox Christian worship. Ben Sira had more currency among Jews than any other text of the Apocrypha, yet contrary to common assumptions, it was not the *only* book of the Apocrypha to experience an after-life among Jews. Fragments of Ben Sira have been found at Qumran, at Masada, and in the Cairo Geniza or synagogue storeroom. This represents quite a wide distribution, although surprisingly, Philo and Josephus seemed unaware of it. The rabbis often criticized the use of Ben Sira, yet in ways that also suggest that it was well known (*t. Yadayim* 2:13; *y. Sanhedrin* 28a); the rabbinic discussions suggest an ambivalent history. Ishay Rosen-Zvi interestingly notes that the rabbis mined Proverbs, Song of Songs, and even Ecclesiastes for passages to elaborate but did not adopt apocalypses, prophecy, or biblical history nearly as much. This, he suggests, is because they thought of themselves as *hakamim,* sages.[19] We also note that a medieval Jewish text, *Alphabet of Ben Sira,* a satire, shows the continuing name of Ben Sira in European Judaism. This may be a response to the Christian Bible, as was the case for medieval texts of Jewish Judith, Susanna, and Tobit.

Wisdom of Solomon

Wisdom of Solomon and 4 Maccabees are the most philosophical books of the Apocrypha, but Wisdom of Solomon is the more beautifully written. The combination of philosophy and literary art is often overlooked, as commentators treat the content of the text but not the tone. Wisdom of Solomon presents philosophical questions in a style that is very personal and unusual, sounding at times like the protest texts Job and Ecclesiastes. It is indeed confessional like Ecclesiastes, but this is quite ironic, since Wisdom of Solomon opposes the theological message of Ecclesiastes. Wisdom of Solomon indeed makes a "shimmering impression," and modern translations often alter the language of the text to, as it were, make it shimmer less.[20] The ancient reader certainly would have been impressed by the philosophical aspirations and the Greek style. Well-known rhetorical techniques include the dialogue with opponents, the piling up of words, and the "ladder" argument (6:17–20, 13:18–19). The author also has a penchant for inventing new, somewhat stilted terms, such as "natalicide" (*nēpioktonou,* 11:7), the author as "create-officer" (*genesiarchēs,* 13:3) or "creatonator" (*genesiourgos,* 13:5), and many other provocative new terms. Its literary quality and influence are considerable, both in their original setting and as a text often seen as transitional to Christianity. Wisdom of Solomon was, for instance, surprisingly included in the New Testament canon in the early Christian Muratorian fragment.

Wisdom of Solomon seamlessly combines Jewish tradition and Greek philosophy, the Jewish side influenced by both wisdom and apocalypticism. There are many references to biblical history, although they are surprisingly anonymized by having the names removed. The anonymizing of the Israelite heroes is generally seen as a way to universalize the message,

whether to include gentile readers or, more likely, to provide a universalizing self-image for Jews. The author envisions a group of philosophically
oriented people—from different ethnic groups?—who can perceive God's
transcendent realm. There is an advantage to being "Israel," but it is not
absolute.[21] The beginning of the text is spoken in the voice of Solomon,
addressing "the rulers of the earth," although his name is not used, and we
only confirm this identity in 7:7–8 and 9:4–12—again, without names.

Wisdom of Solomon can be easily divided into three sections; scholars have given each a descriptive name:

Section one, 1:1–6:21   Book of Eschatology (or end of
                             times)
Section two, 6:22–11:1   Book of Wisdom
Section three, 11:2–19:22   Book of History

Each section emphasizes distinct themes and styles, yet it is the very nature
of this text to merge and gently transform one theme and style into another.
Scholars still disagree, for instance, on where the sections begin and end.
The different natures of the sections also create a challenge for the interpretation of the text. Section three, for instance, is nearly as long as sections
one and two placed together, yet the introductory issue in section one, immortality as God's reward to the righteous, is often taken as the main theme
of the book as a whole. Other important differences among the three sections can be noted:

- The term "wisdom" is found eight times in section one,
  twenty-two times in section two, but only twice in the longer
  section three (14:2, 5). Other important words are also distributed unevenly. *Paideia* and related terms barely occur
  outside of section one.[22] *Athanasia,* immortality, is found
  twice in sections one and two, but in the longer section three
  only once. *Aphtharsia,* incorruption, appears three times in
  section one, the adjective twice in section three, but never
  in section two.

- Important themes are not distributed evenly among the sections. Apocalyptic motifs are influential in sections one and two, but not in section three. The created world is not treated positively in section one, but sections two and three value creation. God is a strict judge in chapters 1–5, while showing mercy in chapters 6–19.

- Section one is concerned with immortality as a resolution of injustice. In section three the narrative is focused on the historical plane, not on a timeless immortality, and Israel is rewarded in a historical context. Corresponding to this, section one emphasizes individual and universal values, and the last section emphasizes Israel versus the nations.

- The protagonist in section one seems disaffected and passive, but this is not the case of the speaker in sections two and three.

- It is often noted that the text as a whole has a distinctive literary style, but this may reflect more a literary tradition than one author, as the striking literary traits are not uniformly distributed in the three sections. Alliteration occurs mainly in section one, yet almost all of the very distinctive, invented compound words occur in the last two sections. Ten of the eighteen Hebraisms that David Winston notes are in the small section one.[23] Section one contains none of the seven examples of iambic meter found in the text.

Scholars often note these differences among the three sections, yet few argue for separate origins. After all, important themes are found in more than one section. Assumed in all three sections is the view that the righteous *perceive* God's nature and the unrighteous *do not*. This reminds one of Plato's emphasis on knowledge: if a person is brought to knowledge, he or she will choose the righteous path. In section one this culminates in the drama of the unrighteous also recognizing the true God, and a similar recognition is found in section three: "They saw and recognized as the true God him whom they had before refused to know" (12:27; compare 15:3,

18:1–2). Other observations also suggest a unity of authorship. Winston's list of Wisdom's "favorite 'theme' words and expressions" fall into all three sections, and James M. Reese lists passages in later sections that echo what was said earlier.[24] And while it was noted above that wisdom was absent in the account of history in section three, it may be significant that it is absent as well in the hymn to the famous men in Ben Sira 44–50; the absence of wisdom may be typical of this subgenre. Ultimately, then, although it is perhaps more likely that the text was composed by one author, we entertain the possibility that at least the first section was written separately.

The opening in a general sense evokes royal autobiographies known throughout the ancient Near East, in addition to the concerns about kingship in Deuteronomy 17–18 and the *Temple Scroll* from Qumran, and also the treatises on kingship like *Letter of Aristeas*. The genre as a whole, however, is more closely compared to Greek models. We begin with the common divisions of Greek rhetoric: (1) forensic arguments: arguing about what happened in the past, often a speech at trial; (2) deliberative rhetoric: arguing a course for the future, often in *polis* debates; and (3) epideictic rhetoric: arguing about what is to be praised or blamed in the present.

Most scholars have categorized Wisdom of Solomon as deliberative rhetoric, and specifically, a subset of deliberative rhetoric called protreptic: a discourse that argues for the adoption of a certain rational philosophy.[25] This subgenre of Greek rhetoric was popular in the ancient world, even among Jews and Christians. The contemporary Jewish philosopher Philo commonly referred to Deuteronomy as *protreptikoi logoi* (protreptic words, teachings, or speech, or simply protreptic) without any explanation, as if it were a title. Fourth Maccabees and Paul's Letter to the Romans are also often classified as protreptic. A problem arises, however, when we turn to section three: it is more like an encomium—praise of a person or thing—a subset of epideictic rhetoric. The rhetorical force of section three seems different from that of section one, although the compelling nature of the first has dictated the judgments about the genre of the whole. We will also encounter an even greater challenge: section one undermines Greek protreptic. In protreptic the speaker typically displays confidence that the philosophy being advocated is superior to others. Here, however, the main figure, the righteous one, is disaffected and passive, incapable of saving himself. He does not even speak! A philosopher who uses protreptic and does not speak? On the surface, he is not a good advertisement for the philosophy. One could argue that even Socrates failed to defend himself, but that fact was treated ironically. Plato also disparaged protreptic, preferring the *elenchos* or "Socratic method" of dialogue and the asking of questions. Yet there is a tradition of passive protagonists in Israel, from Joseph to the Suffering Servant (Isaiah 52–53) to Daniel to Esther to Achior in Judith and even to Jesus in Mark.[26] Wisdom of Solomon—at least, the first section— will present the thesis that immortality is the sought-after reward for life in this world.

The universalizing theme in Wisdom of Solomon is found also in Greek and Roman philosophy. Wisdom of Solomon is therefore not unique in this regard; it is a trend across the Hellenistic world. The text is simply an excellent representative. The author, like his contemporary Philo, presents Judaism as a universal religion, as opposed to popular Greek or especially Egyptian religion. The Greek philosophy that is reflected in Wisdom of Solomon is Middle Platonism, a merging of Platonism with elements of Stoicism and Neo-Pythagoreanism. It began in the first century BCE and continued until the third century CE, evolving at that point into Neoplatonism. The Platonic aspects of Middle Platonism are clear enough in the text: there are two realms, spirit and matter (7:22–8:1). Spirit is the eternally existing realm, and matter is a temporary realm that falls away. For Plato immortality was a characteristic of the soul (*Phaedrus* 245C–E), although in Wisdom of Solomon it is not an *inherent* aspect of the soul, but rather God's gift to the righteous. Later the author will also reflect the Platonic notion that the body encumbers the soul: "a perishable body weighs down the soul, and this earthly tent burdens the thoughtful mind" (9:15). There were other Platonizing transcendence texts written by Jews and Christians at this time, for example, Gospel of John, *Joseph and Aseneth, Odes of Solomon, Gospel of Mary,* and passages from Philo and the Nag Hammadi collection. Like Wisdom of Solomon, some of these combine intentional ambiguity and transcendence of this world. Stoic beliefs, part of Middle Platonism, can also be discerned in the text, for instance, Stoic cosmopolitanism, "a rejection of nationalism in favor of a citizenry of nature (the cosmos)."[27] Wisdom is God's spirit, essentially the same as Stoic *pneuma,* a spirit that pervades the cosmos and all things and is present in each thinking person. Like Stoic *logos,* Wisdom "holds all things together" (Wis 1:7); and following a Stoic argument, because spirit had permeated both the heavens and the earth, God was identified with the universe, just as Cleanthes had said of Zeus: "Zeus is the world as a whole." Thus we can sum up the Greek philosophical view of Wisdom of Solomon in this way: the author combines the strong Platonic distinction between spirit and matter and the Stoic notion of a world-spirit that pervades both the highest realms and the world of matter. The same could be said for other Middle Platonic authors like Philo. Greek philosophy also figures in what Wisdom of Solomon opposes. The beliefs of the unrighteous in section one, although quite similar to those espoused in Ecclesiastes (as noted above), also match up quite well with those of the Epicureans. The later Platonic philosopher Plotinus, for instance, soundly rejected Epicureanism.

Thoroughly merged with these Greek influences are aspects of Jewish wisdom and apocalypticism. Wisdom of Solomon reflects the stage of Jewish wisdom referred to above as "speculative, mystical, or philosophical wisdom." This strand of wisdom dates from the second century BCE to the first century CE. In addition to Wisdom of Solomon, it includes Aristobulus of Alexandria, 4 Maccabees, Philo, and *Prayer of Joseph* and is related to later texts such as *Joseph and Aseneth* and Gnostic texts. Wisdom of Solomon was likely composed during first century BCE–first century CE in Alexandria in Egypt, one of the most important centers of intellectual life in the entire Greek and Roman worlds. Whereas in Ben Sira and Baruch, Wisdom is identified with Mosaic law, that is not the case here; the text even "marginalizes Torah," says Matthew Kraus, and Collins agrees: Wisdom of Solomon is not a Torah-centric text.[28] To be sure, at 18:9, 14–15, the divine law is said to be given at Sinai, but it is not fleshed out at all and appears nowhere else in the text. Wisdom, rather, dominates this picture of the relation of the righteous person to God.

Aspects of Jewish apocalypticism can also be discerned in the text, though they are somewhat muted. The emphasis on two levels and the reality of the heavenly world, for instance, may sound Platonic but is associated with apocalypses as well (3:7–9; Daniel 7–12; 1 Enoch 37–71, 92–105; 2 Baruch 51). It is the marriage of wisdom and apocalypticism in Wisdom of Solomon that has prompted some scholars to insist, rightly, that the boundaries of these genre categories are unclear.[29] The knowledge of divine things (Wisdom 7–8) is emphasized in apocalypses, as well as the *mystēria* of God's hidden plan (Wis 2:22, Daniel 1–6). The exaltation of the righteous (Wis 4:20–5:14) is similar to Dan 12:3, 7:27 and 1 En. 104:2, 4:16–17; and the strong moral judgment, by turns explicit and implicit, is characteristic of apocalypticism (Wisdom 2–5; 1 Enoch 62–63, 102:6–103:15). Even the figure of Enoch is alluded to in Wis 4:10–11. Last, the dialogues about theodicy are similar to that found in 4 Ezra (and compare Dan 7:27, 12:3; 1 En. 104:2; 2 Bar 51:10). We note as well the intermediate state of souls (3:1), the souls' dominion over nations (3:8), and the continuing life of the soul with "saints" (5:5).

Three crucial differences, however, are worth noting. First, traditional wisdom texts continued to affirm that people in general have the ability to perceive God's true divine nature and can learn and repent. Apocalyptic texts, on the other hand, generally assume that the righteous and the wicked are more or less predetermined. In Wisdom of Solomon some tension remains between determinism and the possibility of free will (2:24; 19:1–10), although this is true of Ben Sira as well (15:11–17; 33:10–15). Second, in apocalyptic texts there is often an angel to interpret the truths of what is happening, while here it is Wisdom herself. Third, apocalypticism is often associated with the resurrection of the body (Daniel 12), while Wisdom of Solomon focuses on the immortality of the soul and the spiritual transcendence of matter. Yet even here, while scholars often contrast the resurrection of the body as a Jewish—and Christian—response to death and immortality as a Greek one, this is overly simplistic. Other Jewish texts affirm a belief in the immortality of the soul compatible with Platonism, some among the Apocrypha (4 Macc 7:19, 13:17, 16:25; 1 En. 102:5, 103:3–4, 104:6; Jub. 23:31).[30] Ultimately, one should not expect the Greek philosophical and the Jewish apocalyptic threads to be easily disentangled, and the author would probably be surprised at the notion. Rather, Wisdom of Solomon represents what was probably a common synthesis.

We now turn to a consideration of the three sections of the Wisdom of Solomon.

SECTION ONE (1:1–6:21)

The first section is often called the Book of Eschatology. At the beginning
the speaker—Solomon, we assume—is presented as an internationally re-
spected figure, a king among kings, a king who addresses kings. This co-
incides with the biblical view and perhaps also evokes ancient royal autobiographical inscriptions.[31] It is possible that originally "Solomon" was
considered a fictitious voice, or perhaps this section was considered a sort
of "dream sequence." Be that as it may, the text very soon was received as
another text of Solomon, as reflected in the second section (7:7–9, 9:4–12).
Just as law was associated with Moses and Ezra and revelation with Enoch,
wisdom was associated with Solomon. The opening suggests that righteousness (*dikaiosynē*), not necessarily wisdom, is the main theme, placed
parallel to sincerity (*haplotēs*): "Love righteousness, you rulers of the earth.
Think of the Lord in goodness and seek him with sincerity of heart." The
role of righteousness for the wise person is thus crucial: the soul is not immortal by nature—note that the opponents' souls are not immortal—but
righteousness is immortal.[32] Commitment to righteousness brings God's gift
of immortality of the soul. Chapter one, then, invites the audience to approach God in righteousness, with Wisdom as an intermediary. It contains
a number of philosophical terms, used often in Greek discourse and in Hellenistic Judaism:

> Righteousness: *dikaiosynē*
> Sincerity (or rather, simplicity) of heart: *haplotēs kardias*
> Put to the test: *peirazō*
> Those not distrusting him: *hoi mē apistontes autō*
> Perverse thoughts: *skolioi logismoi*
> Wisdom: *Sophia*
> Holy spirit of discipline: *hagion pneuma paideias*
> Kindly (literally, people-loving) spirit: *philanthrōpon pneuma*
> Spirit of the Lord has filled: *pneuma kyriou peplērōken*
> That which holds all things together: *to sunechon ta panta*

One could add other words to this list, but the point is clear: this chapter is
an overture to the philosophical range of the book. Much of chapter 1 re-

lates to the rest of section one, but to the other sections as well. It brings the philosophical ideas of the three sections together. For example, the fact that God created all things so that they may exist (1:14) is expressed in section three. If the three sections had different origins, then chapter 1 may have been created as an overture to the book as a whole. The text turns in chapters 2–5 to a conflict between the righteous person and the many unrighteous. The unrighteous persecute and kill the righteous one, but what is perhaps worse, they deny that there is any life after death, for the righteous or for themselves. This situation is resolved, however, in a recognition scene (ch. 5) in which the unrighteous discover that the righteous will attain immortality. Michael Kolarcik notes that Wisdom 2–5 is organized as a trial—not a trial reported in the past, but one unfolding in real time, as the actions take place; the recognition scene is a dramatic present. Now it becomes clear that for the righteous there is only the appearance of human mortality, what Kolarcik calls the "ambiguity of death."[33]

Section one seems clear at first in its presentation, but on closer examination, one realizes it is all indirect. Although the modern reader may *remember* the righteous protagonist in the Wisdom of Solomon as the "I" who speaks, in section one the righteous "I" never speaks. The narrator—presumably Solomon, but not the same as the righteous one—reports the words *of the wicked,* and it is *they* who in turn describe the thoughts of the righteous person. The wicked, who do speak, reveal more than they know; they have an active agenda in summoning death on themselves:

> Let us make use of creation to the full as in youth. . . .
> Let our might be our law of right,
>> for what is weak proves itself to be useless. . . .
> Let us test the righteous one with insult and torture,
>> so that we may find out how gentle he is,
>> and make trial of his forbearance. (2:6, 11, 19)

It is ironic, then, that the entire philosophical argument is made through two speeches *by the ungodly;* it is through their eyes that we see both positions presented. The wicked are also active in this life, but the righteous one is passive.[34] Ultimately, God will be active, by rendering the wicked *speechless:*

> The Lord will laugh them to scorn.
> After this they will become dishonored corpses. . . .
> God will dash them *speechless* to the ground,
>   and shake them from the foundations. (4:18–19)

It is also the narrator, not the righteous person, who assures us that the wicked will ultimately fail: "Those who despise wisdom and instruction are miserable. Their hope is vain, their labors are unprofitable, and their works are useless" (3:11). But which works are useless? Their campaigns? Their power? Their persecution of the weak righteous? Surprisingly, no. Rather, "Their *wives* are foolish, and their *children* evil; their *offspring* are accursed" (3:12–13, emphasis added). The wicked are not thwarted in their public lives but have foolish wives and worthless children. There is indeed a comeuppance and shaming of the wicked, over and over, in line after line, concerning the pointlessness of their children: "The branches will be broken off before they come to maturity, and their fruit will be useless, not ripe enough to eat, and good for nothing" (4:5).

Why this surprising focus? In traditional Israelite wisdom, God rewards the wise person with wealth, a long healthy life, and many children (see Ben Sira). Jon Levenson has rightly said that in Israel children and a lineage were considered a functional equivalent of immortality.[35] But here the wicked can expect only bad children. The text then offers an alternative goal:

> For blessed is the barren woman who is undefiled . . .
>   she will have fruit when God examines souls.
> Blessed also is the eunuch whose hands have done no lawless
>   deed. (3:13–14)

The childless woman and the eunuch lack children, the functional equivalent of immortality, but they are compensated with postlife immortality. The

inclusion of the eunuch is likely influenced by Isaiah 56, the surprising acceptance of the eunuch, and Isa 54:1, the vindication of the childless woman;
but Wisdom of Solomon seems to take on the interior perspective of the
shame and loss experienced by the eunuch and the childless woman—the
eunuch perhaps a bit more than the childless woman. The author seems to
feel their pain from the inside:

> . . . for special favor will be shown the eunuch for his
> faithfulness,
>> and a place of great delight in the temple of the Lord.
> For the fruit of good labors is renowned,
>> and the root of understanding does not fail. . . .
> Better than this [the prolific brood of the ungodly] is childless-
> ness with virtue,
>> for in the memory of virtue is immortality. (3:14-15, 4:1)

This treatment of the worthless children of the wicked and the compensa-
tory immortality of the childless woman and the eunuch is surprisingly extensive, covering about a chapter, and is further highlighted by being placed
at the center of section one. Here, Wisdom of Solomon challenges the typical wisdom view: it is the unrighteous who have many bad children, and
immortality is the reward for the righteous childless woman or eunuch, supplanting children. The childless woman and the eunuch will also be joined
by "the righteous who die early" in 4:7—that is, those who do not enjoy
wisdom's reward of long life. But who, then, are the righteous and the unrighteous? Their identity is not stated. Are the unrighteous gentiles who
persecute Jews, or do they actually represent Jews who in the author's mind
are unrighteous? While granting that for some scholars "the apocalyptic
dualism marking Wisdom 1–5 must *reflect* a situation of high tension," David
deSilva rightly counters that "apocalyptic literature . . . may equally seek to
be *productive* of high tension, high boundaries, and mutual antagonism and
rejection between groups." The author may be creating a tension to define
the right course more clearly. Collins also argues that the unrighteous do not
represent those who are actually persecuting the author, but this passage is

rather an illustrative story depicting those who deny immortality of the soul. They are presumably apostates, says Collins, but why then the focus on childless women and the eunuch? The opponents may simply be Jews who are more like Ben Sira, who argue that children are a reward for wisdom and who demean the life of the eunuch.[36]

The Wisdom of Solomon may represent a somewhat withdrawn or sectarian position, and the entire passage may reflect the point of view of the righteous childless marginalized *within* the community of Jews. Is it possible that the author was a eunuch-scribe? Positing eunuchs as authors or audience in this period is quite plausible. Eunuchs are everywhere in our texts, discussed often in Ctesias's *Persica,* the *Story of Ahikar,* Esther, Judith, and the Greek novels.[37] Deuteronomy 23:1 forbade the admission of eunuchs to the assembly of God, although Isa 56:3–5 prophesies that eunuchs shall be accepted. It is possible that Nehemiah was a eunuch ("cupbearer to the king," 1:11), and later Jews and Christians assumed that Daniel and his three friends were all eunuchs (*b. Sanhedrin* 93b; Jerome, *Commentary on Daniel* 1:3). The eunuch was sometimes tasked with protecting the harem, as in Esther, but a eunuch could also be a courtier—or a traitor— within the court. Eunuchs were perceived as ambiguous in terms of gender, and in terms of ethnicity; the eunuch was a boundary-crosser. Ben Sira and Wisdom of Solomon present opposite sides of the coin on eunuchs. In Ben Sira, the eunuch is a despised third gender: every prejudice against the eunuch is expressed. If our author was a eunuch, we may perceive in Wisdom of Solomon "internalized oppression." We may even wonder whether section one was written by a eunuch-scribe for other eunuch-scribes.

SECTION TWO (6:22–11:1)

After the conflict in the first section, the second, the Book of Wisdom, turns to a poetic and philosophical paean to Wisdom and how she functions in the world. Solomon was said to have prayed for wisdom at 1 Kgs 3:5–15, and that is rendered poetically here (Wis 7:7–8; 9:4, 10–12). Solomon models a devotional commitment to righteousness. Here, for the first time in the text, the anonymous speaker is clearly understood to be Solomon. He receives

Wisdom but also "unerring knowledge of what exists, . . . the structure of
the world and the activity of the elements, the beginning and end and middle of times, the alternations of the solstices and the changes of the seasons"
(7:17–18). This amounts to knowledge of the heavens.[38] The list of Wisdom's attributes is like those found in hymns to Isis:

> There is in Wisdom a spirit that is intelligent, holy,
>> unique, manifold, subtle,
>> mobile, clear, unpolluted,
>> distinct, invulnerable, loving the good, keen,
>> irresistible, beneficent, humane,
>> steadfast, sure, free from anxiety,
>> all-powerful, overseeing all,
>> and penetrating through all spirits
>> that are intelligent, pure, and altogether subtle.
>>> (7:22–23)

The similarity to Isis is quite strong (compare Apuleius, *Metamorphoses*
11:3–11). Like Isis, Sophia is present at creation; she orders the cosmos, has
dominion over the earth, establishes law for humanity, and is sent forth from
the mouth of God as in Egyptian creation accounts. Is Wisdom here a consort of God, or simply a personification of God's activity on earth? Her role
as intermediator may be telling: she is a cosmic savior like other cosmic
saviors. James Reese noted these parallels to Isis and argued further that
Wisdom of Solomon explored these similarities in order to co-opt and oppose Isis worship. Collins rightly disagrees, arguing that Isis is not treated
here as a temptation for Jews, but rather, these notions were part of the
philosophical world of Alexandria, shared by Jews and others.[39]

   The phrase "beginning and end and middle of times" calls for com-
ment. Most ancient cultures, including Israel, did not speak of a continuous timeline that included past, present, and future. Hebrew lacks an actual
present tense, and the three aspects of time are not discussed together in the
Hebrew Bible. The Greeks, however, did speak philosophically of past,
present, and future. This is found in Plato and is associated with Orphic

texts.[40] The past, present, and future appear together in Judith 9 as well, and the "beginning and end and middle of times" here may *sound* the same. However, Wisdom of Solomon is referring to cosmic knowledge of origins, of eschatology, and the great "middle of times" of our worldly existence, that is, knowledge of the cosmos that includes God's plan for history. This knowledge is not really a past, present, and future in the modern sense. The passage proceeds, "to know the alternations of the solstices and the changes of the seasons, the cycles of the year and the constellations of the stars." The knowledge of the future may also shade into an apocalyptic eschatology.[41]

In terms of the relationship with Woman Wisdom, Ben Sira had presented this relationship in very sexual terms: Woman Wisdom was a young lad's female object of desire. Wisdom of Solomon, on the other hand, expressed the relation somewhat differently. The desire can be erotic, though not quite the stalking of Wisdom that we saw in Ben Sira. The author at times idealizes the attraction, almost to the point of chivalry: "I loved her and sought her from my youth. I desired to take her for my bride, and became enamored of her beauty" (8:2). The speaker then waits upon God to bestow her—a father giving away a bride: "I perceived that I would not possess wisdom unless God gave her to me" (8:21). Section two also communicates an understanding of spirit and matter different from that in section one. There is no longer a clear transcendence of the body but a negotiation between soul and body, even a discipline about rising above the body, with some ambivalence: "I entered an undefiled body" (8:19–20; cf. 8:13); but "a perishable body weighs down the soul, and this earthly tent burdens the thoughtful mind" (9:15). This notion of discipline of the body is similar to Plato's (*Phaedo* 81c), who was not as anti-body as some of his Middle Platonic and Neoplatonic followers.

After this description of the cosmic, timeless Wisdom, section two concludes with a historical survey of how Wisdom led Israelite heroes. Again, they are unnamed, but figures from Adam to Moses are clearly meant. As noted above, chapter 10 is a transitional poem; some scholars have included it with section two, others with section three. The author likely treats the Israelite heroes as anonymous to universalize the message: all cultures could theoretically learn the lesson of this history. In addition, by anonymizing, it is perhaps emphasized that the heroes did not act on their own, but rather, were guided by Wisdom. One could even go further: Does the anonymized history suggest a transcendence of the world and even mysticism?

SECTION THREE (11:2–19:22)

The third section, or Book of History, recounts the Exodus narrative, also without any names. The list of historical examples would at first appear to continue that of chapter 10—from the Red Sea to the wandering in the wilderness—but that is not quite accurate. First, beginning in chapter 11, there is more detail. Second, Wisdom is no longer the divine element that works for good in the world, but rather God. A third difference is the careful arrangement of seven of the ten plagues of Exodus: aspects of the plagues that were injurious to the Egyptians are matched with similar acts of God that aided the Israelites in the wilderness wandering:

1. The Nile changed to blood is compared to water from the rock (11:6–14) (this is followed by two long digressions; see below)
2. Frogs are compared to quails (16:1–4)
3. Stinging flies and locusts are compared to deliverance from snakes by the raising of the bronze serpent (16:5–14)
4. Storm and hail are compared to manna (16:15–29)
5. Darkness is compared to the light that guides Israel (17:2–18:4)
6. Death of the firstborn is compared to Moses delivering Israel (18:5–25)
7. Egypt drowned in the Red Sea is compared to Israel delivered through the Red Sea (19:1–9)

This pairing of opposites is typical of the *synkrisis* or comparison, common in Greek rhetoric. While the beginning of Wisdom of Solomon is generally categorized as protreptic, now the discourse is more like encomium, in this case the figures of Israelite history. But just as it was ironic in section one to

hear a protreptic speech when the protagonist is passive, so here it is ironic
to hear praise of historical figures who are not named. The author plays with
the expectations of learned rhetoric. And in addition: Why *seven* plagues
and not ten as in Exodus? It is not clear, but a similar phenomenon lies
hidden within the Gospel of John: the seven miracles of Jesus can be contrasted with the seven plagues; turning water into blood, for instance, can
be contrasted to turning water into wine in John 2.[42] The list of examples
from the past is a common rhetorical technique in ancient discourse. In the
Hebrew Bible we note Joshua 24; Nehemiah 9; Psalms 78, 105, 106, 135; and
Ezekiel 20; in the Apocrypha, 1 Macc 2:51–60, 4 Ezra 7:105–11, and Ben Sira
44–50. By tracking the heroes of their history, the audience can discern les-
sons for their generation. The list of examples is sometimes found in Jewish
and Christian texts that were likely sermons, such as Hebrews and 1 Clement;
and the style of section three is indeed homiletic, even if it is not actually a
sermon.[43] At times it can even be "fire and brimstone": the unrighteous
worshipped animals, and animals are brought forth by God to plague them
(11:15–19). An opportunity for repentance is also provided (15:1–6).

Most similar to the lists of examples in Wisdom 11–19 are Ben Sira
44–50 and Hebrews 11. Ben Sira 44–50 also recounts the heroes of Israelite
history, but there are two important differences. First, all of the exemplary
figures in Ben Sira are clearly named. Second, the beginning of Ben Sira's
section (44:11–13) expresses a theme opposite of that in Wisdom of Solomon 2–5: children and wealth are the rewards of the wise. In Hebrews 11
Israelite exempla are also clearly named, but there is a surprising similarity
to Wisdom of Solomon.[44] Hebrews 11:1 states that faith is "the assurance of
things hoped for, the conviction of things not seen," similar in theme to
Wisdom 2–5. In addition, it is sometimes suggested that just as Hebrews 11
repeats that the heroes lived and died "by faith," so Wisdom 11–19 declares
that they led exemplary lives "by wisdom." However, this may be importing
assumptions from the other sections; in section three, "wisdom" appears
only in 14:2, 5, where it is very understated. For Wisdom 11–19, as for Ben
Sira 44–50, God, not Wisdom, is said to guide the heroes.

Interrupting the progression of history in section three is also a long
essay of three chapters on the evils of the worship of idols (13:1–15:19). Cri-

tiques of idol worship can be found in earlier Israelite literature, but this digression is by far the longest and most detailed.[45] It is also one of the most subtle, philosophical, and sophisticated of the critiques, exploring human emotions and foibles. The length of the digression indicates that the reaction to Egyptian animal worship was quite strong. The argument about idols is composed of two arcs, up and down, as it were. By beholding beautiful things, one may move up the ladder of nature to derive the one who created them (13:5, similar to Plato's *Symposium*). By this upward arc, Wisdom affirms "natural theology," the belief that humans, even without a direct revelation, can discern the structure of God's cosmic plan. But there is a danger of a downward arc as well. If one remains fixated on the material representations, one is dragged down, inevitably committing sins. The charge of irrationality here is very Greek in tone. Earlier Israelites condemned idols as representing *other gods,* while Wisdom of Solomon condemns them because they are *material representations.* Matter is unfit for representations of spiritual things. From the time of the pre-Socratic philosophers, Greek intellectuals had tried to eliminate the material representations of gods. Stoics condemned the "error of levels" and insisted that although matter was imbued with spirit, true divinity was spirit at a higher level. "Wisdom of Solomon," says Emma Wasserman, takes a stand on this point and "aspires to the level of an esteemed philosophy."[46]

The parody of idols in Israelite texts now reads as very "Jewish" and opposed to the typical error of the Greeks, but the rejection of images was also a Greek philosophical theme. Following Plato, philosophers increasingly described the gods as immaterial, while it was only the unlettered masses who resorted to images (Pseudo-Heraclitus, Epistle 4). Hecataeus of Abdera even approved of the lack of icons among Jews (Diodorus Siculus 40.3.4). But in the Jewish construction of identity, the elite philosophers could be ignored and the common view of the masses was more in mind. At any rate, the idol parodies in the Apocrypha—here and in Bel, Letter of Jeremiah, and Jubilees—tend to stridently undercut the divinity in the idols, disempowering them by reducing them to natural materials, and even shaming the idols and their creators. Well-meaning modern scholars often insist that ancient Egyptians or others did not really believe that the divinity was present in the idol, but that probably reflects a misguided desire to protect the ancient peoples from the Jewish (and later Christian) charge of superstition. Rather, the ancient worshippers of images likely believed that the gods worked through the images, could see those who were bearing gifts, and could act to bestow blessings upon them. The Jewish idol parodies are insistent and even pedantic *because* they are trying to disempower the images of others. And certainly Jews and Christians were just as capable of believing that material objects, for instance, amulets and *mezuzot,* channeled the power of God.

The providence affirmed in section three—attributed directly to God rather than to Wisdom—creates a more positive and less pessimistic tone about God's activity *in the world* than does section one. The ending of the historical survey at 19:22 resolves the issue: "In everything, O Lord, you have exalted and glorified your people, and you have not neglected to help them at all times and in all places." The triumphalism of the book, most notable in this last section, has been characterized by John Barclay as "an educated and deeply Hellenized exercise in cultural aggression." Other scholars find here a more balanced vision of Jews among the nations. Collins perceives a tone of coexistence, and although Rajak interprets it as ambivalence and negotiation, she also says, "There is an unavoidable contradiction, or at least a tension, between the claim of being as good as everyone else, as Greeks, and the claim of being even better, as the followers of a God who trumps all others."[47] This is another example of colonial universalism.

Crucial differences can be found in the three sections of Wisdom of Solomon, though overarching motifs and themes have persuaded most scholars that we have here the product of one author. The overall poetic style is similar throughout, and as noted, two major, overarching thematic approaches can be traced through all sections. First, there is a need to acknowledge God's transcendence and humans' attainment of that on the basis of righteousness. Second, present in all three sections is the emphasis on the improvement of the moral agent in knowledge. And yet, other observations challenge the assumption that there is only one author. We have already noted that the protagonist in section one is passive in terms of worldly engagement, while the speaker in sections two and three is much more active, even triumphant.

WISDOM OF SOLOMON IN CHRISTIAN
AND JEWISH TRADITION

From earliest times to today, Wisdom of Solomon has held an important place in Christian thought and practice. It may have influenced a number of New Testament texts. The closest parallels are Rom 1:19–32 (compare Wis 13:1–9) and Matt 27:43 (compare Wis 2:17–20). There are other possible allusions that have drawn scholarly attention. The *Novum Testamentum Graece* lists quotations and possible allusions in the New Testament, and though many allusions to Wisdom of Solomon are quite vague, ninety-nine are listed.[48] This might indicate a common cultural matrix more than literary influence, yet it is significant in that the number of parallels is greater than for any other text of the Apocrypha (other than Ben Sira, with which it is tied). The earliest clear reference to Wisdom of Solomon can be found in 1 Clem. 27:5 (compare Wis 12:12), written at the end of the first or beginning of the second century. As already noted, in about 200 CE Wisdom of Solomon was listed in the Muratorian fragment as part of the New Testament, and also similarly in Epiphanius, *Panarion* 76.5 (along with Ben Sira). Over the next three centuries it was included in every known Old Testament. Jerome opposed the canonization of the Greek Apocrypha in general, but Wisdom of Solomon was a favorite of Augustine and was already used in liturgy. It has remained influential in Christian tradition as a poetic, philosophical, and spiritual text. The Montfort Missionaries of the Catholic Church take Wisdom of Solomon as a central text in their religious life. Unlike most of the Apocrypha, it did not pass totally out of use by Jews. It is one of the few Apocryphal texts that may be alluded to in rabbinic literature (*b. Yoma* 75a; compare Wis 16:25–26). In the thirteenth century Nachmanides took the text quite seriously, though he emphasized that it was noncanonical, and the medieval Jewish mystical text *Zohar* may cite it.

Fourth Maccabees

About a century after the writing of 1 and 2 Maccabees, another text was composed that substantially refashioned the tradition. Fourth Maccabees takes up the martyrdom stories found in 2 Maccabees 6–7 but treats them as an opportunity for a philosophical treatise: "a most philosophical subject, whether devout reason rules over the passions" (1:1). On one hand, 4 Maccabees takes its inspiration from 2 Maccabees; more than forty words, not found in the rest of the Greek Bible, are used in common by them. Fourth Maccabees extends some of the storytelling techniques of 2 Maccabees with an intense focus on the sufferings of the martyrs, yet it is also a philosophical text more in common with Wisdom of Solomon. Some of our texts, for instance, offer the hope of resurrection of the body (2 Maccabees), and others an immortality of the soul that transcends the material body (Wisdom of Solomon; compare Philo). Fourth Maccabees is in agreement with the latter view.[49]

The text has two parts. The subject matter of the book is established in 1:1–3:18, and at 3:19–18:24 the author turns to the examples of martyrdom: Eleazar and the mother and her seven sons. Some significant differences from 2 Maccabees are noteworthy here. Fourth Maccabees does not emphasize as strongly that persecution is a result of past sin (although it is still noted, 4:19–21). The elderly hero of virtue, Eleazar, is now not only a priest and an expert in the law but also a philosopher (5:4, 35). The Seleucid leader Antiochus engages Eleazar in a philosophical debate, pitting Jewish law against the demands of the world. The whole of 4 Maccabees, then, is devoted to a topic that takes up only one part of 2 Maccabees. The expansion over 2 Maccabees largely consists in the speeches, and as a result, the genre is now not a history, but a philosophical discourse, presenting the torture of the martyrs as a model of the noble, philosophical death (see especially 13:1–14:10). Eusebius and Jerome even referred to 4 Maccabees as "On the Supremacy of Reason." The first verses make the connection between devout reason (*eusebēs logismos*) and Greek virtue; they treat rational judgment, self-control, justice, and courage, the four cardinal virtues associated with Platonic and Stoic philosophy. This very Greek reflection on the mastery of emotions will be met with a *Jewish*-Greek synthesis: mastery of the emotions can be accomplished through education (Greek *paideia*) and Jewish law (1:17). The fusion of Jewish law and Greek philosophy is seen in an expansive notion of law that is neither traditionally Israelite nor traditionally Greek. Law or *nomos* now functions in multiple ways: it teaches

Jewish culture, it enables one to conduct one's life rationally, it encourages the faithful to persevere in the face of persecution, it condemns people for their behavior, and it issues commands and prohibitions for right living. Many scholars thus remark on the fact that it is *Jewish* law that enables one to live the *Greek* ideal.[50] Fourth Maccabees, like Wisdom of Solomon, also exhibits colonial universalism. The synthesis of Greek and Jewish notions is carried forward at a later moment when Eleazar turns to a plea that is technically not philosophical: he appeals to God to accept his death as an expiation for the sins of Israel (6:26-29; see also *hilastērion*, atoning sacrifice, in 17:22). This develops further the notions of sacrifice and atonement for sins found in 2 Macc 7:37-38 and is similar as well to Rom 3:25.

The exordium or introduction to the treatise is quite typical of Greek philosophical texts, yet it is perhaps overdone in that the topic question, whether reason rules over the emotions, is repeated many times over. Given the repeated message, it is not surprising that 4 Maccabees is composed in educated, even pretentious Greek. Says Robert J. V. Hiebert, "His [the author's] use of extravagant rhetoric and florid prose is presumably intended to arouse pity for the martyrs and to motivate readers to emulate their piety."[51] Still, rhetorical speeches of this period were performance pieces, and the florid style is appropriate for such a text, especially since it likely serves as a public commemoration of the Maccabean martyrs. Fourth Maccabees takes the form of a Greek rhetorical address, but precisely what kind? Often suggested are a combination of diatribe (a strongly argued address that often includes an artificial dialogue with imaginary opponents), protreptic (an address that instructs or persuades; see "Wisdom of Solomon" above), and encomium (praise for someone or something; also see "Wisdom of Solomon"), here specifically a memorial address for the Maccabean martyrs. Yet these categories often overlap. DeSilva presses more in the direction of epideictic rhetoric that praises what is good or condemns what is bad. Yet he rightly adds that "what is at stake for the author is not the philosophical thesis, but the lifestyle defended by the martyr-heroes."[52] The goal might also be said to be deliberative and protreptic: to bring the audience to emulate this philosophical lifestyle. One might argue that 4 Maccabees is not particularly profound as philosophy, yet it is remarkably effective as a somewhat long-winded rhetorical text about reason and piety (*eusebeia,* translated "religion" in the NRSV). This text affirms the belief that *logismos* and God's law can indeed exercise mastery over the appetites and passions. This is not a minor point; it is the claim about the law that Paul would later reject in insisting that the human being, armed with Jewish law, could *not* control the passions (Romans 7). Fourth Maccabees, then, rather calmly states over and over that the law is sovereign over the passions. Also like Wisdom of Solomon, reason comes through education, although here it is more explicitly associated with Mosaic law.

Fourth Maccabees, like the other philosophical text in the Apocrypha, Wisdom of Solomon, argues for the immortality of the soul (14:5–6, 16:13, 18:23), but unlike Wisdom of Solomon, it remains more calmly philosophical.[53] It engages opposing views as arguments to be disproved, not as speeches uttered by wicked antagonists who will ultimately pass away. Wisdom of Solomon is also sometimes considered muddled because it alternates philosophical and apocalyptic passages. Fourth Maccabees does not mix philosophical and apocalyptic motifs in this way, but it is sometimes characterized as muddled in a different way, in mixing Platonic and Stoic ideas. Many Stoics held that emotions should be extirpated from the rational mind, while Platonists maintained that the emotions could not be removed entirely but should rather be moderated. Fourth Maccabees, then, seems comfortably within the Platonic fold in retaining a positive place for emotions. At times this seems clear: "No one of us can eradicate anger from the mind, but reason can help to deal with anger. . . . For reason does not uproot the emotions but is their antagonist" (3:3). Yet Hans Moscicke finds that this is not the end of the discussion.[54] True, the author of 4 Maccabees does not wish to extirpate emotions, since they are planted in the soul by God. Yet 4 Maccabees proceeds to show that the emotions are so firmly under control that there is a functional absence of emotions, a sort of de facto Stoic *apatheia.* "Devout reason" says the author at 14:13, "strengthened the mother to disregard . . . her parental love." This is yet another way in which the comparisons of 4 Maccabees, Wisdom of Solomon, and Philo have remained so intriguing to scholars.

This latter point demonstrates as well what is perhaps the best quality of the work: the intense interest in moral psychology. Steven Weitzman draws our attention to an arresting case of this psychological interest when he compares God's command to sacrifice Isaac in Genesis 22 with 4 Maccabees 14, where the pious mother must observe her seven sons being executed by the Seleucid king:

Gen 22:2-3	4 Macc 14:13-20
God said, "Take your son, your only son Isaac, whom you love, and go to the land of Moriah, and offer him there as a burnt offering on one of the mountains that I shall show you." So Abraham rose early in the morning. . . .	Observe how complex is a mother's love for her children, which draws everything toward an emotion felt in her inmost parts. Even unreasoning animals, as well as human beings, have a sympathy and parental love for their offspring . . . even bees at the time of making honeycombs defend themselves against intruders and, as though with an iron dart, sting those who approach their hive and defend it even to the death. But sympathy for her children did not sway the mother of the young men; she was of the same mind as Abraham.

Genesis, says Weitzman, offers no description of what Abraham was thinking; he simply complies with God's command, "leaving his thoughts for readers to figure out on their own (as they have been trying to do ever since)."[55] How different, then, is 4 Maccabees, even though the author likens the mother to Abraham.

The philosophical language of 4 Maccabees might at first suggest an origin in Alexandria, but the memorializing of the Maccabees suggests that the text could have been written in a literary center closer to Judea, perhaps Antioch in Syria. Fourth Maccabees was likely composed in the first century

CE before the Jewish War (which does not figure at all in the text). Apollonius's title in 4:2, "governor of Syria, Phoenicia, and Cilicia," also suggests a time when these regions were part of a Roman administrative area: 20–54 CE. It is possible that 4 Maccabees was known to Josephus (*Jewish War* 2.152–53), and in the rabbinic corpus *t. Hullin* 2:24 may reflect knowledge of 4 Macc 5:7. Fourth Maccabees was at times transmitted with the Josephus corpus and attributed to him.[56] The example of the mother and seven sons would later appear in *Lamentations Rabbah* 150, but it was not likely known from 4 Maccabees. The tradition also appears in Josippon. The text explores issues of the sacrifice and expiation by blood of the martyrs that Paul treats in Romans (cf. 4 Macc 17:22 and Rom 3:25, 5:10; also 1 Pet 1:19, 1 John 1:7). Similar terminology is used (*hilastērion*), but there is no indication of a direct literary connection. It exercised little influence on later Christian theology but may have contributed to the developing theology of martyrdom (note especially Origen, *Exhortation to Martyrdom*).[57] The fourth-century Latin *Passio Sanctorum Machabaeorum* even treats the martyrs as Christian.

Baruch (1 Baruch) and Letter (or Epistle) of Jeremiah

The outward trappings of Baruch and Letter of Jeremiah might suggest that they should be classified as prophecy, but the frame is really only a literary device. True, the content also sometimes speaks of prophecy, but at other times it relates more to wisdom, and this is how the two books are categorized here. Baruch was an important character in the book of Jeremiah—the prophet's faithful scribe. In the late Hellenistic period many texts bore the names of these two: Baruch (or 1 Baruch), 2 Baruch, 4 Baruch (Paralipomena of Jeremiah), and Letter of Jeremiah are treated in this volume, and in the ancient period there also existed an *Apocryphon of Jeremiah* from Qumran and a 3 Baruch. In addition, Jeremiah was considered an Israelite hero who might rise from the dead (2 Maccabees 15, Matt 16:14). Indeed, the role of Jeremiah in 2 Maccabees and at Qumran indicates that, while the *book* of Jeremiah was surprisingly not treated often, the heroic *figure* was. Since Baruch and Letter of Jeremiah circulated together in ancient Bibles, Letter of Jeremiah was often numbered as Baruch 6; they are treated together here. Hindy Najman has referred to rewritten scripture as "Mosaic discourse"— the channeling and extending of the voice of Moses to a new generation (see the introduction to Chapter 2)—and Judith H. Newman observes a similar pattern in regard to Jeremiah discourse in Baruch. Baruch interweaves Jeremiah's language and extends his message, while pushing toward a different resolution. "Baruch can be understood both to receive and compose 'Jeremiah' with the sense of a new ending that overcomes exile itself."[58] By this process Baruch, the scribe of Jeremiah, is elevated on his own to the status of a cultural hero. Doubtless his role as witness to history contributed to this prominence, but it is also due to his function as a scribe. The contemporary developments in wisdom texts and apocalypses focus on scribalism, and the name Baruch is associated with both wisdom texts and apocalypses.

Baruch and Letter of Jeremiah are, in their different parts, informed by particular biblical books, so much so that they are often treated as inferior re-editions. Still, some value may be found in this. Unlike Qumran texts or Jubilees, Baruch and Letter of Jeremiah are not sectarian. According to Anthony Saldarini, "Baruch's very generality and lack of originality, for which it has often been criticized, made it attractive and available to Jews of every inclination." Both Baruch and Letter of Jeremiah address all Jews and try to raise them to a higher moral standard. These two texts did not focus, for instance, on the divisive calendar issues, and life after death is not mentioned. The divine intervention and restoration of Israel is hoped for in the present worldly context, not in an apocalyptic future. Nations will be punished, but there is no expected messiah nor final judgment: "The desired result of the restoration," Saldarini continues, "is for Israel to dwell in the land in peace."[59] Yet, though he can say that these texts were addressed to "all Jews," we may specify the audience a bit: the texts address the ideal Jew, the free male person of means, the ideal moral agent of wisdom texts. True, women are sometimes mentioned in such texts, and they may have in fact participated in social and political institutions; but the "ideal agent" addressed in Jewish wisdom texts was often the free male head-of-household (see "Ben Sira" above).

Both Baruch and Letter of Jeremiah begin with the tone of prophecy. Baruch 1:1–14 assumes a setting in the exile, although the text was likely written much later. The narrative is not carefully composed, however, for Baruch seems to be present for events at both the beginning of the exile and after, when the temple vessels were returned. The text begins: "These are the words of the book that Baruch son of Neriah son of Mahseiah son of Zedekiah son of Hasadiah son of Hilkiah wrote in Babylon, in the fifth year, on the seventh day of the month, at the time when the Chaldeans took Jerusalem and burned it with fire." It continues by saying that Baruch read his book to the son of the king of Judah and to all the people in exile in Babylon. They then wept, fasted, and prayed before the Lord. This reminds one more of Ezra 8–10 than of Jeremiah, but by this time there was also a merging of pious ideals. Baruch then continues speaking in the tone of Jeremiah, for he prays for King Nebuchadnezzar and his son (1:10–14). The connection with Ezra should be seen also on another level. Around 400 BCE Ezra was reconstituting Judeans by defining them as those who had returned from exile. Baruch 1:1–14, on the other hand, composed several centuries later, attempted whether consciously or unconsciously to provide a prequel by reimagining this same ethno-religious group two centuries before Ezra-Nehemiah.

Following the introduction (1:1–14), Baruch can be divided into three parts, each exhibiting a strong influence of particular biblical texts:

Part and theme	Biblical influence
1. Confession of sin and penitential prayer (1:15–3:8)	Dan 9 and Jeremiah
2. Wisdom poem (3:9–4:4)	Deut 30, Job 28, Sir 24[60]
3. Poem of consolation, or "Zion poem" (4:5–5:9)	Isa 40–66

PART 1: CONFESSION OF SIN AND PENITENTIAL PRAYER (1:15–3:8)

The first part is a confession of Israel's sin, similar in tone to Daniel 9, Ezra 9, and Nehemiah 9: "There is open shame on us today, . . . because we have sinned before the Lord."[61] For such a short book, the confession of sin and prayer for God's deliverance are quite long and repetitive. One wonders whether the litany of confessions here and in these other confessional texts represented an actual liturgy of a group confession, similar to the listing of sins in the Yom Kippur service. The liturgical aspect seems clearest in 2:16–18. Yet in the prayer that follows the confession, it is striking that the list of sins includes failing to serve the king of Babylon (2:21–24). This brings us back to the message of the book of Jeremiah: Israel should adapt to living in a foreign land. The repetitiveness, even tediousness of this part— and Letter of Jeremiah as well—may reflect an attempt to reinforce Jewish identity by resort to rhetorical emphasis. The prayer then draws to a close by restating God's covenant-making: "I will make an everlasting covenant with them to be their God and they shall be my people" (2:35).

PART 2: WISDOM POEM (3:9–4:4)

The tone of this part differs from that of the first: "Hear the commandments of life, O Israel; give ear, and learn wisdom!" (3:9). It is also somewhat artificially connected to the narrative of Baruch in exile: "Why is it, O Israel, that you are in the land of your enemies?" (3:10). The lesson of the exile, which would have been far in the past, was that walking in the way of God and wisdom will save Israel. Somewhat like Wisdom 2–5, the distinction is made between those who courted worldly wealth and power, who "have vanished and gone down to Hades," and the wise who "live in peace forever" (3:13, 19). Finding the place of Wisdom is at first difficult: "She has not been heard of in Canaan or seen in Teman. . . . Who has gone up into heaven, and taken her, and brought her down from the clouds?" (3:22, 29). This theme of the inaccessibility of Wisdom is at first similar to Job:

> Where shall wisdom be found?
>> And where is the place of understanding?
> Mortals do not know the way to it,
>> and it is not found in the land of the living. (Job
>> 28:12–13)

But as in Ben Sira 24, the peoples of the earth could not learn about wisdom on their own; yet in Israel Wisdom can be found:

> God gave her to his servant Jacob,
>   and to Israel whom he loved. . . .
> She is the book of the commandments of God,
>   the law that endures forever.
> Happy are we, O Israel, for we know what is pleasing to God.
>   (Bar 3:36; 4:1, 4)

Still, as Nickelsburg points out, the personification of wisdom is less clear here than in Ben Sira 24: "The poem is *about* her rather than *by* her."[62] Likewise, the cosmic expanse of Wisdom and the suggestion that she is a cosmic savior are less pronounced in Baruch.

PART 3: POEM OF CONSOLATION, OR "ZION POEM" (4:5–5:9)

The more positive ending of the wisdom poem is not continued in the third part. The poem of consolation or Zion Poem returns to the problem of exile. Time and again, there are echoes of Isaiah 40–66:

Isa 50:1b	Bar 4:6–8
	It was not for destruction That you were sold to the nations,
Because of your sins you were sold, And for your transgressions your mother was put away.	But you were handed over to your enemies Because you angered God. You provoked the one who made you By sacrificing to demons and not to God. You forgot the everlasting God who brought you up, And you grieved Jerusalem, who reared you.

Isa 60:2-3	Bar 4:24
The Lord will rise upon you, And his glory will appear over you. Nations shall come to your light, and kings to the brightness of your dawn.	For as the neighbors of Zion have now seen your capture, So they soon will see your salvation by God, Which will come to you with great glory and with the splendor of the Everlasting.

Isa 40:4	Bar 5:7
Every valley shall be lifted up, And every mountain and hill be made low. The uneven ground shall become level, and the rough places a plain.	For God has ordered that every high mountain and the everlasting hills be made low, And the valleys filled up to make level ground.

In this part as in the others, Baruch opens his heart to a rending confession, entreating God to overlook Israel's sins: "I have taken off the robe of peace and put on sackcloth for my supplication; I will cry to the Everlasting all my days" (4:20). As in Second Isaiah, the exile is a low point in Israel's history, but a new day will dawn. God's mercy will outweigh God's judgment, and there will be salvation. In addition to Isaiah 40–66, important parallels can also be found in Deuteronomy (32:17–18, 33:29 LXX) and Psalms of Solomon 11 (see Chapter 5), which likely predates Baruch. The revenge that will be enacted upon Babylon is similar to Isaiah 47, but it is also very different in tone from the conciliatory setting in the introduction (Bar 1:11–12). It could be argued that it simply results from different texts being placed together, but most scholars now assume that we see the work here of only one author, although this person has taken up different genres to compose the various parts. Despite the universal agreement, then, that there are three parts in the work, Odil Hannes Steck and André Kabasele Mukenge can still argue that Baruch is a unitary work, the latter stating that the whole was based on Deuteronomy 28–33 and Jeremiah 27–33 and composed as an appendix to Jeremiah. Jeremy Corley also finds unity in the emotional transformation, the human subject changing from sorrowful shame to glorious joy, and God changing from divine anger to divine consolation toward Israel.[63]

The dating of Baruch is uncertain. It was written long after the events described. The resonance with Daniel 9 would indicate that it is later than 165 BCE, but Daniel 9 may also depend on an earlier prayer. If the wisdom poem is dependent on Ben Sira 24, then a date after 180 is required for that part. The confession of Israel's sins speaks to an experience of being under the control of foreign powers, which suggests a date before the Maccabean Revolt or after the defeat of Judah by Rome in 63 BCE, or even after the fall of Jerusalem and the destruction of the second temple in 70 CE; all three periods have been proposed. But the imaginative or even consciously ficti- tious aspect of the text makes dating difficult. Saldarini was perhaps wise to leave the date as unknown.[64]

Letter or Epistle of Jeremiah

The Letter or Epistle of Jeremiah is not a real letter but takes the form of an epistle to deliver moral instruction. In a precanonical stage, Letter of Jere- miah was independent, but it was included in the Old Testament either as the final chapter of Baruch, numbered as chapter 6 (Vulgate), or as an inde- pendent text coming after Lamentations (Vaticanus and Alexandrinus). The historical setting of the letter actually precedes that of Baruch, which also mixes different time frames in the same text. The moral epistle was a very common genre in the ancient world, but the Letter of Jeremiah has the dis- tinction of being one of the earliest examples in Judaism. The supposed context of the letter—perhaps understood to be fictitious—is clearly ex- pressed: "a copy of a letter which Jeremiah sent to those taken to Babylon as captives by the king of the Babylonians." "A copy of a letter" calls to mind the letters in Jeremiah 29; Ezra 4:7, 11; Neh 2:7; Esth 8:5, 9:26; and many others. The lives of Jews within the great empires were constantly noted in our texts by means of letters and decrees. Sara Raup Johnson ties these ex- amples together and points out the importance of this motif: the Persians had invested in writing as the medium of authority, and this motif was adopted in our texts to communicate the spread of Jewish authority through writing, covering great distances by means of the letter format—ancient mass media.[65] Yet many of these examples were fictitious, so aspects of real political networks were constantly incorporated to depict an ideal, extended Israel. In this case, the letter has the force of Jeremiah's prophecy, but it is now present in the community as a copy—the physical presence of God's prophetic *and* textual authority.

In the book of Jeremiah, the prophet had sent a letter to the exiles exhorting them not to join in rebellion against the Babylonians (Jeremiah 29). The present Letter of Jeremiah opens by taking up the spirit and some of the words of that letter and is similar as well to the opening of Baruch (although in the latter case the invented letter was supposedly sent in the opposite direction, from the exiles to Jerusalem):

Jer 29:1	Let Jer 6:1	Bar 1:1–2
These are the words of the letter that the prophet Jeremiah sent from Jerusalem to the remaining elders among the exiles, and to the priests, the prophets, and all the people, whom Nebuchadnezzar had taken into exile from Jerusalem to Babylon.	A copy of a letter that Jeremiah sent to those who were to be taken to Babylon as exiles by the king of the Babylonians, to give them the message that God commanded them.	These are the words of the book that Baruch son of Neriah . . . wrote in Babylon in the fifth year on the seventh day of the month, at the time when the Chaldeans took Jerusalem and burned it with fire. Baruch read the words of this book to Jeconiah son of Jehoiakim, king of Judah, and to all the people who came to hear the book, and to the nobles, and the princes, and to the elders, and to all the people, small and great, all who lived in Babylon by the river Sud.

The Letter of Jeremiah continues by further channeling the spirit of Jeremiah: "Because of the sins that you have committed before God, you will be taken to Babylon as exiles by Nebuchadnezzar, king of the Babylonians. Therefore when you have come to Babylon you will remain there for many years, for a long time, up to seven generations; after that I will bring you away from there in peace" (6:2–3). After this opening, the letter turns immediately to a parody of idol worship, similar to that found in Isa 44:9–20, Wisdom 13–15, and Bel and the Dragon (see discussion at "Wisdom of Solomon" above). Letter of Jeremiah extends the parody of idols by repeating many examples of the folly of idols: idols are inappropriate images of God, they are a broken dish, an imprisoned criminal, a scarecrow that guards nothing, a useless thorn bush, an abandoned corpse.

Scholars have deemed the repetitive style tedious. Nickelsburg characterizes the argument as inept; it does not progress, but only repeats. The method of this letter is to utilize a rhetorical overkill and what Matthew Goff refers to as "sarcastic humor." Scholars even speculate that it reflects the complacent self-assurance of a mediocre mind; how, asks C. J. Ball, could a work "so formless, so confused, so utterly destitute of the graces of style" be canonized?[66] But it is important to discern how the rhetoric is meant to function. Ten arguments are arrayed to demonstrate that foreign gods—so impressive in their temples, and especially in the processions and festivals— are nothing but richly decked out statuettes that have no power, even for their own people. At the end of each argument there is a repeated refrain, "This shows that they are no gods." The first argument, for example, describes some of the characteristics of the statues and then presents a clever argument as to why the figure cannot represent a true god: "Their tongues are smoothed by the carpenter, and they themselves are overlaid with gold and silver—but they are false and cannot speak!" (6:8). The impressive or beautiful aspects of the idols are then taken up in order and in each case deconstructed by being compared to some aspect of human vanity: "They take gold and make crowns for the heads of their gods, as they would for a girl who loves ornaments, and sometimes the priests secretly take gold and silver from their gods and spend it upon themselves, and even give some of it to the harlots in the brothels" (6:9–11). Each aspect of the icon seen by the other peoples as a symbol of divine power is now revealed to be even more powerless than everyday practices of human beings:

Purported symbol of divine power	Reality of weakness in human terms
Tongues overlaid with gold	but cannot speak
Gold crowns on their heads	like ornaments for a girl
Images possess gold and silver	which priests use for harlots
Images wear fine garments	but cannot protect themselves from
Images hold a scepter	rust or corrosion
Images hold a dagger and axe	but cannot pass judgment
	but cannot save themselves from the ravages of war

In each case the inevitable lesson is drawn: "Therefore, they evidently are not gods; so do not fear them."

Despite the repetition, slight differences can still be observed. In the third and fourth arguments, the depictions of non-Israelite practices also affirm Israelite values: the foreign priests enrich themselves on the offerings, and yet give none to the poor or helpless. Unlike the Jerusalem temple, non-Israelite women bring offerings even if they are in a period of impurity from menstruation or childbirth (v. 29). The other gods cannot enforce vows; they cannot save someone who has made a petition or protect the weak from the strong—yet at v. 41 it is said that the worshippers of Bel *try* to cure those who are suffering. The prophetic and wisdom traditions can also be heard in the denunciations of the other cults: "They cannot take pity on a widow or do good to an orphan." Tessa Rajak also calls attention to what at first appears to be a minor innovation in the critique of idols: idols rot![67] This, she notes, is not so minor. For the first time in the Israelite parody of idols, it is their *material* that is a problem. To be sure, at times some subtlety is introduced into the argument. For instance, since the idols are less powerful than the people who made them, it is concluded that one would be better off living honestly in the human realm, or that it is better to be an honest piece of wood that serves the utility of human beings, such as a utensil, or even a door that protects the contents of a house (v. 59). Or to move in the cosmic direction, the true God *really does* have power to move *truly big things* around—the sun and moon and stars—and can command the lightning, wind, and clouds. The idol, by contrast, cannot even dust itself off.

Other peoples in the ancient world, of course, were not as naive as these idol parodies suggest, but despite well-meaning cautions from scholars, ancient peoples—with the possible exception of elite philosophers—did assume that idols had agency, could see, and were inhabited by divine presences, just as Jews and Christians felt the power of God or Christ emanating through material objects. Idols really were seen by those who revered them to have power and agency, so Letter of Jeremiah is engaged in a program of systematically deconstructing idols, disempowering them. Visible here is a ritual shaming of the idols and the people who made and revered them. We are told that bats, birds, and even cats would lie upon the idols; the idol is like a scarecrow or a thorn bush, sat on by every bird to leave its droppings: "They will be a reproach in the land." We see at play here a rhetorical effort that uses repetition to achieve a sort of mantra: the simplicity of the message comes through, and also the importance of the theme. The arguments are taunt-songs, which heap shame upon the idols and their worshippers; we may wonder whether the *performance* of the text would be viewed as having a quasi-magical effect of "doing things with words." The lines of this text deconstruct the others' idols much as the bodies of enemies were cut apart and spread about so that burial would be impossible. Shaming the other was a means of reversing the shame that Jews felt: "Those who serve the idols will be put to shame" (v. 39).

The repetition can also be illuminated by a consideration of the genre of the text. The rhetoric takes the form of a "word of exhortation" (*logos paraklēseōs*). It typically follows a three-part structure, which is flexible and can be repeated many times: (1) list of examples, quotations, or short arguments; (2) conclusion; and (3) exhortation. Originally a Greek rhetorical pattern, it is found, for instance in the "harangues" of military commanders to their troops in Greek histories.[68] That it is a Greek influence rather than a native Israelite pattern is indicated by the fact that it is not found in the Hebrew Bible, although Deuteronomy 29–30 at times approximates it. Letter of Jeremiah, then, is the earliest example in Jewish literature. After a series of repetitions of the three-part pattern, the final argument moves to a broader exhortation: "Better, therefore, is someone who is upright [*dikaios*] who has no idols; such a person will be far from reproach" (6:73). This is significant: at last we hear a positive declaration and not the repeated negatives exposing the shame of idolatry. This line also reminds us of the theme of Wisdom of Solomon 2–5, where the persecuted just person (*dikaios*) ultimately attains immortality.

The date of composition for the Letter of Jeremiah is uncertain. Although 2 Maccabees may reflect knowledge of the letter, the direction of influence could also be reversed.[69] It has been argued that a small fragment from Qumran (7Q2, dated to about 100 BCE) is from Letter of Jeremiah, but this is not certain. The use of language indicates a Semitic original, but the word of exhortation genre would support a Greek original. The question of original language thus remains open. Baruch was not quoted in the New Testament, but it strongly influenced the structure and themes of the Christian 5 Ezra. Athenagoras, *Legatio pro Christianis* 9, cites Bar 3:36 as Jeremiah, and other Christian authors understand this passage about Wisdom appearing on earth to refer to the incarnation of Christ. Baruch 3:9–15, 3:32–4:4 then became part of the Catholic Easter vigil, the only Apocryphal text to be so included (see also Aquinas, *Summa Theologiae* 3.4.4). Although, as noted above, the Letter of Jeremiah may have shown up at Qumran, it was not alluded to in the New Testament, and it was rarely quoted in the early church, though it was part of the early canons. Jerome, however, who often had independent ideas, insisted on calling it a *pseudepigraphon* (*Commentary on Jeremiah* praef.). Tertullian and Theodoret of Cyrus quoted it when condemning idolatry, and the Catholic Catechism (§2112) quotes it as a warning against idolatry. These texts had no impact on Jews, and aside from the reference concerning the Easter vigil, little impact on Christian tradition as well. Baruch and Letter of Jeremiah have been largely ignored because the two texts read as derivative, borrowing from one text after another. Yet the didactic style reaffirms the authoritative role of Jeremiah and Baruch and would not have been considered unusual in the period.

Fourth Baruch or Paralipomena of Jeremiah

Like the other Jeremiah/Baruch texts, 4 Baruch (or Paralipomena of Jeremiah, "the things omitted from Jeremiah") is set just after the destruction of the first temple at the hands of the Babylonians (Chaldeans). This is a coded way of describing the destruction of the second temple by the Romans. The date of composition, then, must be the end of the first or beginning of the second century CE, that is, soon after the Roman destruction. It may be possible to be more precise. It is said that Abimelech slept for sixty-six years, rather than the usual calculation of seventy years for the Babylonian captivity. Sixty-six years after the fall of Jerusalem would be 136 CE, which would coincide with the further destruction of Jerusalem after the Bar Kochba revolt of 132–136 CE. This text is canonical only in the Ethiopian Bible, which also included other texts with this theme: Meqabyan, Josephus *Jewish War* Book 6, and perhaps Josippon. Despite the lack of canonical status in the West, it was known in several ancient languages.

Fourth Baruch is a wisdom text but has affinities with apocalypses as well. It is somewhat like 4 Ezra and 2 Baruch in its reflection on why God would punish Israel for its sins while allowing Rome to prosper. Chapter 3 provides a vision of how the destruction occurred: angels on the city walls allow the Babylonians/Chaldeans to enter. As in 4 Ezra and 2 Baruch, the fall of Jerusalem results from the sins of the inhabitants. At first, 4 Baruch seems a rambling narrative of unreal images of a destroyed Jerusalem, conjuring the notion of an apocalypse. At 3:1–2 (long version), the temple vessels are consigned to the earth, which swallows them up, and at 4:4 Jeremiah throws the keys to the temple up to the sun. At 7:1 Baruch leaves the tomb and finds an eagle who talks, a semiapocalyptic symbolic vision. "This is the God," it is stated, "who appeared to our fathers in the wilderness through Moses, and now he has appeared to us through the eagle" (7:20). Jeremiah writes a letter for the eagle to take back to Jerusalem for Baruch and Abimelech (the same as Ebedmelech the Ethiopian in Jer 38:7). Borrowing from Ps 136:3–4, he says, "How shall we sing for you, since we are in a foreign land?" (7:33–34). Also present here is a theme from the heroic tradition in Israel: the hiding of the temple vessels or sacred texts. Nehemiah was said to have hidden away sacred texts (2 Macc 1:13), and here Jeremiah asks God what is to be done with the temple vessels. God delivers a beautiful response: "Consign them to the earth, which the Lord created: Earth, receive your ornaments. Guard them until the gathering of the beloved" (4 Bar 3:9–11, short version).

After the destruction of the second temple, a program for the recon-struction of Jewish society was needed. Views of a future intervention by God were common, and one such contribution is found in chapter 8. When Jews return to Jerusalem from Babylon, some have foreign wives. Jeremiah, Baruch, and Abimelech deny them entrance. These Jews then return to Babylon, but there they are denied entrance as well, where it is said, "You hated us and you left us secretly." At 8:1–11 they then go to the desert and build Samaria. It is difficult to say whether this renegotiation of identity reflects an actual contemporary friction with Samarians or a retelling of the conflicts between Jews and northern Israelites (Samarians) found in such texts as Ezra-Nehemiah. At the end there is an addition consisting of Chris-tian predictions, written in a different style. Some scholars suggest that the text as a whole could have been a Christian composition, but the themes of putting away foreign wives in order to enter the revived city of Jerusalem, as well as Samaria as the place of assimilation, indicate a non-Christian Juda-ism. Jens Herzer has argued that this conclusion is not an anti-Jewish redac-tion, but reflects rather a missionary interest toward Jews: learn from your history, it suggests, and you will come around. Dale C. Allison rightly re-sponds, however, that the tone is not conciliatory. Rather, it gives voice to a supersessionist theology in the early Christian tradition of *Adversus Judaeos:* "One fails to see how 4 Baruch's unqualified contrast of condemned Jews over against believing gentiles can have missionary potential. Not only is Judaism characterized as judged or condemned (9:15) . . . without qualifi-cation, but no attempt is made to lay out common ground between Jews and Christians."[70] Even if the intent were to lead Jews to conversion, that would also bear an anti-Jewish intent, in that it has the goal of making Juda-ism disappear into Christianity.

FOUR

Apocalypses and Visionary Literature

IN PERIODS OF NATIONAL DISASTER AND great social up-
heaval, the questioning of God's action in the world can take a drastically pessimistic turn. Rather than prophesy that Israelites in general should repent
and redeem themselves, or that God may redeem the people through a reversal in historical circumstances—compare the classical biblical prophets—the
early apocalypses communicated the overwhelming sense that human institutions are controlled by evil forces. But for the righteous few there exists a
ray of hope: secret knowledge of the schedule of coming events or of the
structure of the cosmos is available in inspired texts purportedly written by
visionaries from a much earlier period. In these texts one will learn about
God's angels in heaven and how they will vanquish the evil heavenly powers and overturn their earthly minions as well. The small remnant of God's
chosen people will witness this revolution. The conditions that existed at
the beginning of time will now be re-created, in two distinct stages. First,
there will be a destruction that is a return to the original chaos, the "formless void" that existed before God's creation (Gen 1:2). This will be followed by a return to a peaceful and simpler Eden. As the German theologians
described it, *Endzeit = Urzeit,* the end of time will reproduce the conditions
present at the beginning of time.

Although much debate remains about the nature of the apocalypse
genre, we begin by listing some of the typical elements of apocalypses. Many
scholars have addressed the longer history of apocalypses, but here we are
concerned with a subset of Jewish apocalypses that were composed between 300 BCE and 100 CE. A special edition of the journal *Semeia* (volume 14) brought a team of scholars together to map the motifs that appeared

in texts generally considered to be apocalypses.[1] Several traits were perceived to be common in the texts: the narrative introduction that provides a
context for what follows, the emphasis on revelation, and a transcendent
reality that governs the world. The panel of *Semeia* 14 also found that apocalypses could be divided into those that emphasized the temporal axis—
world history from a very early period until its final resolution in the near
future—and the spatial axis, which looked upward to describe the nature
of the heavens.[2] In addition, five elements were in virtually all of the fifteen
Jewish apocalypses listed in *Semeia* 14: dreams or visions, the attribution of
the vision to an ancient author (for example, Enoch, Daniel, or Ezra), an
otherworldly or angelic interpreter, judgment, and an afterlife. Other traits
appeared in many but not all of the texts: an array of named angels and demons, an imminent cosmic catastrophe, the resurfacing of ancient mythical
content ("recrudescence of myth"), and future predictions with a rigid, deterministic timeline. On the social and political scale, there is often, but not
always, a critique of empire and a radical, sectarian doctrine of salvation;
that is, only a righteous minority—those "in the know"—will be saved. The
deterministic predictions also offer a means of dating apocalypses. The predictions are supposedly in the ancient author's future, but they are mainly
in the actual author's past. The point at which the "predictions" go wrong
is then likely the date of the composition. A clear example of this can be
found at Dan 11:40, where the recitation of supposedly future events, which
had been accurate, now becomes inaccurate. Also associated with apocalypses are aspects of Israelite wisdom: scribalism, knowledge, teaching, and
books. At the end of most apocalypses, for instance, there is a strong emphasis on how the visionary has *written* a text that is either *hidden* or *passed
on* to the audience's generation—fictitious though that transmission may be.
The association of the apocalyptic visionaries with scribes is so strong that
Gerhard von Rad argued that apocalypticism arose out of the wisdom tradition. The scribes, he assumed, simply became more pessimistic in response
to the domination of empires and created a revelation-based genre. This
thesis now seems too simplistic, since different streams evidently flowed into
apocalypticism, yet remained separate as well. Still, the mutual relations of
wisdom and apocalypticism are undeniable.[3]

Semeia 14 and the listing of common motifs provided an essential first step in discussing the genre systematically, but it was only a beginning, and it was clear that important modifications were also called for. Some scholars voiced dissatisfaction with the attempt to define the essence of apocalypses by means of elaborating typical motifs and moved back one step to ask what kind of discourse constitutes these texts. For Christopher Rowland, the mode of discourse of apocalypses was the revelation of the secrets of heaven. The revealed knowledge of the visionary, communicated to a special audience— again, those in the know—was the essence of apocalypses. The key to apocalypses is not the motifs but how humans receive it as revealed knowledge. Putting it in slightly different terms, Michael Wolter defined apocalypse as "a speech-form in which the speaker announces, in the first-person singular, that he will mediate a truth that has been heretofore hidden from human knowledge, but is now realized by breaking through a cognitive boundary. Apocalyptic texts affirm a reality that is understood to be expressed *for the first time* in human consciousness."[4] As noted in the introductions to Chapters 1 and 2, genres are perceived by audiences on many levels and are rightly described in different ways. The two approaches—common motifs on one hand and mode of discourse on the other—need not be considered mutually exclusive. They are complementary means that humans use to perceive the different facets of a genre. However, another influential approach cannot be harmonized so easily. Some scholars insist that the essence of the apocalypse can be reduced to one theme—a mythical account of the origin of evil. This is indeed a strong theme in the Enochic tradition but does not appear at all in Daniel. In that case, Daniel could not be considered an apocalypse. The field remains split on this aspect of the definition of apocalypses, although in the present book the origin of evil is not taken as the one defining motif of apocalypses.

What were apocalypses called? The texts are often filled with terms relating to scribes and wisdom, but we generally distinguish apocalypses from wisdom texts. The term "apocalypse" is derived from Rev 1:1, *apokalypsis,* revealing, but that text was written two to three centuries after the first apocalypses, and even in Revelation the word refers not to a kind of text but to the process of revealing. (Josephus, *Antiquities* 12.9, uses *apokalypsis* to describe the unwrapping of the covering on sacred scrolls.) As we have seen elsewhere, genres often function in society without a clear name. The term "film noir," for instance, was applied to this genre of film only after it was essentially over, and as one might guess, it was coined by French film critics to describe US films. Just as there was no term for film noir as these films were being created, there was evidently no special term for the earlier texts. However, a root commonly associated with apocalypses was *hazah*, to see or have a vision, and its noun form, *hazōn* (Dan 1:17, 7:11). Apocalypses may have been perceived as part of a visionary tradition in Israel, and this may be related to the international body of mantic or oracular wisdom that these scribes tapped into.

Other observations of recent scholarship on the apocalypses can be noted. That apocalypses condemn foreign domination is often explicit, yet first, they differ on this point, and second, apocalypses, like all other Jewish literature, are also influenced by Greek intellectual trends. Carol Newsom sees the mapping of the heavens in 1 Enoch as similar to royal dominion and Hellenistic map-making. The historical apocalypses can equally be said to be influenced by the rise of Greek history writing, especially the notions of "universal history," as a sort of resistance literature (see the introduction to Chapter 2 and also the discussion of 2 Baruch below). John J. Collins also points out a contrast between apocalypses and wisdom literature. Wisdom texts approximate the Greek notion of general knowledge ordered for learning. The texts reveal a pattern of transmission from father to son, even if that is but a pretense of the texts, and discipline (Hebrew *musar*, Greek *paideia*): the student must listen and learn through great effort, guided by a discipline of the head-of-household that never ends (Ben Sira). Apocalypses, however, do not emphasize discipline but the passing on of the keys of knowledge to those who are spiritually open to it. Knowledge is dispensed, then, not through a general educational program, but in an ad hoc way through revelation. Collins states the distinction in this way: "Wisdom's salvation is inherent in the world order, while apocalyptic posits a sharp break between the heavenly regions and rejects the earthly and the present world order. The Jewish sapiential [= wisdom] tradition is based on the premise that wisdom can be found in all creation, whereas in apocalyptic wisdom has retired to heaven and can be known only by heavenly revelations."[5]

Another important recent observation is that apocalypses are not as dualistic as once thought. Loren Stuckenbruck cautions that apocalypses do not really posit a strict *dualism* of two ages, the present world and the next, but the future *culmination* and *resolution* of one age. In a similar way, Emma Wasserman argues that apocalypses do not present a strict dualism of *equal* opposing forces, good and evil, but depict conflict between unequal adversaries, the dominant power of God and the lesser power of the rebellious forces in heaven. Satan, it turns out, often is not a looming chief of the demons as much as a stock adversary. Wasserman also suggests that visions of conflict could theoretically serve to quiet discontent, to channel it away, to provide an alternative experience to earthly battle. If apocalypses provide a compensation for being disempowered, can they lead to accommodation? In addition, even the ruling foreign powers, no matter how sinful, are not "equal" opponents to God, but servants of the divine will. Although apocalypses seem at first to be very culture-specific, scholars have also noted the international similarities. Ancient Near Eastern and Greek parallels to many of the motifs can be found. Yet why did apocalypses appear in some ancient kingdoms and not in others? Long ago S. K. Eddy tried to answer this question, and his conclusions still reverberate.[6] Apocalypse-like texts and significant resistance to Hellenistic rule appeared in Persia, Egypt, and Judah, but little resistance arose in Syria, Samaria, Parthia, and Bactria. What did Persia, Egypt, and Judah have in common? They exhibited strong notions of cosmic kingship, unity, a chosen people, ethical dualism, and future reward and punishment. In addition, there were fewer large Hellenistic cities in those regions. The common assumption that only Israel resisted, and did so only because of their loyalty to the idea of one true God, should be attributed to the success of the propaganda of 1 and 2 Maccabees and Judith—and of the theological assumptions of later Jewish and Christian scholars.

Did apocalypses, then, die out in Judaism? The rabbis chose the path of avoiding the radical, sectarian response to empire and tried to live peacefully under foreign rule. Prophecy was consigned by the rabbis to the past, the contents of a closed canon; no new prophecy could occur: "Until Alexander the prophets prophesied in the holy spirit, but from now on turn your ear to hear the words of the sages" (*Seder Olam Rabbah* 30; cf. *m. Hagigah*

2:1). This strategy at first afforded little role for apocalypses, although later Jewish mysticism took up many of their visionary and symbolic motifs. Christian authorities also attempted to declare prophecy a closed channel, consigned to the past, but again, prophetic and apocalyptic voices did continue to arise.

First Enoch and Its Parts

A large number of texts in in the Hellenistic and Roman periods are attributed to Enoch or show interest in him, although he is mentioned in only one short, inscrutable passage in Genesis. There it is said that he lived 365 years—is this why he was associated with a solar calendar?—and that he did not die but "walked with God; and he was not, for God took him" (Gen 5:24). Abraham, Noah, Moses, Daniel, and Ezra also became visionary figures, so for a biblical figure to take on a visionary role was not unique. Yet Enoch rises to a level of tremendous importance in a large and developing visionary tradition and has no other known "backstory" than the single verse in Genesis. Perhaps analogous to the Enoch tradition is the voluminous Gnostic tradition that surrounds Seth, a son of Adam and Eve, who is likewise mentioned in only one verse, Gen 4:25. The one stray line concerning Enoch, however, may signal that there was at one time a larger tradition concerning this ancient figure, now lost in the editing of the biblical tradition yet surviving and growing to appear in the 1 Enoch texts and elsewhere.

What we refer to as 1 Enoch or Ethiopic Enoch is the text found in the Bible of the Ethiopian Orthodox Tewahedo Church. "For Ethiopic literature," says Ephraim Isaac, "the book of Enoch is like Pushkin for Russian literature and Shakespeare for English literature." It is known in its entirety only in this Eastern Christian context, although it is composed of five Jewish texts that were written between the third century BCE and first century CE (or possibly later). Scholars sometimes speak as if a full text of "1 Enoch" existed in the ancient period, but it most likely circulated as separate Enochic texts, as indeed the Qumran fragments indicate. The earliest part of 1 Enoch was composed before the latest part of the Hebrew Bible, Daniel 7–12. It is also possible, though unprovable, that the five parts that made up

1 Enoch were meant to complement or even supplant the five books of Moses. Still, the image of a unitary "1 Enoch" in this early period remains a subconscious problem. Annette Yoshiko Reed asks, "To what degree does the unity within 1 Enoch reflect the production of its parts within a single socio-religious sphere, and to what degree is the appearance of unity created retrospectively by the act of collection?"[7] However, although there was not likely a unitary text, there probably was a connected tradition associated with Enoch, much as Noah, Isaiah, Daniel, or Seth generated connected traditions.

Despite, then, the meager information in Genesis—or perhaps *because* the short notice allowed a sense of mystery to surround this figure—Enoch is associated with many ancient legends. He is similar, for instance, to ancient Near Eastern figures, especially King Enmeduranki in Mesopotamian tradition. In the lists of ancient heroes, Enoch and Enmeduranki were both the seventh figure before the flood, and just as Enoch was associated with the solar calendar, Enmeduranki revered Shamash, the sun god. A knowledge of omens, divination, dreams, astronomy, and mantic wisdom also unites them.[8] Within Israelite tradition, 1 Enoch is first of all indebted to the biblical prophets. His call is similar to that of Jeremiah or Ezekiel, with one important difference: he is not called to prophesy to the people but to the heavenly Watchers (12:3-6). As in the case of other apocalypses, the seer is also indebted to wisdom and scribalism. He is a "righteous scribe" (12.3) and "scribe of truth" (15:1). The emphasis on written texts is common in the Enoch texts (81:1-6, 82:1-2; see the introduction to Chapter 3). Like Daniel, Enoch is associated with court life (13:4-7), and it is not just Enoch himself who is wise and scribal; those who receive his wisdom are as well (100:6). The vision of an enlightened, sectarian group is strong, even if it exists solely in the minds of the readers: "Then wisdom will be given to all the chosen; and they will all live, and they will sin no more through godlessness or pride. In the enlightened man there will be light, and in the wise man, understanding. And they will transgress no more, nor will they sin all the days of their life, nor will they die in the heat of God's wrath" (5:8). Outside of the Enoch texts, the book of Jubilees also exhibits a strong reverence for this figure: "Enoch was the first among humans born on earth who learned writing, knowledge, and wisdom, and who wrote down the signs of heaven in a book according to the order of their months" (4:17). At Qumran 1 Enoch and Jubilees were both revered texts, and *Genesis Apocryphon* as well contains a significant treatment of Enoch (2:12–25).

Although there was no collected book of 1 Enoch before the turn of the era, there was a distinctive and developing Enoch tradition. The distinctive features include (1) an elevated role for Enoch, (2) an astronomical orientation, and (3) a mythic account of the origin of evil. As Anathea Portier-Young says, 1 Enoch provides a visionary guide to the cosmos achieved by "mapping the places of judgment and reward and the seat of God's power. . . . Visionary mapping puts the powers 'in their place.'" Stars that have transgressed "are confined to a no-space."[9] The growth of an Enochic textual tradition is somewhat analogous to that of Daniel: a number of important parts were created in succession, revered by many, and collected into various editions. They were not really closed as a composite text until much later. As a result, the books of Daniel and Enoch become "train-car" texts into which new sections could be added at will. This comparison becomes even more interesting when we note that at Qumran, where four of the Enoch sections were discovered, there was also found another Enochic book, *Book of the Giants,* which never became part of the later 1 Enoch.

Remarkable in 1 Enoch is the lack of any mention of the law of Moses. There is, for example, no reference to pentateuchal commandments. It is difficult to imagine that the law of Moses was not central for all ancient Jews, yet a number of scholars have suggested that there were other major streams in ancient Judaism. We are given a sense of a personality, Enoch, who challenges the Mosaic tradition of rewritten scripture that was proliferating at this time. Although seemingly aware of the books of Moses and Mosaic tradition, Enoch simply circumvents it. As Collins says, "By choosing to attribute vital revelation to a figure who lived long before Moses, long before the emergence of Israel as a people, the authors of the Enoch literature chose to identify the core revelation, and the criteria for judgment, with creation, or the order of nature as they understood it, rather than with anything distinctively Mosaic." The Enochic texts even may have played the role of a countertradition, outside of the mainstream. The story of the Watchers

and the origins of evil found there was perhaps the basis of such a move-
ment, separate from and even counter to the Mosaic tradition. One prominent recent theory would even speak of "Enochic Judaism" as a protest
against Zadokite Judaism, the priestly party that formed the basis of the Jerusalem priesthood. A struggle between Enoch and Moses as guarantors of
revelation is perceived here. Other scholars, however, while acknowledging
the difference between Mosaic and Enochic Judaism, do not perceive an
actual opposition. James VanderKam, for instance, simply posits a different
emphasis between the two streams. "The Enochic tradition," he says, "finds
its cornerstone not in the Sinaitic covenant and law but in the events around
the time of the flood."[10]

Each section of 1 Enoch holds a peculiar fascination. Coming in and
out of view are different aspects of revelation, different roles for the Enoch
figure, and different senses of those initiated into these mysteries. The slight
differences among the texts produce a kaleidoscopic effect; placed together,
they provide a visionary show. The parts of 1 Enoch were most likely composed in this order:

Chs. 72–82	Book of the Luminaries	Third century BCE
Chs. 1–36	Book of the Watchers	Third or early second century BCE
Chs. 83–90	Animal Apocalypse or Dream Vision	Early second century BCE
Chs. 92–105	Epistle of Enoch and the Apocalypse of Weeks	Early second century BCE?
Chs. 37–71	Parables (or Similitudes) of Enoch	First century CE?

BOOK OF LUMINARIES (1 ENOCH 72–82)

As parts of the Book of Luminaries were reused in the Book of the Watchers, this section is likely the oldest of 1 Enoch, written in the third century
BCE. Luminaries describes Enoch's tour through the heavens, guided by
the archangel Uriel. The heavens take the form of a huge vault, with twelve
gates through which the sun and moon emerge and exit at different times in
the seasons. Windows are also interspersed in the vault, and here the stars

make their orbit. These movements follow a 364-day year: twelve months of thirty days, with a day added four times a year, or fifty-two weeks exactly. The first law of Luminaries is thus not time but cosmos: the sun rises in the east, crosses, and sets in the west. The sun is the principal heavenly luminary, which is why the solar calendar is so important. The resulting solar calendar, found also in Jubilees, was followed by some Jewish groups, especially at Qumran, but opposed by the Jerusalem temple authorities. They had long followed the lunar-based calendar found in the Hebrew Bible, which was followed by the rabbis and by Jews thereafter to this day. The struggle over which calendar was correct—that is, which calendar God was following—was intense, somewhat analogous to the later Christian disputes over the date of Easter. The misalignment of the calendar was blamed for the state of sin. According to Michael Stone, "human evil will be connected profoundly with a perversion not merely of the computation of the calendar, but of the very astronomical cycles themselves."[11] Because sinners were incapable of recognizing the true nature of the stars, they erred and took the stars as gods. This was the origin of Babylonian astronomy. Three aspects of the Luminaries section are thus significant here. First, the descriptions of heavenly phenomena are revealed rather than learned through astronomical observation. Second, this is all cast as *knowledge* of the heavens, precise and in detail, and knowledge is one of the overlapping aspects of wisdom and apocalypticism. Third, the archangel Uriel, whose name means "El is my light," figures prominently here, as Raphael will below (compare Raphael in Tobit).

Like most of the other sections, Luminaries contains a prediction of human sinfulness—that is, an "ancient" prediction of sinfulness that would become obvious at the time when the text was actually written and transmitted. As a result of this sin, "punishment shall come upon them so as to destroy all" (80:8). Nevertheless, there is a hope for life after death (81:4, 7–8), likely the resurrection of flesh as in 2 Maccabees, 4 Ezra, 2 Baruch, and Meqabyan and not bodiless immortality as in Wisdom of Solomon 2–5 and 4 Maccabees (see Conclusions). The connection of life and righteousness, or life and knowledge, however, is similar in 1 Enoch and Wisdom of Solomon. Also, as in Jubilees and the *Temple Scroll* from Qumran, it was believed here that the calendar is a bit off—a solar year is in fact 364 *and one-quarter* days—because humans have not observed the correct times. At a future time, near the end, the years will be shortened, and orbits will be corrected by some of the chiefs of stars.

BOOK OF THE WATCHERS (1 ENOCH 1–36)

The Enochic myth as a whole is defined largely by what happens in the Book of the Watchers. Likely the second oldest section of 1 Enoch, it is dated to the third or early second century BCE. Two interesting subsections, chapters 1–5 and 6–11, may have had a separate origin, with the latter perhaps earlier, as early as third century BCE. Chapters 1–5 now provide an introduction for the entire collection of what we know as 1 Enoch: "The words of the blessing with which Enoch blessed the righteous chosen who will be present on the day of tribulation, to remove all the enemies, and the righteous will be saved" (1:1).[12] The motifs of crisis, future judgment, punishment of the wicked, and salvation of the righteous are quickly introduced, and in the chapters to follow many motifs associated with apocalypses will be presented: a radicalized version of Israelite wisdom (see the introduction to Chapter 3), judgment against "all flesh," human ignorance of the order of the heavenly bodies, and future blessings and curses. All of this comprises the message of Enoch, the visionary of old, who, as a faithful scribe, wrote the revelation down for future generations of the righteous.

But all of that is merely an opening act for what follows, the fall of the Watchers (chs. 6–11).[13] There are two parts, one concerning Shemihazah and one concerning Azael. The first part concerns the fall of Shemihazah, the corruption of humanity, and the destruction that the giants, their offspring, and the spirits produced, along with the flood. The second part recounts the corruption of humanity by the teaching of secret and forbidden acts, also culminating in the flood. The fall of the Watchers is central to the Enoch tradition and, as noted, may be the oldest core. It provided a mythical explanation for the origin of evil in the world, and indeed some scholars have argued that such an account of the origin of evil is *the* defining characteristic of apocalypses (see the chapter introduction above). The myth of the Watchers here either is based on or perhaps shares a common source with Gen 6:1–4. When people multiplied on the earth, says Genesis 6, heavenly figures called sons of God "saw that the human daughters were fair, and they took wives for themselves" (6:2). This short Genesis account then concludes: "The *Nephilim* were on the earth in those days, when the sons of God went in to the daughters of humans, who bore children to them. These were the heroes of old, warriors of renown" (6:4). The identities of both the "sons of Gods" and the Nephilim are unclear. Genesis 6 is likely a radically pared-down telling of a myth well known at the time, and 1 Enoch, familiar with this mythical tradition, has restored it to its prior importance. The sons of God, now called Watchers, have a leader, Shemihazah. These figures revealed to humans sorcery and charms, but they went further: they devoured the produce of the human men and then began to devour the men themselves. They even cannibalistically began to devour each other. They also revealed to humans various metallurgical arts, both those for weapons and those for gold and silver ornaments. All sorts of knowledge was thus revealed, which seems to have led to conditions favoring a powerful but evil nation of beings on the earth. The humans raised a cry for help, and when the four archangels of heaven heard this, they turned to God for permission to intervene. In response, God sent the archangels to destroy the sons of the Watchers and save the human race from destruction. The archangel Michael was also to plant righteousness and truth (11:16). A vision of eschatological blessings follows: "All of the human beings will become righteous, and all the peoples will worship me." (11:20–21).

The Christian doctrine of the fall of Adam and Eve and original sin is so pervasive in Western culture that it is difficult to read the Genesis narrative without seeing "original sin" in every chapter (compare also 4 Ezra). Israelite tradition, however, and later Jewish belief as well, did not place the fall and the origin of human sin with the Adam and Eve narrative, but in Genesis 6, the same myth that lies behind the Watchers. In Jewish interpretation, the expulsion from Eden did not place humans in a position of extreme sin; it was a first, partial fall. Only in Genesis 6 do humans suffer a more serious fall, and the story of Noah's ark follows in Genesis as a partial solution to the problem. First Enoch is thus expanding this important segment of early Israelite myth, which indeed becomes the foundation of the Enochic tradition. For Genesis and for Jewish tradition, the human error that led to the fall was not sex but knowledge of heavenly things. At the center of this story is the belief that the Watchers have passed along knowledge that humans cannot handle. But an even greater disaster is also unfolding. In Israel, simply *mixing* different categories was often prohibited: two kinds of plants in the same field, two kinds of material worn together, two kinds of animals yoked together, and so on. (The prohibition of eating milk and meat together comes much later but follows this pattern.) The Watchers, then, by mixing with the daughters of humans, produced a race of "giants, half-breeds" (1 En. 9:8–9; cf. 10:9). In Israelite law, a *mamzer,* or illegitimate child, was not a child born out of wedlock, as in European culture, but a child of two parents who were not supposed to "mix" (Deut 23:2–3; compare *m. Yevamot* 4:13). The mixing of Watchers and human women was just such a mixing of different orders and produced bastards in the Israelite sense, *mamzerim.* Enoch is commissioned as a prophet to announce that the Watchers will be judged. In chapters 17–32 he must pass through the heavens and witness the places of judgment and punishment, as well as the Mountain of God, Jerusalem, and Eden.

How are we to understand these Watchers and their offspring? Do they refer to political figures, such as the Seleucid kings and overlords? Perhaps, but this is not clear. Stuckenbruck provides some background information on them. Watchers (Aramaic *'irin, 'yryn;* Greek *egrēgoroi*) were angelic beings, in Gen 6:2 associated with the "sons of God." They are sometimes seen as positive (1 En. 12:2–3; Dan 4:13, 17, 23), sometimes negative (1 Enoch 6–11). In 1 Enoch 8 they reveal knowledge to humans that was negative: weaponry, cosmetics that led to fornication, magic, and astrological divination. Reprehensible human practices are traced back to Asael, leader of the rebellious angels. "In this way," says Stuckenbruck, "the tradition 'demonizes' expressions of culture that pose a threat to the religious identity of the author(s) and the pious community envisioned behind the text." Wasserman nuances this somewhat by cautioning against taking a dualistic view of a cataclysmic battle between good and evil. The rebellion of heavenly figures and the origin of evil is only *one* of many themes in the Enoch texts, and the Watchers are not equal opponents of God and his angels, nor consistently demonic. They are subordinates of God, finally placed back under control. God rules in heaven and on earth, and the power of Enochic texts lies in their emphasis on knowledge, not time and evil.[14]

ANIMAL APOCALYPSE OR DREAM VISIONS (1 ENOCH 83–90)

After examination of the origin of sin in the Book of Watchers, the Animal Apocalypse or Dream Visions may seem closer to what modern readers associate with the genre of apocalypse. Here Enoch speaks in the first person to address his son, Methuselah, grandfather of Noah. Because Enoch lived before the flood, he predicts the flood that is to come:

> Heaven was thrown down and taken away,
> And it fell down upon the earth.
> And when it fell down upon the earth,
> I saw how the earth was swallowed up in the great abyss. . . .
> I cried out and said,
> "The earth has been destroyed." (83:3–5)

After the flood, there is a second vision of the long arc of history in which human figures represent seven archangels, and animals represent various groups of humans. Three ages are represented in succession: from Adam to the flood, from the renewal of creation (Noah) to a first period of judgment, and from the second renewal to an unclear future.[15] Genesis 6, now understood in light of the Watchers story, is replayed in allegorical form: a star fell from heaven, representing the fallen angels, and they mate with the cattle (human beings) and produce elephants, camels, and asses—mixed peoples, now of a status inferior to the earlier generations (chs. 86–87). The Animal Apocalypse is thus not content to recount only the early period of the world as in chapters 6–11 but constructs a long view of how the fall of angels affects the empires that ruled over Judah in the author's present.

The drama of human history is played out in symbolic fashion. In Genesis 10 there was already an account of how the three sons of Noah become the fathers of the peoples of the earth: Shem is the progenitor of the ancestors of Israel ("Semites"), Ham is the progenitor of Canaan and the enemy peoples of the land, and Japheth is the progenitor of the peoples farther away, such as Greece. In the Animal Apocalypse, these groups are now represented by white, red, and black bulls (89:9). The cattle diversify and produce various animals—the present peoples—and then disappear. Isaac, however, bears a black boar, Esau, and a white sheep, Jacob. The sheep produced in this way from Jacob are sometimes blind and go astray and are sometimes set upon by animals representing gentiles. The troubled state of Israel's position, reflecting Judah under the Seleucids, is followed by a promise of God's deliverance. Seventy angels come forward as shepherds of Israel but are not successful, and so another angel, likely Michael, intervenes on Israel's behalf. The notion that apocalyptic visions require a symbolic key to tie them to world events is borne out here, perhaps the clearest case among the Enoch texts. This vision of world history represented by animals is also one of the most explicitly political sections of 1 Enoch, and perhaps the part that most justifies the term "crisis literature."[16] The next part seems similar to Daniel 10–12 and Jubilees 23: a lamb grows a great horn, representing Judah Maccabee. The correspondence to known events breaks down at this point, and so the dating of this section is usually reckoned as the period just before the Maccabean Revolt, with an update during Judah Maccabee's campaigns. At any rate, what is envisioned is a judgment against the rebellious angels, the negligent shepherds, and the wicked Jews. Jerusalem will also be restored, with some ambiguity about the role of gentiles. The people of Israel are represented by white bulls and cattle, yet the red and black cattle of the other peoples do not appear. Also lacking in the crisis period or in the restoration is any mention of the temple. Typical of Enochic literature, the focus is on neither Mosaic law nor the temple, but the secret knowledge of the recipients is emphasized, suggesting that they engage a sectarian identity within Israel.

EPISTLE OF ENOCH AND APOCALYPSE OF WEEKS (1 ENOCH 92-105)

Like the Letter of Jeremiah, Epistle of Enoch begins as an artificial epistle and transitions into an exhortation. The epistle is not, by itself, an apocalypse and does not maintain the preflood setting of other parts of 1 Enoch. Vander-Kam categorizes this section as "wisdom," and indeed three categories—artificial epistle, testament, and wisdom—apply.[17] The immortality of the soul, found in Wisdom of Solomon and 4 Maccabees, may also be affirmed in the epistle at 1 En. 102:5, 103:3–4, 104:6. A section within the epistle, 93:3–10, 91:11–17, is called the Apocalypse of Weeks. It summarizes the course of all history, including the end, by dividing it into ten periods called weeks, each lasting 490 years. Curiously, however, it is evidently now out of order, as weeks eight–ten come before weeks one–seven. Most editions thus reverse the two parts to restore what was likely the proper reading. Whether the Apocalypse of Weeks section near the beginning was originally part of the epistle is debated, but the bulk of the epistle consists of a set of woes and exhortations.

Likely composed with the Enochic tradition in mind, it includes some of the motifs of apocalypses, and in its present location it contributes to the reading of the larger collection as an apocalypse. (There is an epistle at the end of 2 Baruch as well.) Yet should the *genre* of the Epistle of Enoch be more appropriately associated with nonapocalyptic genres? If we look forward in time, we find that this section of 1 Enoch is similar to the didactic programs of testaments on one hand and artificial epistles like Letter of Jeremiah, Epistle of James, *Didache,* and Epistle of Barnabas on the other. The woes in Epistle of Enoch are similar to those in Luke 6:24–26. The Epistle of Enoch may be the first "artificial epistle with testamentary elements" in Jewish tradition, but the theme and function may also be related to Greek protreptic. There is renewed interest among classicists in the origins of Greek protreptic—the philosophical discourse that tries to lead the reader to virtue or to the life of philosophy. It is, for instance, often mentioned in regard to Wisdom of Solomon, 4 Maccabees, and Paul's Letter to the Romans.[18] The genre category of protreptic is now also understood to be broader, often including more Greek texts. The function of the Epistle of Enoch is similar to that of protreptic: to remake the reader into an ideal moral agent. But in addition—and unlike Greek protreptic—Jewish protreptic defines ideal group boundaries much more directly. Some scholars here note the similarity to later Christian church orders, or we may suggest a broad category of community exhortation. A community exhortation is related to the larger category of didactic literature, but unlike Proverbs, it is not written as though addressed to an individual scribe or scribe-in-training, but rather to members, plural, of a defined group. A bounded group is assumed, and a strong awareness of those others who are outside. Viewed another way, Epistle of Enoch can be seen as standing at the midpoint between some biblical texts—Deuteronomy, Exodus 20-23, and Leviticus 18-20—and the later community exhortations—Qumran *Community Rule,* James, and Epistle of Barnabas. They all construct the ideal moral agent as a righteous member of the community. The Jewish protreptic texts emphasize the relation between the urgent moral demand of God and group boundaries. This is true for Epistle of Enoch even if, as many argue, the group that is constructed may exist only as an ideal. The Epistle of Enoch, then, although assimilated to the apocalypse of 1 Enoch, was composed according to a different generic model.

PARABLES (OR SIMILITUDES) OF ENOCH (1 ENOCH 37-71)

Although this section came to be known as the Parables or Similitudes of Enoch, it was actually introduced as Enoch's "vision of wisdom" (37:1). The word "parable" does occur, where it suggests a prophetic idiom, and more specifically, a revelatory discourse. All of the sections of 1 Enoch have been found at Qumran with the exception of the parables, and so it may have been written later, although this is not clear. Suggestions for the date have ranged from first century BCE to first to second century CE, although early first century CE seems most likely. As in the Book of Luminaries, Enoch is once again taken on heavenly journeys. He observes the heavenly throne room, the celestial phenomena, and the places of punishment. His special knowledge of the cosmos includes secrets concerning lightning, thunder, winds, and the sun and moon (ch. 41). Noah and the flood, now symbolizing a future, final judgment, are also treated, and the chief demon Azazel is encountered. This name appears in Lev 16:8 as the scapegoat released on Yom Kippur, although a demonic spirit may lie behind the scapegoat tradition (cf. Asael in chs. 6-11). There are orders of beings in this section on the side of good and evil. On the side of good are God, the heavenly attendants, the Chosen One, agents of judgment, and those people who are chosen, righteous, and holy. On the side of evil are Azazel, his attendants, kings, and the mighty. The kings and the mighty will be punished, and so this section also contains some of the more explicitly political condemnations. The Enochic texts also emphasize the group identity of the righteous ones, as opposed to the individual righteous person of Wisdom of Solomon 2–5. But despite some dualism of righteous and sinners, chapter 48 also exhibits openness to the salvation of gentiles, as elsewhere in 1 Enoch. This is in contrast to Jubilees and may indicate that parts of 1 Enoch are not as sectarian.[19]

The tendency of apocalyptic texts to offer a hidden wisdom is in evidence here. The channel to the heavens that Enoch has opened and made available to those who receive and transmit his knowledge can be contrasted with the more mainstream views of Ben Sira and Baruch 3–4. In the latter texts, God's wisdom descends to earth and becomes manifested in Jewish law; it is available to anyone. In 1 Enoch, however, wisdom is not found in the law or proverbial sayings, but in the knowledge of the operations of the heavens. In a few words 1 Enoch 42 even offers a powerful satire of the more mainstream narrative of the descent of Wisdom as found in Ben Sira 24 and Baruch 3–4:

> Wisdom did not find a place where she might dwell,
>> So her dwelling was in the heavens.
> Wisdom went forth to dwell among the sons of men,
>> But she did not find a dwelling.
> Wisdom returned to her place,
>> And sat down in the midst of the angels.
> Iniquity went forth from her chambers,
>> Those whom she did not seek she found,
> And she dwelt among them
>> Like rain in a desert
>> And dew in a thirsty land.

This passage is deceptively constructed. Verse 1 functions more as a title of the poem: Wisdom found no place to dwell so she is now in heaven. Verses

2–3 then act out the narrative of the myth: Wisdom's descent does not result in a boon for humans because there is none to accept her. An influence here may possibly be found in the earlier Hellenistic poet Aratus, who spun a story of the goddess Justice. Appalled at human wickedness, she departed and ascended into the heavens. The greater literary interest here, however, is found not in Wisdom and her actions, but in the descent of Iniquity: "those whom she did not seek she found." There is irony, even sarcasm, in this little myth, and humor in the simile that suggests that human beings desperately swallow up iniquity, "like dew in a thirsty land." But it all redounds to the figure of Enoch as well: though Wisdom is not with the wise on earth, Enoch has ascended to the heavens, to Wisdom's heavenly abode. Through secret texts such as this, Enoch reveals what true wisdom is like.

In the chapters following this, a series of titles are applied to Enoch that suggest he is being elevated to a new level as a heavenly agent. The title "Chosen One" combines the elements from a rich Jewish tradition: the one like a son of man in Dan 7:13–14, the Servant in Isaiah 52–53, the Davidic messiah, and heavenly Wisdom. This will culminate in Enoch's description of his ascent to the heavens and his vision of angels, the four archangels, and the Head of Days (compare Ancient of Days in Dan 7:9). God informs Enoch that he is the Son of Man (71:14). As in Daniel 7, so here the Son of Man may be a collective figure who represents the righteous. "His ascent to heaven," says Nickelsburg, "and his exalted status are a promise of the deliverance and vindication of the righteous in the coming judgment." Yet another development has intrigued New Testament scholars. In the parables the heavenly, preexistent figure is called Son of Man, Chosen One, Righteous One, and Messiah, which combines a surprisingly large number of titles, and in chapter 71—which may be a later addition—this heavenly figure is identified with Enoch. It is striking that these titles do not occur in the other Enoch texts, yet we do find them attached to Jesus. In addition, Enoch of the parables section and Jesus both ground these titles by reference to wisdom, messianic, and apocalyptic motifs. It is likely, asserts Gabriele Boccaccini, that the Enoch Messiah/Son of Man and the Jesus Messiah/Son of Man overlapped with each other, influenced each other, perhaps even competed with each other. Intriguing as this is, Matthias Henze points out that the two traditions rarely mention each other at the early stage (although they do later on). It is, rather, remarkable "that Enoch and Enochic literature, generally speaking, play so small a role in early Christianity." Yet even if these two contemporary developments do not arise in response to each other, they are still significant. They may simply reflect a natural development of apocalyptic texts. "The apocalyptic literature," says Collins, "envisions a layered, hierarchical universe, where agents on different levels act in synergy with each other." At roughly the same time, Enoch and Jesus both came to combine what had been separate identities and could move up and down between heaven and earth. But despite the intriguing similarities between the Enochic and Jesus traditions at just this same time, significant differences must also be noted. First, Enoch was not killed, while Jesus was. Second, Enoch was understood as an ancient figure, the author of an ancient tome, while Jesus was a real, contemporary figure who did not write texts. Third, Enoch was supposedly revered by a small community of those who had received and comprehended his text, while Jesus was revered by a broader community of followers (although the Gospel of John may reflect a situation closer to that of the Parables of Enoch).[20]

1 ENOCH IN LATER TRADITION

Few texts of the Apocrypha, even Ben Sira, have enjoyed as rich an afterlife among Jews as the Enochic texts. The parts of 1 Enoch may not have been assembled into a single text until the rise of the Ethiopian Orthodox Tewahedo Church, for whom it was fully canonical, yet the parts (except for the parables) were very popular at Qumran. First Enoch and Jubilees were found at Qumran in more copies than almost any book of the Hebrew Bible. In Ben Sira's paean to the ancestors of Israel, Enoch is lauded twice (44:16, 49:14), and Wis 4:10–11 holds out Enoch as a paradigm of the righteous person. *Apocryphon of Jannes and Jambres* continued the myth of the giants from 1 Enoch, while Philo, *On the Giants,* opposed this mythical elaboration. Other Enochic texts appeared, called now 2 Enoch and 3 Enoch, which made use of motifs of 1 Enoch—and recall that the parts of 1 Enoch did not originally constitute a single book. The figure of Enoch was also revered among the rabbis as one of the nine who entered Eden while alive (*Derek Eretz Zuta* ch. 1). The rabbis, however, did not endorse the Watchers myth and tended to treat the fallen angels as simply lower figures (*Genesis Rabbah* 26:6). It is difficult to keep powerful myths at bay, however, and aspects of the Enoch myth are reintroduced at *Pirqe de-Rabbi Eliezer* 22. It is possible that the Enoch figure is merged with the heavenly figure Metatron in Jewish mystical texts.[21]

In the New Testament, the Letter of Jude 14–15 quotes 1 En. 1:9 as scripture, although when this passage was used as a source for 2 Pet 2:4, 3:6, the quotation was removed, presumably because the Enoch text was not considered canonical. Hebrews 11:5 features Enoch as one who would not see death because he pleased God. The index of quotations and allusions in the Greek New Testament (*Novum Testamentum Graece* 26) lists more references to 1 Enoch than to any of the Apocrypha except Ben Sira and Wisdom of Solomon—more, even, than many Hebrew Bible books! The second-century Epistle of Barnabas 4:2 quotes 1 En. 89:55, 66, 67 also as scripture. Tertullian, who affirmed the role of continuing prophecy in the Christian church, argued for the inclusion of 1 Enoch in the Bible (*On Female Fashion* 1.3). We may wonder, however, why Enoch was *not* featured in Christian Gnostic texts; Seth, rather, is the principal biblical "father" of Gnostic insight. The Ethiopian Church elevated 1 Enoch to a central place in its Bible, and the figure Enoch was popular in Armenian apocrypha.[22] Finally, we note that this figure enjoyed an enduring role in Jewish and Christian speculation and was revered in Manichean tradition and Islam as well. William Blake created two moving illustrations of Enoch (fig. 12).

Jubilees

In addition to texts that rewrote the Israelite histories (1 and 2 Chronicles, 1 Esdras), a number of ancient Jewish texts are referred to as rewritten Bible or rewritten scripture (see Chapter 2). These texts—Jubilees, *Temple Scroll, Genesis Apocryphon,* and the so-called *Reworked Pentateuch*—retold quite freely parts of the books of Moses. Jubilees is likely the earliest of these, and also the longest. Despite its relative obscurity in the West, its importance

Figure 12. William Blake, *Enoch,* 1806–1807. The Metropolitan Museum of Art, New York

should not be underestimated; indeed, James Kugel says that "Jubilees is arguably the most significant of all Jewish writings of the Second Temple period." It is a large and fascinating text and the beginning, as Kugel notes, of the "flowering of biblical commentary."[23] It expands upon selected parts of Genesis 1–Exodus 24, sometimes copying faithfully, sometimes changing or clarifying, and sometimes adding entire subplots. By simply renarrating parts of the biblical narrative, Jubilees can at first seem tedious, but at many points it changes and supplements the text in fascinating ways. We are jolted into a recognition that something new is afoot.

   Although Jubilees also circulated under the name *The Little Genesis,* the earliest known title was *The Book of the Divisions of the Times According to Their Jubilees and Weeks* (found in *Damascus Document* 16:2–4 from Qumran).[24] The text also ends with a similar phrase. Times and calendrical issues were not only paramount for the author, but they structure the text precisely, from beginning to end. Much of the special halakhic concern of Jubilees is for the faithful following of a solar calendar of 364 days, found also in 1 Enoch 72–82, *Temple Scroll,* and other texts at Qumran. In this reckoning, there are exactly fifty-two weeks in the year with no days left over. This was deemed crucial, for annual holidays would now always fall on the same day of the week, as God surely arranged it. The lunar-based calendar, followed in the Jerusalem temple, lacked this regularity and was considered contrary to both God's designs and the angels' worship of God (6:36–37; contrast Sir 43:6–7). By this process, the significance of the week for Jewish time reckoning is also projected onto the calculation of all time. If the week is the basic unit of time, then the jubilee, seven weeks of years or forty-nine years, is now perceived to be the larger unit of history: Israel, for instance, enters the promised land on the fiftieth jubilee, or year 2450. Yet Israel failed to maintain this meticulous system. Disobeying God's laws directly resulted in calendrical errors; keeping Sabbath and worshipping at the same time as God and the angels was crucial, and it was not observed (1:14, 2:18, 6:23).

The laws of God are here revealed to Israel as an eternal covenant written on tablets in heaven; even the patriarchs prior to Moses observed these commandments and indeed, performed priestly duties. By taking the long view of history, over the course of many jubilees, God's relationship with Israel is seen as eternal and not merely a temporary disruption. Although the patriarchs appear to initiate festivals and other matters, the conception of these events can be seen as both higher than the patriarchs and effectively eternal. Jubilees 23:32 is also the first passage to assert that Moses wrote the entire Pentateuch, even the ending that describes his death. The boundaries of those who are considered Israel must also be strictly maintained. Opposition to intermarriage with gentiles, introduced in Ezra-Nehemiah, is now emphasized even more strongly. An extra step—quite an extra step—is taken in Jubilees, when it intimates that the higher orders of angels are circumcised (15:23–34). The circumcision of male Israelites thus renders them similar to angels, and gentiles are excluded from worship with the angels. In a move parallel to later midrashic texts, Jubilees also ties some legal judgments to events in the narrative of Genesis. That Adam and Eve began to wear clothing, for instance, becomes a basis for sternly prohibiting nudity (3:31); the intervention of Simeon and Levi in preventing the marriage of

Dinah to Shechem authorizes the prohibition of intermarriage.[25] The moral stature of the patriarchs is also established more clearly. In the Bible they were often not models of morality; they were patriarchs not because they were good but because they were chosen, and their principal good act was to marry their first cousins to create an endogamous lineage. By contrast, Jubilees—and indeed most of the rewritten scriptures—champion the deeds of the patriarchs. They are heroes of virtue.

There are a number of ways, then, in which the narratives of Genesis and Exodus are altered. An overriding theme of Jubilees is that God's law transcends a particular historical moment in Israel. The patriarchs are depicted as obedient to the law before God's revelation of the Ten Commandments at Sinai, even to the extent of observing holidays that had not yet been commanded. The patriarchs themselves, whose stories are now slightly edited, become better models of obedience. The story of Shechem's rape of Dinah (Genesis 34), for instance, also provides an early justification for prohibiting Jews from marrying gentiles, which actually entered as a principle only with Ezra-Nehemiah. In keeping with this, purer genealogical lines in Israel are established, at the same time that there is a much stronger separation from gentiles. Israel becomes a sect, with strict genealogical boundaries (6:35, 22:16–22, 25:3–10). Details are often adjusted to improve on aspects of the narrative: some passages are abbreviated (the Joseph story, the plagues of Exodus), some are expanded by the addition of other narrative traditions (Noah), perceived difficulties are eliminated (Abraham pretending that his wife was his sister), some motivations are clarified (Judah's repentance for having sex with Tamar), nations are updated to reflect the conflicts of the period (the rendering of Esau is more negative to account for his descendants, the Edomites/Idumeans). Details are changed so that the patriarchs do not lie and Jacob is not a trickster. Abraham's wife, Keturah, is no longer a foreigner, and here it is the Satan figure Mastema and not God who proposes the idea of testing Isaac by demanding that Abraham kill him. Abraham is said here to introduce agriculture to the Chaldeans but perceives the folly of idolatry and burns down the local temple. Patriarchs and matriarchs pronounce important blessings (chs. 25, 31) and deliver more deathbed testaments to their children (chs. 7, 20). It is interesting that Abraham's testament (ch. 22) includes prohibitions of fornication, intermarriage, idolatry, and the consuming of blood, similar to what is emphasized in Leviticus 17–26 (the Holiness Code), and it evidently influences the tradition of the "Noachic covenant," those divine requirements that were determined to be binding on all human beings (compare Acts 15). A combination of prophetic and scribal communications is also often on display. "Every major patriarch," says Eva Mroczek, "has become a recipient of textual revelation, a writer of sacred text, or a keeper of books that play a part in Israel's unfolding relationship with God."[26] The spirit of prophecy descends on the patriarchs and matriarchs at the time of their testaments and blessings (chs. 20, 25, 31, 36), but it is a very discrete prophecy: only publicly recognized leaders receive it, and it is directed to the transmission of approved leadership. This is not the more unpredictable world of inspired prophets that we find in the biblical tradition. Rather, it is more like a *scribal* phenomenon. Indeed, Enoch, who learned writing from the angels, is the first scribe, and the patriarchs in general are literate scribes, their books handed down carefully (10:13–14, 12:27). The addition of speeches and prayers paints a fuller picture of the character of the protagonists, and the role of women is increased when compared with Genesis. Both of these developments are similar to the Jewish novellas.

Yet if Jubilees is the earliest example of rewritten scripture, it is as a result not simply conforming to an already existing literary pattern; it is creating something new. Indeed, it touches on other genres as well. Although lacking the typical introduction of apocalypses, it includes many of the motifs characteristic of that genre. The spirit of the entire book can be summed up in this command of God to Moses on Sinai: "Write for yourself this entire account which I proclaim to you on this mountain: the first things, the last things, and that which happens throughout all the divisions of the times with respect to the law and the testimony, and during the weeks of their jubilees until eternity, until the time when I descend and live with them throughout all the eternal ages" (1:26). It continues as a revelation to Moses from the chief angel, the Angel of the Presence. The angel speaks in the first person, and Moses is addressed in the second person, with the result that, as Matthew Goff notes, "The reader is in a sense, on Sinai with

Moses, listening to the angel as he speaks with him." The author constantly weaves in claims to a higher revelation. "Lurking beneath every aspect of the book of Jubilees," sees Hindy Najman, "is its fascination with the importance and authorizing power of sacred writing."[27] In the prologue and chapter 1, the angel displays tablets of *all* of history, not just the scriptural history to come—creation to Sinai—but creation to judgment (1:27–29). Jubilees focuses on the visionary scribe who records the revelation in books. Heavenly tablets contain not only the Torah of Moses, but world history and deeds, future events, calendar and feasts, and even interpretations of biblical law. In addition to the law that is recorded in the Pentateuch, God and one of the archangels dictate past and future events and special commandments that Moses is to record for future generations. The text also renders Enoch a superhuman, even semidivine person:

> He was the first among humans born on earth who learned writing, knowledge, and wisdom, and who wrote down the signs of heaven in a book according to the order of their months. . . . What was and what will be he saw in a vision of his sleep: just as it will happen to humankind throughout their generations until the day of judgment. . . . He was taken from human society and [the angels] brought him into the garden of Eden for greatness and honor. (4:15–26)

It focuses on heavenly characters with supernatural powers, such as Mastema and demons. There is an eschatological judgment for the righteous and unrighteous (23:16–32, 30:22, 36:9–10) and a sectarian division of the world typical of apocalypses; the "future," that is, the audience's present, is characterized as a wicked generation. Finally, Jubilees features the Watchers myth as an explanation of the origin of evil, and it advocates the solar calendar that is found in 1 Enoch and at Qumran but is opposed by the Jerusalem authorities. As a result of these observations, Jubilees is placed here with the apocalypses rather than with the histories. To be sure, it seems to play with the expectations of the genre. It treats the typical issues, all the while presenting atypical views on these subjects.[28] Apocalyptic themes are presented in a muted way and do not overwhelm the reader, as is their usual function. Also, many of the motifs appear in a more restrained manner, and the account is surprisingly *clear*, not an interpretation by an angel of cryptic dreams or visions. The future predictions are present but not emphasized, and there is no bizarre imagery. It is, as it were, a long, sometimes tedious, low-voltage near-apocalypse that stresses a more earnest view of the patriarchs and stricter notions of halakhic purity.

In addition to apocalypses, Jubilees also shares some traits with the Jewish histories of the period that followed the newer Greek practice of making sense of the dates in the biblical record by placing them on one continuous timeline (see the introduction to Chapter 2). The author of Jubilees devises an absolute chronology, and apparent inconsistencies in the Bible are solved through creative exegesis. About seventy-five years earlier, in Alexandria in Egypt, the Jewish historian Demetrius the Chronographer had attempted to develop an absolute chronology. In Alexandria and in Judea, therefore, Demetrius and the author of Jubilees, writing in two different languages, ordered by two different chronological schemes and using two different historical models, both played with notions of universal history. The broader Hellenistic rationalization of history had evidently influenced both authors. Paul J. Kosmin would in fact explain Jubilees' conception of time as a postcolonial *protest* against the Seleucid universal chronology.[29] Members of other ethnic groups were devising similar schemes. In about 270 BCE Berossus of Babylon had devised a world history based on divisions of sixty, six hundred, and thirty-six hundred years (*FGH* 2.498, fr. 4). Where the Jew Demetrius engaged Greek intellectuals in Alexandria, the author of Jubilees digested, perhaps unconsciously, certain Hellenistic assumptions and turned them back on the Hellenistic rulers with an ethnic exclusivism.

Michel Testuz noted Jubilees' relation to other genres and suggested that it was a "composite genre," a "compendium, a summary of the religious information of the author's community."[30] Yet, is Jubilees an exploratory text that plays with styles borrowed from many other genres, or is that an illusion that results from our partial knowledge of the literary landscape? We are in danger of imposing twenty-first-century notions of normative versus experimental. What looked to Testuz like a carry-all was perhaps a coherent *new* genre, with important resonances with other genres. To be sure, the text *appears* experimental, while, say, 1 Enoch on one hand and Tobit on the other *appear* to lie clearly within their generic categories. Yet their authors may have been "first founders" of genres as well. Further, Jubilees is often said to "belong" to the genre of rewritten scripture, yet this is a genre that the author *invented.* As with many of the young genres of this period— novella, history, apocalypse, rewritten scripture—genre "borrowing," "influence," or "belonging" is difficult to define precisely.

Much of the attention that Jubilees receives from scholars relates to its discussion of Jewish law. There are parallels to later rabbinic law and midrash, but here often stated in more extreme ways. Although the view of gentiles is actually more negative than is usually presented within Jewish tradition, it is a view in keeping with the stereotyped Christian view of *general* Jewish exclusivism. Very few Jewish texts condemned all gentiles; negative statements are reserved for those gentiles who opposed Israel, especially the peoples who resided in the land of Canaan.[31] Gentiles "in good standing," those who had not specifically opposed Jews, were not generally condemned. Jubilees, however, extends Ezra-Nehemiah's prohibition of *intermarriage* with gentiles to a comprehensive *condemnation* of gentiles, evidently without exception: "Anyone who is born whose own flesh is not circumcised on the eighth day is not from the sons of the covenant that the Lord made for Abraham, since he is from the sons of destruction. There is therefore no sign upon him so that he might belong to the Lord, because he is destined to be destroyed and annihilated from the earth" (15:26). This reads like the coming judgment on the wicked that we find in many apocalypses, but here "gentile" and "wicked" become synonymous. There is also often a repetition and rhetorical overkill in the use of language, turning obsessive and violent (chs. 30, 33). Jubilees does not specifically prohibit contact, but the text is a blueprint for separatism. The author constructs a bounded world in which heavenly tablets announce an eternal covenant between God and those who are circumcised on the eighth day and who worship in the company of circumcised angels. Those who are not circumcised do not have the mark of being God's own. As a result of this emphasis on circumcision as a boundary marker, the story of Shechem's rape of Dinah (Genesis 34) is altered. In Genesis, Simeon and Levi trick Shechem and his male tribesmen into circumcising themselves to join in a covenant and only then slaughter them while they are sore, but in Jubilees that would imply that the Shechemites indeed received the mark of covenant. As a result, this section of the story is omitted. Further, it is foretold that Israel will stray in the future by leaving some skin and not circumcising all boys.

The dating of Jubilees has been debated. Since the text is found at Qumran, it was probably written before about 100 BCE, probably before the split between the Essenes and the Jerusalem leadership around 135 BCE. Jonathan Goldstein sees in the text references to the events of the early 160s, before the more drastic actions of Antiochus IV and their aftermath. This is plausible, and in this scenario the revulsion to gentiles would be explained as a reaction to Antiochus's interference in temple administration and prohibition of circumcision. However, VanderKam counters that the somewhat vague references are meant to characterize the period as a whole and that the text was composed during the period after the Maccabean Revolt, when a pious scribe might hope for a higher degree of observance.[32]

A large number of fragments of Jubilees were found among the Dead Sea Scrolls; in fact, more manuscripts of this text are found at Qumran than of any other, biblical or nonbiblical, except Psalms, Deuteronomy, Isaiah, and Genesis. It seems related to the same groups who produced parts of 1 Enoch, and both of these writings found a home among the Qumran sectarians. In addition, fragments of a similar textual tradition were discovered at Qumran, so-called pseudo-Jubilees, which may have been considered as authoritative as Jubilees. Jubilees was not cited by the rabbis, although there are intriguing parallels in the medieval *Midras Tadshe* or *Book of Asaph*. Despite its extreme views on the relation of Jews and gentiles, Jubilees has enjoyed interest by scholars of rabbinic Judaism. It engages issues of Jewish law head-on, with creative new interpretations. The rabbis had indeed wondered why the Bible begins at Gen 1:1 with creation and not at Exod 12:2, where the issue of laws is first raised. Goff responds to this ancient question: "The gap between Genesis and the rest of the Torah essentially disappears if scripture is understood in the manner presented by

Jubilees. The composition reconfigures stories from Genesis so that the patriarchs carry out halakhic practices that are grounded in scriptural law."[33] Although Jubilees has retained an importance in the Ethiopian Orthodox Church, it does not figure often in Western Christian tradition.

2 Esdras or 4 Ezra

Fourth Ezra is one of a number of texts composed in the name of Ezra who, with Nehemiah, restored the temple and city of Jerusalem in the fifth–fourth century BCE. Many books were associated with this figure. It is not necessary to rehearse all the details, but in brief: The name 1 Esdras—Esdras being the Greek and Latin form of Ezra—refers to the history book included in Chapter 2, and 2 Esdras to the present apocalypse. The Jewish core of the book, chapters 3–14, is now generally called 4 Ezra. Early on, Christian authors added an introduction, chapters 1–2, now known as 5 Ezra, and also a conclusion, chapters 15–16, known as 6 Ezra. So although the text as a whole is called 2 Esdras, the Jewish part, chapters 3–14, is called 4 Ezra. The Jewish apocalypse 4 Ezra was written in about 100 CE by a scribe near Jerusalem who was deeply mourning the destruction of the temple by the Romans. Originally written in Hebrew, neither that version nor the first main translation in Greek has survived. We know the text only through a series of subsequent translations into Latin, Syriac, Ethiopic, Georgian, Armenian, Arabic, and Coptic. Once again, the Eastern translations remind us of the global distribution of Christians and their texts (and Jews as well, although these translations were Christian). The Latin translation was included in an appendix to the Catholic Vulgate, and so that version has dominated in the West.[34]

The text places Ezra in Babylon thirty years after the destruction of the first temple. Karina Martin Hogan notes that this setting creates an anachronism: the visionary's plaint is set during the exile, while the historical Ezra was active between 70 and 150 years later (the dating of biblical Ezra is unclear) and was associated with a successful restoration. Perhaps, she suggests, it is an intentional signal to the audience that 4 Ezra is a fictional text. Jason Zurawski, however, counters that the anachronism might not have been perceived as a problem. The author and audience of 4 Ezra may have been less precise about earlier history, viewing 4 Ezra more as "heroic narrative" than historical. The author is providing a heroic prequel—the experience of the future leader of Jerusalem as a young man.[35] Be that as it may, the setting of 4 Ezra after the fall of the first temple creates an experience parallel to the period after the fall of the second. Ezra has been moved backward in time to render his predictions more compelling for the situation at the end of the first century CE. Because the setting is presented as thirty years after the first destruction, it is even possible to specify that the text was written thirty years after the second destruction, about 100 CE. At any rate, 4 Ezra is an apocalypse that demonstrates that a clear set of historical predictions is not necessary to the genre.

Fourth Ezra consists of seven visions—seven being a structuring number in 2 Baruch and Revelation as well—yet the first three are unusual for an apocalypse in that they are dialogues. The remaining four visions can be divided into waking visions and dream visions: vision four is a waking vision of the heavenly Jerusalem, visions five and six are symbolic dreams more typical of apocalypses, and vision seven is a waking vision about secret and public books. When we examine the content of the visions, we see that, as in some of the other apocalyptic texts, the condemnation of the oppressive ruling empires is explicit and absolute. This is indeed the theme of the book: "I did not wish to inquire about the ways above, but about those things that we daily experience: why Israel has been given over to the Gentiles in disgrace; why the people whom you loved has been given over to godless tribes, and the law of our ancestors has been brought to destruction and the written covenants no longer exist" (4:23). And later: "O Lord, behold, these nations, which are reputed to be as nothing, domineer over us and devour us" (6:57). When Ezra's visions survey the course of world history, the most terrifying segment, and one of the most detailed, is the one that predicts the final kingdom, Rome:

> There came up from the sea an eagle that had twelve wings and three heads. And I looked, and behold, he spread his wings over all the earth, and all the winds of heaven blew upon him, and the

clouds were gathered around him. . . . And I looked, and behold, the eagle flew with his wings to reign over the earth and
over those who dwell in it. And I saw how all things under
heaven were subjected to him. (11:1–2, 5–6)

The situation of Israel is thus grim in 4 Ezra. People as a whole have
been sinful, yet gentiles have prospered, oppressing the fallen Jews. In the
similar situation of the Maccabean Revolt, Daniel 11–12 found hope in the
doctrine of resurrection: the persecuted righteous would be raised for everlasting life, and the wicked oppressors raised for everlasting judgment.
Fourth Ezra is in this tradition and fills out the details of the process. Upon
death, people first go to Hades as a shadowy place of waiting (4:35, 39).
This is not the purgatory that we encounter in much later Christian tradition, but simply a staging area where human beings await the final resurrection and judgment. From here, both those who have been good and those
who have been evil can survey the course of the world. This stage features a
recognition scene—compare Wisdom of Solomon 2–5—as both groups come
to know what is in store for them. For the good, "the root of evil is sealed up
from you, illness is banished from you, and death is hidden; Hades has fled
and corruption has been forgotten; sorrows have passed away, and in the end
the treasure of immortality is made manifest" (8:53–54). At the end, all will
be sent to either eternal reward or punishment.

A dominant question in 4 Ezra, as also in 1 Enoch and 2 Baruch, concerns the origin of sin. In this text, God placed an evil inclination within
Adam that was passed on to all humanity (3:20–21): "For an evil heart has
grown up in us, which has alienated us from God, and has brought us into
corruption and the ways of death, and has shown us the paths of perdition
and removed us far from life" (7:48). We also see here a possible influence
on early Christian notions of the origin of sin, but there is an important
difference. In Christianity, at least from the time of Augustine, original sin
was identified with sexual desire, while for Jews the origin of sin was not
particularly associated with sex.[36] Yet for 4 Ezra sin is still inevitable, and all
are predestined to sin. Other voices in ancient Judaism, perhaps more mainstream voices (e.g., Sir 15:11–20), pushed back against this predestinarian

view. For the rabbis, the evil inclination that God has placed within each person is balanced by a good inclination as well. As a result, humans would be capable of choosing between them—or more precisely, of keeping them in balance. Fourth Ezra also brings forward some very negative statements about gentiles, such as: "As for the other nations that have descended from Adam, you have said that they are nothing, and that they are like spittle, and you have compared their abundance to a drop from a bucket" (6:56). To be sure, the view of gentiles here may not be quite as negative as that found in Jubilees. Those here who are "like spittle" are the Roman rulers who had destroyed the temple that had stood for six hundred years. Further, the rhetorical shaming of an enemy was very common in the ancient world; it was assumed that the shaming words actually reduced the opponent. Apocalypses generally exhibit many connections to the wisdom tradition, and 4 Ezra and 2 Baruch are both "wisdom" texts in this sense: they reflect an attempt to understand, and the bestowal of secret knowledge. The hope of fully understanding is ultimately impossible for human beings, yet some insights—troubled as they are—were given to Ezra and preserved in this book. They are sometimes in the form of parables. As to the question, for instance, of why the resolution of chaos does not come sooner, the angel replies that it is like a woman who is in labor: she longs to escape the pangs of childbirth. And the question of why people were created over time and not all at once is partially answered at 5:43-49: as a woman cannot give birth to ten children at once, but only over time, just so the earth can hold only a limited number of people at once. Through such parables certain insights concerning God's plan for history are communicated.

But some problems cannot be so easily resolved. Ezra seeks consolation and understanding from Uriel but is not satisfied by the explanations. Three visions are recounted in chapters 9–13 that seek to provide new awareness: a mother grieving for her son, an eagle destroyed by a lion, and a figure like a man who comes out of the sea to destroy his enemies. The eagle, for instance, is quite significant: "This is the Messiah whom the Most High has kept until the end of days, who will arise from the offspring of David, and will come and speak with them" (12:32). Both 4 Ezra and 2 Baruch exhibit an intense psychological interest. The speaker in 4 Ezra often condemns himself, even offering up a rather authoritarian pronouncement against himself, but the angel attempts to temper Ezra's self-condemnation (8:46–50). With some poignancy, then, the author touches on the state of the person as individual, and the discipline of the self that was developing during this period, transitioning into ascetic theology. As noted, at times the speaker sounds like Job: "You have nurtured it [the created body] in your righteousness, and instructed it in your law, and reproved it in your wisdom. You put it to death as your creation, and make it live as your work. If then you will suddenly and quickly destroy what with so great labor was fashioned by your command, to what purpose was it made?" (8:12–14). But, unlike Job, who suffers a *personal* fall from his position of wealth, the author here turns to the condition of Israel among the nations: "About all humankind you know best; but I will speak about your people, for whom I am grieved, and about your inheritance, for whom I lament, and about Israel, for whom I am sad, and about the seed of Jacob, for whom I am troubled" (8:15–16). Also as in the book of Job, the problems posed by the human figure are compelling, yet the heavenly voice does not resolve them. "Fourth Ezra," says Lisbeth S. Fried, "like the book of Job, asks where God's justice is, and like the book of Job, it provides various answers, none of which satisfy." There are limits to human knowledge, and this is a tragic conclusion (4 Ezra 4:1–12, 5:36–40; compare Job 38–41). Yet Hogan nuances this dramatic problem. The dialogue between Ezra and the angel Uriel gives voice to two opposing positions—typical views of the period—neither of which really represents the author's own theology. Ezra recounts the assertions of traditional wisdom as found in Ben Sira and Baruch, and Uriel responds with a more radical eschatological wisdom position found also in *4QInstruction* from Qumran. Neither position is by itself compelling or satisfactory, yet there is a resolution in the more strongly expressed position of the later visions and the epilogue: belief in divine revelation offers a hope of a higher perspective that can illuminate the chaos of earthly events. Not a logical resolution of the two former positions, this perspective calls upon the higher knowledge based on visionary insight—a typical theme of apocalypses. For Hogan, the author thereby undergoes a certain transformation. The secret teachings do not entirely resolve the crisis of loss; it is a deep trauma and grief that cannot be totally healed.[37] Yet the text itself is a path—even a ritual?—that moves the reader toward a new awareness. And as an apocalypse, the text provides a kind of resolution to which Job does not have access: "The Most High," says Uriel, "has revealed secrets to you" (10:38). The angel then instructs Ezra to record the revelations for later generations of the wise—the audience's generation.

The extreme depression of Ezra the speaker, however, makes it difficult to discern exactly where a change might come in his outlook, and scholars have disagreed about how much progress there is in his therapy session with the angel. Michael Stone grants that we are confronted by a cycle of visions with answers that are not really satisfactory—each seems to simply repeat the previous visions—and yet the cycle may be progressive. The fourth vision, he asserts, is a turning point, and Ezra is now receptive to Uriel's words. But other scholars have pushed the turning point farther along the series of visions. Hogan argues that while Ezra is not transformed by the fourth vision, he does show development over the course of the next visions. The seventh, however, is merely an epilogue. Meredith J. C. Warren urges us to think again, however, about the seventh vision. To be sure, it is different, but the drinking of the fiery heavenly liquid provides the culmination of Ezra's emotional development. Najman proposes a new direction in this debate—to rise above the cycle of visions, as it were, and view them from a different perspective. Fourth Ezra mourns the destruction of the temple, but the author is not searching for reassurance about a rebuilding of the temple. She argues that this author sought, rather, to "reboot" the relation with God that was not focused as before on the temple, but rather on a renewal of the text of scripture and the apocalyptic vision in textual form. There will be a restoration of Torah to "resume its covenantal life with God." This new Ezra does not return to Jerusalem but moves instead to uninhabited land, the wilderness, as an appropriate place for revelation (9:24–25). Hope for a continuing covenant with God was affirmed "not in spite of destruction and exile, but *as transformed by them*."[38] The dynamic of the visions, then, is not what we might expect—finding hope for renewal of the fallen temple, but finding a new set of symbolic centers.

Who was this man Ezra, then, that he could embody such a persona?

In the biblical book of Ezra, this leader was revered for bringing the Jerusa-
lemites back to a recommitment to God's covenant. A priest and a latter-day
Moses, he was also the scribe par excellence: "the scribe, a scholar of the
text of the commandments of the Lord and the statutes for Israel. . . . scribe
of the law of the God of heaven" (Ezra 7:11–12, cf. 7:25). The biblical Ezra
was also one of the first figures associated with "Torah" as a term for Israelite law. Although Torah is better translated in the Bible as instruction rather
than simply law, it is easy to see how 4 Ezra, as also Ben Sira, could place
wisdom and law so fundamentally together. Torah, in fact, includes law
and instruction about wisdom, the natural order, and "the way of the Most
High." Fourth Ezra takes up the name of the Ezra who participated in the
restoration of the first temple and who contributed to the teaching of the
law, but the new Ezra also borrows from Moses, Daniel, Ezekiel, Job, and
Enoch. In addition to the usual education of the scribe, Ezra has a mystical
connection to knowledge. He is commanded to assemble scribes and to
dictate texts: "When you have finished, some things you shall make public,
and some you shall deliver in secret to the wise. . . . Make public the twenty-
four books [the canon of the Hebrew Bible], and let the worthy and the
unworthy read them, but keep the seventy that were written last, in order to
give them to the wise of your people. For in them is the spring of understanding, the fountain of wisdom, and the river of knowledge" (14:26, 45–
47). He is thus commanded to write down *both* the public books of the
Bible *and* the secret books. When he is finally taken up into heaven, he
is called "the scribe of the knowledge of the Most High forever" (14:50,
printed as a textual variant in the NRSV). This may have an esoteric component. As letters of the alphabet were used for numbers in the ancient
world, seventy may represent Hebrew *sōd* or secret, and some of the twenty-
four books of the Bible were at times combined to arrive at twenty-two, the
number of letters in the Hebrew alphabet. At 14:39 Ezra is also given a po-
tion that is "like fire," perhaps like a hallucinogen: "My heart poured forth
understanding, and wisdom increased in my breast, and my spirit retained
its memory, and my mouth was opened, and no longer closed." Najman also
perceives here another dimension: the Torah is both textual and hypertext;
that is, the reverence for the earlier Torah of Moses is maintained, but the

Torah has been burned (14:21).[39] It is ironic, however, since the lost *text* is followed by a *new, secret text*. The newer revelation is now Ezra's *textual* report of his dialogues with the angel Uriel. The interpretation of the biblical text that had become so central in Israel is supplanted by an interpretation of visions. This, of course, is similar to other apocalypses.

Fifth and Sixth Ezra

The first two and last two chapters of 2 Esdras were Christian additions, composed at different times. Numbered as 2 Esdras 1–2 and 15–16, they are also known as 5 Ezra and 6 Ezra. They appear only in the Latin edition and are not part of the Eastern translations. When added to 4 Ezra they changed the interpretive context for the Jewish apocalypse. Fifth Ezra—the new beginning of the book as a whole—resonates like a biblical prophetic book: "The word of the Lord came to me" (1:4). The figure of Ezra is introduced with information known from the Hebrew Bible books of Ezra and Nehemiah and has a prestigious priestly genealogy. But whereas the Jewish apocalypse of 4 Ezra creates a persona of Ezra as a very contemporaneous seer—rendering him "present" for the distraught audience—this Christian introduction returns Ezra back to his historical past.

Fifth Ezra exhibits a careful six-part structure, based somewhat surprisingly on the book of Baruch (1 Baruch). The author draws out a Christian meaning in each section, sometimes emulating Baruch and sometimes altering the message.

Baruch	**5 Ezra**
1. 1:15–2:29, 3:1–8	1. 1:5–27
Baruch's prayer: national confession of sins	Recounting of exodus and God's acts of salvation, which Israel ignored
2. 3:9–4:4 (out of order)	2. 1:28–34
Paean to Wisdom	Prophetic and wisdom motifs
3. 2:30–35	3. 1:24, 35–40
Ideal qualities of Jewish exiles in Babylon	Ideal qualities of Christians
4. 4:5–20	4. 2:1–7
Destruction of Jerusalem	Destruction of Jerusalem

5. 4:21–35	5. 2:15–32
Jerusalem addresses exiles as mother	Mother Church
6. 4:36–5:9	6. 2:33–48
Jewish exiles returning from Babylon	Future glory of Christians

Fifth Ezra is also influenced by Gal 4:21–31, where Paul contrasts the children of the slave woman, Hagar, with the children of the free woman, Sarah, or Israel and Christians.[40] Fifth Ezra repeats Paul's contrast of Hagar as earthly Jerusalem and Sarah as heavenly and contrasts as well Sinai as the mountain of the old covenant with Zion as the mountain of the new.

By reasserting the ancient, biblical Ezra over the very "present" apocalyptic seer of 4 Ezra, 5 Ezra places the entire book in the context of a prediction from long ago on the present punishment of Israel, the destruction of the temple, and the coming of Christianity. It is part of the Christian *adversus Judaeos* tradition, in which the sins of Israel are emphasized as an explanation for the transfer of God's favor from Jews to Christians: "Pull out the hair of your head and hurl all evils upon Israel, for they have not obeyed my law—they are a rebellious people" (1:8). God further says definitively, "I will turn to other nations [gentiles] and will give them my name, that they may keep my statutes. Because you have forsaken me, I also will forsake you. . . . I have rejected your feast days, and new moons, and circumcisions of the flesh. . . . I will give your houses to a people that will come, who without having heard will believe" (1:24–25, 31, 35). Ezra himself quotes God's lasting punishment for Jews: "Let them be scattered among the nations; let their names be blotted out from the earth, because they have despised my covenant" (2:7); and God concludes this section with a prediction of the coming of Jesus Christ: "Tell my people [the new nations, that is, Christians] that I will give them the kingdom of Jerusalem, which I was going to give to Israel. . . . I say to you, O nations that hear and understand, 'Await your shepherd; he will give you everlasting rest, because he who will come at the end of the age is close at hand'" (2:10, 34).

Sixth Ezra begins with God addressing a word of prophecy to an unnamed prophet. If it is read in the context of 4 Ezra, the prophet is Ezra, but it is more likely that 6 Ezra was written independently and added at the end of 4 Ezra, probably in about the fourth century CE. Sixth Ezra also may have been composed before 5 Ezra and perhaps added to 4 Ezra prior to the addition of 5 Ezra. Sixth Ezra is similar to apocalypses in containing visions and warnings, but it is unlike apocalypses in that there is no interpreting angel, nor a narrative frame that provides the seer's context (though this may have been lost). And so this work "is, through and through, a writing in the classical, biblical prophetic style," albeit an eschatological prophecy.[41] It consists of repetitive images of the destruction that awaits, a prediction of the destruction of Jerusalem and the second temple at the time of the Jewish War (66–70 CE). The images of destruction, without any apparent structuring, are overwhelming. The tone might suggest an eyewitness to the rebellion or one near in time to it, but this is not likely. After the longer set of predictions of the catastrophe that awaits, the second, shorter part (16:35–78) exhorts the elect to withdraw from the world and abstain from sin in order to be saved. Unlike 5 Ezra, which reveals a clear Christian interpretation at various points, 6 Ezra is not as easily characterized. There is no clearly Christian reference, and indeed the text could conceivably be Jewish. Yet two passages suggest a Christian provenance. First, the discussion of Babylon, here meaning Rome, is similar to that in Revelation.[42] Second, the persecution of "the elect" in 16:68–74 is similar to Christian discourse about persecution in the second and third centuries. Sixth Ezra as a whole in fact reminds one of the so-called Little Apocalypse in Mark 13. The dualism of the saved and the damned is strongly emphasized and repeated often in this section. Sixth Ezra ends abruptly, repeating the message that those who are righteous will be saved, while those who are not will be judged and punished: "'Hear, my elect,' says the Lord. 'Behold the days of tribulation are at hand, and I will deliver you from them. . . . Woe to those who are choked by their sins and overwhelmed by their iniquities, as a field is choked with underbrush and its path overwhelmed with thorns, so that no one can pass through! It is shut off and given up to be consumed by fire'" (16:74, 77–78). These two Christian additions were probably written around the second to third centuries, 6 Ezra perhaps a bit earlier than 5 Ezra.

Despite the ambiguity of 4 Ezra's place in the Western canon, it retained some popularity. The doctrine of sin found there comported with Paul's views—though the author was not likely familiar with Paul's writings.[43]

The Christian introduction (5 Ezra) assimilates the text to the doctrine that Israel was appropriately punished by God. Epistle of Barnabas 12:2 quotes 4 Ezra 4:33, 5:5 as a "prophet" in a long series of biblical quotations with interpretation. Ambrose was fond of 4 Ezra, and it was quoted by Clement of Alexandria (*Stromateis* 3:16) and translated into many languages. Other texts may allude to 4 Ezra: *Greek Apocalypse of Ezra, Apocalypse of Sedrach, Revelation of the Blessed Ezra, Questions of Ezra, Questions of St. Gregory about the Souls of Men,* and *Expansions of Ezra* in the Armenian version of 2 Esdras.

Second Baruch, or Syriac Apocalypse of Baruch

Fourth Ezra and 2 Baruch are a matched set in many ways. They are both apocalypses, written at about same time—the end of the first century or beginning of the second CE—and they share another aspect: they feature a dialogue-dispute between a seer and a divine figure.[44] Written soon after the destruction of the second temple, they are both narrated in the voice of a famous figure prominent after the destruction of the first temple. They are also similar in being weakly attested in the various canons: 4 Ezra was marginally present in the Western Bibles, and 2 Baruch only included in the Syriac Bible (Peshitta). However, 4 Ezra has often been considered the superior text and 2 Baruch a derivative copy, although 2 Baruch does exhibit many interesting qualities and should not be overlooked.

We begin with what immediately resonates as a strong similarity between the two. In 2 Baruch the speaker, as in 4 Ezra, poses the same question to God, and it also gives rise to a poignant reflection: "What will be after these things? For if you destroy your city, and you hand your land over to those who hate us, how will the name of Israel again be remembered? Or how will we speak about your glories? Or to whom will be explained what is in your Torah?" (3:5–6). Yet despite this similar statement of the theme, the differences between the two texts are significant. Fourth Ezra opens (that is, 2 Esdras 3:1) with a typical apocalyptic visionary introduction, but 2 Baruch begins more in the manner of the prophetic books: "The word of the Lord was upon Baruch, . . . and he said to him. . . ."[45] Second Baruch also expresses more interest in ancient figures and motifs, connecting the discourse to the biblical tradition. Furthermore, it utilizes a number of different genres—prayers, laments, dialogues, public speeches, dream visions, and epistles. It is somewhat like a symphony, creating distinct tones in each section. These sections are at times comforting, but the repetition of some of these forms can seem overlong, as if an overactive author did not know when to stop. Second Baruch may then appear weaker in terms of apocalyptic imagery; that is, the images are not very provocative, and the explanations are more rationalistic. Still, this may simply reflect a value judgment on the part of the modern reader.

Some of the most important differences between 2 Baruch and 4 Ezra revolve around the role of Baruch. An angelic interpreter is an expected part of an apocalypse, but in 2 Baruch there is more direct communication with God.[46] God speaks to Baruch as to a prophet, and Baruch in turn addresses Jeremiah with authority (2:1) and is even like Moses in interceding for the people (21:20–25, 48:11–24). Baruch is at times even the superior of Jeremiah. We may perceive three phases in the relation of Jeremiah and Baruch within this tradition. In the Hebrew Bible, Jeremiah was dominant and Baruch his scribe. Baruch then ascends in this apocalypse as the voice of a higher revelation. In the Peshitta, Baruch once again regresses and becomes a mere scribe in a Jeremianic corpus of books. Balázs Tamási sees in this complex relation between Baruch and the tradition an attempt by the author of 2 Baruch to build authority for the text.[47] Here Baruch, in Jerusalem, is presented as a second Jeremiah, as the latter is now away in Babylon. Baruch is also seen as a second Moses who affirms the law. He is presented as prophet, seer, Torah sage, and community leader. In addition, he utilizes three different genres: apocalypse, letter, and testament. Finally, the end of the book characterizes the textual revelation of the whole: "a letter of instruction and a book of hope" (77:12).

For the modern reader, 4 Ezra and 2 Baruch both present significant psychological interest, yet 4 Ezra is more depressive and the visionary more inconsolable; he plays the Job not just for himself but for the entire nation. Second Baruch, however, finds some hope and looks to a brighter outcome (1:5, 73:1–74:3), communicating a stronger message of consolation. The people's loss and disillusionment, and the loss of their leaders, are poignantly communicated: "The shepherds of Israel have perished, and the lamps which gave light are extinguished" (44:1–3). The pressing question of the author, and thus of the audience, is: How will the people be able to survive without such leaders as the biblical prophets and their prophetic successors like Baruch? The author consoles the audience: Torah abides; the commitment to God's law can continue in Israel, and it is this that defines the land, not Rome's occupation. Slowly it is also shown how there will be hope for the people in a future restoration. It is indeed possible that 2 Baruch is responding to and even trying to improve upon the thoroughly negative message of 4 Ezra. Liv Ingeborg Lied sums up the attitude of 2 Baruch: "No one will survive unless they live according to the Torah, but neither will they survive the destructive consequences of the fall of the Jerusalem temple unless they also learn to see the post-destruction world through the lenses of Baruch's teaching."[48]

Related to the stronger theme of consolation in 2 Baruch is the sense that this text is also less sectarian, less emphatic about dividing the human race into a small group who are saved—because they alone have the proper revelation—and the large mass of humanity who are ignorant and doomed. We may compare here the sectarian view of 4 Ezra, which is indeed similar to the sectarian view of the Qumran texts or Gospel of John. Shannon Burkes, however, finds a difference here between 4 Ezra and 2 Baruch. The temple, Israel's center, had been destroyed, and so worldly wisdom clearly failed. Possible rewards are now focused on direct, revealed knowledge of God's plan for the end of history. Although both texts are sectarian to some extent, Burkes asserts rightly that 4 Ezra is more pessimistic and sectarian, insisting on the necessity of knowing the secret texts. Second Baruch pulls back from this strict dualism, providing assurances about the larger arc of time and how periods of suffering—the period after the first destruction of the Jerusalem temple and after the second—will be followed by the vindication of righteous Israel: "If you prepare your hearts and sow in them the fruits of the Torah, the Mighty One will protect you in that time to come, who will shake up all of creation" (32:1). Consider also 46:5–6: "Only prepare your hearts, so that you will obey the Torah and subject yourselves to those who in fear are wise and understanding; and prepare your soul, lest you withdraw from them. For if you do these, those good tidings will come to you of which I spoke to you." Susan Docherty notes that the distinction between Israel and the gentiles is renegotiated: "Gentiles who have not harmed God's people will be spared in the final judgment (72:4–5), and proselytes can be included in the future salvation, while Israelites who choose not to keep the commandments will be excluded from it (42:1–8). In answering the question, 'Who will be saved?,' then, this author subtly redefines the meaning of 'Israel' so that it relates to observance of the law and is no longer a strictly ethnic entity." Burkes also notes that for 2 Baruch life is still available in a new, revealed wisdom that informs one about how to keep the law. Esoteric books are not required as in 4 Ezra, so the role of Torah is different: "Life . . . is gained through the Law, which is identified with wisdom more frequently than in Fourth Ezra. In addition, the Law in Second Baruch appears to refer to the biblical corpus, while in Fourth Ezra it extends to the esoteric seventy books which he is to reveal only to 'the wise.' The greater accessibility of the complete Law in Second Baruch implies that more people may put it to use effectively." Scholars have pondered the literary relationship between these two similar apocalypses, but with little consensus. Although some have suggested that 2 Baruch simply rewrites what is found in 4 Ezra, Henze has argued against this: 2 Baruch is in an engaged dialogue with the earlier text and in fact extends it. Hogan allows that 2 Baruch is in dialogue with 4 Ezra but does not perceive much extension of the themes. Be that as it may, however, Henze still posits mutual influence between the texts at a very early stage, including oral transmission of similar motifs.[49]

We should not pass from 2 Baruch without noting some interesting passages that relate to other texts of the period. As we have seen, the two common responses in the Apocrypha to the problem of an unjust death are immortality of the soul in Wisdom of Solomon, 4 Maccabees, and perhaps Epistle of Enoch, and resurrection and judgment in 4 Ezra, the rest of 1 Enoch, 2 Maccabees, and Meqabyan. Second Baruch follows the latter affirmation, yet the recognition scene of the righteous and the wicked will remind readers of Wisdom 2–5: "Therefore, when they will see those, over whom they are now exalted, will then be exalted and glorified more than they, and that they have all been transformed, these into the splendor of the angels and those into startling apparitions, then at the sight of these shapes they will waste away even more" (51:5). Chapters 53–74, the narration of all Israelite history down to the destruction of the second temple, is also a longer, fuller, more rationalized version of world history, influenced perhaps by the Greek universal histories like Diodorus Siculus. Another point of interest is the statement that Abraham and the patriarchs received the unwritten Torah (57:1–2). The unwritten Torah, revealed along with the written Torah, was a Pharisaic belief that became central in rabbinic and later Judaism. Relating to Christian theology is also the assertion that human sinfulness resulted from Adam's sin (56:5–6). Finally, at 73:2 there is a vision of renewal not unlike Luke's reuse of Isaiah 61 (Luke 4:18–19): "Then healing will be descending in the dew, and disease will vanish, and concern and sorrow and groans will pass from among humans, and gladness will walk about the entire earth." Second Baruch is thus a long, somewhat repetitive sermon, a deep reflection on the destruction of Jerusalem, and a *joint* performance of the author/speaker and the audience: "Therefore, when you receive this letter, read it in your assemblies with care, and meditate thereon, above all on the days of your fasts. And remember me through this letter, as I, too, remember you through it, always" (86:1–2). In this respect it is similar to the Epistle of Enoch in 1 Enoch, but the community invitation is like Paul's First Letter to the Thessalonians 2–3 as well.

Just as there are a surprising number of parallels between 1 Enoch and the New Testament texts, so also for 2 Baruch, although there are no direct quotations. The common motifs evidently arise from the same thought world. Henze presses this point in a profound way: "It would be difficult to miss the parallels that exist between *2Bar*'s expectations of the end time and similar beliefs in the New Testament, particularly in Paul's Epistles and Matthew's Gospel. . . . The affinities are so salient, the common ground of their rhetoric so striking, that it becomes questionable whether such distinctions between 'Jewish' and 'Christian' are not distorting more than they clarify." Goff goes so far as to say that the resurrection and end of time discussion in 1 Corinthians 15 is very similar to 2 Baruch 29–30.[50] Possible parallels can also be discerned in Epistle of Barnabas 11:9, which may be attributed to a common source, and *Odes of Solomon* expresses some of the motifs found in 2 Bar 77:18–26: "I wrote these two letters: one I sent by means of an eagle to the nine and a half tribes, and the other I sent to those who were in Babylon by means of three men." Beyond these references, however, 2 Baruch did not enjoy the rich afterlife in Christian tradition that accrued to 1 Enoch. In rabbinic texts, Baruch is sometimes treated as a prophet (*b. Megillah* 14b), but in other passages this status is denied him (*Mekhilta de-Rabbi Ishmael* Bo' 1).

Psalms, Prayers, and Odes

A NUMBER OF EXTRA PSALMS AND ODES are found in differ-
ent versions of the Old Testament, often placed together, yet there is little
consistency. The fluidity is even greater than for the rest of the canon. It is
no accident that Eva Mroczek takes Psalms as her main example of the unfixed nature of the Bible. But as fluid as the collections of psalms and odes
are, it is also no accident that Psalms are quoted more in the New Testament
than any other biblical book, and quoted often in the Mishnah. The expanding collections of psalms doubtless reflect this popularity. Extra psalms
were also discovered among the Qumran texts, in addition to those composed at Qumran for the community (*Songs of the Sabbath Sacrifice*). What
Randall D. Chesnutt and Judith Newman say about late prayers applies
to psalms and odes as well: there is a "scripturalization" process in which
older biblical Psalms and texts such as Exod 34:6 and Isa 6:3 are reused
often.[1] Here we treat the extra psalms of the larger Old Testaments: Psalms
151–155, Prayer of Manasseh, and Psalms of Solomon. The short collection
of prayers and songs known as Odes (not the same as the *Odes of Solomon*)
was included in Codex Alexandrinus but not in the other early versions.
It was canonized as a separate book in the Eastern Orthodox Church. The
Odes consist of Old and New Testament texts and thus are not new to the
Bible but simply drawn together as a liturgical book. As a result, they will
not be treated here. Also, although Prayer of Azariah and Song of the Three
originated as separate texts, they function within the book of Daniel and
thus were treated in Chapter 1.

Psalm 151

The book of Psalms in the Hebrew Bible consists of 150 psalms, but in the Greek versions of the Bible an extra psalm, Psalm 151, appears at the end. It is counted as one of the Psalms in Sinaiticus but labeled as extracanonical in Vaticanus and Alexandrinus. In the Syriac translation, this psalm and four others are placed at the end of the book of Psalms, numbered 151–155. In the *Psalms Scroll* found at Qumran (11Q5 or 11QPs³), there is a fuller version of this psalm, divided in two parts and now numbered by scholars as 151A and 151B. The two Qumran psalms likely represent the older version and were edited together to form Psalm 151 of the Christian Bibles. Nothing suggests that the Qumran psalms were an Essene composition; rather, the two psalms were transmitted with other extracanonical psalms. Because this psalm tradition appears at Qumran, it is clear that a Hebrew version circulated before the Jewish War. Although the biblical Psalms were at times ascribed to David, some were especially known as "historical psalms" because they were understood to reflect the voice of David.[2] Psalm 151 takes up this literary assumption more explicitly and is the only one that mentions events of David's life as recounted in 1 Samuel 16–17: his ability in playing the harp and the lyre, his selection by God, and his defeat of Goliath that saves his people. Somewhat like 1 Esdras 3–5 and Susanna, Psalm 151 presents David as a young hero. Its literary tone matches that of heroic poetry cross-culturally: a voice "sings" the story; a hero comes forth, and though he is not impressive, he defeats the giant. Minor, concrete details communicate important parts of the legend of David (here from the LXX version):

> I was small among my brothers,
>> and the youngest in my father's house;
> I would shepherd my father's sheep. (v. 1)

The conclusion is told with great flair, indeed, with the music of epic:

> I went out to meet the Philistine,
>> and he cursed me by his idols.

But I drew his own sword;
> I beheaded him,
> and took away disgrace from the people of Israel. (vv.
>> 6–7)

Irony and understatement increase the epic sway of events: the youngest of the brothers, David slays Goliath with the giant's own sword. In many ways, the style here is the opposite of the novella: the action is not in "mundane time" but in "epic time" or "ancient time." Despite the ancient tone of heroic epic, however, Tessa Rajak notes that it contains late elements as well: the visitation by an angel and the fact that Goliath is explicitly associated with idols.[3] The poem was likely a Maccabean triumph song, despite its appearance among the scrolls of the anti-Hasmonean Qumran sect. The small David and the older brothers connote Israel among the nations.

Two matters of great interest have attached to the study of Psalm 151, especially in the Qumran version. Psalm 151A adds a clause (v. 2d): "I spoke to myself," literally, "I, indeed I, spoke in my soul" (*'amarty 'any benafshy*). This interiorizing expression, perhaps addressing a separate inner self, has suggested similarities to other developments of the period. The intense focus on one's sinful self has been observed at Qumran and to some extent in Greek Esther, foreshadowing the marked Christian discipline of the self. Yet speaking "in the heart" or "in the soul," though rare in the Hebrew Bible, is not unknown. The expression, however, may reflect a greater interest in interior reflection (see the introduction to Chapter 1 and the Conclusion). A second interest in this psalm concerns the emphasis on David's playing of musical instruments and his singing before God, stated more strongly in the Qumran Psalm 151A:

> My hands fashioned a reed pipe,
>> And my fingers a lyre;
> And so I gave glory to the Lord.
>> I said in my mind,
> "The mountains cannot testify to him,
>> Nor can the hills proclaim—

Lift up my words, you trees,
   And my compositions, you sheep." (lines 2–3)

The singing and playing to God, coupled with the possible introspective consciousness, have reminded some of the Greek tradition of Orpheus, whose playing of the lyre has divine qualities. As James A. Sanders says:

> The tone is quite non-biblical; the [Bible] clearly speaks of mountains and hills witnessing to God. . . . David, by contrast [to his brothers] is a small, humble shepherd whose shepherd's music is appreciated by no one save his dumb flock and the trees among which they graze. Unattractive and a lonely figure, fully unappreciated save by nature, David nonetheless says in his soul that he will render glory to God. . . . For hellenized Judaism then to take the obvious next step of seeing in David, the musician, the orphic talents and virtues is both logical and reasonable.[4]

Syriac Psalms 151–155

The Syriac Old Testament (Peshitta) combined Psalm 151 with four others, numbered 152–155. In addition to Psalms 151A and 151B, Psalms 154 and 155 were also found in the Qumran psalter, but as Psalms 152 and 153 were not, the latter could date from a later period and derive from Christian hands. As interesting as these psalms are for discussions of an unfixed canon of Psalms, Psalms 152–155 seem to reflect more typical psalm motifs than do Psalms 151A and 151B. Psalm 152 is at first typical of biblical hymns of praise, albeit with intriguing differences: "Join your soul to the good and the perfect to glorify the Most High." Is this a further example of a discipline of the self, perhaps even influenced by Greek abstract philosophy concerning "the good and the perfect"? Perhaps, and since this psalm was not found at Qumran, it could date from several centuries later. This psalm also intones the biblical motif that praise of God is the equivalent of sacrifices (see discussion of the Prayer of Azariah in Chapter 1). Psalm 153 is an individual lament and prayer for healing and rescue, which features the consciousness of sin: "Do not judge me according to my sins, because no human being ['no flesh'] is innocent before you." Psalms 154–155, likewise prayers for rescue, can be dated earlier than the Jewish War as a result of their presence at Qumran. They both mention tending the flocks and attacks by wild beasts—images of David as shepherd. The speaking voice prays as well for deliverance from death and Sheol.

Prayer of Manasseh

A continuing theme of the so-called Deuteronomic theology of the biblical histories is the characterization of the kings of Israel and Judah as either good or bad depending on whether they remained steadfastly loyal to God's covenant with Israel. Ironically, Manasseh ruled longer than any other king in Judah—fifty-six years!—but was deemed the worst of the kings: he brought on God's punishment and the fall of Judah. In 2 Kings 21 he was not taken captive to Babylon, but when 1 and 2 Chronicles reworked this history, he was exiled to Babylon and was the only one who was actually rehabilitated (2 Chr 33:12–13). At this point some early Christian biblical manuscripts insert a prayer of this king, which takes advantage of Chronicles' new narrative—the bad king repents—and this added prayer lived on in the Christian tradition as the prayer of a penitent. There had long existed a tradition of confession of Israel's sin and a petition for God's forgiveness (see Baruch, and also Ezra 9, Nehemiah 9, and Daniel 9). David Lambert, however, notes an important innovation in this prayer. Although the mercies of God had often been extolled in the tradition (Exod 34:6–7, Deut 4:30), the tone here is of a prepared or fixed channel of forgiveness, and a path for the individual, not Israel as a whole: "You, O Lord, God of the righteous, have not appointed repentance for the righteous, for Abraham and Isaac and Jacob, who did not sin against you, but you have appointed repentance for me, who am a sinner" (vv. 6–8). Says Lambert, "With this praise, Manasseh establishes the basis, as a penitent, on which he can expect, even demand, to have his petition favorably received." Even further, for Judith Newman, that "the Jewish God is a 'God of those who repent,' as distinct from a God of the righteous, is another unique feature."[5]

Like some other biblical texts, Prayer of Manasseh is expressed in the tones of a liturgical prayer, "something at the nexus of liturgy and scripture," say Newman and van der Horst, "between the praxis of worship and the instruction of adherents." Along with William Schniedewind, they make some far-reaching claims about the Manasseh tradition: Manasseh lives through his own "Babylonian exile" and becomes a paradigm for the people as a whole.[6] The similar Manasseh fragments at Qumran (in 4Q380–81) suggest a broader tradition as well. As David was increasingly the source for psalms, Manasseh was the figure associated with repentance. But despite these similar traditions at Qumran, Prayer of Manasseh may have been written somewhat later, in Greek, and perhaps by Christians.

Prayer of Manasseh has been much more influential in Jewish and Christian tradition than the other texts treated in this chapter. Similar versions of Prayer of Manasseh were found at Qumran and in the Cairo Genizah. The latter indicates broader Jewish use, but it is not clear how the prayer was understood. In *Lives of the Prophets* 1:1, Manasseh is blamed for killing Isaiah by sawing him in two; it was for this act that God allowed Manasseh to be defeated. In rabbinic tradition he is viewed in an ambivalent or negative way. The targum to 2 Chr 33:10–13, for instance, adds significant details: angels tried to prevent Manasseh's prayer from reaching God, but God nevertheless heeded the prayer and allowed his rehabilitation. Among Christians, Prayer of Manasseh was found in *Didaskalia Apostolorum* and *Apostolic Constitutions* and became a typical "prayer of the penitent." The Christian use expresses a doctrine of individual repentance and forgiveness, not unlike Prayer of Azariah. Lambert also suggests that, as in *Joseph and Aseneth,* repentance and forgiveness may here be considered in a context of conversion.[7] One may imagine that Manasseh was specifically chosen as an example for converts: if a channel for repentance was established for a king as wicked as Manasseh, then it was open as well for the potential convert. It was also included as one of the Odes and thus enjoyed a very prominent role in early church worship. Later texts of the Syriac Peshitta contained it, as did the Luther Bible of 1534, but not the French Zwingli Bible of 1527–1529.[8] Since the Council of Trent (1546), it has been included in an appendix to the Vulgate.

Psalms of Solomon

A heading at the end of Codex Alexandrinus states that Psalms of Solomon and the letters of Clement of Rome were part of an appendix, but that appendix is now lost. Psalms of Solomon was not part of any other early manuscript, but in the tenth century, Codex Vindobenensis Theol. 11 included it between Wisdom of Solomon and Ben Sira, indicating it was a fully biblical text. In the Leiden Syriac Peshitta it is found with the extra psalms.[9] In recognition of these later canons, Alfred Rahlfs included Psalms of Solomon in his edition of the Septuagint. It was likely Rahlfs's editorial decision that brought Psalms of Solomon more into the discussion of the Apocrypha. It is included in NETS and treated fully in *T&T Clark Companion to the Septuagint* and Otto Kaiser's *Old Testament Apocrypha,* even though it is understandably barely mentioned in David deSilva, *Introducing the Apocrypha,* and not introduced at all in Daniel Harrington, *Invitation to the Apocrypha.*

The text takes the name of Solomon most likely because he was traditionally said to have composed many proverbs and songs (1 Kgs 4:32). The most common psalm type in this collection is the judgment doxology (2:15–21, 8:25–34, 10:5–8). There are similarities to the laments in the book of Psalms and also the book of Lamentations, written after another national calamity, the fall of the first temple. After an opening lament on Jerusalem, there is an alternation of individual and communal psalms: five individual (2–6), five collective (7–11), and five individual (12–16), concluding with two other collective psalms (17–18) and a hymnic closing in 18:10–12. The Psalms of Solomon have been especially interesting to scholars for a number of reasons. First, there are specific, datable references to important historical events. Second, there are indications that the psalms were composed by and for Pharisees. Third, the psalms combine traditional psalm themes with wisdom concerns, especially *paideia* or education, and also eschatological predictions. Fourth, of the Jewish texts of this period, the Psalms of Solomon probably exhibit the most similarities to early Christian theology. This statement should not be pressed to conclude that there was some sort of special path from Jewish texts *to* early Christianity. The Psalms of Solomon probably receive a greater share of attention by scholars because of the important parallels to New Testament texts, but we may consider this relationship in a way somewhat analogous to, say, the observation that Ben Sira is the most similar to rabbinic Judaism. And indeed, we also note that Psalms of Solomon exhibit similarities to rabbinic Judaism as well.

We begin with the first observation, the datable references to the political context. A strong scholarly consensus holds that the Psalms of Solomon refer to the Roman invasion of Judea led by Pompey, which resulted in his taking of the temple in 63 BCE, ending a hundred years of independent Hasmonean rule.[10] (Although Pompey captured the temple and entered it, he did not destroy it. This did not occur until the Jewish War, 66–70 CE.) According to the text, it was the sins of Israel, particularly the role of the Hasmonean kings, that caused the calamity (Pss. Sol. 1, 8, 18). It had often been assumed that the king would be in the line of David, but the Hasmoneans, from a different lineage, had usurped the role. The Essenes at Qumran had also objected to the fact that the Hasmoneans had taken on the role of high priest. The intervention of Pompey in Israel's politics was thus explained as God's punishment of the Hasmoneans, and Psalm of Solomon 17 looks forward to the rise of the true Davidic messiah. The author takes up the language of Davidic fulfillment from Ps 2:7–9 and Isa 11:2–5: the one in the line of David will embody certain messianic features—wisdom, righteousness, no taint of sin, and his word is powerful like God's. The text even uses the word *christos* or messiah: the messiah will reign as God's representative on earth. An eschatological hope of renewal can also be discerned here, consisting of true kingship, the gathering of Israel, and the reverence of Jerusalem by the nations, although the text stops just short of the two-eras thinking of apocalypses (granting, as noted in the introduction to Chapter 4, that the historical dualism of apocalypses is sometimes exaggerated). There is, for example, also no transcendent reality that is specified, no knowledge of time and cosmos that is revealed, no angelic interpreter. As George Nickelsburg says, "We miss here the white heat of apocalyptic expectation, stoked by revelation."[11] Several themes have also suggested to scholars that this text was written by Pharisees. First, resurrection of the flesh, a Pharisaic belief, may be assumed at Pss. Sol. 3:12 (compare 13:10).

Second, the text is negative toward the Jerusalem leaders (Pss. Sol. 4), which would be priests and Sadducees, criticized by the Pharisees. Third, there are no aspects that correspond to the known views of the Sadducees or Essenes; for instance, there is no high-priestly messiah (along with a Davidic messiah) as at Qumran. Also, no text of Psalms of Solomon was found at Qumran (although this could be coincidental). Yet it must be admitted that we know very little about the Pharisees in the first century BCE, and the connection is weak. The Psalms of Solomon, then, contains many moving passages, made all the more poignant by the fact that the historical situation is definite and compelling. A clear window is created that provides a view of the end of independent Jewish rule—shorter than, but still similar to, Josephus's account of the defeat of Jewish rebels a century later and the destruction of the temple. Alongside a powerful evocation of Israelite communal theology, the reader gets a sense of the individual author, haunted by the calamity of Israel's fall, which is attributed here to the author's sins. Says Otto Kaiser, "The intentional alternation between individual and collective psalms reveals both the artfulness of the book's composition as well as its message."[12]

Moral, theological, and psychological aspects are emphasized. *Hosios,* pious, is used often, especially in the phrase *synagōgai hosiōn,* congregations of the pious, referring to Jerusalem. This expression, says Nickelsburg, "indicates that these psalms were created and used in circles that considered themselves to be especially pious, righteous, and God-fearing and who gathered for purposes of worship, which probably included the recitation of some of these psalms." Further, the mixture of moods and motifs among the psalms would affect the audience at times as if it were a wisdom text and at others almost as if it were an apocalypse. The latter was noted above, but Daniele Pevarello also marks the prominence of the *paideia* root, education or discipline: the righteous who have sinned should embark on a path of fasting and self-affliction. "The *Psalms of Solomon,*" Kaiser continues, "is admittedly not an eschatological pamphlet, but a book of comfort and a school of prayer for the pious battered by the chaos of their time."[13] Yet an eschatological element is expressed often enough to keep this theme in the community's mind.

Because of the relative clarity concerning the events described in the text, a fairly precise date is possible: between Pompey's victory (63 BCE; Pss. Sol. 8, 17) and his death (48 BCE; Pss. Sol. 2). Although the text exists only in Greek and in Syriac texts translated from the Greek, scholarly consensus has long maintained that it was originally composed in Hebrew. Despite its inclusion in some of the medieval manuscripts, Psalms of Solomon is rarely cited in Judaism or Christianity. Still, because of its importance for historical studies and for motifs that are common in the New Testament, it is studied quite closely.

Conclusion

Common Themes in the Books of the Apocrypha

THE APOCRYPHA ARE INDEED A SOMEWHAT arbitrary grouping of changing texts, defined differently over the centuries. Yet because most of them arose within a few centuries of each other, during Greek and Roman rule, we can reasonably ask what recurring themes or literary aspects are encountered. One of the most prominent characteristics of Apocryphal literature, says Steven Weitzman, "is precisely the way they resemble the texts found in the Hebrew Bible, often involving the very same characters and kinds of situations, appearing to follow the same style and genres."[1] They often use older scriptural texts but rarely quote them explicitly. Even the attribution to a named author in Ben Sira and the "channeling" of Solomon in Wisdom of Solomon seem to assume the authority of the predecessor text, the book of Proverbs, thought at the time to be composed by Solomon. The Apocryphal texts were thus likely considered secondary to the Bible, although this assumes that both "Bible" and "secondary" were clear conceptions. We should perhaps say that the Apocrypha extended and played upon older Israelite literature, partly by utilizing similar genres.

One might assume that in these texts we would find variations from the Hebrew Bible in terms of theology, but the Apocrypha of the Western Old Testament were mostly "mainstream Judaism." David deSilva lists some themes from the Hebrew Bible that are taken up in the Apocrypha:[2]

- "Deuteronomic theology," that is, the view of history found in Deuteronomy: when Israel is faithful to God, the people flourish, and when they are not faithful, they fall. This is treated in Judith, Baruch, and 2 Maccabees, yet this view is challenged in the apocalyptic texts of 4 Ezra, 1 Enoch, Jubilees, and 2 Baruch (texts *not* accepted in the Western Apocrypha).

- Related to this is the penitential theology of Ezra 9, Nehemiah 9, and Daniel 9, which is developed in Judith, Greek Esther, Prayer of Azariah, Baruch, and Prayer of Manasseh.
- The recurring conflict between Judea and the "nations roundabout," treated in 1 Maccabees and in various ways in the other Maccabees texts and Judith.
- The personified role of Woman Wisdom in Ben Sira and Wisdom of Solomon developed beyond the role found in Proverbs 8–9 and referred to briefly in 1 Enoch 42.

We may extend this list with other observations. The combination of the transcendence of God and penitential theology, for instance, worked together in an unexpected way: the God who is more transcendent is yet responsive to prayer, and a stricken heart may elicit God's intervention. Prayer becomes more strongly emphasized, preparing the way for ascetic practices and theology, further developed in early Christianity.

Myths and legends of semidivine heroes were often recounted in Greece and Rome. If we simply remove the adjective "semidivine," we find that Israel had told similar stories concerning Abraham, Isaac, and Jacob; Sarah, Rebecca, and Rachel; Moses; Samson and Gideon; and so on. In the process, the Jewish heroes may also become semidivine. Many of the narratives attributed miraculous powers to them, as when the bones of Elisha bring a man back to life (2 Kgs 13:21). The role of heroes is continued in the Apocrypha, as other figures are considered to have extraordinary abilities, for instance, Enoch, Ezra, Daniel, and Jeremiah.[3] The last even appears from the dead, though perhaps in a dream, along with a dead hero from the recent past, the high priest Onias, and prays for the people (2 Macc 15:14–16; compare Matt 16:14). Yet, the possibility of intercessory prayer is also denied at 4 Ezra 7:102–5. Judith, although a fictitious character, is patterned after the judges-as-heroes and receives similar honors (Jdt 16:23–25). Further, it came to be assumed that Enoch, Abraham, Moses, Baruch, Ezra, and Daniel possessed extraordinary abilities that made them friends with God and allowed them heavenly insights. Merely the act of writing apocalypses or reading them was treated as access to the divine, a theme strongly emphasized in Jubilees, 1 Enoch, and 2 Baruch.

Although the Apocrypha differ among themselves on the fundamental question of the origin of evil, the three main views found in these texts have some background in biblical texts. Ben Sira and 1 and 2 Maccabees, in agreement with Deuteronomy, are very this-worldly: evil in the world can be combatted by humans committing more strongly to a righteous standard before God. Other texts, however, follow in the tradition of Ezekiel or Daniel 7–12 and are more pessimistic about combatting evil. They look for a solution from God. First Enoch, for instance, provides a radical explanation of the origin of evil and its ultimate resolution. The theme of the judgment of good and evil people at the end of the present age, found in Daniel 12, is also expressed in Jub. 5:11–12; 2 Esd 6:18–28, 7:113–114; 2 Baruch 48, 50; and 1 Meqabyan. A somewhat different response to evil is visible in the very tone of the novellas; they provide a romanticized happy ending. Tobit depicts the protection of the innocent by an angel (although a more judgmental ending has likely been added to the text), Susanna is protected by Daniel and indirectly by God, and in Judith we find an unstoppable heroine aided by God. These narratives find some kinship with the biblical stories of Joseph and Esther, but in the Apocrypha the book of Esther is expanded to give God a more explicit role in providing a happy ending.

Only in Daniel 11–12 does the Hebrew Bible register a clear belief in immortality, but this issue is greatly increased in the Apocrypha. There are two ways of obtaining immortality in the texts: through resurrection and judgment on one hand (2 Maccabees, 1 Enoch, 4 Ezra, 2 Baruch, Meqabyan) and immortality of the soul on the other (Wisdom of Solomon and 4 Maccabees). In some texts, immortality can also be achieved through writing: apocalypses emphasize that the scribe, by passing on his secret knowledge, attains a kind of immortality.[4] This affirmation can be found in the conclusions of 1 Enoch, 4 Ezra, and 2 Baruch.

As God became more removed above the human realm, not only did the female figure of Wisdom receive a prominent role, but also named angels, both good and bad. When the angel Raphael visits Tobit, he states that he is one of the seven angels who serve before God (12:15). This likely assumes traditions such as 1 Enoch 20, where seven archangels are listed: Michael, Raphael, Gabriel, Uriel, Saraqael, Raguel, and Remiel. Other Jewish literature features Michael (Daniel 10 and 12, *Testament of Abraham*), and Gabriel is encountered in Luke 1:19. The eschatological conflict between good and evil forces, or God's angels and the fallen angels, is encountered in 2 Esdras and 1 Enoch. Ben Sira 15:15–17 may perhaps respond to this by reemphasizing a this-worldly responsibility: the law protects one from sin (21:11).[5]

A developing political philosophy can also be found in some of the Apocryphal texts, a Jewish response to the rule of the Seleucids to the north of Judea and the Ptolemies in Egypt. The world of Hellenism can be perceived in many of the texts, but the attitude expressed was not a simple choice between resistance and assimilation. The Jewish court narratives, such as Esther and Daniel, tell the story of the negotiation of the faithful Jew under foreign kings. These stories register a pronounced threat from foreign courtiers, while retaining a surprising tone of loyalty to the foreign kings. This creates a narrative world in which Jews can be good citizens under foreign kings, even though they will face competition with and even persecution from those at their same social level. The books of 2 and 3 Maccabees also express the need for resistance to oppression, while finally remaining hopeful about coexistence in the Greek world. Wisdom of Solomon affirms a sort of Jewish philosophical superiority but uses the language of the Greek intellectual tradition. As an example of the more positive view, we also witness in some texts what may be termed colonial universalism: the affirmation by the colonized group that, far from being barbarians, they actually embody a higher form of philosophical universalism than the colonizers. These texts, then, communicate a sense of engaged and even confident, but ambivalent, negotiation with Hellenism.[6] On the other hand, the apocalyptically oriented texts—4 Ezra, 1 Enoch, Jubilees, and 2 Baruch—exhibit much stronger negative reactions: there is little hope for the foreign rulers.

The texts of the Apocrypha also expanded upon a fascinating literary theme begun in earlier texts. Israelite literature had already shown an unusual interest in an understated, even passive protagonist: Joseph (Genesis 37–50), Ezra, and the mysterious Suffering Servant of Isaiah 52–53. In the Apocrypha we find examples where a passive protagonist models behavior, and we are given insights into people's inner emotions and the dramas of everyday Jews as opposed to kings and patriarchs. This is especially noteworthy in the novellas, where we have access to the inner emotions of more passive protagonists, such as Esther (more so in Greek than in Hebrew Esther), Susanna, Achior (but not Judith!) in Judith, and Sarah in Tobit. This same interest is revealed in thoughts of the "righteous one" in Wisdom of Solomon 2–5, the expressions of anxiety by the male head-of-household in Ben Sira, and the psychological approach to virtue in 4 Maccabees. This examination of inner emotions, a psychological interest that is almost modern, is related to the rise of a new kind of moral agent: not a larger-than-life hero, but an everyday protagonist whose main achievement is simply remaining faithful to God.[7] The protagonist could be male or female, and the texts were likely aimed at both male and female Jews.

The very word that is usually translated "Jew"—*Yehudi* in Hebrew or *Ioudaios* in Greek—receives new treatment during this period, reflecting a more explicit emphasis on "Jewish" identity. The term *Yehudi/Ioudaios* (and the Aramaic and feminine forms) is surprisingly rare in Jewish texts before the turn of the Common Era. This observation has provoked an energetic scholarly debate: How can we speak of "Jewish identity" before the word "Jew" appears, and further, did *Yehudi/Ioudaios* really mean "Jew," or simply "Judean," that is, one from Judea? The texts of the Apocrypha provide material for this debate. While it is true that the terms *Yehudi* and *Ioudaios* are rare before the turn of the era, they do occur in significant ways in the Jewish novellas. Both Hebrew Esther and Greek Esther use *Yehudi/Ioudaios* often. Judith's name is the feminine form of Judah and means "Jewish woman." In Bel and the Dragon, the Babylonian courtiers deride the king by exclaiming, "The king has become a Jew!" Two novelistic Jewish stories from Qumran, *Prayer of Nabonidus* and *Tales of the Persian Court*, both identify the protagonists using forms of *Yehudi*. At this same time,

2 Maccabees invents two terms that provide a way of thinking about what *Ioudaios* means: "Judaism" (*Ioudaismos*) and "Hellenism" (*Hellēnismos*). So although *Yehudi* and related terms were not common, they were enlisted as strong identity terms in these texts, almost rallying cries for a new identity of the colonized, indigenous members of Israel. The archaeological evidence from this period corroborates the sense that the Apocrypha and other Jewish texts were exploring a new emphasis on everyday morality. The archaeologist Andrea Berlin tracks changes at this time in regard to everyday aspects of Jewish life that provide evidence of what she calls "household Judaism": *mikvaot* or ritual bathing pools, the new synagogues that provided a means of individual piety away from the temple, the simple "Herodian lamps" that replaced ornate Greek lamps, hewn stone vessels that were assumed not to be susceptible to impurity.[8] This archaeological evidence corroborates the evidence from our texts. Many Jews, living in the expansive Hellenistic and Roman empires, began to define a clearer sense of Jewish identity—the colonized negotiating a new, assertive identity.

These themes, then, can be found in many of the texts of the Apocrypha, but they are not consistently distributed over all of them. And as we have seen, there is not one set of extra texts beyond the Jewish canon, but many different sets. From the beginning, "Apocrypha" has been a boundary category, and the set of the texts at issue has expanded and contracted. Yet this boundary nature of the Apocrypha has sparked interest as well. The different authority that the texts have had forces the modern reader to consider them from divergent perspectives. If different religious traditions grant authority to a Bible as a sort of constitution, the extra texts then indicate a shadow zone where the constitution is negotiated or expanded. As the world witnesses more global movements of peoples and interactions, the extra texts will be debated anew.

Notes

Introduction

1. Harrington, *Invitation to the Apocrypha*. In general, see also Siegert, *Einleitung in die hellenistisch-jüdische Literatur;* and Hengel, *Septuagint as Christian Scripture*.

2. Harrington, *Invitation to the Apocrypha*, 5; see also 1–8; deSilva, *Introducing the Apocrypha*, 1–14.

3. The term pseudepigrapha can also be misleading; see Annette Yoshiko Reed, "The Modern Invention of 'Old Testament Pseudepigrapha,'" *JTS* 60 (2009): 403–36. The term will appear in this book but always as a term used in the past that should also be questioned.

4. Klawans and Wills, eds., *Jewish Annotated Apocrypha*.

5. Reed, "Canon," in Klawans and Wills, eds., *Jewish Annotated Apocrypha*, 570–74, at 570. In the same volume see also Eva Mroczek, "The Incredible Expanding Bible: From the Dead Sea Scrolls to Haile Selassie," 614–20.

6. Rajak, *Translation and Survival*, 216. Michael L. Satlow, *How the Bible Became Holy*, 3, argues even more strongly that the biblical books had "only very limited and specific kinds of authority" until the third century CE. Others, however, see a growing authority for some texts at a much earlier date. We will also have occasion to ask whether it was the historical memory and the reverence of heroes that was authoritative rather than the texts themselves.

7. Barton, "The Old Testament Canons," in Paget and Schaper, eds., *New Cambridge History of the Bible*, 145–64, at 147.

8. Figures for the churches vary, but see the data for member churches at the World Council of Churches website, https://www.oikoumene.org/en/member-churches.

9. *Global Bible Commentary*, ed. Daniel Patte et al. (Nashville: Abingdon, 2004).

10. Pentiuc, *Old Testament in Eastern Orthodox Theology*, 132.

11. Rajak, "The Hasmoneans and the Uses of Hellenism," in *The Jewish Dialogue with Greece and Rome: Studies in Cultural and Social Interaction,* ed. Rajak (Leiden: Brill, 2001), 61–80, at 67; see also Seth Schwartz, "The Hellenization

of Jerusalem and Shechem," in *Jews in a Graeco-Roman World,* ed. Martin
Goodman (Oxford: Clarendon, 1998), 37–46.

12. Honigman, *Septuagint and Homeric Scholarship,* 41; see also Wright, *Letter of
Aristeas;* Wasserstein and Wasserstein, *Legend of the Septuagint;* and Klawans,
"Identities Masked: Sagacity, Sophistry and Pseudepigraphy in *Aristeas,*" *JAJ*
10 (2020): 395–415.

13. Rajak, *Translation and Survival,* 7–8, 313. See also the introduction to NETS.

14. Rahlfs, ed., *Septuaginta.* Seventy is an important number in Jewish tradition,
for instance, seventy elders in Exod 24:1–7, Num 11:24–30, and Ezra 8. In Luke
10 Jesus sends out seventy disciples, and in rabbinic tradition God thundered
in seventy languages at Sinai so that all would understand (*Midrash Rabba* 5.9
on Exod 4:27; Philo, *On the Decalogue* 46–47).

15. Hanhart, "Introduction: Problems in the History of the LXX Text from Its
Beginnings to Origen," in Hengel, *Septuagint as Christian Scripture,* 1–18. See
also de Lange, *Japheth.* Satlow, *How the Bible,* 153–70, takes a rather opposite
view: this intellectual, scribal activity may have been limited to the library at
Alexandria and to a few elite Jewish intellectuals like Philo. There is now a
large body of scholarship on the Septuagint that sheds important light on the
Apocrypha; as an entry point, see NETS and Aitken, ed., *T&T Clark Companion to the Septuagint.*

16. Jonathan Conant, "Memories of Trauma and the Formation of an Early Christian Identity," in *Memories of Utopia: The Revision of Histories and Landscapes
in Late Antiquity,* ed. Bronwen Neil and Kosta Simic (New York: Routledge,
2019), 36–55.

17. See Mroczek, "Incredible Expanding Bible."

18. Beckwith, *Old Testament Canon,* 401–5, and deSilva, *Introducing the Apocrypha,* 15, argue that Jude is merely quoting an important text, not a canonical
one, but see Philip R. Davies, *Scribes and Schools: The Canonization of the
Hebrew Scriptures* (Louisville: Westminster John Knox, 1998), 164–65, and
Lee Martin McDonald, *The Biblical Canon* (Grand Rapids, MI: Baker Academic, 2007), 106. For other possible allusions to Apocrypha, cf. also Rom
9:20–23 and Wis 12:12, 20; 2 Cor 5:1, 4 and Wis 9:15; and James 1:13, 19 and Sir
15:11–12 and 5:11. See deSilva, *Introducing the Apocrypha,* 22–23, for a stronger
argument of influence on the New Testament.

19. Rufinus, *Exposition of the Creed* 30; see Gallager, "Writings Labeled 'Apocrypha.'"

20. Origen, *Commentary on Matthew* 10.18, 13.57; *Prologue to Song of Songs.* For
Melito, see Eusebius, *Ecclesiastical History* 4.26.7. According to Robert Han-
hart, *Text und Textgeschichte des Buches Judith* (Mitteilungen des Septuaginta-
Unternehmens 14; Göttingen: Vandenhoeck & Ruprecht, 1979), 16, Origen

cites Judith as scripture, even though it is not present in his canon list (as recorded by Eusebius, *Ecclesiastical History* 6.25.2).

21. Cf. Cyril of Jerusalem, *Catechetical Lectures* 4.33–36; Athanasius, *Festal Letter* 39, and see Pentiuc, *Old Testament,* 346 n. 60, and Irenaeus, *Against Heresies* 1.20.1. See Collins, "The Apocryphal/Deuterocanonical Books: A Catholic View," in Kohlenberger, ed., *Parallel Apocrypha,* xxxi–xxxvii, at xxxi.

22. Tertullian, *On Women's Dress* 1.3; Augustine, *On Christian Doctrine* 2.8.12–13; Augustine, like many theologians, believed that the main Greek translation was sacred (*City of God* 18.43, *On Christian Doctrine* 2.22; *Epistle* 28).

23. Vincent T. M. Skemp, *The Vulgate of Tobit Compared with Other Ancient Witnesses,* SBLDS (Atlanta: Society of Biblical Literature, 2000), 17; Edwin Voigt, *The Latin Versions of Judith* (Leipzig: Drugulin, 1925), 46; Johann Gamberoni, *Die Auslegung des Buches Tobias in der griechisch-lateinischen Kirche der Antike und der Christenheit des Westens bis zum 1600* (Munich: Kösel, 1969), 78; and Gallager, "Writings Labeled 'Apocrypha.'"

24. Collins, "Apocryphal/Deuterocanonical Books," xxxi. See also Collins, "Penumbra of the Canon."

25. Charles C. Torrey, "A New Era in the History of the 'Apocrypha,'" *Monist* 25 (1915): 286–94, at 287.

26. Karin Schöpflin, "Susanna's Career in Reformation Drama: A Reception Historical Perspective with an Outlook on Fine Art," in Xeravits and Zsengellér, eds., *Deuterocanonical Additions,* 143–70, at 152.

27. Collins, "Apocryphal/Deuterocanonical Books," xxxiii.

28. Demetrios J. Constantelos, "The Apocryphal/Deuterocanonical Books: An Orthodox View," in Kohlenberger, ed., *Parallel Apocrypha,* xxvii–xxx, at xxviii.

29. DeSilva, *Introducing the Apocrypha,* 14–31.

30. Letter of Jeremiah was included as part of Baruch, and the Additions to Esther and Daniel with those books.

31. The order is not the same as that of the Catholic Bible; texts are arranged in historical order. As in the case of the Ethiopian canon, there are versions of the Syriac Bible that contain other texts, for instance, Odes of Solomon and Psalms of Solomon together; see Naomi Koltun-Fromm, "The Peshitta and the Syriac Biblical Context," in Klawans and Wills, eds., *Jewish Annotated Apocrypha,* 588–92. See also Gallager and Meade, *Biblical Canon Lists.*

32. On a broader and a narrower Ethiopian Orthodox canon, see Cowley, "Biblical Canon of the Ethiopian Orthodox Church," and Mroczek, "Incredible Expanding Bible."

33. Dönitz, "Sefer Yosippon and the Greek Bible," 233. On the continuing Jewish use of texts from the Greek Bible, see de Lange, *Japheth.*

Chapter 1. Novellas

1. J. T. Milik, "Les modèles araméens du livre d'Esther dans la grotte 4 de Qumrân," *RQ* 59 (1992): 321–406, at 363–65.
2. Cicero, *On Invention* 1.19.27; Pseudo-Cicero, *To Herrennius* 1.8.12–13; Quintilian 2.4.2. See David Konstan, "The Invention of Fiction," in *Ancient Fiction and Early Christian Narrative*, ed. Ronald F. Hock, J. Bradley Chance, and Judith Perkins (Atlanta: Scholars, 1998), 3–18.
3. Wills, *Jew in the Court;* Tawny L. Holm, *Of Courtiers and Kings: The Biblical Daniel Narratives and Ancient Story-Collections* (Winona Lake, IN: Eisenbrauns, 2013), 45–183; Stephanie Dalley, "Assyrian Court Narratives in Aramaic and Egyptian: Historical Fiction," in *Proceedings of the XLVe recontre assyriologique internationale, 1: Historiography in the Cuneiform World,* ed. T. Abusch et al. (Bethesda, MD: CDL, 2001), 149–62; Dalley, "Semiramis in History and Legend," in *Cultural Borrowings and Ethnic Appropriations in Antiquity,* ed. Erich Gruen (Stuttgart: Steiner Franz, 2005), 11–22.
4. Nickelsburg, "The Genre and Function of the Markan Passion Narrative," and Wills, "Response," in *George W. E. Nickelsburg in Perspective: An Ongoing Dialogue of Learning,* ed. Jacob Neusner and Alan J. Avery-Peck (Leiden: Brill, 2003), 473–503 and 504–12.
5. Corinne Jouanno, "Novelistic Lives and Historical Biographies: The *Life of Aesop* and the *Alexander Romance* as Fringe Novels," in *Fiction on the Fringe: Novelistic Writing in the Post-Classical Age,* ed. Grammatiki Karla (Leiden: Brill, 2009), 42–46; T. P. Wiseman and Christopher Gill, eds., *Lies and Fiction in the Ancient World* (Exeter: University of Exeter Press, 1993); Niklas Holzberg, "Genre: Novels Proper and the Fringe," in *Novel in the Ancient World,* ed. Gareth Schmeling (rev. ed.; Boston: Brill, 2003), 11–28; J. R. Morgan and Richard Stoneman, eds., *Greek Fiction: The Greek Novel in Context* (London: Routledge, 1994); Susan A. Stephens and John J. Winkler, eds., *Ancient Greek Novels: The Fragments* (Princeton: Princeton University Press, 1995).
6. William F. Hansen, *Anthology of Ancient Greek Popular Literature* (Bloomington: Indiana University Press, 1998), xx–xxi.
7. Van Gennep, *The Rites of Passage* (Chicago: University of Chicago Press, 1960); see also Victor Turner, "Betwixt and Between: The Liminal Period in *Rites de passage,*" in *Forest of Symbols: Aspects of Ndembu Ritual* (Ithaca: Cornell University Press, 1967), 93–111. Saul M. Olyan, *Biblical Mourning: Ritual and Social Dimensions* (Oxford: Oxford University Press, 2004), 18, notes that a common part of the mourning ritual, or the petitionary mourning ritual, involves undressing and redressing (cf. 2 Sam 12:16–23). This is indeed related,

but the woman's scene in the novellas is a "novelized," applied case. The signs of mourning are marked carefully: the type of clothes, how she takes off the clothes and puts on mourning garments, the meaning of the "mourning" phase and what happens in it, the type of clothes she puts on, and finally, the change in the agent and her acceptance of mission.

8. Cohen, *Beginnings of Jewishness;* Wills, "Jew, Judean, Judaism"; Cynthia M. Baker, *Jew* (New Brunswick, NJ: Rutgers University Press, 2017), and the literature cited there.

9. Crawford, "Additions to Esther," 3.945–46.

10. Bickerman, "Colophon," 346–47. The options for dating are discussed by Bickerman, and see Moore, *Daniel, Esther, and Jeremiah,* 250; Crawford, "Additions to Esther," 3.970–71.

11. Clines, *Esther Scroll, passim.* For an interesting exploration of how the priority of Gk A illuminates one motif, see Halvorson-Taylor, "Secrets and Lies." In addition, the Old Latin version was also somewhat different from the Greek texts; see Simon Bellmann, "The Theological Character of the Old Latin Version of Esther," *JSP* 27 (2017): 3–24.

12. Fox, *Character and Ideology,* 145; Boyd-Taylor, "Esther's Great Adventure," 113. On the possible Greek influences, see Wills, *Jewish Novel,* 93–131; Sara Raup Johnson, "Novelistic Elements," 588–89.

13. Maxine Grossman, "Expanded (Greek) Esther," in Klawans and Wills, eds., *Jewish Annotated Apocrypha,* 125–47, at 138, notes that "menstrual rag" as a symbol of disgust also occurs in Ezek 7:19–20, and Lam 1:17, although in the biblical laws (Leviticus 15) menstruation is treated very matter-of-factly. Note that Judith 8–10 is a contemporaneous reference to a woman's bathing ritual that may be related. On the gendering of the prayers, see Schorch, "Genderising Piety"; and Menn, "Prayer of the Queen," 76. Cf. also Heliodorus 8.9, Chariton 2.11.

14. Menn, "Prayer of the Queen." True, the notion of sex with the king is condemned in Esther's prayer, but that likely reflects a different author from the narrative of her audience before the king; see also Day, *Three Faces of a Queen,* 214–21; LaCocque, *Feminine Unconventional: Four Subversive Figures in Israel's Tradition* (Eugene, OR: Wipf and Stock, 2005), 73. Crawford, "Additions to Esther," 962, and Stone, *Empire and Gender,* 37–38, 231–32, both assume that Esther is *acting* a role to negotiate a new power relation within the empire. Yet this seems unlikely: she faints twice (15:7, 15), and it is God who alters the king's disposition (15:8). But different voices may be detected in the various layers of the Greek versions. Boyd-Taylor, "Esther's Great Adventure," argues that where Greek Esther 2:7 says that Mordecai raised up Esther

in his house, it is to become his wife—a "romance" motif. The similarity in Hebrew of *bat,* daughter, and *bayit,* house, caused this question to be explored in rabbinic sources as well (*b. Megillah* 13a). Yet this connection is not stated in Esther, and there is none of the attraction or lovesickness between Mordecai and Esther that is typical of the Greek novels.

15. The translation is from Susan A. Stephens and John J. Winkler, eds., *Ancient Greek Novels: The Fragments* (Princeton: Princeton University Press, 1995), 41–42.

16. David Konstan, *Sexual Symmetry: Love in the Ancient Novel and Related Genres* (Princeton: Princeton University Press, 1994); Rachel Adelman, *The Female Ruse: Women's Deception and Divine Sanction in the Hebrew Bible* (Sheffield: Sheffield Phoenix Press, 2017), 198–230; T. M. Lemos, "'They Have Become Women:' Judean Diaspora and Postcolonial Theories of Gender and Migration," in *Interpreting Exile: Displacement and Deportation in Biblical and Modern Contexts,* ed. Brad E. Kelle et al. (Atlanta: Society of Biblical Literature, 2011), 377–93; Day, *Three Faces of a Queen;* cf. also Wisdom of Solomon 2–5.

17. Literally, "brother." Cf. Tobit where "brother" and "sister" are used for spouses and marriageable kin. It evidently arises from the preferred Jewish marriage within the *mishpachah,* clan or extended family.

18. Randall L. Bytwerk, *Landmark Speeches of National Socialism* (College Station: Texas A&M University Press, 2008), 91.

19. Boyd-Taylor, "Esther and Additions to Esther," in Aitken, ed., *T&T Clark Companion,* 203–21, at 215.

20. Boyd-Taylor, "Esther and Additions to Esther," 219. Josephus includes echoes of Esther's and Mordecai's prayers from Addition C (*Antiquities* 11.239–53). See also Carruthers, *Esther through the Centuries.*

21. "Yahweh is good" is a common biblical refrain: Nah 1:7, Jer 33:11, Pss 100:5, 106:1. Richard Bauckham, "Tobit as a Parable for the Exiles of Northern Israel," in Bredin, ed., *Studies in the Book of Tobit,* 140–64, at 150–51, notes that Tobi, a shortened form of Tobiyah, is found in Aramaic and Hebrew fragments from Qumran. Note also that in our story a son bears the name of a living father, unlikely in this period. Otzen, *Tobit and Judith,* 47, points out that Raphael in 1 En. 10.4 also has a healing role, as his name implies. On translation issues in general in Tobit, see Alexander A. Di Lella, "Tobit," NETS, 456–57.

22. Nickelsburg, *Jewish Literature,* 31–32; see also Novick, "Biblicized Narrative"; Machiela and Perrin, "Tobit and the *Genesis Apocryphon.*"

23. Vladimir Propp, *Morphology of the Folktale* (Austin: University of Texas Press, 1968), 79–83. On the similarity of Tobit to the Grateful Dead story, see Otzen, *Tobit and Judith,* 8–14; Wills, *Jewish Novel,* 68–92; Gordon Hall Gerould,

The Grateful Dead: History of a Folk Story (Urbana: University of Illinois Press, 2000), 47–75. Some folktale motifs from Tobit also appear in rabbinic sources; so Noah Bickart and Christine Hayes, "The Apocrypha in Rabbinic Literature," in Klawans and Wills, eds., *Jewish Annotated Apocrypha*, 593–97, at 596.

24. Simkovich, *Making of Jewish Universalism*, 70–80.

25. Collins, "The Judaism of the Book of Tobit," in Xeravits and Zsengellér, eds., *Book of Tobit*, 23–40, at 29; see also 26–27, 40; Zsengellér, "Topography as Theology: Theological Premises of the Geographical References in the Book of Tobit," in Xeravits and Zsengellér, eds., *Book of Tobit*, 179–86. Nineveh and Media are important in arc two, Jerusalem and Israel in arcs one and three. Naomi S. Jacobs, "'You Did Not Hesitate to Get Up and Leave the Dinner': Food and Eating in the Narrative of Tobit with Some Attention to Tobit's Shavuot Meal," in Xeravits and Zsengellér, eds., *Book of Tobit*, 121–32, finds a comic fixation with food in Tobit, alluded to thirty-one times, but all in the second arc. See also her *Delicious Prose*. Hicks-Keeton, "Already/Not Yet," provides a possible explanation for the discrepancy between the prophetic predictions in the last section of Tobit and the book as a whole: the author of Tobit suggests that a tension remains between the predictions and their non-fulfillment. However, the distance in tone between the great middle section of the book and the prophetic ending is still significant.

26. Van der Toorn, *Scribal Culture and the Making of the Hebrew Bible* (Cambridge, MA: Harvard University Press, 2007), 23.

27. It is noticeable, however, that although they do appear in the proverbs, these three virtues from arcs one and three are not the same as the angel Raphael's three virtuous practices at 12:6–10: prayer, fasting, almsgiving with righteousness. The latter likely represent the ethical emphasis of a separate arc two.

28. On the integrity of the three arcs, see Moore, *Tobit*, 21–22; Nickelsburg, "Search for Tobit's Mixed Ancestry," 342; Fitzmyer, *Tobit*, 42–46; and Soll, "Tobit and Folklore Studies." The chiastic structure is presented in Engel, "Auf zuverlässigen Wegen," 89–92; and Engel, "Das Buch Tobit" (slightly modified). See also Ego, *Das Buch Tobit*, 892–93. Deselaers, *Das Buch Tobit*, and Rabenau, *Studien zum Buch Tobit*, both find insertions and supplementation throughout the book but do not treat the three arcs separately and do not imagine a fairy-tale-to-novella evolution.

29. On genre, see the discussion in Deselaers, *Das Buch Tobit*, 262–79, and his conclusion of *romanhafte Lehrerzählung*, 278; Ego, "Das Buch Tobit," 884: *weisheitliche Lehrerählung*. See also "short Jewish romance," Moore, *Tobit*, 21, and Wills, *Jewish Novel*, 68–92.

30. Otzen, *Tobit and Judith*, 2. Through a detailed consideration of fairy tale parallels, Otzen posits a more detailed folktale source than is warranted; still, he raises interesting suggestions. The dog that accompanies Tobias and Raphael may derive from a Persian folktale and is an opponent of demons. MacDonald, "Tobit and the *Odyssey*," suggests, however, that the source may be found in the two dogs that accompany Telemachus in *Odyssey* 2.10–11. The mysterious dog may also enter as the companion of the angel; so Naomi Jacobs, "Tobit," in Klawans and Wills, eds., *Jewish Annotated Apocrypha*, 149–75, at 163.

31. Collins, "Judaism of the Book of Tobit," 40.

32. Genette, *Palimpsests: Literature in the Second Degree* (Lincoln: University of Nebraska Press, 1997). The term "refictionalize" is from Gerhardus van den Heever, "Novel and Mystery: Discourse, Myth, and Society," in Brant, Hedrick, and Shea, eds., *Ancient Fiction*, 85–94, at 91.

33. Deselaer, *Das Buch Tobit*, 292–302. Nickelsburg, "Search for Tobit's Mixed Ancestry," 341: Tobit is similar to Abraham in that they both send a son to secure an endogamous marriage, and a principal character is named Sarah. Raphael is also similar to Abraham's servant who accompanies Isaac. More contemporaneous to Tobit, Jub. 23:13–18 recounts the scene of Isaac comforting Rebekah while Jacob is away, using language almost identical to Tobit's words to Anna; see Jacobs, "Tobit." Some scholars who grant these biblical influences also find broad parallels in folklore and Greek culture. As in *Antigone*, for instance, the universal humane goal to bury the dead supersedes human laws, and as in both the *Odyssey* and the somewhat later Greek novels, the theme of travel and marriage dominates; so Cynthia Baker, "Jewish Identity," in Klawans and Wills, eds., *Jewish Annotated Apocrypha*, 649–53, at 651; Nickelsburg, "Search for Tobit's Mixed Ancestry."

34. Weitzman, "Allusion, Artifice, and Exile," 59; Weitzman, *Song and Story*, 67–68: Tobit's hymn is similar to the Song of Moses. See also Anderson, "Does Tobit Fear God?," 115: "Tobit . . . was a type of the elected nation"; "the divine testing of Tobit" is parallel to that of Job.

35. Soll, "Tobit and Folklore," 216. Soll's use of Propp's methods would seem to argue against his conclusions: the elements of the first arc do not give rise to responses or resolutions in the large middle arc. Rather, new issues are introduced in the second arc, and resolved there, with very little relation to the first arc. The same is true for the transition from the second to the third arc. Otzen, *Tobit and Judith*, 45, finds the eschatological vision of arc three a tremendous addition theologically, which also suggests a different author; without it, says Otzen, Tobit is merely "an innocent tale."

36. Jensen, "Family, Fertility and Foul Smell: Tobit and Judith," in Bredin, ed.,

Studies, 129–39, at 130–31; the following quotation is from p. 132. In the case of Judith as well, does the theology merely protect the story from censure? Similar questions may be asked about other biblical theological themes in Tobit. Otzen, *Tobit and Judith,* 27, finds that providence recalls the law of Moses, seen in *euodoō* and *hodos,* told through romanticizing relationships, the stuff of the novella, as at 5:17. But is this a theological emphasis or simply narrative coloring?

37. Weeks, "A Deuteronomic Heritage in Tobit?," in *Changes in Scripture: Rewriting and Interpreting Authoritative Traditions in the Second Temple Period,* ed. Hanne von Weissenberg, Juha Pakkala, and Marko Marttila (Berlin: de Gruyter, 2011), 389–404, at 403–4. The Deuteronomic interpretation had been largely assumed since Di Lella, "Deuteronomic Background." Weeks provocatively but helpfully wonders (395–96) whether Weitzman is adumbrating a clear *Deuteronomic* theology in Tobit or simply perceiving some vague Deuteronomic-like notions among the *literary* connections. See also Kiel, *"Whole Truth."*

38. Weeks, "Deuteronomic Heritage," 395.

39. Otzen, *Tobit and Judith,* 18, 51–52.

40. The interesting exception is Cousland, "Tobit," who argues that what we perceive as problematic or humorous would not have been perceived in that way by the original audience. For instance, while modern readers may perceive Tobit's anger at his wife Anna for taking in domestic work as exceptionally rigid, in an ancient context this may have resonated as an *appropriate* reaction to her shaming of Tobit by taking in work. Ben Sira 25:22 says, "There is wrath and impudence and great disgrace when a wife supports her husband." Equally, we may read the fact that Sarah is rebuked by her slaves as part of her suffering, but it is also shameful to be rebuked by slaves. Still, few scholars have been won over by Cousland's argument.

41. Nowell, "Book of Tobit," 983–87; Nowell, "The Book of Tobit: An Ancestral Story." Scholars who propose an earnest comic interpretation also include Anderson, "Does Tobit Fear God?"; and Bow and Nickelsburg, "Patriarchy with a Twist," 128–30.

42. Gruen, *Diaspora,* 157–58: "The humor that enlivens the narrative also modifies, compromises, and gently subverts the nobler messages." Although Gruen (319 n. 87) dismisses the possibility that the third arc has been added, his satirical interpretation of the whole would seem to require this conclusion: there is nothing funny in the first and third arcs. Gruen also posits a self-righteous Tobit in the first arc, but it is not at all clear that it is satirical; it is more the typical self-presentation of the royal autobiographical tradition that is visible

in much rhetoric, even in Nehemiah or Paul. And when Gruen argues that Tobit does not reflect a defensive posture toward gentiles, he is correct in regard to most of Tobit, but not in regard to the third arc. Portier-Young, "Alleviation of Suffering," 41, agrees with Gruen that the story pokes fun at Tobit's character: "the greatest single cause of Tobit's suffering is his inability correctly to perceive and appreciate the extent of his connectedness in this human community." In *Jewish Novels,* 68–92, I argued for a more satirical interpretation, but as will become clear, I now leave open the possibility of a multilevel audience response. The interpretation here may also find some agreement in the article by Schellenberg, "Suspense, Simultaneity, and Divine Providence."

43. See Jacobs, "'You Did Not Hesitate'"; Levine, "Diaspora as Metaphor"; and Wills, *Jewish Novel,* 68–92. On the general Jewish preference for marriage within the extended family, cf. Philo, *Spec. leg.* 3.125–36, and see Michael L. Satlow, *Jewish Marriage in Antiquity* (Princeton: Princeton University Press, 2018), esp. 58–61, 111–16, 133–61, 173–80.

44. Moore, *Tobit,* 130. On family terms, see Rabenau, *Studien,* 122, 175–82.

45. This is in contrast to what I argued in *Jewish Novel,* 81.

46. Bolyki, "Burial as an Ethical Task in the Book of Tobit, in the Bible and in the Greek Tragedies," in Xeravits and Zsengellér, eds., *Book of Tobit,* 89–98. Tobit's endorsement of provisioning the dead (4:17) has surprised some, considering the condemnation of this practice in Deut 26:14, Ps 106:28, and esp. Sir 30:18, yet it was considered a positive practice by some in the care for patriarchal burial sites (and see Amos 6:10; Jer 16:5; Isa 57:6, 65:4; Ps 16:3–4). On family memory as a kind of "immortality," see Jon D. Levenson and Kevin J. Madigan, *Resurrection: The Power of God for Christians and Jews* (New Haven: Yale University Press, 2008), 107–20.

47. Soll, "Family," 171. Macatangay, *When I Die,* 74, rightly gathers all of these issues of family, marriage, burial, and inheritance but treats them as positive affirmations rather than as humorous or satirical explorations, and argues that the fact that the story is set in northern Israel still rules the geographical hopes of the author: there is a hope of gathering the exiles back to the south. However, the values of the second arc are probably those of the wealthy patron class in a more international setting, but see also Dimant, "Tobit in Galilee."

48. Jozef T. Milik, "La patrie de Tobie," *RB* 73 (1966): 522–30.

49. C. C. Ji, "A New Look at the Tobiads in 'Iraq al-Amir," *Liber Annuus* 48 (1998): 417–40; B. Mazar, "The Tobiads," *Israel Exploration Journal* 7 (1957): 137–45, 229–38.

50. When the earliest version of Tobit (Sinaiticus) is compared with the later ones (Vaticanus/Alexandrinus/Venetus/Vulgate), it is observed that the love match,

marriage within family, and inheritance issues are tempered; so Tobias Nicklas, "Marriage in the Book of Tobit: A Synoptic Approach," in Xeravits and Zsengellér, eds., *Book of Tobit*, 139–54; Geoffrey David Miller, *Marriage in the Book of Tobit* (Berlin: de Gruyter, 2011).

51. Moore, *Tobit*, 42–43; Fitzmyer, *Tobit*, 54.

52. Bauckham, "Tobit as a Parable," 154; see also Milik, "La patrie de Tobie." More in agreement with the position advocated here are József Zsengellér, "Topography as Theology: Theological Premises of the Geographical References in the Book of Tobit," in Xeravits and Zsengellér, eds., *Book of Tobit*, 177–88, and Collins, "Judaism of the Book of Tobit," 26–28, who questions whether exile is really a "problem" in arc two rather than a story setting.

53. Dimant, "Tobit in Galilee"; see also Machiela and Perrin, "Tobit and the *Genesis Apocryphon.*" In response, it should be noted that it is entirely possible that the core of Tobit originated in the east within the extended Tobiad family, and part—perhaps the last part—was added in the same context of the other Qumran texts.

54. Bickart and Hayes, "Apocrypha in Rabbinic Literature," 596.

55. Shalom Goldman, "Tobit and the Jewish Literary Tradition," in Bredin, ed., *Studies*, 90–97; Weeks, Gathercole, and Stuckenbruck, eds., *Book of Tobit*; Loren T. Stuckenbruck, "The 'Fagius' Hebrew Version of Tobit: An English Translation of the Constantinople Text of 1519," in Xeravits and Zsengellér, eds., *Book of Tobit*, 189–99.

56. Otzen, *Tobit and Judith*, 40, 65–66. See also Anderson, "Does Tobit Fear God?"; Gary A. Anderson, *Sin: A History* (New Haven: Yale University Press, 2009), 164–88; Anderson, *Charity: The Place of the Poor in Biblical Tradition* (New Haven: Yale University Press, 2013), 15–34, 136–61.

57. Trevor Hart, "Tobit in the Art of the Florentine Renaissance," in Bredin, ed., *Studies*, 72–89; Elizabeth Philpot, *Old Testament Apocryphal Images in European Art* (Göteborg: University of Gothenburg, 2009), 129–76.

58. *Luther's Works*, ed. Jaroslav Pelikan (St. Louis: Concordia, 1955-), 3.345.

59. John Beer, *Coleridge the Visionary* (London: Chatto and Windus, 1959), 116, and on Kierkegaard, see Hugh Pyper, "'Sarah as Hero': Kierkegaard's Reading of Tobit in *Fear and Trembling*," in Bredin, ed., *Studies*, 59–71.

60. Judith is now well served by a number of substantial commentaries; see esp. Moore, *Judith;* Schmitz and Engel, *Judit;* and Gera, *Judith.*

61. Otzen, *Tobit and Judith*, 120–21. This is clearly a reaction to Antiochus IV, but also suggestive of Hasmonean politics is the parallel with Nicanor at 1 Macc 7:26–50 and 2 Macc 15:1–36.

62. Coined by Stocker, *Judith*, 11.

63. Jensen, "Family, Fertility and Foul Smell," 130–31. See also Amy-Jill Levine, "Sacrifice and Salvation: Otherness and Domestication in the Book of Judith," in VanderKam, ed., *"No One Spoke Ill,"* 17–27.
64. Significantly, Judith's words mirror the Greek version as opposed to the Hebrew Bible. This has been taken as evidence that Judith was written in Greek, although the evidence on this is mixed; see Wills, *Judith,* 17–23; Cameron Boyd-Taylor, "Ioudith," in NETS, 441–42.
65. Van Henten, "Judith as Alternative Leader: A Rereading of Judith 7–13," in Brenner, ed., *Feminist Companion,* 224–52. On the biblical traditions, see Dubarle, *Judith;* Haag, *Studien zum Buche Judith,* 118–24; Schmitz, *Gedeutete Geschichte;* Rakel, "'I Will Sing'"; Sidnie Ann White (Crawford), "In the Steps of Jael and Deborah: Judith as Heroine," in VanderKam, ed., *"No One Spoke Ill,"* 5–16; and Stocker, *Judith, passim,* but esp. 150. Judith also bears some similarities to Esther, but these may pertain to genre as much as to any direct dependence of one on the other; see Sidnie Ann Crawford, "Esther and Judith: Contrasts in Character," in *The Book of Esther in Modern Research,* ed. Crawford and Leonard J. Greenspoon (London: Clark, 2003), 60–76.
66. Gera, *Judith,* 39.
67. Gera, *Warrior Women: The Anonymous* Tractatus de mulieribus (Leiden: Brill, 1997). On the Xerxizing of Nebuchadnezzar, see Mark Caponigro, "Judith, Holding the Tale of Herodotus," in VanderKam, ed., *"No One Spoke Ill,"* 47–59.
68. Gera, *Warrior Women;* Weststeijn, "Wine, Women, and Revenge"; Weststeijn, "Zenobia of Palmyra." On the depictions of Seleucid kings, see M. Rahim Shayegan, *Arsacids and Sasanians: Political Ideology in Post-Hellenistic and Late Antique Persia* (Cambridge: Cambridge University Press, 2011), 169–72. On Xerxizing, see Caponigro "Judith, Holding the Tale of Herodotus," in VanderKam, ed., *No One Spoke Ill,* 47–59.
69. I am grateful to Nicole Brown for alerting me to this visual parallel. At Pergamon the giant Agrios is also clubbed to death by a female Fate, one of the Moirai.
70. Cf. only Wis 7:17–18: God taught Solomon knowledge of "the beginning, end, and middle of times"—although in Wisdom of Solomon knowledge *of the cosmos* is meant, not simply history.
71. Otzen, *Tobit and Judith,* 90, 122.
72. Alonso-Schökel, *Narrative Structures;* Craven, *Artistry and Faith.*
73. Jacobus, "Judith, Holofernes." On the wave of feminist studies, see Wills, *Judith,* 50–71; Bal, "Head-Hunting"; and Stocker, *Judith.* See now as the culmination of these interests, Wright and Edwards, "'She Undid Him.'"

74. Craven, *Artistry and Faith*, 60–63.
75. Fusillo, "Modern Critical Theories and the Novel," in *Novel in the Ancient World*, ed. Gareth Schmeling (rev. ed.; Boston: Brill Academic, 2003), 277–305, at 300–301.
76. Alonso-Schökel, *Narrative Structures*, 7.
77. Wills, *Judith*, 107–66; Brine, Ciletti, and Lähnemann, eds. *Sword of Judith*.
78. Paul Stenhouse, "Further Reflections on the Falasha," in *Between Africa and Zion: Proceedings of the First International Congress of the Society for the Study of Ethiopian Jewry*, ed. Steven Kaplan et al. (Venice: University of Venice; Jerusalem: Ben-Zvi Institute, 1995), 94–102; Martha Himmelfarb, "The Apocrypha in Medieval Hebrew Literature," in Klawans and Wills, eds., *Jewish Annotated Apocrypha*, 598–602, at 599, 601.
79. Wills, *Judith*, 50–71.
80. Modern English translations of the Apocrypha are based on the Th version, but English translations of both the OG and Th versions of Susanna and Bel can be found in *APOT*, NETS, and Collins, *Daniel*, 435–45. See also Steussy, *Gardens in Babylon;* DiTommaso, *Book of Daniel;* Wills, *Jew in the Court*, 75–152; and Wills, *Jewish Novel*, 76–77
81. DiTommaso, "4QPseudo-Daniel a–b (4Q243–4Q244) and the Book of Daniel," *DSD* 12 (2005): 101–33, at 105 n. 17.
82. See Stith Thompson, *Motif-Index of Folk Literature: A Classification of Narrative Elements in Folktales, Ballads, Myths, Mediaeval Romances, Exempla, Fabiaux, Jest Books and Local Legends* (6 vols.; Bloomington: Indiana University Press, 1966), at K2112; and Thompson and Antti Aarne, *The Types of the Folktale: A Classification and Bibliography* (2nd ed.; Helsinki: Suomalainen Tiedeakatemia, 1987), at Type 883A, Innocent slandered maiden. Note, however, that Thompson, *The Folktale* (Berkeley: University of California Press, 1946), 110, also insists that as it stands Susanna is a literary telling that may have at times reentered oral telling. See also Moore, *Daniel, Esther, and Jeremiah*, 88–89.
83. Lahey, "The Additions to Daniel," in Aitken, ed., *T&T Clark Companion*, 555–66, at 560–62. A parallel, explained on either biblicist or historicist criteria, is Jub. 23:16, where it is said that children will reproach their parents and elders on account of sin.
84. Grillo, "Showing Seeing in Susanna."
85. Steussy, *Gardens in Babylon*, 101–43, esp. 140.
86. Cf. Hos 4:15, Jeremiah 3, Ezekiel 23. See Japhet, *I & II Chronicles: A Commentary* (OTL; Louisville: Westminster John Knox, 1993), 46; Grillo, "'You Will Forget,'" 20–21.

87. Engel, *Die Susanna Erzählung;* Moore, *Daniel, Esther, and Jeremiah,* 90 n. 23; Wills, *Jewish Novels,* 53–60.

88. Though rare in the LXX, *haplotēs* is important at Wis 1:1; 1 Macc 2:37, 60; 1 Clem. 60:2; Barn. 8:2, 17:1; see the discussion at "Wisdom of Solomon," Chapter 3.

89. Lahey, "Additions to Daniel," 557–58. In rabbinic sources examination of witnesses and the problem of false judges is sometimes emphasized (*m. Avot* 1:8–9; *y. Sanh.* 6:3).

90. De Wet, "Reception of the *Susanna,*" 238. On the history of reception in general, see Spolsky, ed., *Judgment of Susanna;* and Clanton, *The Good.* Susanna was sometimes grouped with Noah, Jonah, Daniel and his three friends, and Thecla; see Annewies van den Hoek and John J. Herrmann, Jr., "Celsus' Competing Heroes: Jonah, Daniel, and Their Rivals," in *Poussières de christianisme et de judaïsme antiques: Études réunies en l'honneur de Jean-Daniel Kaestli et Éric Junod,* ed. Albert Frey and Rémi Gounelle (Lausanne: Éditions du Zèbre, 2007), 307–39, at 307–11; van den Hoek and Herrmann, "Thecla the Beast Fighter: A Female Emblem of Deliverance in Early Christian Popular Art," *Studia Philonica Annual* 13 (2001): 212–49; and Robin Jensen, *Understanding Early Christian Art* (London: Routledge, 2000), 25, 69.

91. Amy-Jill Levine, "Susanna," in Klawans and Wills, eds., *Jewish Annotated Apocrypha,* 333–37, at 333; Susanna Drake, *Slandering the Jews: Sexuality and Difference in Early Christian Texts* (Philadelphia: University of Pennsylvania Press, 2013), 59–77.

92. Karin Schöpflin, "Susanna's Career in Reformation Drama: A Reception Historical Perspective with an Outlook on Fine Art," in Xeravits and Zsengellér, eds., *Deuterocanonical Additions,* 143–70, at 143–44. It is significant that Luther was one of the few Christian figures to state that Susanna, Judith, and Tobit were imaginative stories rather than biblical history. Schöpflin, 152, considers Clanton's suggestion that the freedom demonstrated in treating Susanna can be attributed to the fact that her text comes from the Apocrypha, but she rightly disagrees. The three women, Judith, Esther, and Susanna, provided material for multiple characterizations, not primarily because they were from the Apocrypha (Esther was also in the proto-canonical Bible), but because they were "novel women" whose presence could be manipulated in different and even contradictory ways.

93. Robert J. V. Hiebert, "Syriac Bible Textual History," in *The Old Greek Psalter: Studies in Honor of Albert Pietersma,* ed. Robert J. V. Hiebert, Peter J. Gentry, and Claude E. Cox (Sheffield: Sheffield Academic Press, 2001), 178–204, at 194–96.

94. Michael E. Stone, *Armenian Apocrypha Relating to Biblical Heroes* (Atlanta: Society of Biblical Literature, 2019), 209–14.

95. Margaret R. Miles, *Carnal Knowing: Female Nakedness and Religious Meaning in the Christian West* (Boston: Beacon, 1989), 123; Grillo, "Showing Seeing in Susanna"; Glancy, "The Accused"; Bal, "Elders and Susanna."

96. Garrard, "Artemisia and Susanna"; Grillo, *Reception*.

97. Combining prose narrative with poetry was common in ancient Israel though very rare in Greece and Rome; see 1 Samuel 2, 2 Samuel 22, Jonah 2, Judith 16, and Add Esth 14:11–19, and Weitzman, *Song and Story,* esp. 65–67. See also Jennifer Grillo, "'Sages Standing in God's Holy Fire': Prayer as Mnemonic for the Book of Daniel," in Harkins and Schmitz, eds., *Selected Studies,* forthcoming.

98. Van der Horst and Newman, *Early Jewish Prayers,* 186, 190. See also Rodney Alan Werline, *Penitential Prayer in Second Temple Judaism: The Development of a Religious Institution* (Atlanta: Scholars, 1998).

99. Collins, *Daniel,* 198.

100. The song also exhibits patterns similar to those in Ben Sira 43, and from Qumran, *4QBerakhot,* and the Thanksgiving Hymn for the Sabbath in *4QWords of the Luminaries* (4QDibHama 1–2 recto vii 4–9); see Noah Hacham, "Creational Blessings in Second Temple Prayer and Psalmody," in Harkins and Schmitz, eds., *Selected Studies.*

101. Collins, *Daniel,* 198–200; see also David Lambert, "The Prayer of Azariah and the Song of the Three," in Klawans and Wills, eds., *Jewish Annotated Apocrypha,* 327–331, at 327.

102. Van der Horst and Newman, *Early Jewish Prayers,* 180.

103. Grillo, *Reception;* Collins, *Daniel,* 202.

104. Bickart and Hayes, "Apocrypha in Rabbinic Literature," 597; Dönitz, "Sefer Yosippon," 233–34.

105. Montgomery, *A Critical and Exegetical Commentary on the Book of Daniel* (ICC; Edinburgh: T&T Clark, 1927), 270; see also Hartmann and Di Lella, *Daniel,* 21, 197; Wills, *Jew in the Court,* 129–38. See also Collins, *Daniel,* 418.

106. Lahey, "Additions to Daniel," 561. At Jer 51:44 God says, "I will punish Bel in Babylon, and make him disgorge what he has swallowed." On "living God," see Deut 5:26 and Jer 10:10.

107. Bergmann, "Idol Worship in Bel," 209–10; Rajak, *Translation and Survival,* 198–99.

108. Susan Niditch, *Underdogs and Tricksters: A Prelude to Biblical Folklore* (San Francisco: Harper & Row, 1987), 103–4.

109. Dönitz, "Sefer Yosippon," 231–33; Himmelfarb, "Apocrypha in Medieval Hebrew Literature," 600–601.

110. Among the early Western Bibles, this text appears only in Alexandrinus and Venetus; it is not included in Sinaiticus or the Vulgate. It was later included in the Syriac (Peshitta) and Armenian Bibles.

111. Cousland, "Reversal, Recidivism and Reward," 44; see also Hacham, "3 Maccabees"; and Noah Hacham, "3 Maccabees," in Klawans and Wills, eds., *Jewish Annotated Apocrypha*, 289–308.

112. See deSilva, *Introducing the Apocrypha,* 340–44; Alexander and Alexander, "Image of the Oriental Monarch," 92–93; Williams, "3 Maccabees."

113. Croy, *3 Maccabees,* xiv. He responds to the negative view of the style expressed by Hadas, *Third and Fourth Books,* 22. See also Johnson, "Third Maccabees"; Wills, *Jewish Novel,* 201–10; Nickelsburg, *Jewish Literature,* 202; and Gruen, *Heritage and Hellenism,* 234–36.

114. Wright, "Ben Sira," 91 n. 17.

115. Alexander and Alexander, "Image of the Oriental Monarch," 97. Much of the discussion here and in regard to Holofernes in Judith is indebted to this article. See also Wills, *Jewish Novel,* 204, and on Simon II, see Ben Sira 50.

116. Hacham, "3 Maccabees and Esther," 782–84.

117. DeSilva, *Introducing the Apocrypha,* 348; see also 345–51.

118. Johnson, "3 Maccabees," in Aitken, ed., *T&T Clark Companion,* 292–305, at 302; see also Gruen, *Heritage and Hellenism,* 222–36. On dating, see Collins, *Between Athens and Jerusalem,* 124–25; and Alexander and Alexander, "Image of the Oriental Monarch," 92–93. Collins argued for Caligula's reign, but see Johnson, "3 Maccabees," 294–95, and deSilva, *Introducing the Apocrypha,* 338–39, who summarize counterarguments. In addition, 3 Macc 3:18, 5:20, 6:23–28, 7:2 may reflect parallels with Greek Esth 16:3–6, 10–16, but it is not clear in which direction the influence may have run.

Chapter 2. Historical Texts

1. Goodman, with Géza Vermes, "La littérature juive intertestamentaire à la lumière de recherches et de découvertes," in *Études sur le judaïsme hellénistique: Congrès de Strasbourg,* ed. R. Kuntzmann and J. Schlosser (Paris: Cerf, 1984), 19–39, at 37–38.

2. On the ambiguity of "historical novels," see the introduction to Chapter 1 and Wills, "Differentiation of History"; Wills, *Judith,* 78–106.

3. Certeau, "History: Science and Fiction," in *The Certeau Reader,* ed. Graham Ward (Malden, MA: Blackwell, 2000), 37–52. This approach is related to what

has been called social memory or collective memory, and the theories of Maurice Halbwachs. See the introduction in Chapter 1 for the distinctions among *historia,* a true account of events that actually occurred; *plasma,* an account narrating events that did not occur but are like real events; and *mythos,* an account that narrates events that are not true and not similar to real events.

4. Emilio Gabba, "True History and False History in Classical Antiquity," *Journal of Roman Studies* 71 (1981): 50–62.

5. Van Seters, *In Search of History: Historiography in the Ancient World and the Origins of Biblical History* (New Haven: Yale University Press, 1986), 357. There is no ancient Israelite word for "history," although *toledot,* generations, overlaps to some extent.

6. To be sure, Ezra-Nehemiah, which was roughly contemporary with Herodotus, explicitly notes sources and can perhaps be considered a midpoint between Israelite and Greek methods. Yet Honigman, *Septuagint and Homeric Scholarship,* 38–41, 65–91, insists that ancient authors in general did not assume the same criteria for truthfulness in history that modern readers would seek.

7. Najman, *Seconding Sinai.*

8. Although it has been argued that the ancients lacked a clear sense of a continuous timeline, the intellectuals, especially the authors of history, seemed quite capable of considering the orderly connection of events. It may be true, however, that some authors did not think of the narrative as the passage of *abstract time* per se in the modern, Newtonian sense, but as the succession of *events,* each of which could have lasted six minutes or six months.

9. Bartlett, *1 Maccabees,* 18–19. See also deSilva, *Introducing the Apocrypha,* 280–81, 298–99; Nickelsburg, *Jewish Literature,* 106; and Goldstein, *I Maccabees,* 76, 377.

10. Doran, *Temple Propaganda,* 20; see also deSilva, *Introducing the Apocrypha,* 275–86. Gregory Mobley alerted me to the similarity of the heroic poetry and Judges; see also his *The Empty Men: The Heroic Tradition in Ancient Israel* (New Haven: Yale University Press, 2005).

11. Nickelsburg, *Jewish Literature,* 105; see also deSilva, *Introducing the Apocrypha,* 271; Harold W. Attridge, "Historiography," in Michael E. Stone, ed., *Jewish Writings of the Second Temple Period,* CRINT II:3 (Assen, Netherlands: Van Gorcum; Philadelphia: Fortress, 1984), 157–84, at 172.

12. This is similar to the Acts of the Apostles: when the followers of Jesus are not explicitly guided by the spirit, their efforts come to naught; see Wills, "The Depiction of the Jews in Acts," *JBL* 110 (1991): 631–54.

13. Schwartz, "1 Maccabees," in Klawans and Wills, eds., *Jewish Annotated Apocrypha,* 203–49, at 203.

14. Cf. 2 Macc 7:24, 15:11; Heb 13:22; Acts 13:13–41, and see at Letter of Jeremiah; also see Wills, "Form of the Sermon."

15. Paul J. Kosmin, *Time and Its Adversaries in the Seleucid Empire* (Cambridge, MA: Harvard University Press, 2018).

16. Bartlett, *1 Maccabees*, 21–36.

17. Williams, *Structure of 1 Maccabees*, 131, 137.

18. See deSilva, *Introducing the Apocrypha*, 273–75, for a summary of the texts.

19. Cohen, *Beginnings of Jewishness*, 92; Wills, *Not God's People*, 90. Hasmoneans introduced a Jewish constitution in those cities that they defeated (1 Macc 13:47–48).

20. Goldstein, *I Maccabees*, 21.

21. Schwartz, "1 Maccabees," 204.

22. Gruen, *Heritage and Hellenism*, 254–65; Wills, *Not God's People*, 87–100.

23. Goldstein, *I Maccabees*, 16–17; see also Bartlett, *1 Maccabees*, 33–34.

24. Williams, "1 Maccabees," in Atkins, ed., *T&T Clark Companion*, 261–72, at 263–64.

25. Schwartz, "1 Maccabees," 203–5; deSilva, *Introducing the Apocrypha*, 267; see also Doran, "Independence or Coexistence," 102–3. That it was written in Hebrew was also attested by Origen (Eusebius, *Church History* 6.25) and Jerome (*Prologus Galeatus*).

26. Kosmin, "Indigenous Revolts."

27. DeSilva, *Introducing the Apocrypha*, 288.

28. Eyal Regev, "2 Maccabees," in Klawans and Wills, eds., *Jewish Annotated Apocrypha*, 251–88, at 251.

29. Doran, *Temple Propaganda;* cf. Judith.

30. Klawans, *Josephus and the Theologies*, 101–6.

31. Although Polybius 2.56.7–12, 3.31.13 criticized historians such as Duris and Phylarchus for their exploitation of *psychagōgia,* he is upholding a more elite standard of history. He had also championed usefulness, *ōpheleia,* as contrasted with enjoyment, *terpsis,* and pragmatic history, *pragmatikos tropos.* Even the theological motifs in 2 Maccabees are similar to some Greek histories. Second Maccabees 9:11–12 calls to mind the role of *Tychē,* the goddess Fortuna, in Polybius; so Doran, *Temple Propaganda,* 90–91.

32. History *kata meros.* Polybius criticized those who wrote such smaller histories (29.12.1–3, 8; 16.14.1; 12.23.7, 24.5). See Martin Hengel, *Acts and the History of Earliest Christianity* (Philadelphia: Fortress, 1980), 36–37, on Acts of the Apostles and the *Tobiad Romance.*

33. See the discussion in Doran, *Temple Propaganda,* 84–90; Collins, *Between Athens and Jerusalem,* 78–83; Schwartz, *Judeans and Jews,* 67–84; Simkovich, "Greek Influence."

34. It is interesting that the letters plead for Hanukkah, but the body of the history barely notes it, and the miracle of the oil appears only in later rabbinic accounts (*b. Shabb.* 21b). On ancient accounts of the transfer of a cult, see Elizabeth R. Gebhard, "The Gods in Transit: Narratives of Cult Transfer," in *Antiquity and Humanity: Essays on Ancient Religion and Philosophy: Presented to Hans Dieter Betz on His 70th Birthday,* ed. Adela Yarbro Collins and Margaret M. Mitchell (Tübingen: Mohr Siebeck, 2001), 451–76.

35. Cohen, *Beginnings of Jewishness,* 3–4, 92.

36. Gruen, *Heritage and Hellenism,* xiv, 5–6; Wills, *Not God's People,* 87–100; Seth Schwartz, "Israel and the Nations Roundabout: 1 Maccabees and the Hasmonean Expansion," *JJS* 42 (1991): 16–38.

37. Gruen, *Heritage and Hellenism,* 3–4, 29–31. He tends to dissolve the *ambivalent* attitudes toward the Greeks into an overall *positive* interpretation.

38. Cohen, *Beginnings of Jewishness,* 69–105.

39. Wills, "Jew, Judean, Judaism."

40. 2 Macc. 2:21, 10:4, 13:9. See also Philip A. Harland, "Climbing the Ethnic Ladder: Ethnic Hierarchies and Judean Responses," *JBL* 138 (2019): 665–86.

41. Doran, *Temple Propaganda,* 105–9, arguing against Arnaldo Momigliano, "The Second Book of Maccabees," *CP* 70 (1975): 81–88.

42. Attridge, "Historiography," 182–83; Goldstein, *I Maccabees,* 32–36.

43. Schwartz, *2 Maccabees,* 50; see also Doran, *2 Maccabees,* 164–66; Rajak, "Reflections on Jewish Resistance"; and Henten, *Maccabean Martyrs,* 128. On the angry tyrant, cf. Judith 5 and see Wills, *Judith,* 270–75; Tessa Rajak, "Angry Tyrant," in Rajak, Pearce, Aitken, and Dines, eds., *Jewish Perspectives on Hellenistic Rulers,* 110–27; Alexander and Alexander, "Image of the Oriental Monarch."

44. Attridge, "Historiography," 177. Arguing for Judea are van Henten, *Maccabean Martyrs,* 50; and Lee I. Levine, *Judaism and Hellenism in Antiquity: Conflict or Confluence?* (Seattle: University of Washington Press, 1998), 79; but Schwartz, *Judeans and Jews,* 45, favors the diaspora.

45. Noah Bickart and Christine Hayes, "The Apocrypha in Rabbinic Literature," in Klawans and Wills, eds., *Jewish Annotated Apocrypha,* 593–97, at 596–97; and Martha Himmelfarb, "The Apocrypha in Medieval Hebrew Literature," in Klawans and Wills, eds., *Jewish Annotated Apocrypha,* 598–602, at 601.

46. Origen, *Exhortation to Martyrdom* 22–27; Cyprian, *On Fortune* 11; John Chrysostom, *On the Maccabees;* Gregory of Nazianzus homily 15, *On the Maccabees.* This literature influenced early Christian identity terms like *Hellēnismos* and *paganus.* See Douglas Boin, "Hellenistic 'Judaism' and the Social Origins of the 'Pagan-Christian' Debate," *JECS* 22 (2014): 167–96; and Joslyn-Siemiatkoski, *Christian Memories.*

47. Schwartz, "1 Maccabees," 206. On the medieval songs and prayers, see Satlow, *How the Bible Became Holy,* 124–25; Aaron D. Panken, "Hanukkah in the Apocrypha," in Klawans and Wills, eds., *Jewish Annotated Apocrypha,* 629–32. Bickart and Hayes, "Apocrypha in Rabbinic Literature," emphasize that the rabbinic traditions did not rely directly on 1 and 2 Maccabees.

48. See also the apocalypse known as 4 Ezra and 2 Esdras. In the Vulgate, the texts are numbered differently: 1 Esdras = biblical Ezra; 2 Esdras = biblical Nehemiah; 3 Esdras = the Greek Old Testament 2 Esdras; 4 Esdras = 4 Ezra.

49. Tamara Cohn Eskenazi, "1 Esdras," in Klawans and Wills, eds., *Jewish Annotated Apocrypha,* 99–123, at 99.

50. Talshir, *1 Esdras,* 106–9. Nehemiah, it should be noted, is heroized at 1 Maccabees 1, 2 Maccabees 2, and Sir 49:13. See Eskenazi, "1 Esdras," 99; Lisbeth S. Fried, "Why the Story of the Three Youths in 1 Esdras?," in Fried, ed., *Was 1 Esdras First?,* 83–92; and Jacob L. Wright, "Remember Nehemiah: 1 Esdras and the *Damnatio Memoriae Nehemiae,*" in Fried, ed., *Was 1 Esdras First?,* 145–63, and also the other essays in the same volume.

51. Eric Myers, *I and II Esdras,* 6, 13–16; Jellicoe, *Septuagint and Modern Study,* 291.

52. Fried, "Why the Story?," 105.

53. Johnson, *Historical Fictions;* Johnson, "Novelistic Elements."

54. Similar also is *Life of Aesop* 51–55, but it is even more satirical.

55. Loader, *Pseudepigrapha on Sexuality,* 145; Nickelsburg, *Jewish Literature,* 28. Cf. Ben Sira 19:2–3, 31:26–31, and see deSilva, *Introducing the Apocrypha,* 176–77; Wills, *Judith,* 337. In Ctesias (at Plutarch, *Artaxerxes* 15.4), generals are arguing at a symposium, and one says, "As the Greeks say, there is truth in wine."

56. Truth as a supreme value in Persian court tradition is reported by Herodotus 1.136, 138; 7.101; 1 Kgs 22:16 uses truth ironically. *'Emet* is derived from *'aman,* to confirm, as in *amen,* and so in Israel truth is more about the person's affirmation of it than an objective and independent truth. But see Pss 117:2, 146:6, and cf. the "Greek" moment in John 18:38 when Pilate asks, "What is truth?" See also Myers, *1 and 2 Esdras,* 53–56. See also Fried, "Why the Story?"

57. Klawans, "Jewish Theology and the Apocrypha," in Klawans and Wills, eds., *Jewish Annotated Apocrypha,* 640–44, at 642.

58. Scholarly literature is very sparse, but note Witakowski, "Zena Ayhud"; Kamil, *Josef Ben Gorion;* Flusser, "Josippon"; Flusser, *The Josippon;* and Bowman, "Tenth-Century Byzantine?" The best modern edition of Hebrew text, with German translation, is Börner-Klein and Zuber, *Josippon.*

59. Yerushalmi, *Zakhor: Jewish History and Jewish Memory* (Seattle: University of Washington Press, 2011); Robert Bonfil, "Jewish Attitudes toward History

and Historical Writing in Pre-Modern Times," in *Jewish History* 11 (1997): 7–40. See also Himmelfarb, "Apocrypha in Medieval Hebrew Literature," 600.

60. Börner-Klein and Zuber, *Josippon,* 12. See also Binyam, "Studies in Sefer Yosippon."

61. Dönitz, "Sefer Yosippon (Josippon)," in *A Companion to Josephus,* ed. Honora Howell Chapman and Zuleika Rodgers (Oxford: Oxford University Press, 2016), 382–89, at 386; see also Dönitz, "Sefer Yosippon and the Greek Bible"; Bowman, "'Yosippon' and Jewish Nationalism," 48; and Bowman, "*Sefer Yosippon.*" On the ambiguity of the Ethiopian canon, see Asale, "Ethiopian Orthodox Tewahedo Church Canon." I am also indebted to Ted Erho for information on the Ethiopian Orthodox canon.

62. Binyam, "Ethiopic Books." There is almost no scholarly treatment to be found, and translations in European languages are rare. A nonscholarly English translation of all three texts exists (Selassie, *Ethiopian Books*) and a more scholarly English translation of 1 Meqabyan (Curtin, *First Book*). The translations here are taken from both of these, with slight alterations for clarity. One may occasionally also find Rastafarian (Lyaric) translations available.

63. Bausi, "Maccabees." Binyam uses this title as well but notes that it is not quite accurate. The Maccabean texts of the other canons are lacking in the Ethiopian Bible, Bausi suggests, because they were absent from Vaticanus and Athanasius's list. The Ethiopian Church had perhaps adopted this version of the Bible.

64. Binyam, "Ethiopic Books."

65. Curtin, *First Book,* 5, 37.

66. Ullendorff, *Ethiopia and the Bible,* 73; see also Isaac, "Bible in Ethiopic," 119.

67. The translation is that of H. St. J. Thackeray in the LCL (1979). On the structure of the text, see Steve Mason, "Pathos and Passions in Josephus' Judaean War: A Tragic Vision of History and Politics," in *Passion, Persecution and Epiphany in Early Jewish Literature,* ed. Nicholas Peter Legh Allen, Pierre Johan Jordaan, and József Zsengellér (Oxford: Routledge, 2020), 150–73. Mason notes that the crescendo actually begins in Book 5.

68. The prophecy here, however, is not likely one of the biblical prophecies, but perhaps *Sibylline Oracles* 4.115–18.

Chapter 3. Wisdom Texts

1. Wills, *Jew in the Court,* 23–38. The Assyrian *Story of Ahikar* is a non-Israelite example; cf. also *Prayer of Nabonidus* and *Tales of the Persian Court* from Qumran.

2. Lang, *Wisdom and the Book of Proverbs: An Israelite Goddess Redefined* (New York: Pilgrim Press, 1986); Gilbert, *Sagesse de Salomon,* 108.

3. Wills, "Wisdom and Word"; Kloppenborg, "Isis and Sophia." See esp. Apuleius, *Metamorphoses* 11.3–6.

4. These types of wisdom were based on categories presented by my first professor on wisdom, Dieter Georgi. Cornelis Bennema, "The Strands of Wisdom Tradition in Intertestamental Judaism: Origins, Developments and Characteristics," *Tyndale Bulletin* 52 (2001): 61–82, develops a somewhat different division of wisdom into Torah-centered, spirit-centered (prophetic inspiration), and apocalyptic. See also John J. Collins, "The Court-Tales in Daniel and the Development of Apocalyptic," *JBL* 94 (1975): 218–34; and Thomas, "Eternal Writing."

5. Hartmut Gese, "Wisdom Literature in Persian Period," in *Cambridge History of Judaism,* ed. W. D. Davies and Louis Finkelstein (Cambridge: Cambridge University Press, 1984), 189–218, at 190. See also Kynes, *Oxford Handbook.* On the discipline of the self, see Wills, "Ascetic Theology?"; Arjen Bakker, "Sages and Saints: Continuous Study and Transformation in *Musar le-Mevin* and *Serek ha-Yahad,*" in *Tracing Sapiential Traditions in Ancient Judaism,* ed. Hindy Najman, Jean-Sébastien Rey, and Eibert J. C. Tigchelaar (Leiden: Brill, 2016), 106–18.

6. Wright, *No Small Difference,* 232.

7. DeSilva, *Introducing the Apocrypha,* 173–76; Skehan and Di Lella, *Wisdom of Ben Sira,* 50. See also Sanders, *Ben Sira and Demotic Wisdom.* On schools and Ben Sira's school, see Collins, *Jewish Wisdom,* 35–39.

8. William Riehl Poehlman, "Addressed Wisdom Teaching in *The Teachings of Silvanus:* A Form-Critical Study" (PhD diss., Harvard University, 1974). Clifford, *Wisdom Literature,* 117–20, goes further to outline the sayings into sixty-three topic units and eight larger sections, each beginning with a poem to wisdom: 1:1, 4:11, 6:18, 14:20, 24:1, 33:19, 38:24, 44:1. In addition, there is a conclusion beginning at 50:25.

9. Satlow, "Ecclesiasticus, or the Wisdom of Jesus, Son of Sirach (Ben Sira)," in Klawans and Wills, eds., *Jewish Annotated Apocrypha,* 427–98, at 431–32. Ben Sira was closely allied with the Jerusalem priesthood, perhaps even a priest himself. See Olyan, "Ben Sira's Relationship to the Priesthood"; Wright, "'Fear the Lord'"; Wright, "Putting the Puzzle Together: Some Suggestions Concerning the Social Location of the Wisdom of Ben Sira," in Wright and Wills, eds., *Conflicted Boundaries,* 89–112.

10. Goering, "Wisdom in the Apocrypha," in Klawans and Wills, eds., *Jewish Annotated Apocrypha,* 603–8, at 606; Rad, *Wisdom in Israel,* 241; cf. 243, 259; Nickelsburg, *Jewish Literature,* 58, and see Sir 1:10, 24:33.

11. Conzelmann, "Mother of Wisdom"; Kloppenborg "Isis and Sophia"; Collins, *Jewish Wisdom,* 50; Wills, "Wisdom and Word." Wisdom is related to the cosmic order of creation (16:24–18:14, 33:7–15, 39:16–35), and there are clear parallels to Ma'at, the Egyptian goddess of order, as well.

12. Collins, "Reinterpretation," 144; Klawans, *Josephus,* 28.

13. On the opposition of Ben Sira and 1 Enoch, see Wright, "Fear the Lord," 218–22; Argall, *1 Enoch and Sirach;* Boccaccini, *Middle Judaism,* 80, 104–19. See Ben Sira 34:1–8 on the deception caused by dreams and visions. Ben Sira 44:16 on Enoch is likely a later expansion; so Skehan and Di Lella, *Wisdom of Ben Sira,* 499.

14. Hengel, *Judaism and Hellenism,* 1.159–60. Hengel also states, 1.150, that in Ben Sira Wisdom and law co-opt the functions of *Logos.* Mattila's views are found at "Ben Sira and the Stoics." In Proverbs we already find emphasis on the discipline of education (*musar* in Hebrew, *paideia* in Greek). "*Paideia* of the mouth," added in the Greek version as a heading for an entire section, 23:7–15, may seem very Greek, but it does not appear in the Hebrew texts. However, we may consider it a legitimate part of the grandson's translated version for Alexandrian Jews. See also David Winston, "Theodicy in Ben Sira and Stoic Philosophy," in *Of Scholars, Savants, and Their Texts: Studies in Philosophy and Religious Thought: Essays in Honor of Arthur Hyman,* ed. Ruth Link-Salinger (New York: Lang, 1989), 239–49, at 241–43.

15. DeSilva, "Wisdom of Ben Sira," *CBQ* 58 (1996): 433–55. See also Newman, *Before the Bible,* 23–52, where she speaks of the daily discipline of Ben Sira the scribe as decentering and recentering.

16. Ben Sira 9:1–9, 19:2–3, 22:3–6, 23:22–27, 25:16–26, 26:1–18, 31:25, 36:21–25, 37:27–31, 42:9–14. Wright, "From Generation to Generation." A number of scholars have mapped out the interrelationship of some of the topics treated so far, from God, Wisdom, and Torah at the idealized end, to wives, women, daughters, and slaves at the more concrete level; see Balla, *Ben Sira on Family,* 153, 230. Wright and Edwards, "'She Undid Him.'" To be sure, Ellis, *Gender in the Book of Ben Sira,* argues that Ben Sira is not as demeaning of women as most scholars have judged, but few scholars would agree.

17. Berquist, *Controlling Corporeality: The Body and Household in Ancient Israel* (New Brunswick, NJ: Rutgers University Press, 2002), 188; Balla, review of Claudia V. Camp, *Ben Sira and the Men Who Handle Books: Gender and the Rise of Canon-Consciousness, RBL* [http://www.bookreviews.org] (2014).

18. Camp, "Honor and Shame," 182. See Sir 16:1–4, 41:5–9, and cf. below regarding Wisdom of Solomon. See also Bolle and Llewelyn, "Intersectionality," and the discussion of eunuchs at "Wisdom of Solomon" below. Ben Sira reflects

less anxiety on the topic of friends; see Saul M. Olyan, *Friendship in the Hebrew Bible* (New Haven: Yale University Press, 2017), 87–107.

19. Kurt Aland et al., eds., *Novum Testamentum Graece* (26th ed.; Stuttgart: Deutsche Bibelgesellschaft, 1979), 772–73. See deSilva, *Introducing the Apocrypha,* 157–60. The many variants in the textual tradition indicate that Ben Sira was "an open-ended project in both Hebrew and Greek"; so Newman, *Before the Bible,* 43. See also Wright, "Character in Search." All the extant Hebrew manuscripts of Ben Sira are available online at The Book of Ben Sira, www.bensira .org, created by Gary A. Rendsburg and Jacob Binstein. See also Rosen-Zvi, "The Wisdom Tradition in Rabbinic Literature and Mishnah *Avot,*" in Najman, Rey, and Tigchelaar, eds., *Tracing Sapiential,* 172–90. See also Labendz, "Book of Ben Sira."

20. "Shimmering impression," *schillernden Eindruck,* was Dieter Georgi's description (*Weisheit Salomos,* 391). See also Matthew Kraus, "Wisdom of Solomon," in Klawans and Wills, eds., *Jewish Annotated Apocrypha,* 390–425, at 391.

21. This view has been likened to that of Philo, who mistakenly believed that "Israel" derives from Hebrew *Ish-ra-el,* man-sees-God, and argued both an Israelite advantage and a gentile option. See Winston, *Wisdom of Solomon,* 59–63, and cf. also John 4:22–23. To be sure, anonymity can also be a "hidden transcript," a rhetorical strategy to express strongly held beliefs secretly in a hostile world; see James C. Scott, *Domination and the Arts of Resistance: Hidden Transcripts* (New Haven: Yale University Press, 1990), 91; and Portier-Young, *Apocalypse against Empire,* 3–47. Yet our text reads more as a brilliant literary project than as an attempt to fly under the radar. Jason M. Zurawski, "Crafted Ambiguity in the Philosophy of the Wisdom of Solomon: The Case(s) of Epistemology and Cosmology," presentation at the Society of Biblical Literature Annual Meeting, November 23, 2019, sees intentional ambiguity in this text as a didactic strategy, a *paideia* through ambiguity. On the structure of Wisdom, see Clifford, *Wisdom Literature,* 139–40; Winston, *Wisdom of Solomon,* 4; and Nickelsburg, *Jewish Literature,* 205–12.

22. Only at 7:14 (section two) and 11:9, 12:22 (section three). To be sure, righteousness (*dikaiosynē*) and related terms are distributed evenly among the three sections, giving support to Winston's thesis above that this is the main theme.

23. Forty-three invented and strikingly unusual compound words are listed by Winston, *Wisdom of Solomon,* 15 n. 5, and Kraus, "Wisdom of Solomon," 391. Of these, only four are found in section one (aside from the introduction): *autoschediōs* (2:2), *anapodismos* (2:5), *polychronios* (2:10, 4:8), and *petrobolos* (5:22). I do not count *philanthrōpos* because, although it is compound, it is not

unusual, nor do I count the odd assemblage of words in 4:12. On the Hebraisms, see Winston, *Wisdom of Solomon*, 15 n. 2. The examples of iambic meter are listed in Winston, *Wisdom of Solomon*, 15 n. 6.

24. Winston, *Wisdom of Solomon*, 16–17 n. 15; Reese, *Hellenistic Influence*, 123–40; Mack, *Logos und Sophia*, 169. The argument for separate origins is associated with Friedrich Focke, *Die Entstehung der Weisheit Salomos* (Göttingen: Vandenhoeck & Ruprecht, 1913). Georgi, *Weisheit Salomos*, 392–95, suggested that it was written over time by different authors. Opposed are Winston, *Wisdom of Solomon*, 12–15, and Kaiser, *Old Testament Apocrypha*, 114–15.

25. Reese, *Hellenistic Influence*, 117–21; Winston, *Wisdom of Solomon*, 18–20; Collins, *Jewish Wisdom*, 181–82; S. R. Slings, *Plato, Clitophon* (Cambridge: Cambridge University Press, 1999), 59–60, 90. Examples of protreptic include Plato, *Euthydemus* 278e–282d; (Pseudo?)-Plato, *Clitophon*; Aristotle, *Protreptic*; Isocrates, *To Nicocles*; Cicero, *On Duties* 2.2–8 and *Tusculan Disputations* 5.5–11; Seneca, *Letter to Lucilius*; Galen, *Protreptic*; Philo, *On Joseph*; and Clement of Alexandria, *Protreptic*. Clifford, *Wisdom Literature*, 142, argues that protreptic was a species of epideictic rhetoric. Protreptic was associated with other kinds of rhetoric as well; so Helen Rhee, *Early Christian Literature: Christ and Culture in the Second and Third Centuries* (London: Routledge, 2005), 24.

26. Wills, "Why the Passive Protagonist?"; George W. E. Nickelsburg, "The Genre and Function of the Markan Passion Narrative," in *George W. E. Nickelsburg in Perspective: An Ongoing Dialogue of Learning*, ed. Jacob Neusner and Alan J. Avery-Peck (2 vols.; Leiden: Brill, 2004), 2.504–12, with response by Wills.

27. Kraus, "Wisdom of Solomon," 410. Cf. Philo, *That the Worse Is Wont to Attack*, 83, and see Hogan, "Exegetical Background," 4–6; Clifford, *Wisdom Literature*, 138. See Philo, *Special Laws* 3.22.72, and Plato, *Phaedo* 81c. In addition, the philosopher, by a sort of mystical ascent, could also approach the highest levels of divinity. A Middle Platonic phrase, *homoiōsis theō*, means becoming more similar to God (from Plato's *Theaetetus* 176b, picked up by Philo, *On Flight* 63). The initiate to Isis has aspirations to a similar higher spirituality in Apuleius's *Golden Ass* Book 11. See also Wills, "Wisdom and Word."

28. Kraus, "Wisdom of Solomon," 392; Collins, *Jewish Wisdom*, 220–22. The laws, plural, at Wisdom 6:17–18 may not be the same as the law of Moses.

29. Wright and Wills, eds., *Conflicted Boundaries*; Nickelsburg, *Jewish Literature*, 207, 216–17. Stone, "Apocalyptic Literature," 388, notes that one place where wisdom forms and apocalyptic eschatology are both represented is Wis 7:17–21; see also Stone, "Lists of Revealed Things"; Kaiser, *Old Testament Apocrypha*, 122; and Collins, "Cosmos and Salvation."

258 Notes to Pages 141–146

30. See deSilva, *Introducing the Apocrypha,* 147; Collins, *Jewish Wisdom,* 185–87; and Burkes, "Wisdom and Apocalypticism," 40–41.

31. In an Isis hymn, the goddess calls to rulers of the earth; see Vera Frederika Vanderlip, *The Four Greek Hymns of Isidorus and the Cult of Isis* (Toronto: Hakkert, 1972), 50.

32. Winston, *Wisdom of Solomon,* 116. On *haplotēs,* see also the Old Greek ending of Susanna.

33. Kolarcik, *Ambiguity of Death,* 185–86; Hogan, "Exegetical Background." At 2 Baruch 50–51 there will also be a recognition scene at the resurrection of the righteous and the wicked. Fourth Ezra 7:83–84 is also similar. Cf. also Psalm 14 and note that at Plato, *Theaetetus* 176e–77a, the unrighteous do not realize that "the penalty they pay is the life they lead." Job enacts a trial setting as well, and like Wisdom, grants the interlocutors a real voice. The Gospel of John similarly introduces trial motifs throughout (not just in the Passion) to present a similar distinction between those who attain eternal life and those who do not and are convicted of an identity in unrighteousness. It is the function of trials— forensic rhetoric—drawn into literary contexts to distinguish facts from appearances, truth from illusion.

34. There is a rich background in Judaism of the righteous person, the *dikaios* (Greek) or *zadik* (Hebrew), as the *suffering* righteous person, who is often passive: the Joseph story in Genesis 37–50, Job, and the Suffering Servant passage in Isaiah 52–53 are early examples, and the theme evolves further in the court narratives of Esther, Daniel 3 and 6, Susanna, 2 Maccabees 7, 3 Maccabees, and in non-Israelite texts as well, such as *Ahikar.* The second half of *Testament of Joseph* is perhaps the closest parallel. See Nickelsburg, "Genre and Function"; and Wills, "Ascetic Theology?"

35. Jon D. Levenson and Kevin J. Madigan, *Resurrection: The Power of God for Christians and Jews* (New Haven: Yale University Press, 2008), 107–20. Note also Candida R. Moss and Joel S. Baden, *Reconceiving Infertility: Biblical Perspectives on Procreation and Childlessness* (Princeton: Princeton University Press, 2015), 136: "If, for the author of the Wisdom of Solomon, barrenness is compatible with virtue, for Philo it is practically identical."

36. DeSilva, *Introducing the Apocrypha,* 138, 147–53; see also Collins, *Jewish Wisdom,* 194–95.

37. Cf. also *Tales of the Persian Court;* Matt 19:10–12; Acts 8; and see Collins, *Daniel,* 133–36; Peter Guyot, *Eunuchen als Sklaven und Freigelassene in der griechisch-römischen Antike* (Stuttgart: Klett-Cotta, 1980); Samuel Cheon, "Three Characters in the Wisdom of Solomon 3–4," *JSP* 12 (2001): 105–13; Shaun Tougher, ed., *Eunuchs in Antiquity and Beyond* (London: Classical Press of

Wales, 2002); Sakkie Cornelius, "'Eunuchs'? The Ancient Background of *Eunouchos* in the Septuagint," in *Septuagint and Reception,* ed. Johann Cook (Leiden: Brill, 2009), 321–33; Wills, *Judith,* 333–35; and Deborah Levine Gera, *Xenophon's Cyropaedia: Style, Genre, and Literary Technique* (Oxford: Clarendon; New York: Oxford University Press, 1993), 254–59, on Greek suspicions of the emotional eunuchs. See Sir 16:1–4, 41:5–9 on having good and bad children, and the discussion of eunuchs there.

38. Stone, "Lists of Revealed Things."

39. Reese, *Hellenistic Influence,* 40; Collins, *Jewish Wisdom,* 203–4. Reese, 46–49, lists verbal parallels to Isis hymns; see also pp. 39–41; Collins, *Jewish Wisdom,* 50; Wills, "Wisdom and Word." Kloppenborg, "Isis and Sophia," 68, 71, emphasizes that the activities of Wisdom in Wisdom 10 transfer the traditional role of God (as *sōtēr,* savior) to Wisdom and include actions that are parallel to Isis, yet not found in other Israelite recitations of the saving acts of God.

40. Winston, *Wisdom of Solomon,* 173–74, gives ample references.

41. So Stone, "Apocalyptic Literature," 388.

42. The others are close enough to suggest that a similar Exodus tradition is at work; see Robert Houston Smith, "Exodus Typology in the Fourth Gospel," *JBL* 81 (1962): 329–42; Douglas K. Clark, "Signs in Wisdom and John," *CBQ* 45 (1983): 201–9; Wills, *Quest of the Historical Gospel: Mark, John, and the Origins of the Gospel Genre* (London: Routledge, 1997), 162. See also Glicksman, *Wisdom of Solomon 10,* 82–89. Egyptians and Canaanites, who appear as the opponents in section three—also without being named—may represent the contemporary Alexandrians and Romans. On the other hand, perhaps they are abstract depictions of a negative Other functioning as foils to affirm a stronger Jewish identity. This text ultimately strengthens the ideal of the righteous Jew as moral agent, in contrast to the wicked Other. See Winston, *Wisdom of Solomon,* 45.

43. Wills, "Form of the Sermon."

44. Pamela Eisenbaum, *The Jewish Heroes of Christian History: Hebrews 11 in Literary Context* (Atlanta: Scholars, 1997), 32–33, 178–79; Alan D. Bulley, "Death and Rhetoric in the Hebrews 'Hymn to Faith,'" *Studies in Religion/ Sciences Religieuses* 25 (1996): 409–23. Peter Enns, *Exodus Retold,* 391–92, 397, states that the reciting of history in section three demonstrates the role of personified Wisdom to exact justice.

45. Biblical examples are Isa 40:18–41:7, 44:9–20, 46:5–8; Jer 10:3–8; Hab 2:18–19; Pss 115:4–8, 135:15–18; Daniel 5; Bel; Letter of Jeremiah; Jub. 12:2–5, 20:8–9; see also *Aristeas* 135–38, and Philo's extended critique of idol worship (*On the Decalogue* 52–81), which rivals Wisdom in length. This is a possible influence

on Romans 1, although they may both reflect Jewish thought of the period; see Kaiser, *Old Testament Apocrypha*, 3–10; Collins, "The Apocryphal/Deuterocanonical Books: A Catholic View," in Kohlenberger, ed., *Parallel Apocrypha*, xxxi–xxxvii, at xxxiii–xxxiv.

46. Wasserman, "Along a Marvelous Way: The Significance of Middle Platonism for Understanding Wisdom of Solomon's Soteriology," presentation at Society of Biblical Literature Annual Meeting, Denver, November 17, 2018. See also Dell, *"Get Wisdom,"* 138–39. For Roman sources, cf. Cleanthes in Cicero, *On the Nature of the Gods* 2.12–15, and Horace, *Satire* 1.8. Michael Wojciechowski, "Ancient Criticism of Religion in Dan 14 (Bel and Dragon), Bar 6 (Epistle of Jeremiah), and Wisdom 14," in Xeravits and Zsengellér, eds., *Deuterocanonical Additions*, 60–76.

47. Barclay, *Jews in the Mediterranean Diaspora: From Alexander to Trajan (323 BCE–117 CE* (Berkeley: University of California Press, 1996), 186, see also 183, 191; Collins, *Between Athens and Jerusalem*, 201; Collins, *Jewish Wisdom*, 212–13; Rajak, *Translation and Survival*, 63, 209; Gruen, *Diaspora*, 64, 217, 239; Greg Schmidt Goering, "Election and Knowledge in the Wisdom of Solomon," in Xeravits and Zsengellér, eds., *Studies*, 163–82. Jason Zurawski, "Paideia," 211, emphasizes the trans-ethnic view of the author; paideia is "an ideal, universal educational system which leads, ultimately, to immortality. . . . Ethnic particularism has no place in this text."

48. Aland et al., eds., *Novum Testamentum Graece*, 772–73. See the discussion in deSilva, *Introducing the Apocrypha*, 157–60, and on Jewish tradition, Kraus, "Wisdom of Solomon," 392.

49. Cf. 2 Maccabees 7 and 4 Macc 9:22, 14:5–6, 16:13, 17:12, 18:23. See deSilva, *4 Maccabees*, 124–56, esp. 137; Nickelsburg, *Jewish Literature*, 256–57.

50. Robert J. V. Hiebert, "4 Maccabees," in Aitken, ed., *T&T Clark Companion*, 306–19, at 314, notes the irony that the author associates Antiochus's assaults with a "Greek way of life," when the entire philosophical message is Stoic! See also Redditt, "Concept of *Nomos*," 251–54; and deSilva, "Using the Master's Tools," 99–127. The same irony may be found in Paul's views of being "in Christ"; this allows one to master the passions; see David C. Aune, "Mastery of the Passions: Philo, 4 Maccabees, and Early Christianity," in Wendy E. Helleman, ed., *Hellenization Revisited: Shaping a Christian Response with the Greco-Roman World* (Lanham, MD: University Press of America, 1994), 125–58. The *hilastērion* and sacrifice take up the effective death of the hero in Greek culture; see Wills, *Quest of the Historical Gospel*, 23–50.

51. Hiebert, "4 Maccabees," 307; Klauck, "Hellenistische Rhetorik," 451–65; deSilva, "Noble Contest."

52. DeSilva, *4 Maccabees,* 27; see also 21–28. DeSilva also notes the language associated with epideictic, *epideiknymi,* at 1:1 and elsewhere. Aristotle's *Protrepticus* is a eulogy to reason and exhorts people to "exercise moral virtue for the sake of wisdom, for which wisdom is the supreme end" (B21). The protreptic nature of 4 Maccabees is very similar to Wisdom of Solomon, but the former emphasizes law more explicitly (4 Macc 2:23; 5:24, 34). Although reason is the stated subject of the treatise, *eusebeia* is almost as common. The summary of the treatise at 18:1 features both terms; see also Hiebert, "4 Maccabees," 311.

53. The immortality of the soul is often distinguished from the resurrection of the body, as in 2 Macc 7:7–14, yet 4 Macc 9:26–10:21 remains unclear on this issue; see Hiebert, "4 Maccabees," 315.

54. Moscicke, "Concept of Evil," 163–95. Also see 1:28–30. Winston, "Hellenistic Jewish Philosophy," in Daniel H. Frank and Oliver Leaman, eds., *History of Jewish Philosophy,* 46, takes the more common view that 4 Maccabees is an example of the Middle Platonism that had already merged Platonic, Stoic, and Peripatetic elements. Perhaps a less academic-sounding aspect of the argument can be found in the mother's sermon, which affirms emotions by including a list of biblical texts on suffering and God's care for the suffering; see Rajak, *Translation and Survival,* 226. On the suppression of emotions, see Cicero, *Tusculan Disputations* 3.22; 4.38, 57; Plato, *Phaedo* 93–94; deSilva, *4 Maccabees,* 52–55.

55. Weitzman, personal communication.

56. Eusebius, *Ecclesiastical History* 3.10.6, and Jerome, *On Illustrious Men* 13; see Rajak, "Angry Tyrant," in Rajak, Pearce, Aitken, and Dines, eds., *Jewish Perspectives on Hellenistic Rulers,* 110–27, at 126 n. 32; Hiebert, "4 Maccabees," 307; Nickelsburg, *Jewish Literature,* 258; Collins, *Between Athens and Jerusalem,* 187.

57. Hiebert, "4 Maccabees," 313; Joslyn-Siemiatkoski, *Christian Memories.*

58. Newman, *Before the Bible,* 61, 74. See also Kipp Davis, *The Cave 4 Apocryphon of Jeremiah and the Qumran Jeremianic Traditions: Prophetic Persona and the Construction of Community Identity* (Leiden: Brill, 2014); and Adams, *Baruch and the Epistle of Jeremiah.*

59. Saldarini, "Letter of Jeremiah," 6.934–35. See also Steck, *Apockryphe Baruchbuch,* 312: "Originalität ist überhaupt nicht der Anspruch der Schrift. . . . Bar will gar nichts Neues präsentieren." On aspects of the Greek in Baruch, see Tony S. L. Michael, "Barouch," in NETS, 925–26.

60. Cf. also Psalms of Solomon 11.

61. The so-called confessions of Jeremiah are really complaints: Jer 11:18–12:6, 15:10–21, 17:14–18, 18:18–23, and 20:7–18. Steck, *Apockryphe Baruchbuch,* 88–92,

286, draws a close relation between the Baruch prayer and Daniel 9, both perhaps based on an older prayer. See also Newman, *Before the Bible,* 53–74.

62. Nickelsburg, *Jewish Literature,* 96.

63. Steck, *Apockryphe Baruchbuch;* Kabasele Mukenge, *L'unité littéraire;* Corley, "Emotional Transformation." See also Daniel Ryan, "Baruch," in Aitken, ed., *T&T Clark Companion,* 487–99.

64. Saldarini, "Letter of Jeremiah," 931; Moore, *Daniel, Esther, and Jeremiah,* 260, argues for the early second century. Steck, *Apokryphe Baruchbuch,* 294–303, perceives references to the détente with the Seleucids after the Maccabean Revolt. Rajak, *Translation and Survival,* 199, places it still later, after 70 CE.

65. Johnson, *Historical Fictions;* Johnson, "Novelistic Elements." Regarding the epistle frame, the Epistle of Enoch, part of 1 Enoch, is the only other artificial epistle in this period. See Irene Taatz, *Frühjüdische Briefe: Die paulinischen Briefe im Rahmen der offiziellen religiösen Briefe des Frühjudentums* (Göttingen: Vandenhoeck & Ruprecht, 1991); and Marvin Lloyd Miller, *Performances of Ancient Jewish Letters: From Elephantine to MMT* (Göttingen: V&R Academic, 2015), for the history of real and artificial letters in ancient Israel.

66. Nickelsburg, *Jewish Literature,* 37; Goff, "The Letter of Jeremiah," in *New Oxford Annotated Bible,* ed. Michael Coogan (5th ed.; Oxford: Oxford University Press, 2018), 1559–63, at 1559; C. J. Ball, "Epistle of Jeremy," *APOT,* 596–611, at 597. On matters of translation and style, see Benjamin G. Wright, "Letter of Ieremias," in NETS, 942–44.

67. Letter of Jeremiah 6:20–21; Rajak, *Translation and Survival,* 200. It is assumed here that worship of God includes care for the poor and helpless—cf. Deut 15:11—but this was hardly unique to Israel. Still, note the creation of one's identity by the condemnation of the Other.

68. F. W. Walbank, "Speeches in Greek Historians," in his *Selected Papers: Studies in Greek and Roman History and Historiography* (Cambridge: Cambridge University Press, 1985), 242–61, at 253, discerned three kinds of speeches in Greek histories: debating speeches of politicians (*dēmēgoriai*), harangues of commanders (*paraklēseis*), and discourses of ambassadors (*presbyterikoi logoi*). Cf. Thucydides's military harangues, e.g., 2.11, and Plato, *Menexenus* 236d–48e. Jews and Christians further developed the word of exhortation (1 Macc 10:24; 2 Macc 7:24, 15:11; Heb 13:22; Acts 13:14–41; Hebrews and 1 Clement repeat the pattern often); see Wills, "Form of the Sermon"; Tomes, "Heroism," 182 n. 32. If the word of exhortation is the generic pattern adopted by Letter of Jeremiah, this might argue for a Greek original, although an influence of the Greek pattern on Hebrew literature is also possible. See Benjamin G.

Wright, "The Epistle of Jeremiah: Translation or Composition?," in Xeravits and Zsengellér, eds., *Deuterocanonical Additions,* 126–42, on the arguments for and against Hebrew composition.

69. Adams, *Baruch and the Epistle of Jeremiah,* 149, argues that the earliest reference to our text is 2 Macc 2:1–4; see also Wright, "Epistle of Jeremiah," in Aitken, ed., *T&T Clark Companion,* 520–27. But a date of around the second century BCE is still indicated.

70. Herzer, *4 Baruch,* xxxv; Allison, "Paraleipomena Jeremiou," 345, see also 327–28. In general, see also Purinton and Kraft, *Paraleipomena Jeremiou.* On the similar disappearance of Judaism in Acts, or rather the co-optation of Judaism by Christians, see Wills, "The Depiction of the Jews in Acts," *JBL* 110 (1991): 631–54; and Christopher Stroup, *The Christians Who Became Jews: Acts of the Apostles and Ethnicity in the Roman City* (New Haven: Yale University Press, 2020). Another interesting theory propounded by Marc Philonenko, "Simples observations sur les Paralipomènes de Jérémie," *RHPhR* 76 (1996): 157–77, suggests that our text was a Christian gnostic composition, but Herzer, "Die Paralipomena Jeremiae," correctly refutes this possibility.

Chapter 4. Apocalypses and Visionary Literature

1. Collins, ed., *Apocalypse* (*Semeia* 14). What follows is based upon *Semeia* 14 and Stone, "Apocalyptic Literature." See also Collins, *Apocalyptic Imagination;* and Portier-Young, *Apocalypse against Empire.*

2. However, Martha Himmelfarb, *Tours of Hell: An Apocalyptic Form in Jewish and Christian Literature* (Philadelphia: University of Pennsylvania Press, 1983), 60–61, n. 68, and Seth Schwartz, *Imperialism and Jewish Society* (Princeton: Princeton University Press, 2001), 14–15, and esp. 75–76, distinguish the historical apocalypses and cosmological apocalypses as separate genres.

3. Von Rad, *Wisdom in Israel,* 263–83. Similarities between wisdom and apocalypticism can be seen, for instance, in Wis 7:17–21; 2 Baruch 59; 4 Ezra 4:5–9, 5:36–37; and cf. Job 38. See also Stone, "Apocalyptic Literature," 388; and Wright and Wills, eds., *Conflicted Boundaries.*

4. Rowland, *Open Heaven;* Wolter, "Apokalyptik als Redeform im Neuen Testament," *NTS* 51 (2005): 171–91, at 181. The translation is my own. See also Sacchi, *Jewish Apocalyptic.* There is an interesting *Endzeit = Urzeit* aspect of this, since Gen 2:16–17, 3:22 states that the transgression of Adam and Eve was not sexual awakening, as Christians would later interpret it, but knowledge of good and evil that was now illegitimately made available to humans. Genesis, the *Urzeit,* will be replayed in the *Endzeit,* and knowledge will again be chan-

neled to humans—but only to some, and only through special visionaries like Enoch, Daniel, or Ezra, who are guided by angels.

5. Newsom, "The Development of *1 Enoch* 6–19: Cosmology and Judgment," *CBQ* 42 (1980): 310–29; Collins, "Cosmos and Salvation," 141–42.

6. Stuckenbruck, *Myth of Rebellious Angels,* 81, see also 1, 13; Wasserman, *Apocalypse as Holy War, passim;* Eddy, *The King is Dead: Studies in the Near Eastern Resistance to Hellenism, 334–31 B.C.* (Lincoln: University of Nebraska Press, 1961), esp. 135–36, 163–64, 327–31.

7. Isaac, "Bible in Ethiopic," 117; Nickelsburg, *1 Enoch,* 44; Reed, "Interrogating 'Enochic Judaism': 1 Enoch as Evidence for Intellectual History, Social Realities, and Literary Tradition," in Boccaccini, ed., *Enoch and Qumran Origins,* 336–44, at 341.

8. VanderKam, *Enoch,* 37–42, 151–72; Collins "Cosmos and Salvation," 131–32.

9. Portier-Young, *Apocalypse against Empire,* 289. See also Horsley, *Scribes,* 151–72.

10. Collins, *The Invention of Judaism: Torah and Jewish Identity from Deuteronomy to Paul* (Oakland: University of California Press, 2017), 74; VanderKam, "The Interpretation of Genesis in 1 Enoch," in *The Bible at Qumran: Text, Shape, and Interpretation,* ed. Peter W. Flint (Grand Rapids: Eerdmans, 2001), 129–48, at 142. See also Portier-Young, *Apocalypse against Empire,* 296–97, 304; Wright, "Ben Sira and the Book of the Watchers." The term "Sadducee," the main temple-oriented party at the turn of the era, may derive from Zadokite. See Boccaccini, *Beyond the Essene Hypothesis;* cf. Martha Himmelfarb, *A Kingdom of Priests: Ancestry and Merit in Ancient Judaism* (Philadelphia: University of Pennsylvania Press, 2006), 41; Nickelsburg, "Enochic Wisdom."

11. Stone, "Apocalyptic Literature," 403–4. Technically, the biblical calendar was a combination lunar/solar calendar: a lunar calendar formed the basis but was corrected to correspond to the solar year by the intercalation of extra months. Although Jubilees, which was a favorite text at Qumran, adamantly favored the solar calendar alone, the Enoch literature includes some references to lunar reckonings and so is more moderate on this issue; see James C. VanderKam, *Calendars in the Dead Sea Scrolls: Measuring Time* (Oxford: Routledge, 1998), 113–16.

12. The translation is that of George W. E. Nickelsburg and James C. VanderKam, *1 Enoch: The Hermeneia Translation* (Minneapolis: Fortress, 2012), with minor changes. See also Collins, "Enochic Judaism"; Harkins and Bautch, eds., *Watchers in Jewish and Christian Tradition.* In terms of who will be saved, the small circle of the elect are emphasized in 1 Enoch 1:1, 7–8; 5:5–10, but in 10:21 all Israel will become righteous.

13. According to Stone, "Apocalyptic Literature," 400, the Watchers section may be either chapters 6–11 or 6–16. On the continuing use of the Book of the Watchers to explain aspects of the origin of sin, and even the sin of women in particular, see Reed, "Gendering Heavenly Secrets? Women, Angels, and the Problem of Misogyny and 'Magic,'" in *Daughters of Hecate: Women and Magic in the Ancient World,* ed. Kimberley B. Stratton and Dayna S. Kalleres (Oxford: Oxford University Press, 2014), 108–51.

14. Stuckenbruck, *Myth of Rebellious Angels,* 1, 13, 81. In Greece and Rome the mating of gods and human women produces heroes, as mentioned briefly in Gen 6:4, but in Genesis and here as well there appear to be positive and negative memories. Enoch, for instance, intervenes on behalf of the Watchers but then pronounces judgment against them. See also Wasserman, *Apocalypse as Holy War,* 68–72, 106–7. Benjamin G. Wright, "Putting the Puzzle Together: Some Suggestions Concerning the Social Location of the Wisdom of Ben Sira," in Wright and Wills, eds., *Conflicted Boundaries,* 89–112, finds here only a mild critique of the Jerusalem priesthood, not a thoroughly sectarian critique. The emphasis on revealed knowledge in apocalypticism was also emphasized as a theme by Rowland, *Open Heaven.*

15. Nickelsburg, *Jewish Literature,* 83–86.

16. Patrick A. Tiller, "Israel at the Mercy of Demonic Powers: An Enochic Interpretation of Postexilic Imperialism," in Wright and Wills, eds., *Conflicted Boundaries,* 113–22. In contrast, however, Olson, *New Reading,* argues that the text does not concern the nations but God and universal salvation.

17. VanderKam, "Studies in the Apocalypse of Weeks"; see also Stuckenbruck, *1 Enoch 91–108.*

18. S. R. Slings, *Plato: Clitophon* (Cambridge: Cambridge University Press, 1999), 58–92. Although Plato preferred the dialogue (*elenchus*) over protreptic, he incorporated aspects of the latter in his works, sometimes in parody. Regarding Deuteronomy, see Weitzman, "Sensory Reform." According to Karl-Wilhelm Niebuhr, *Gesetz und Paränese: Katechismusartige Weisungsreihen in der frühjüdischen Literatur* (Tübingen: Mohr Siebeck, 1987), 12–15, the three Pentateuchal texts mentioned above become summaries of the entire law of Israel; Leviticus 19 even summarizes the summary laws of the Ten Commandments. See also Patrick Pouchelle, *Dieu éducateur: une nouvelle approche d'un concept de la théologie biblique entre Bible Hébraïque, Septante et littérature grecque classique* (Tübingen: Mohr Siebeck, 2015).

19. Cf. 10:21, 90:38, 91:14. See Nickelsburg, *Jewish Literature,* 248–51; and see Wright, "1 Enoch and Ben Sira"; Nickelsburg, "Parables of Enoch."

20. Nickelsburg, *Jewish Literature,* 254; see also Nickelsburg and VanderKam,

1 Enoch: The Hermeneia Translation, 4. Collins, "Enoch and the Son of Man: A Response to Sabino Chialà and Helge Kvanvig," in Boccaccini, ed., *Enoch and the Messiah*, 216–27, at 226–27. In this same volume, see also Helge S. Kvanvig, "The Son of Man in the Parables of Enoch," 179–215. On the gospel Son of Man, see Gabriele Boccaccini, "Finding a Place for the Parables of Enoch within Second Temple Jewish Literature," 263–89, at 278; and Mathias Henze, "The Parables of Enoch in Second Temple Literature: A Response to Gabriele Boccaccini," 290–98, at 297, both in Boccaccini, ed., *Enoch and the Messiah*. Stone, "Apocalyptic Literature," 402, also finds similarities between this text and the gospels in that the Son of Man is transcendent, exists before creation or before selection, there is an enthronement theme, and there is judging. These characteristics go beyond the Davidic messiah. To make proper sense of this comparison with the New Testament, however, the dating of the Book of Parables (and ch. 71 separately, if it is an addition) becomes quite important, since it may be later than the gospels. Yet it is likely somewhat earlier than the gospels, and either way the resonances are significant.

21. Rachel Adelman, *The Return of the Repressed: Pirqe de-Rabbi Eliezer and the Pseudepigrapha* (Leiden: Brill, 2009), 70; Andrei A. Orlov, *The Enoch-Metatron Tradition* (Tübingen: Mohr Siebeck, 2005). In general see Reeves and Reed, eds., *Enoch from Antiquity;* Himmelfarb, *Apocalypse;* James C. VanderKam, "1 Enoch, Enochic Motifs, and Enoch in Early Christian Literature," in VanderKam, ed., *Jewish Apocalyptic*, 33–100; Adler, *Time Immemorial;* and Kraft, *Exploring the Scripturesque*.

22. Annette Yoshiko Reed, "Enoch in Armenian Apocrypha," in *The Armenian Apocalyptic Tradition: A Comparative Perspective,* ed. Kevork Bardakjian and Sergio La Porta (Leiden: Brill, 2014), 149–86.

23. Kugel, review of James C. VanderKam, *Jubilees: A Commentary on the Book of Jubilees, Review of Biblical Literature,* https://www.bookreviews.org/pdf/12938_14428.pdf (2020). On rewritten scripture, see Sidnie White Crawford, *Rewriting Scripture in Second Temple Times* (Grand Rapids, MI: Eerdmans, 2008); Najman, *Seconding Sinai*. On the teachings in Jubilees, see VanderKam, *Jubilees,* 41–84.

24. But see now also on this passage Dimant, "Two 'Scientific' Fictions." See also VanderKam, *Textual and Historical Studies,* 84, also 24–26, 87; and Docherty, *Jewish Pseudepigrapha,* 15–22.

25. Nickelsburg, *Jewish Literature,* 70; Kugel, "Early Interpretation," in *Early Biblical Interpretation,* ed. Kugel and Rowan A. Greer (Philadelphia: Westminster, 1986), 9–105, at 60–61; Kugel, *A Walk through Jubilees: Studies in the Book of Jubilees and the World of Its Creation* (JSJSup; Leiden: Brill, 2012), 6–17.

26. Mroczek, "The Incredible Expanding Bible: From the Dead Sea Scrolls to Haile Selassie," in Klawans and Wills, eds., *Jewish Annotated Apocrypha*, 614–20, at 616. Regarding the role of women, Pseudo-Philo, *Biblical Antiquities*, increases their prominence as well; see Betsy Halpern-Amaru, *The Empowerment of Women in the Book of Jubilees* (Leiden: Brill, 1999), 147–59.

27. Goff, "Jubilees," in Klawans and Wills, eds., *Jewish Annotated Apocrypha*, 1–97, at 3; Najman, "Interpretation as Primordial Writing: Jubilees and Its Authority Conferring Strategies," *JSJ* 30 (1999): 379–410, at 381.

28. Hanneken, *Subversion of the Apocalypses;* O. S. Wintermute, "*Jubilees,*" in Charlesworth, ed., *Old Testament Pseudepigrapha*, 2.46–48; Davenport, *Eschatology*, 47–71, 81–87.

29. Kosmin, *Time and Its Adversaries in the Seleucid Empire* (Cambridge, MA: Harvard University Press, 2018).

30. Testuz, *Les idées religieuses du livre des Jubilés* (Geneva: Druz, 1960), 11–12.

31. Wills, *Not God's People*, 21–52.

32. Goldstein, "The Date of the Book of Jubilees," *Proceedings of the American Academy for Jewish Research* 50 (1983): 63–86; VanderKam, *Book of Jubilees*, 18. It is also possible that the eschatological predictions were composed in the early 160s and the rest somewhat later; so Davenport, *Eschatology*, 10–18.

33. Goff, "Jubilees," 4. On the afterlife of Jubilees in Christian tradition, see Adler, *Time Immemorial*.

34. Stone and Henze, *4 Ezra and 2 Baruch*, 4–5, have rightly cautioned against taking that version as the only source for understanding the precise words of the text. For Jerome, Nehemiah was named 2 Esdras, and what in the Apocrypha is now called 1 Esdras he numbered 3 Esdras; the present text became 4 Esdras. Later, the Latin Bible began to use 2 Esdras for the present text, and it has been referred to by this name in the Catholic tradition.

35. Hogan, *Theologies in Conflict*, 220–21; Zurawski, "Ezra Begins."

36. Henze, "On the Anthropology of Early Judaism," 30–31. That Adam's sin was the cause of sin and mortality for all humans is found in 4 Ezra and 2 Baruch and was shared by Paul (Romans 5, 1 Corinthians 15), but it was still the *exception* in the Jewish literature of this period; 4 Ezra 3:7; 7:118; 2 Bar 48:42–47, 54:15–22, 56:5–7. Cf. Jub. 5:2, also based on Gen 6:5. It is possible that the early Christian Letter of James (1:15) responds to this attribution of sin to an evil inclination. On the balanced good inclination, see *m. Ber.* 9:5, *m. Avot* 4:1; cf. *b. B. Bat.* 16a. Fourth Ezra 7:21–24 assumes that people can choose, and 2 Bar 48:42–43, 54:19 state both sides of the matter.

37. Fried, "4 Ezra," in Klawans and Wills, eds., *Jewish Annotated Apocrypha*, 345–84, at 346. See also in the same volume, Greg Schmidt Goering, "Wisdom

in the Apocrypha," 603–8. Hogan, *Theologies in Conflict,* 229; see also 37–42. To be sure, Matthias Henze, in reviewing her book (*JR* [2010]: 65–66), questions whether the first two positions can be clearly identified as separate schools of thought, especially if the position of Uriel is identified with only one text, *4QInstruction,* and this attested only in the separated community of Qumran. But even if that is true, there still seems present in this text a dialogue of one traditional sort of wisdom and another more radical and eschatological wisdom, which are then resolved to some extent by appeal to a direct visionary connection to the divine. On ascetic theology, see Wills, "Ascetic Theology?"

38. Stone, *Commentary,* 28–36; Hogan, *Theologies in Conflict, passim;* Warren, *Food and Transformation,* 37–58; Najman, *Losing the Temple,* 6 (italics original).

39. Najman, *Seconding Sinai,* 70. See also Hogan, "The Meanings of *tôrâ* in *4 Ezra,*" *JSJ* 38 (2007): 530–52; Najman, *Losing the Temple,* 26–66; Mroczek, "Incredible Expanding Bible"; and Stone, *Commentary,* 437; cf. Philo, *On Drunkenness,* 146–48.

40. The term "Christians" is anachronistic in Galatians, where Paul is thinking of a new access of gentiles *within* Israel, but by the time of 5 Ezra, this dynamic is understood as the replacement of Israel by a separate group, Christians. The translations, and much of the discussion here of 5 and 6 Ezra, are based on Theodore Bergren, "Fifth Ezra" and "Sixth Ezra," in Bauckman, Davila, and Panayatov, eds., *Old Testament Pseudepigrapha,* 467–97.

41. Bergren, "Sixth Ezra," 486.

42. Cf. 6 Ezra 15:43–16:1 with Rev 14:8, 16:19–19:3; however, cf. also 4 Ezra 3:28–36. See Bergren, "Sixth Ezra," 484–86. The prediction of the destruction of Babylon or Rome (15:34–45) also remind one of the opening of Greek Esther, although the latter is clearly a fictional vision played for literary effect.

43. Stone and Henze, *4 Ezra and 2 Baruch,* 6–7. See also Bergren, "Christian Influence on the Transmission History of 4, 5, and 6 Ezra," in VanderKam, ed., *Jewish Apocalyptic Heritage,* 102–27.

44. Stone and Henze, *4 Ezra and 2 Baruch,* 10–11, propose a date after the destruction by Rome (e.g., 7:1–8:5) but before the Bar Kokhba revolt of 132–135, which is not mentioned. A Jerusalem location for the writing is also likely. The translations here, with exceptions, are from the volume by Stone and Henze. See also Liv Ingeborg Lied, "Recent Scholarship on 2 Baruch," *CBR* 9 (2011): 238–76.

45. Second Baruch is not as clearly structured as 4 Ezra, although it is also divisible into seven sections, six demarcated by a fast: 5:7, 9:1, 12:5, 21:1, 47:2, 35:1. To maintain this pattern, a fast would presumably be necessary at 35:1; so Stone, "Apocalyptic Literature," 409. This structure suggests one editor for

the whole, but independent sources may have been incorporated, some more similar to 4 Ezra. On the different genres of the component parts, see Stone and Henze, *4 Ezra and 2 Baruch*, 12.

46. Although the angel Ramiel does appear at times to function as an interpreting angel (55:3); see Docherty, *Jewish Pseudepigrapha*, 149–52. On the subordinate role of Jeremiah, see 2 Bar 2:1, 5:5, 9:1, 10:2, and Nickelsburg, *Jewish Literature*, 277.

47. Tamási, "Sources," esp. 244; see also 2 Bar 46:1–3, 77:13–16, 85:1–5. See also Henze and Lied, "Jeremiah, Baruch."

48. Lied, "Those Who Know," 445. Similar is Henze, "Torah and Eschatology," 202–3, and Nickelsburg, *Jewish Literature*, 283.

49. Burkes, "'Life' Redefined," 69; Docherty, *Jewish Pseudepigrapha*, 154; Henze, *Jewish Apocalypticism*, 181–86. See also Murphy, *Structure and Meaning*, 140; and Hogan, "Mother Zion."

50. Henze, *Jewish Apocalypticism*, 373–74; Goff, "Mystery of God's Wisdom." On the later reception of 2 Baruch, see J. Edward Wright, "Baruch," 281.

Chapter 5. Psalms, Prayers, and Odes

1. Mroczek, *The Literary Imagination in Jewish Antiquity* (Oxford: Oxford University Press, 2016), esp. 26; Chesnutt and Newman, "Prayers in the Apocrypha," 40–41. According to Harold W. Attridge, "Giving Voice to Jesus: Use of the Psalms in the New Testament," in *Psalms in Community: Jewish and Christian Textual, Liturgical, and Artistic Traditions*, ed. Attridge and Margot E. Fassler (Atlanta: Society of Biblical Literature, 2003), 101–12, 129 of the 150 biblical Psalms are quoted or alluded to in the New Testament. See also Eileen Schuller, *Non-Canonical Psalms from Qumran: A Pseudepigraphic Collection* (Atlanta: Scholars, 1986).

2. Harrington, *Invitation to the Apocrypha*, 170, follows the consensus in stating that the Hebrew text from Qumran is more coherent than the Greek, but note that Segal, "Literary Development," maintains that the LXX version is prior. The historical psalms are Psalms 3, 7, 18, 34, 51, 52, 54, 56, 57, 59, 60, 63, and 142, most of which are found in the second of the five sections of Psalms, or 42–72. The last of these concludes, "The prayers of David son of Jesse are ended." See Vivian L. Johnson, *David in Distress: His Portrait through the Historical Psalms* (London: T&T Clark, 2009). On David as hero, see Gregory Mobley, *The Empty Men: The Heroic Tradition of Ancient Israel* (New Haven: Yale University Press, 2005); and Wills, "Jewish Heroes."

3. Rajak, *Translation and Survival*, 195–96. The translation of Psalm 151 is by

Peter W. Flint, at https://www.bibleodyssey.org/en/passages/related-articles
/psalm-151-and-the-dead-sea-scrolls.

4. Smith, "How to Write a Poem," 188, prefers a less interiorizing translation: "I
   truly said to myself." Sanders, "Ps. 151 in 11QPss," 81–83. The Jewish philosopher Aristobulus had already appropriated Orphism; see Eusebius, *Preparation for the Gospel* 13.12. On the sinful soul at Qumran, see Wills, "Ascetic
   Theology." On speaking "to my heart" or "to my soul," cf. Deut 13:6–7; Pss
   14:1, 42:5, Qoh 2:1, 3:17, and see Saul M. Olyan, *Friendship in the Hebrew Bible*
   (New Haven: Yale University Press, 2017), 97. Retaining the inward perspective in Ps 151 is Eric D. Reymond, *New Idioms*, 51–74.

5. Lambert, "The Prayer of Manasseh," in Klawans and Wills, eds., *Jewish Annotated Apocrypha*, 387–89, at 387; Newman, "Form and Settings," 124. Cf. also
   m. Avot 2:10. The penitential themes may also have been influenced by Psalm
   51; so Werline, "Prayer in the Apocrypha," in Klawans and Wills, eds., *Jewish
   Annotated Apocrypha*, 625–628, at 628.

6. Van der Horst and Newman, eds., *Early Jewish Prayers*, 148; Schniedewind,
   "Source Citations."

7. Lambert, "Prayer," 387.

8. Van der Horst and Newman, *Early Jewish Prayers*, 147–49.

9. Kaiser, *Old Testament Apocrypha*, 80–81.

10. Atkinson, *"I Cried to the Lord,"* argues that 4, 7, 12, and 15 are pre-Pompey and
    13 is mixed; the rest reflect the incursion of Pompey.

11. Nickelsburg, *Jewish Literature*, 243. See also Docherty, *Jewish Pseudepigra-
    pha*, 76–77; and Simkovich, *Discovering*, 183–87.

12. Kaiser, *Old Testament Apocrypha*, 81. On p. 83 Kaiser presses the connection
    to Pharisees with some confidence. In agreement are Mikael Winninge, *Sin-
    ners and the Righteous: A Comparative Study of the Psalms of Solomon and
    Paul's Letters* (Stockholm: Almkvist & Wiksell, 1995), 171–78, but the position
    is criticized by Joseph L. Trafton, "The Bible, the *Psalms of Solomon,* and
    Qumran," in *The Bible and the Dead Sea Scrolls,* ed. James H. Charlesworth
    (3 vols.; Waco, TX: Baylor University Press, 2006), 2.427–46, at 431–34. Dan-
    iele Pevarello, "Psalms of Solomon," in Aitken, ed., *T&T Clark Companion,*
    425–37, at 433, considers it uncertain.

13. Nickelsburg, *Jewish Literature*, 247; Pevarello, "Psalms of Solomon," 434;
    Kaiser, *Old Testament Apocrypha*, 84. See Pss. Sol. 3:8; cf. 10:1, 14:1, and
    W. Horbury, "The Remembrance of God in the *Psalms of Solomon*," in *Mem-
    ory in the Bible and Antiquity,* ed. S. C. Barton (Tübingen: Mohr Siebeck,
    2007), 111–28; Patrick Pouchelle, "Prayers for Being Disciplined: Notes on
    paideuō and *paideia* in the Psalms of Solomon," in *Psalms of Solomon: Lan-*

guage, History, and Theology, ed. Eberhard Bons and Patrick Pouchelle (Atlanta: SBL, 2015), 115–31.

Conclusion

1. Weitzman, "Literary Approaches to the Apocrypha," in Klawans and Wills, eds., *Jewish Annotated Apocrypha,* 608–13, at 611. See also Katell Berthelot, "Hellenization and Jewish Identity in the Deuterocanonical Literature: A Response to Ben Wright," in *Canonicity, Setting, Wisdom in the Deuterocanonicals,* ed. Géza G. Xeravits, József Zsengellér, and Xavér Szabó (Berlin: de Gruyter, 2014), 69–88, at 79.
2. DeSilva, *Introducing the Apocrypha,* 37–57.
3. Wills, "Jewish Heroes."
4. Thomas, "Eternal Writing." In general, see Collins, "The Apocryphal/Deuterocanonical Books: A Catholic View," in Kohlenberger, ed., *Parallel Apocrypha,* xxxi–xxxvii, at xxxiii–xxxiv; Klawans, *Josephus,* 111–15.
5. Miryam Brand, "Evil and Sin," in Klawans and Wills, eds., *Jewish Annotated Apocrypha,* 645–48.
6. Gruen, *Diaspora,* argues correctly that many Jewish texts express an overall positive attitude toward the Hellenistic ruling powers, but he tends to smooth over the edges of conflict and ambivalence and ignores the apocalypses altogether. Naomi Seidman, *Faithful Renderings: Jewish-Christian Difference and the Politics of Translation* (Chicago: University of Chicago Press, 2006), 123, 154, outlines the powers of colonized writing, although the Apocrypha differ in the extent to which they participate in intentional "foreignization" and resistance; see also Portier-Young, *Apocalypse against Empire.* The term "colonial universalism" was coined by Partha Chatterjee, *Nationalist Thought and the Colonial World: A Derivative Discourse* (London: Zed; Totowa, NJ: Biblio Distribution Center, 1986), but he used it in a one-directional way: the colonizing center imposes a notion of universalism upon the colonized margins. Homi Bhabha, *Location of Culture* (London: Routledge, 1994), 85–92, saw universalizing ideals proceeding in both directions, mutually influencing and hybridizing each other, but did not use the term colonial universalism. See also Honigman, "'Jews as the Best'"; and deSilva, *Introducing the Apocrypha,* 303.
7. See also Tob 2:2, 14:7; cf. 2:6. See also Matthew Rindge, "Jewish Identity under Foreign Rule: Daniel 2 as a Reconfiguration of Genesis 41," *JBL* 129 (2010): 85–104, esp. 90.
8. Wills, "Jew, Judean, Judaism." The Greek term *Ioudaios* is common in *some* texts of the New Testament, in *some* books of Philo, and in Josephus, but this

may reflect Roman usage. On the archaeological evidence, see Berlin, "Manifest Identity: From Ioudaios to Jew," in *Between Cooperation and Hostility: Multiple Identities in Ancient Judaism and the Interaction with Foreign Powers*, ed. Rainer Albertz and Jacob Wöhrle (Göttingen: Vandenhoeck & Ruprecht, 2013), 151–75.

Bibliography

Adams, Sean A. *Baruch and the Epistle of Jeremiah: A Commentary Based on the Texts in Codex Vaticanus.* Leiden: Brill, 2014.

———. "Epistle of Jeremiah or Baruch 6: The Importance of Labels." *Journal for Septuagint and Cognate Studies* 44 (2011): 26–30.

Adler, William. *Time Immemorial: Archaic History and Its Sources in Christian Chronography from Julius Africanus to George Syncellus.* Dumbarton Oaks Studies 26. Washington, DC: Dumbarton Oaks, 1989.

Aitken, James K., ed. *T&T Clark Companion to the Septuagint.* London: Bloomsbury T&T Clark, 2015.

Alexander, Philip, and Loveday Alexander. "The Image of the Oriental Monarch in the Third Book of Maccabees." Pages 92–109 in *Jewish Perspectives on Hellenistic Rulers.* Edited by Tessa Rajak, Sarah Pearce, James Aitken, and Jennifer Dines. Berkeley: University of California Press, 2007.

Allison, Dale C. "The Paraleipomena Jeremiou and Anti-Judaism." Pages 325–52 in *The Ways That Often Parted: Essays in Honor of Joel Marcus.* Edited by Lori Baron. ECL 24. Atlanta: Society of Biblical Literature, 2018.

Alonso-Schökel, Luis. *Narrative Structures in the Book of Judith.* Berkeley: Center for Hermeneutical Studies in Hellenistic and Modern Culture, 1975.

Anderson, Gary A. "Does Tobit Fear God for Naught?" Pages 115–43 in *The Call of Abraham: Essays on the Election of Israel in Honor of Jon D. Levenson.* Edited by Gary A. Anderson and Joel S. Kaminsky. South Bend, IN: University of Notre Dame Press, 2013.

Argall, Randal A. *1 Enoch and Sirach: A Comparative Literary and Conceptual Analysis of the Themes of Revelation, Creation, and Judgment.* SBLEJL 8. Atlanta: Scholars, 1995.

Asale, Bruk A. "The Ethiopian Orthodox Tewahedo Church Canon of the Scriptures: Neither Open nor Closed." *Bible Translator* 67 (2016): 202–22.

Atkinson, Kenneth. *"I Cried to the Lord": A Study of the Psalms of Solomon's Historical Situation and Social Setting.* SupplJSJ 84. Leiden: Brill, 2004.

Bal, Mieke. "The Elders and Susanna." *BibInt* 1 (1993): 1–19.

———. "Head-Hunting: 'Judith' on the Cutting Edge of Knowledge." Pages 253–85 in *A Feminist Companion to Esther, Judith, and Susanna*. Edited by Athalya Brenner. FCB 7. Sheffield: Sheffield Academic Press, 1995.

Balla, Ibolya. *Ben Sira on Family, Gender, and Sexuality*. Berlin: de Gruyter, 2011.

Bartlett, John R. *1 Maccabees*. Guides to the Apocrypha and Pseudepigrapha. Sheffield: Sheffield Academic Press, 1998.

Bauckham, Richard, James Davila, and Alexander Panayatov, eds. *Old Testament Pseudepigrapha: More Noncanonical Scriptures*. Volume 1. Grand Rapids, MI: Eerdmans, 2013.

Bausi, Alessandro. "Maccabees, Ethiopic Book of." Pages 3.621–22 in *Encyclopaedia Aethiopica*. Edited by Siegbert Uhlig. 5 vols. Wiesbaden: Harrassowitz, 2003–2014.

Beckwith, Roger T. *The Old Testament Canon of the New Testament Church and Its Background in Early Judaism*. Grand Rapids, MI: Eerdmans, 1986.

Beentjes, Pancratius C., ed. *The Book of Ben Sira in Modern Research: Proceedings of the First International Ben Sira Conference, 28–31 July 1996, Soesterberg, Netherlands*. BZAW 255. Berlin: de Gruyter, 1997.

Bergmann, Claudia. "Idol Worship in Bel and the Dragon and Other Jewish Literature from the Second Temple Period." Pages 207–23 in *Septuagint Research: Issues and Challenges in the Study of the Greek Jewish Scriptures*. Edited by Wolfgang Kraus and R. Glenn Wooden. SBLSCS 53. Atlanta: Society of Biblical Literature, 2006.

Bickerman, Elias. "The Colophon of the Greek Book of Esther." *JBL* 63 (1944): 339–62.

Binyam, Yonatan. "The Ethiopic Books of Maccabees." In *Textual History of the Bible: Deuterocanonical Scriptures*. Edited by Matthias Henze and Frank Fader. Textual History of the Bible 2B. Leiden: Brill, forthcoming.

———. "Studies in Sefer Yosippon: The Reception of Josephus in Medieval Hebrew, Arabic, and Ethiopic Literature." PhD diss., Florida State University, 2017.

Boccaccini, Gabriele. *Beyond the Essene Hypothesis: The Parting of the Ways between Qumran and Enochic Judaism*. Grand Rapids, MI: Eerdmans, 1998.

———, ed. *Enoch and Qumran Origins: New Light on a Forgotten Connection*. Grand Rapids, MI: Eerdmans, 2005.

———, ed. *Enoch and the Messiah Son of Man: Revisiting the Book of Parables*. Grand Rapids, MI: Eerdmans, 2007.

———. *Middle Judaism: Jewish Thought 300 B.C.E. to 200 C.E.* Minneapolis: Fortress, 1991.

Bolle, Helena M., and Stephen R. Llewelyn. "Intersectionality, Gender Liminality and Ben Sira's Attitude to the Eunuch." *VT* 67 (2017): 546–69.

Börner-Klein, Dagmar, and Beat Zuber. *Josippon: Jüdische Geschichte vom Anfang der Welt bis zum Ende des ersten Aufstands gegen Rom*. Wiesbaden: Marix, 2010.

Bow, Beverly, and George W. E. Nickelsburg. "Patriarchy with a Twist: Men and Women in Tobit." Pages 127–43 in *"Women Like This:" New Perspectives on Jewish Women in the Greco-Roman World*. Edited by Amy-Jill Levine. Atlanta: Scholars, 1991.

Bowman, Steven. "*Sefer Yosippon:* History and Midrash." Pages 280–94 in *The Midrashic Imagination: Jewish Exegesis, Thought, and History*. Edited by Michael Fishbane. Albany: SUNY Press, 1993.

———. "A Tenth-Century Byzantine–Jewish Historian?" Review of David Flusser, *Studies on the Josippon and Its Authors. Byzantine Studies/Études Byzantines* 10 (1983): 133–36.

———. "'Yosippon' and Jewish Nationalism." *Proceedings of the American Academy of Jewish Research* 61 (1995): 23–51.

Boyd-Taylor, Cameron. "Esther's Great Adventure: Reading the LXX Version of the Book of Esther in Light of Its Assimilation to the Conventions of the Greek Romantic Novel." *BIOSCS* 30 (1997): 81–113.

Brant, Jo-Ann A., Charles W. Hedrick, and Chris Shea, eds. *Ancient Fiction: The Matrix of Early Christian and Jewish Narrative*. SymS 32. Atlanta: Society of Biblical Literature, 2006.

Bredin, Mark, ed. *Studies in the Book of Tobit: A Multidisciplinary Approach*. LSTS 55. London: T&T Clark, 2006.

Brenner, Athalya. *A Feminist Companion to the Bible: Esther, Judith, Susanna*. FCB 7. Sheffield: Sheffield Academic Press, 1995.

Brenner-Idan, Athalya, with Helen Efthimiadis-Keith. *A Feminist Companion to Tobit and Judith*. FCB Second Series 20. London: Bloomsbury T&T Clark, 2015.

Brine, Kevin R., Elena Ciletti, and Henrike Lähnemann, eds. *The Sword of Judith: Judith Studies across the Disciplines*. Cambridge: Open Book, 2010.

Burkes, Shannon. "'Life' Redefined: Wisdom and Law in Fourth Ezra and *Second Baruch*." *CBQ* 63 (2001): 55–71.

———. "Wisdom and Apocalypticism in the Wisdom of Solomon." *HTR* 95 (2002): 21–44.

Camp, Claudia V. *Ben Sira and the Men Who Handle Books: Gender and the Rise of Canon-Consciousness*. Hebrew Bible Monographs 50. Sheffield: Sheffield Phoenix Press, 2013.

———. "Honor and Shame in Ben Sira: Anthropological and Theological Reflections." Pages 171–88 in *The Book of Ben Sira in Modern Research: Proceedings*

of the First International Ben Sira Conference, 28–31 July 1996, Soesterberg,
Netherlands. Edited by Pancratius C. Beentjes. BZAW 255. Berlin: de Gruyter, 1997.

Carruthers, Jo. *Esther through the Centuries.* Hoboken, NJ: Wiley-Blackwell, 2008.

Charles, R. H., ed. *The Apocrypha and Pseudepigrapha of the Old Testament.* 2 vols. Oxford: Clarendon, 1913.

Charlesworth, James H., ed. *Old Testament Pseudepigrapha.* 2 vols. New York: Doubleday, 1983.

Chesnutt, Randall D., and Judith Newman. "Prayers in the Apocrypha and Pseudepigrapha." Pages 38–42 in *Prayer from Alexander to Constantine: A Critical Anthology.* Edited by Mark Kiley. London: Routledge, 1997.

Clanton, Dan W., Jr. *The Good, the Bold, and the Beautiful: The Story of Susanna and Its Renaissance Interpretations.* LHBOTS 430. London: T&T Clark, 2006.

Clifford, Richard J. *The Wisdom Literature.* Interpreting Biblical Texts. Nashville: Abingdon, 1998.

Clines, David J. A. *The Esther Scroll: The Story of the Story.* SupplJSOT 30. Sheffield: JSOT Press, 1984.

Cohen, Shaye J. D. *The Beginnings of Jewishness: Boundaries, Varieties, Uncertainties.* Berkeley: University of California Press, 1999.

———. *From the Maccabees to the Mishnah.* 3rd ed. Philadelphia: Westminster John Knox, 2014.

Collins, John J., ed. *Apocalypse: The Morphology of a Genre.* Semeia 14. Atlanta: Society of Biblical Literature, 2003.

———. *The Apocalyptic Imagination: An Introduction to Jewish Apocalyptic Literature.* 3rd ed. Grand Rapids, MI: Eerdmans, 2016.

———. *Between Athens and Jerusalem: Jewish Identity in the Hellenistic Diaspora.* Grand Rapids, MI: Eerdmans, 2000.

———. "Cosmos and Salvation: Jewish Wisdom and Apocalypticism in the Hellenistic Age." *HR* 17 (1977): 121–42.

———. *Daniel: A Commentary on the Book of Daniel.* Hermeneia. Minneapolis: Fortress, 1994.

———. "Enochic Judaism: An Assessment." Pages 219–34 in *The Dead Sea Scrolls and Contemporary Culture.* Edited by Adolfo D. Roitman, Lawrence H. Schiffman, and Shani Tzoref. STDJ 93. Leiden: Brill, 2011.

———. *Jewish Wisdom in the Hellenistic Age.* Louisville: Westminster John Knox, 1997.

———. "The Penumbra of the Canon: What Do the Deuterocanonical Books Represent?" Pages 1–18 in *Canonicity, Setting, Wisdom in the Deuterocanonicals.*

Edited by Géza G. Xeravits, József Zsengellér, and Xavér Szabó. DCLS 22. Berlin: de Gruyter, 2014.

———. "The Reinterpretation of Apocalyptic Traditions in the Wisdom of Solomon." Pages 143–58 in *Jewish Cult and Hellenistic Culture: Essays on the Jewish Encounter with Hellenism and Roman Rule*. Edited by John J. Collins. SupplJSJ 100. Leiden: Brill, 2005.

Conzelmann, Hans. "The Mother of Wisdom." Pages 230–43 in *The Future of Our Religious Past*. Edited by James M. Robinson. New York: Harper, 1971.

Corley, Jeremy. "Emotional Transformation in the Book of Baruch." Pages 225–52 in *Emotions from Ben Sira to Paul*. Edited by Renate Egger-Wenzel and Jeremy Corley. DCL Yearbook 2011. Berlin: de Gruyter, 2012.

Cousland, J. R. C. "Reversal, Recidivism and Reward in 3 Maccabees: Structure and Purpose." *JSJ* 24 (2003): 39–51.

———. "Tobit: A Comedy in Error?" *CBQ* 65 (2001): 535–53.

Cowley, Roger. "The Biblical Canon of the Ethiopian Orthodox Church Today." *Ostkirchliche Studien* 23 (1974): 318–23.

Craven, Toni. *Artistry and Faith in the Book of Judith*. SBLDS 70. Chico, CA: Scholars, 1983.

———. "The Book of Judith in the Context of Twentieth-Century Studies of the Apocryphal/Deuterocanonical Books." *CurBR* 1 (2003): 187–229.

Crawford, Sidnie White. "The Additions to Esther." Pages 3.943–71 in *The New Interpreter's Bible*. Edited by Leander E. Keck. 12 vols. Nashville: Abingdon, 1999.

Croy, N. Clayton. *3 Maccabees*. Septuagint Commentary Series. Leiden: Brill, 2005.

Curtin, D. P. *First Book of Ethiopian Maccabees*. Philadelphia: Dalcassian, 2018.

Davenport, Gene L. *The Eschatology of the Book of Jubilees*. Leiden: Brill, 1971.

Day, Linda. *Three Faces of a Queen: Characterization in the Books of Esther*. LHBOTS. Sheffield: Sheffield Academic Press, 1995.

De Lange, Nicholas. *Japheth in the Tents of Shem: Greek Bible Translations in Byzantine Judaism*. Texts and Studies in Medieval and Early Modern Judaism 30. Tübingen: Mohr Siebeck, 2016.

De Lange, Nicholas, Julia Krivoruchko, and Cameron Boyd-Taylor, eds. *Jewish Reception of the Greek Bible Versions: Studies in Their Use in Late Antiquity and the Middle Ages*. Texts and Studies in Medieval and Early Modern Judaism 23. Tübingen: Mohr Siebeck, 2009.

de Wet, Chris L. "The Reception of the Susanna Narrative (Dan. XIII; LXX) in Early Christianity." Pages 229–44 in *Septuagint and Reception: Essays Prepared for the Association for the Study of the Septuagint in South Africa*. Edited by Johann Cook. SVT 127. Leiden: Brill, 2009.

Dell, Katharine. *"Get Wisdom, Get Insight": An Introduction to Israel's Wisdom Literature.* London: Darton, Longman & Todd, 2000.

Deselaers, Paul. *Das Buch Tobit: Studien zu seiner Entstehung, Komposition und Theologie.* OBO. Freiburg: Universitätsverlag; Göttingen: Vandenhoeck & Ruprecht, 1982.

DeSilva, David A. *4 Maccabees.* Guides to Apocrypha and Pseudepigrapha 7. Sheffield: Sheffield Academic Press, 1998.

——. *Introducing the Apocrypha: Message, Context, and Significance.* 2nd ed. Grand Rapids, MI: Baker Academic, 2018.

——. "The Noble Contest: Honor, Shame, and the Rhetorical Strategy of 4 Maccabees." *JSP* 13 (1995): 31–57.

——. "Using the Master's Tools to Shore Up Our House: A Postcolonial Analysis of 4 Maccabees." *JBL* 127 (2007): 99–127.

Di Lella, Alexander A. "The Deuteronomic Background of the Farewell Discourse in Tob 14:3–11." *CBQ* 41 (1979): 380–89.

Dimant, Devorah. "Tobit in Galilee." Pages 347–59 in *Homeland and Exile: Biblical and Ancient Near Eastern Studies in Honour of Bustenay Oded.* Edited by Gershon Galil, Mark Geller, and Alan Millard. SVT 130. Leiden: Brill, 2009.

——. "Two 'Scientific' Fictions: The So-Called Book of Noah and the Alleged Quotation of Jubilees in CD 16:3–4." Pages 230–49 in *Studies in the Hebrew Bible, Qumran, and the Septuagint: Essays Presented to Eugene Ulrich on the Occasion of His Sixty-Fifth Birthday.* Edited by Peter W. Flint, Emanuel Tov, and James C. VanderKam. SVT 101. Leiden: Brill, 2006.

DiTommaso, Lorenzo. *The Book of Daniel and the Apocryphal Daniel Literature.* SVTP 20. Leiden: Brill, 2005.

Docherty, Susan. *The Jewish Pseudepigrapha: An Introduction to the Literature of the Second Temple Period.* Minneapolis: Fortress, 2015.

Dönitz, Saskia. "Sefer Yosippon and the Greek Bible." Pages 223–34 in *Jewish Reception of the Greek Bible Versions: Studies in Their Use in Late Antiquity and the Middle Ages.* Edited by Nicholas de Lange, Julia Krivoruchko, and Cameron Boyd-Taylor. Texts and Studies in Medieval and Early Modern Judaism. Tübingen: Mohr Siebeck, 2009.

Doran, Robert. "Independence or Coexistence: The Responses of 1 and 2 Maccabees to Seleucid Hegemony." Pages 1.94–103 in *Society of Biblical Literature Seminar Papers 38.* Edited by Kent Harold Richards. SBLSPS 38. 2 vols. Atlanta: Society of Biblical Literature, 1999.

——. *2 Maccabees.* Hermeneia. Minneapolis: Fortress, 2012.

——. *Temple Propaganda: The Purpose and Character of 2 Maccabees.* Washington, DC: Catholic Biblical Association, 1982.

Dubarle, A. M. *Judith: Formes et sens des diverses traditions.* 2 vols. Rome: Pontifical Biblical Institute, 1966.

Edwards, Matthew. *Pneuma and Realized Eschatology in the Book of Wisdom.* FRLANT 242. Göttingen: Vandenhoeck & Ruprecht, 2012.

Ego, Beate. *Das Buch Tobit.* JSHRZ II.6. Gütersloh: Gerd Mohn, 1999.

———. "Prayer and Emotion in the Septuagint Esther." Pages 83–94 in *Ancient Jewish Prayers and Emotions.* Edited by Stefan C. Reif and Renate Egger-Wenzel. DCLS 26. Berlin: de Gruyter, 2015.

Ellis, Teresa Ann. *Gender in the Book of Ben Sira: Divine Wisdom, Erotic Poetry, and the Garden of Eden.* BZAW 453. Berlin: de Gruyter, 2013.

Engel, Helmut. "Auf zuverlässigen Wegen und in Gerechtigkeit, Religiöses Ethos in der Diaspora nach dem Buch Tobit." Pages 83–100 in *Biblische Theologie und gesellschaftlicher Wandel: Für Norbert Lohfink SJ.* Edited by Georg Braulik, Walter Gross, and Sean McEvenue. Freiburg: Herder, 1993.

———. "Das Buch Tobit; Das Buch Judit." Pages 184–87 in *Einleitung in das Alte Testament.* Edited by Erich Zenger, Heinz-Josef Fabry, and Georg Braulik. Stuttgart: Kohlhammer, 1995.

———. *Die Susanna Erzählung: Einleitung, Übersetzung und Kommentar zum Septuaginta-Text und zur Theodotion-Bearbeitung.* OBO 61. Freiburg: Universitätsverlag; Göttingen: Vandenhoeck & Ruprecht, 1985.

Enns, Peter. *Exodus Retold: Ancient Exegesis of the Departure from Egypt in Wis 10:15–21 and 19:1–9.* HSM 57. Atlanta: Scholars, 1997.

Feldman, Louis H., James L. Kugel, and Lawrence H. Schiffman, eds. *Outside the Bible: Ancient Jewish Writings Related to Scripture.* 3 vols. Philadelphia: Jewish Publication Society; Lincoln: University of Nebraska Press, 2013.

Fitzmyer, Joseph. *Tobit.* CEJL. Berlin: de Gruyter, 2003.

Flusser, David. "Josippon, a Medieval Hebrew Version of Josephus." Pages 386–97 in *Josephus, Judaism, and Christianity.* Edited by Louis H. Feldman and Gohei Hata. Detroit: Wayne State University Press, 1987.

———. *The Josippon (Josephus Gorionides)* [in Hebrew]. 2 vols. Jerusalem: Bialik Institute, 1980–1981.

Fox, Michael V. *Character and Ideology in the Book of Esther.* 2nd ed. Grand Rapids, MI: Eerdmans, 2001.

Fried, Lisbeth S., ed. *Was 1 Esdras First? An Investigation into the Priority and Nature of 1 Esdras.* Ancient Israel and Its Literature 7. Atlanta: Society of Biblical Literature, 2011.

Gallager, Edmon L. "Writings Labeled 'Apocrypha' in Latin Patristic Sources." Pages 1–14 in *Sacra Scriptura: How "Non-Canonical" Texts Functioned in Early Judaism and Early Christianity.* Edited by James H. Charlesworth, Lee Martin McDonald, and Blake A. Jurgens. London: Bloomsbury, 2014.

Gallager, Edmon L., and John D. Meade. *The Biblical Canon Lists from Early Christianity: Texts and Analysis.* Oxford: Oxford University Press, 2017.

Garrard, Mary D. "Artemisia and Susanna." Pages 246–71 in *Feminism and Art History: Questioning the Litany.* Edited by Norma Broude and Mary D. Garrard. New York: Westview, 1982.

Georgi, Dieter *Weisheit Salomos.* JSHRZ III.4. Gütersloh: Gerd Mohn, 1980.

Gera, Deborah Levine. *Judith.* CEJL. Boston: de Gruyter, 2014.

Gilbert, Maurice. *La Sagesse de Salomon.* Rome: Gregorian & Biblical Press, 2011.

Glancy, Jennifer. "The Accused: Susanna and Her Readers." *JSOT* 58 (1993): 103–16.

Glicksman, Andrew T. *Wisdom of Solomon 10: A Hellenistic Reinterpretation of Early Israelite History through Sapiential Lenses.* DCLS 9. Berlin: de Gruyter, 2011.

Goering, Greg Schmidt. *Wisdom's Root Revealed: Ben Sira and the Election of Israel.* SupplJSJ 139. Leiden: Brill, 2009.

Goff, Matthew. "The Mystery of God's Wisdom, the Parousia of a Messiah, and Visions of Heavenly Paradise." Pages 175–92 in *The Jewish Apocalyptic Tradition and the Shaping of New Testament Thought.* Edited by Benjamin E. Reynolds and Loren T. Stuckenbruck. Minneapolis: Fortress, 2017.

Goldstein, Jonathan A. *I Maccabees.* AB 41. Garden City, NY: Doubleday, 1976.

Goswell, Greg. "The Order of the Books in the Greek Old Testament." *JETS* 52 (2009): 449–66.

Grabbe, Lester L. *An Introduction to Second Temple Judaism: History and Religion of the Jews in the Time of Nehemiah, the Maccabees, Hillel, and Jesus.* London: Bloomsbury T&T Clark, 2010.

Grillo, Jennifer. *The Reception of the Additions to Daniel.* New York: Oxford University Press, forthcoming.

———. "Showing Seeing in Susanna: The Virtue of the Text." *Prooftexts* 35 (2015): 250–70.

———. "'You Will Forget Your Ancient Shame': The Innocence of Susanna and the Vindication of Israel." Pages 7–22 in *Women and Exilic Identity in the Hebrew Bible.* Edited by Katherine E. Southwood and Martien Halvorson-Taylor. Library of Hebrew Bible/Old Testament Studies 631. London: Bloomsbury T&T Clark, 2018.

Gruen, Erich S. *Diaspora: Jews amidst Greeks and Romans.* Cambridge, MA: Harvard University Press, 2004.

———. *Heritage and Hellenism: The Reinvention of Jewish Tradition.* Berkeley: University of California Press, 1998.

Haag, Ernst. *Studien zum Buche Judith: Seine theologische Bedeutung und literarische Eigenart.* Trier theologische Studien 16. Trier: Paulinus, 1963.

Hacham, Noah. "3 Maccabees: An Anti-Dionysian Polemic." Pages 167–83 in *Ancient Fiction: The Matrix of Early Christian and Jewish Narrative.* Edited by Jo-Ann A. Brant, Charles W. Hedrick, and Chris Shea. Symposium Series 32. Atlanta: Society of Biblical Literature, 2006.

———. "3 Maccabees and Esther: Parallels, Intertextuality, and Diaspora Identity." *JBL* 126 (2007): 765–85.

Hadas, Moses. *Third and Fourth Books of Maccabees.* Philadelphia: Dropsie College, 1953.

Halvorson-Taylor, Martien. "Secrets and Lies: Secrecy Notices (Esth 2:10, 20) and Diasporic Identity in the Books of Esther." *JBL* 131 (2012): 467–85.

Hamilton, Alastair. *The Apocryphal Apocalypse: The Reception of the Second Book of Esdras (4 Ezra) from the Renaissance to the Enlightenment.* Oxford-Warburg Studies. Oxford: Oxford University Press, 1999.

Hanneken, Todd R. *The Subversion of the Apocalypses in the Book of Jubilees.* Early Judaism and Its Literature 34. Atlanta: SBL, 2012.

Harkins, Angela Kim, and Kelley Coblentz Bautch, eds. *The Watchers in Jewish and Christian Tradition.* Minneapolis: Fortress, 2014.

Harkins, Angela Kim, and Barbara Schmitz, eds. *Selected Studies on Deuterocanonical Prayers.* Contributions to Biblical Exegesis and Theology. Leuven: Peeters, forthcoming.

Harrington, Daniel J. *Invitation to the Apocrypha.* Grand Rapids, MI: Eerdmans, 1999.

Hengel, Martin. *Judaism and Hellenism: Studies in Their Encounter in Palestine during the Early Hellenistic Period.* 2 vols. Philadelphia: Fortress, 1974.

———. *The Septuagint as Christian Scripture: Its Pre-History and the Problem of Its Canon.* Edinburgh: T&T Clark, 2002.

Henten, Jan Willem van. *The Maccabean Martyrs as Saviours of the Jewish People: A Study of 2 and 4 Maccabees.* SupplJSJ 57. Leiden: Brill, 1997.

Henze, Matthias. *Jewish Apocalypticism in Late First Century Israel.* Tübingen: Mohr Siebeck, 2001.

———. *Mind the Gap: How the Jewish Writings between the Old and New Testament Help Us Understand Jesus.* Minneapolis: Fortress, 2017.

———. "On the Anthropology of Early Judaism: Some Observations." Pages 27–42 in *Anthropology and New Testament Theology.* Edited by Jason Maston and Benjamin E. Reynolds. London: Bloomsbury T&T Clark, 2018.

———. "Torah and Eschatology in the Syriac Apocalypse of Baruch." Pages 201–15 in *The Significance of Sinai: Traditions about Sinai and Divine Revelation in Judaism and Christianity.* Edited by George J. Brooke, Hindy Najman, and Loren Stuckenbruck. Leiden: Brill, 2008.

Henze, Mathias, and Gabriele Boccaccini, eds. *Fourth Ezra and Second Baruch: Reconstruction after the Fall.* SupplJSJ 164. Leiden: Brill, 2013.

Henze, Mathias, and Liv Ingeborg Lied. "Jeremiah, Baruch, and Their Books: Three Phases in a Changing Relationship." Pages 330–53 in *Jeremiah's Scriptures: Production, Reception, Interaction, and Transformation.* Edited by Hindy Najman and Konrad Schmid. SupplJSJ 173. Leiden: Brill, 2017.

Herzer, Jens. *4 Baruch (Paraleipomena Jeremiou).* SBLWGRW 22. Atlanta: Society of Biblical Literature, 2005.

———. "Die Paralipomena Jeremiae—eine christlich-gnostische Schrift? Eine Antwort an Marc Philonenko." *JSJ* 30 (1999): 25–39.

Hicks-Keeton, Jill. "Already/Not Yet: Eschatological Tension in the Book of Tobit." *JBL* 132 (2013): 97–117.

Himmelfarb, Martha. *The Apocalypse: A Brief History.* Hoboken, NJ: Wiley-Blackwell, 2010.

Hogan, Karina Martin. "The Exegetical Background of the 'Ambiguity of Death' in the Wisdom of Solomon." *JSJ* 30 (1999): 1–24.

———. "Mother Zion and Mother Earth in 2 Baruch and 4 Ezra." Pages 203–24 in *Intertextual Explorations in Deuterocanonical and Cognate Literature.* Edited by Jeremy Corley and Geoffrey Miller. Berlin: de Gruyter, 2019.

———. *Theologies in Conflict in 4 Ezra: Wisdom Debate and Apocalyptic Solution.* SupplJSJ 130. Leiden: Brill, 2008.

Honigman, Sylvie. "'Jews as the Best of All Greeks': Cultural Competition in the Literary Works of Alexandrian Judeans of the Hellenistic Period." Pages 207–32 in *Shifting Social Imaginaries in the Hellenistic Period: Narrations, Practices, and Images.* Edited by Eftychia Stavrianopoulu. Supplements to Mnemosyne 363. Leiden: Brill, 2013.

———. *The Septuagint and Homeric Scholarship in Alexandria: A Study in the Narrative of the "Letter of Aristeas."* London: Routledge, 2003.

Horsley, Richard A. *Scribes, Visionaries, and the Politics of Second Temple Judea.* Louisville: Westminster John Knox, 2007.

Humphrey, Edith M. *The Ladies and the Cities: Transformation and Apocalyptic Identity in Joseph and Aseneth, 4 Ezra, the Apocalypse and the Shepherd of Hermas.* SupplJSP. London: Bloomsbury T&T Clark, 1995.

Isaac, Ephraim. "The Bible in Ethiopic." Pages 110–22 in *New Cambridge History of the Bible: Volume 2: From 600 to 1450.* Edited by Richard Marsden and E. Ann Matter. Cambridge: Cambridge University Press, 2012.

Jacobs, Naomi S. S. *Delicious Prose: Reading the Tale of Tobit with Food and Drink: A Commentary.* SupplJSJ 188. Leiden: Brill, 2018.

Jacobus, Mary. "Judith, Holofernes, and the Phallic Woman." Pages 110–36 in *Reading Women: Essays in Feminist Criticism.* New York: Columbia University Press, 1986.

Jellicoe, Sidney. *The Septuagint and Modern Study.* Oxford: Oxford University Press, 1968.

Johnson, Sara Raup. *Historical Fictions and Hellenistic Jewish Identity: Third Maccabees in Its Cultural Identity.* Berkeley: University of California Press, 2004.

———. "Novelistic Elements in Esther: Persian or Hellenistic, Jewish or Greek?" *CBQ* 67 (2005): 571–89.

———. "Third Maccabees: Historical Fictions and the Shaping of Jewish Identity in the Hellenistic Period." Pages 185–97 in *Ancient Fiction: The Matrix of Early Christian and Jewish Narrative.* Edited by Jo-Ann A. Brant, Charles W. Hedrick, and Chris Shea. Symposium Series 32. Atlanta: Society of Biblical Literature, 2006.

Joslyn-Siemiatkoski, Daniel. *Christian Memories of the Maccabean Martyrs.* New York: Palgrave Macmillan, 2009.

Kabasele Mukenge, André. *L'unité littéraire du livre de Baruch.* Études Bibliques 38. Paris: Gabalda, 1998.

Kaiser, Otto. *The Old Testament Apocrypha: An Introduction.* Peabody, MA: Hendrickson, 2004.

Kamil, Murad. *Der Josef Ben Gorion (Josippon) Geschichte der Juden nach den Handschriften in Berlin, London, Oxford, Paris und Strasburg.* New York: J. J. Augustin, 1937.

Kiel, Micah D. *The "Whole Truth": Rethinking Retribution in the Book of Tobit.* Library of Second Temple Studies 82. London: T&T Clark, 2002.

Klauck, Hans-Josef. "Hellenistische Rhetorik im Diasporajudentum: das Exordium des vierten Makkabäerbuchs (4 Makk 1:1–12)." *NTS* 35 (1989): 451–65.

Klawans, Jonathan. *Josephus and the Theologies of Ancient Judaism.* Oxford: Oxford University Press, 2012.

Klawans, Jonathan, and Lawrence M. Wills, eds. *Jewish Annotated Apocrypha.* New York: Oxford University Press, 2020.

Kloppenborg, John S. "Isis and Sophia in the Book of Wisdom." *HTR* 75 (1982): 57–84.

Kohlenberger, John R. III, ed. *The Parallel Apocrypha.* New York: Oxford University Press, 1997.

Kolarcik, Michael. *The Ambiguity of Death in the Book of Wisdom 1–6.* AnBib 127. Rome: Pontifical Biblical Institute, 1991.

Kosmin, Paul J. "Indigenous Revolts in 2 Maccabees: The Persian Version." *CP* 111 (2016): 32–53.

Kraft, Robert Alan. *Exploring the Scripturesque: Jewish Texts and Their Christian Contexts.* SupplJSJ. Leiden: Brill, 2009.

Kynes, Will J. *The Oxford Handbook of Wisdom and Wisdom Literature*. New York: Oxford University Press, forthcoming.

Labendz, Jenny. "The Book of Ben Sira in Rabbinic Literature." *AJS Review* 30 (2006): 1–45.

Levine, Amy-Jill. "Diaspora as Metaphor: Bodies and Boundaries in the Book of Tobit." Pages 105–17 in *Diaspora Jews and Judaism: Essays in Honor of, and in Dialogue with, A. Thomas Krabel*. Edited by J. Andrew Overman and R. S. MacLennan. Atlanta: Scholars, 1992.

Lied, Liv Ingeborg. "Those Who Know and Those Who Don't: Mystery, Instruction, and Knowledge in 2 *Baruch*." Pages 427–46 in *Mystery and Secrecy in the Nag Hammadi Collection and Other Ancient Literature: Ideas and Practice*. Edited by Christian H. Bull, Liv Ingeborg Lied, and John D. Turner. Nag Hammadi and Manichaean Studies. Leiden: Brill, 2012.

Loader, William R. G. *The Pseudepigrapha on Sexuality: Attitudes toward Sexuality in Apocalypses, Testaments, Legends, Wisdom, and Related Literature*. Grand Rapids, MI: Eerdmans, 2011.

Macatangay, Francis M. *When I Die, Bury Me Well: Death, Burial, Almsgiving, and Restoration in the Book of Tobit*. Eugene, OR: Pickwick, 2016.

MacDonald, Dennis R. "Tobit and the *Odyssey*." Pages 11–40 in *Mimesis and Intertextuality in Antiquity and Christianity*. Edited by Dennis R. MacDonald. Harrisburg, PA: Trinity Press International, 2001.

Machiela, Daniel A., and Andrew B. Perrin. "Tobit and the Genesis Apocryphon: Toward a Family Portrait." *JBL* 133 (2014): 11–32.

Mack, Burton. *Logos und Sophia: Untersuchungen zur Weisheitstheologie im hellenistischen Judentum*. Göttingen: Vandenhoeck & Ruprecht, 1973.

Mattila, Sharon Lea. "Ben Sira and the Stoics: A Reexamination of the Evidence." *JBL* 119 (2000): 473–501.

McDonald, Lee Martin. *The Formation of the Biblical Canon*. 2 vols. London: Bloomsbury T&T Clark, 2017.

Menn, Esther. "Prayer of the Queen: Esther's Religious Self in the Septuagint." Pages 70–90 in *Religion and the Self in Antiquity*. Edited by David Brakke, Michael L. Satlow, and Steven Weitzman. Bloomington: Indiana University Press, 2005.

Moore, Carey A. *Daniel, Esther, and Jeremiah: The Additions*. New York: Doubleday, 1977.

———. *Judith: A New Translation with Introduction and Commentary*. AB 40. Garden City, NY: Doubleday, 1985.

———. *Tobit*. AB 40A. Garden City, NY: Doubleday, 1996.

Moscicke, Hans. "The Concept of Evil in 4 Maccabees: Stoic Absorption and Adaptation." *Journal of Jewish Thought and Philosophy* 25 (2017): 163–95.

Murphy, Fredrick J. *The Structure and Meaning of Second Baruch.* SBLDS. Atlanta: Scholars, 1985.

Myers, Eric. *I and II Esdras: A New Translation with Introduction and Commentary.* AB 42. Garden City, NY: Doubleday-Anchor, 1974.

Najman, Hindy. "Interpretation as Primordial Writing: Jubilees and Its Authority Conferring Strategies." *JSJ* 30 (1999): 379–410.

———. *Losing the Temple and Recovering the Future: An Analysis of 4 Ezra.* Cambridge: Cambridge University Press, 2014.

———. *Seconding Sinai: The Development of Mosaic Discourse in Second Temple Judaism.* SupplJSJ 77. Leiden: Brill, 2003.

Newman, Judith H. *Before the Bible: The Liturgical Body and the Formation of Scriptures in Early Judaism.* Oxford: Oxford University Press, 2018.

———. "The Form and Settings of the Prayer of Manasseh." Pages 105–25 in *Seeking the Favor of God. Volume 2: The Development of Penitential Prayer in Second Temple Judaism.* Edited by Mark Boda, Daniel K. Falk, and Rodney A. Werline. SBLEJL 22. Atlanta: Society of Biblical Literature, 2007.

Nickelsburg, George W. E. "Enochic Wisdom: An Alternative to the Mosaic Torah." Pages 123–32 in *Hesed Ve-Emet: Studies in Honor of Ernest S. Frerichs.* Edited by Jodi Magness and Seymour Gitin. Atlanta: Scholars, 1998.

———. *1 Enoch.* Hermeneia. Minneapolis: Fortress, 2001.

———. *Jewish Literature between the Bible and the Mishnah.* 2nd ed. Minneapolis: Fortress, 2005.

———. "The Parables of Enoch and the Manuscripts from Qumran." Pages 2.655–68 in *A Teacher for All Generations: Essays in Honor of James C. VanderKam.* Edited by Eric F. Mason. 2 vols. Leiden: Brill, 2012.

———. "The Search for Tobit's Mixed Ancestry: A Historical and Hermeneutical Odyssey." *CBQ* 17 (1996): 339–49.

Nickelsburg, George W. E., and James C. VanderKam. *1 Enoch 2: A Commentary on the Book of 1 Enoch, Chapters 37–82.* Hermeneia. Minneapolis: Fortress, 2011.

Novick, Tzvi. "Biblicized Narrative: On Tobit and Genesis 22." *JBL* 126 (2007): 755–64.

Nowell, Irene. "The Book of Tobit." Pages 3.973–1071 in *The New Interpreter's Bible.* Edited by Leander E. Keck. 12 vols. Nashville: Abingdon, 1999.

———. "The Book of Tobit: An Ancestral Story." Pages 3–13 in *Intertextual Studies in Ben Sira and Tobit: Essays in Honor of Alexander A. Di Lella, O.F.M.* Edited by Jeremy Corley and Vincent Skemp. CBQMS 38. Washington, DC: Catholic Biblical Association, 2005.

Olson, Daniel C. *A New Reading of the Animal Apocalypse of 1 Enoch: "All Nations Shall Be Blessed."* SVTP 24. Leiden: Brill, 2013.

Olyan, Saul M. "Ben Sira's Relationship to the Priesthood." *HTR* 80 (1987): 261–86.

Otzen, Benedikt. *Tobit and Judith*. Guides to the Apocrypha and Pseudepigrapha. London: Sheffield Academic Press, 2002.

Paget, James Carleton, and Joachim Schaper, eds. *The New Cambridge History of the Bible. Volume 1: From the Beginnings to 600*. Cambridge: Cambridge University Press, 2013.

Pentiuc, Eugen. *The Old Testament in Eastern Orthodox Theology*. Oxford: Oxford University Press, 2014.

Pietersma, Albert, and Benjamin G. Wright, eds. *A New English Translation of the Septuagint*. Oxford: Oxford University Press, 2007.

Portier-Young, Anathea. "Alleviation of Suffering in the Book of Tobit: Comedy, Community, and Happy Endings." *CBQ* 63 (2001): 35–54.

———. *Apocalypse against Empire: Theologies of Resistance in Early Judaism*. Grand Rapids, MI: Eerdmans, 2011.

Purinton, Ann-Elizabeth, and Robert A. Kraft. *Paraleipomena Jeremiou*. Texts and Traditions 1. Missoula, MT: Society of Biblical Literature, 1972.

Rabenau, Merten. *Studien zum Buch Tobit*. BZAW 220. Berlin: de Gruyter, 1994.

Rad, Gerhard von. *Wisdom in Israel*. Nashville: Abingdon, 1972.

Rahlfs, Alfred, ed. *Septuaginta: Id est Vetus Testamentum graece iuxta LXX interpretes*. 2 vols. Stuttgart: Deutsche Bibelstiftung, 1935.

Rajak, Tessa. "Reflections on Jewish Resistance and the Discourse of Martyrdom in Josephus." Pages 165–80 in *Judaea-Palaestina, Babylon and Rome: Jews in Antiquity*. Edited by Benjamin Isaac and Yuval Shahar. Tübingen: Mohr Siebeck, 2012.

———. *Translation and Survival: The Greek Bible of the Ancient Jewish Diaspora*. Oxford: Oxford University Press, 2009.Rajak, Tessa, Sarah Pearce, James Aitken, and Jennifer Dines, eds. *Jewish Perspectives on Hellenistic Rulers*. Berkeley: University of California Press, 2007.

Rakel, Claudia. "'I Will Sing a New Song to My God': Some Remarks on the Intertextuality of Judith 16.1–7." Pages 27–47 in *A Feminist Companion to the Bible: Judges*. Edited by Athalya Brenner. FCB Second Series 4. Sheffield: Sheffield Academic Press, 1999.

Redditt, Paul L. "The Concept of *Nomos* in Fourth Maccabees." *CBQ* 45 (1983): 249–70.

Reese, James M. *Hellenistic Influence on the Book of Wisdom and Its Consequences*. Rome: Biblical Institute Press, 1970.

Reeves, John C., and Annette Yoshiko Reed, eds. *Enoch from Antiquity to the Middle Ages, Volume 1*. Oxford: Oxford University Press, 2018.

Reymond, Eric D. *New Idioms within Old Poetry and Parallelism in the Non-Masoretic Poems of 11Q5 (= 11 QPsa)*. Leiden: Brill, 2011.

Rowland, Christopher. *The Open Heaven: A Study of Apocalyptic in Judaism and Early Christianity*. London: SPCK, 1982.

Sacchi, Paolo. *Jewish Apocalyptic and Its History*. Sheffield: Sheffield Academic Press, 1997.

Saldarini, Anthony J. "Letter of Jeremiah." Pages 6.927–82 in *The New Interpreter's Bible*. Edited by Leander E. Keck. 12 vols. Nashville: Abingdon, 2001.

Sanders, Jack T. *Ben Sira and Demotic Wisdom*. SBLMS 28. Chico, CA: Scholars, 1983.

Sanders, James A. "Ps. 151 in 11QPss." *ZAW* 75 (1963): 73–86.

Satlow, Michael L. *How the Bible Became Holy*. New Haven: Yale University Press, 2014.

Schellenberg, Ryan S. "Suspense, Simultaneity, and Divine Providence in the Book of Tobit." *JBL* 130 (2011): 313–27.

Schmitz, Barbara. *Gedeutete Geschichte: Die Funktion der Reden und Gebete im Buch Judit*. HBS 40. Freiburg: Herder, 2004.

Schmitz, Barbara, and Helmut Engel. *Judit*. Freiburg: Herder, 2014.

Schniedewind, William M. "The Source Citations of Manasseh: King Manasseh in History and Homily." *VT* 41 (1991): 450–61.

Schorch, Stefan. "Genderising Piety: The Prayers of Mordecai and Esther in Comparison." Pages 30–42 in *Deuterocanonical Additions of the Old Testament Books: Selected Studies*. Edited by Géza G. Xeravits and József Zsengellér. DCLS 5. Berlin: de Gruyter, 2010.

Schwartz, Daniel R. *Judeans and Jews: Four Faces of Dichotomy in Ancient Jewish History*. Toronto: University of Toronto Press, 2014.

———. *2 Maccabees*. CEJL. Berlin: de Gruyter, 2008.

Segal, Michael. "The Literary Development of Psalm 151: A New Look at the Septuagint Version." *Textus* 21 (2002): 139–58.

Selassie, Feqade. *Ethiopian Books of Meqabyan 1–3, in Standard English*. Lulu Press (print on demand).

Siegert, Folker. *Einleitung in die hellenistisch-jüdische Literatur: Apokrypha, Pseudepigrapha und Fragmente verlorener Autorenwerke*. Berlin: de Gruyter, 2016.

Simkovich, Malka Z. *Discovering Second Temple Literature: The Scriptures and Stories That Shaped Early Judaism*. Philadelphia: Jewish Publication Society, 2018.

———. "Greek Influence on the Composition of 2 Maccabees." *JSJ* 42 (2011): 293–310.

———. *The Making of Jewish Universalism: From Exile to Alexandria.* Lanham, MD: Lexington, 2017.

Skehan, Patrick, and Alexander Di Lella. *The Wisdom of Ben Sira: A New Translation with Notes.* Garden City, NY: Doubleday, 1987.

Smith, Mark S. "How to Write a Poem." Pages 182–208 in *The Hebrew of the Dead Sea Scrolls and Ben Sira: Proceedings of a Symposium Held at Leiden University, 11–14 December 1995.* Edited by T. Muraoka and J. F. Elwolde. Studies on the Texts of the Desert of Judah 26. Leiden: Brill, 1997.

Soll, William. "The Family as a Scriptural and Social Construct in Tobit." Pages 166–75 in *The Function of Scripture in Early Jewish and Christian Tradition.* Edited by Craig A. Evans and James A. Sanders. Sheffield: Sheffield Academic Press, 1998.

———. "Tobit and Folklore Studies, with Emphasis on Propp's Methodology." Pages 39–53 in *Society of Biblical Literature 1988 Seminar Papers.* Edited by David J. Lull. SBLSP. Atlanta: Scholars, 1988.

Spolsky, Ellen. *Judgment of Susanna: Authority and Witness.* EJL 11. Atlanta: Scholars, 1996.

Steck, Odil Hannes. *Das apockryphe Baruchbuch: Studien zu Rezeption und Konzentration "kanonischer" Überlieferung.* FRLANT 160. Göttingen: Vandenhoeck & Ruprecht, 1993.

Steussy, Marti J. *Gardens in Babylon: Narrative and Faith in the Greek Legends of Daniel.* SBLDS 141. Atlanta: Scholars, 1993.

Stocker, Margarita. *Judith: Sexual Warrior: Women and Power in Western Culture.* New Haven: Yale University Press, 1998.

Stone, Meredith J. *Empire and Gender in LXX Esther.* EJL 48. Atlanta: Society of Biblical Literature, 2018.

Stone, Michael E. "Apocalyptic Literature." Pages 383–441 in *Jewish Writings of the Second Temple Period.* Edited by Michael E. Stone. CRINT II:3. Assen, Netherlands: Van Gorcum; Philadelphia: Fortress, 1984.

———. *A Commentary on the Fourth Book of Ezra.* Hermeneia. Minneapolis: Augsburg Fortress, 1990.

———. "Lists of Revealed Things in Apocalyptic Literature." Pages 414–52 in *Magnalia Dei: The Mighty Acts of God: Essays on the Bible and Archaeology in Memory of G. Ernest Wright.* Edited by Frank Moore Cross, Jr., Werner E. Lemke, and Patrick D. Miller. Garden City, NY: Doubleday, 1976.

Stone, Michael E., and Matthias Henze. *4 Ezra and 2 Baruch: Translations, Introductions, and Notes.* Minneapolis: Fortress, 2013.

Stuckenbruck, Loren T. *1 Enoch 91–108.* CEJL. Berlin: de Gruyter, 2007.

———. *The Myth of Rebellious Angels: Studies in Second Temple Judaism and New Testament Texts.* Grand Rapids, MI: Eerdmans, 2017.

Stuckenbruck, Loren T., and Daniel M. Gurtner, eds. *T&T Clark Encyclopedia of Second Temple Judaism*. 2 vols. London: Bloomsbury T&T Clark, 2019.

Talshir, Zipora. *1 Esdras: From Origin to Translation*. Septuagint and Cognate Studies 47. Atlanta: SBL, 1999.

Tamási, Balázs. "The Sources of Authority in Second Baruch." Pages 225–50 in *Scriptural Authority in Early Judaism and Ancient Christianity*. Edited by Géza G. Xeravits, Tobias Nicklas, and Isaac Kalimi. DCLS 16. Berlin: de Gruyter, 2013.

Thomas, Samuel I. "Eternal Writing and Immortal Writers: On the Non-Death of the Scribe in Early Judaism." Pages 2.573–88 in *A Teacher for All Generations: Essays in Honor of James C. VanderKam*. Edited by Eric F. Mason. 2 vols. Leiden: Brill, 2011.

Tomes, Roger. "Heroism in 1 and 2 Maccabees." *BibInt* 15 (2007): 171–99.

Ullendorff, Edward. *Ethiopia and the Bible*. London: Oxford University Press, 1968.

Van der Horst, Pieter, and Judith H. Newman, eds. *Early Jewish Prayers in Greek*. CEJL. Berlin: de Gruyter, 2008.

VanderKam, James C. *The Book of Jubilees*. Guides to the Apocrypha and Pseudepigrapha. Sheffield: Sheffield Academic Press, 2001.

———. *Enoch and the Growth of an Apocalyptic Tradition*. CBQMS 16. Washington, DC: Catholic Biblical Association of America, 1984.

———, ed. *The Jewish Apocalyptic Heritage in Early Christianity*. CRINT 3.4. Assen, Netherlands: Van Gorcum; Minneapolis: Fortress, 1996.

———. *Jubilees: A Commentary on the Book of Jubilees*. Hermeneia. Minneapolis: Fortress, 2018.

———, ed. *"No One Spoke Ill of Her": Essays on Judith*. EJL 2. Atlanta: Scholars, 1992.

———. "Studies in the Apocalypse of Weeks (1 Enoch 93:1–10, 91:11–17)." *CBQ* 46 (1984): 511–23.

———. *Textual and Historical Studies in the Book of Jubilees*. HSM 14. Missoula, MT: Scholars, 1977.

Warren, Meredith J. C. *Food and Transformation in Ancient Mediterranean Literature*. SBLWGRW 14. Atlanta: Society of Biblical Literature, 2019.

Wasserman, Emma. *Apocalypse as Holy War: Divine Politics and Polemics in the Letters of Paul*. Anchor Yale Bible Reference Library. New Haven: Yale University Press, 2018.

Wasserstein, Abraham, and David J. Wasserstein. *Legend of the Septuagint: From Classical Antiquity to Today*. Cambridge: Cambridge University Press, 2006.

Weeks, Stuart, Simon Gathercole, and Loren T. Stuckenbruck, eds. *The Book of Tobit: Texts from the Principal Ancient and Medieval Traditions: With Syn-*

opsis, Concordance, and Annotated Texts in Aramaic, Hebrew, Greek, Latin, and Syriac. Fontes et Subsidia ad Bibliam Pertinentes 3. Berlin: de Gruyter, 2004.

Weitzman, Steven. "Allusion, Artifice, and Exile in the Hymn of Tobit." *JBL* 115 (1996): 49–61.

———. "Sensory Reform in Deuteronomy." Pages 123–39 in *Religion and the Self in Antiquity.* Edited by David Brakke, Michael L. Satlow, and Steven Weitzman. Bloomington: Indiana University Press, 2005.

———. *Song and Story in Biblical Narrative: The History of a Literary Convention in Ancient Israel.* Indiana Studies in Biblical Literature. Bloomington: Indiana University Press, 1997.

Weststeijn, Johan. "Wine, Women, and Revenge in Near Eastern Historiography: The Tales of Tomyris, Judith, Zenobia, and Jalila." *JNES* 75 (2016): 91–107.

———. "Zenobia of Palmyra and the Book of Judith: Common Motifs in Greek, Jewish, and Arabic Historiography." *JSP* 22 (2013): 295–320.

Williams, David S. "3 Maccabees: A Defense of Diaspora Judaism?" *JSP* 13 (1995): 17–29.

———. *The Structure of 1 Maccabees.* CBQMS 31. Washington, DC: Catholic Biblical Association, 1999.

Wills, Lawrence M. "Ascetic Theology before Asceticism? Jewish Narratives and the Decentering of the Self." *JAAR* 74 (2006): 902–25.

———. "The Differentiation of History and Novel: Controlling the Past, Playing with the Past." Pages 13–30 in *Early Christian and Jewish Narrative: The Role of Religion in Shaping Narrative Forms.* Edited by Ilaria Ramelli and Judith Perkins. WUNT 348. Tübingen: Mohr Siebeck, 2015.

———. "The Form of the Sermon in Hellenistic Judaism and Early Christianity." *HTR* 77 (1984): 278–80.

———. *The Jew in the Court of the Foreign King: Ancient Jewish Court Legends.* HDR 26. Minneapolis: Augsburg Fortress, 1990.

———. "Jew, Judean, Judaism in the Ancient Period: An Alternative Argument." *JAJ* 7 (2016): 169–93.

———. "Jewish Heroes in the Apocrypha." Pages 633–36 in *Jewish Annotated Apocrypha.* Edited by Jonathan Klawans and Lawrence M. Wills. New York: Oxford University Press, 2020.

———. *The Jewish Novel in the Ancient World.* Myth and Poetics. Ithaca, NY: Cornell University Press, 1995.

———. "Jewish Novellas in a Greek and Roman Age: Fiction and Identity." *JSJ* 42 (2011): 141–65.

———. *Judith.* Hermeneia. Minneapolis: Fortress, 2019.

———. *Not God's People: Insiders and Outsiders in the Biblical World.* Religion in the Modern World 1. Lanham, MD: Rowman & Littlefield, 2008.

———. "Why the Passive Protagonist in Wisdom of Solomon 2–5?" *Journal of Religious Competition in Antiquity* 1 (2019): 48–61.

———. "Wisdom and Word among the Hellenistic Saviors: The Function of Literacy." *JSP* 24 (2014): 118–48.

Winston, David. "Hellenistic Jewish Philosophy." Pages 30–48 in *History of Jewish Philosophy.* Edited by Daniel H. Frank and Oliver Leaman. London: Routledge, 1997.

———. *The Wisdom of Solomon: A New Translation with Introduction and Commentary.* AB 43. Garden City, NY: Doubleday, 1979.

Witakowski, Witold. "Zena Ayhud." Pages 5.176–78 in *Encyclopaedia Aethiopica.* Edited by Siegbert Uhlig. 5 vols. Wiesbaden: Harrassowitz, 2003–2014.

Wright, Benjamin G. III. "Ben Sira and the Book of the Watchers on the Legitimate Priesthood." Pages 241–54 in *Intertextual Studies in Ben Sira and Tobit: Essays in Honor of Alexander A. Di Lella, O.F.M.* Edited by Jeremy Corley and Vincent Skemp. CBQMS 38. Washington, DC: Catholic Biblical Association of America, 2005.

———. "Ben Sira on Kings and Kingship." Pages 76–91 in *Jewish Perspectives on Hellenistic Rulers.* Edited by Tessa Rajak, Sarah Pearce, James Aitken, and Jennifer Dines. Berkeley: University of California Press, 2007.

———. "A Character in Search of a Story: The Reception of Ben Sira in Early Medieval Judaism." Pages 377–395 in *'Wisdom Poured Out like Water': Studies in Jewish and Christian Antiquity in Honor of Gabriele Boccaccini.* Edited by J. Harold Ellens, Isaac W. Oliver, Jason von Ehrenkrook, James Waddell, and Jason M. Zurawski. DCLS 38. Berlin: de Gruyter, 2018.

———. "'Fear the Lord and Honor the Priest': Ben Sira as Defender of the Jerusalem Priesthood." Pages 189–22 in *The Book of Ben Sira in Modern Research: Proceedings of the First International Ben Sira Conference, 28–31 July 1996, Soesterberg, Netherlands.* Edited by Pancratius C. Beentjius. BZAW 255. Berlin: de Gruyter, 1997.

———. "1 Enoch and Ben Sira: Wisdom and Apocalypticism in Relationship." Pages 159–76 in *The Early Enoch Literature.* Edited by Gabriele Boccaccini and John J. Collins. SupplJSJ. Leiden: Brill, 2007.

———. "From Generation to Generation: The Sage as Father in Early Jewish Literature." Pages 309–32 in *Biblical Traditions in Transmission: Essays in Honour of Michael Knibb.* Edited by Charlotte Hempel and Judith M. Lieu. SupplJSJ 111. Leiden: Brill, 2006.

———. *The Letter of Aristeas: 'Aristeas to Philocrates' or 'On the Translation of the Law of the Jews.'* CEJL. Berlin: de Gruyter, 2015.

———. *No Small Difference: Sirach's Relationship to Its Hebrew Parent Text.* Septuagint and Cognate Studies 26. Atlanta: Scholars, 1989.

Wright, Benjamin G., and Suzanne M. Edwards. "'She Undid Him with the Beauty of Her Face' (Jdt 16.6): Reading Women's Bodies in Early Jewish Literature." Pages 73–108 in *Religion and the Female Body in Ancient Judaism and Its Environments.* Edited by Géza Xeravits. DCLS 38. Berlin: de Gruyter, 2015.

Wright, Benjamin G. III, and Lawrence M. Wills, eds. *Conflicted Boundaries in Wisdom and Apocalypticism.* SymS 35. Atlanta: Society of Biblical Literature, 2005.

Wright, J. Edward. "Baruch: His Evolution from Scribe to Apocalyptic Seer." Pages 264–89 in *Biblical Figures outside the Bible.* Edited by Michael E. Stone and Theodore A. Bergren. Harrisburg, PA: Trinity Press International, 1998.

Xeravits, Géza G., and József Zsengellér, eds. *The Book of Tobit: Text, Tradition, Theology.* SupplJSJ 98. Leiden: Brill, 2005.

———, eds. *Deuterocanonical Additions of the Old Testament Books: Selected Studies.* DCLS 5. Berlin: de Gruyter, 2010.

———, eds. *Studies in the Book of Wisdom.* Leiden: Brill, 2010.

Zurawski, Jason M. "Ezra Begins: *4 Ezra* as Prequel and the Making of a Superhero." Pages 289–304 in *Old Testament Pseudepigrapha and the Scriptures.* Edited by Eibert Tigchelaar. BETL 270. Leuven: Peeters, 2014.

———. "Paideia: A Multifarious and Unifying Concept in the Wisdom of Solomon." Pages 195–214 in *Pedagogy in Ancient Judaism and Early Christianity.* Edited by Karina Martin Hogan, Matthew Goff, and Emma Wasserman. EJL 41. Atlanta: Society of Biblical Literature, 2017.

Index of Subjects

Abraham, 36, 38, 45, 76–77, 99, 103, 120, 157, 177, 195, 199, 215, 221, 228–29, 240

Adam, 121, 148, 177, 183, 185, 194, 203–4, 215, 263, 267

Alexandria. *See* Egypt

Alexandrinus, 10–11, 19–20, 41, 76, 108, 164, 217–18, 223, 242, 248

angels, 66, 74–75, 81, 83–84, 102, 120, 219, 222, 224, 229–30, 239, 240, 264, 269; in Tobit, 34, 37, 38, 45–46, 49–51

apocalypses and apocalypticism, 19, 27–28, 64, 88, 127, 130, 134, 135, 137, 140–41, 145, 156, 159, 170, 172–216, 224, 225, 228, 229, 230, 254, 263, 265, 271

Apocrypha as term (including deutero-canonical), 1–18, 48, 51–52, 65, 82, 90, 91, 111, 134, 151, 153, 169, 191, 192, 214, 223, 227–32, 234, 246, 271

Arabic, 116, 117, 201

Armenian, 4, 5, 6, 9, 70, 87, 192, 201, 211, 248

calendar, 7, 57, 91–92, 96, 131, 159, 177, 178, 181–82, 193–94, 197, 249–50, 264; and time, 57, 96, 136, 147–48, 172, 180, 182, 185, 193–94, 198, 202, 219, 224, 244

canon, 1–20, 33, 90, 111, 116, 118, 120, 133, 135, 153, 164, 166, 169–70, 176, 191–92, 207, 210, 211, 217, 218, 220, 223, 232, 233, 234–35, 246, 253

Catholic Church, 1–20, 49, 108, 121, 134, 153, 169, 201, 235, 267

circumcision, 94, 120, 194–95, 199–200, 209

colonial universalism and postcolonial theory, 7–8, 57, 86, 106, 115, 132, 152, 155, 198, 230, 232, 271

Coptic, 4–5, 6, 9, 118, 201

covenant, 2, 44, 74, 94, 98, 103–4, 115, 117, 120, 130, 161, 180, 194, 196, 199–200, 202, 206, 207, 209, 221

David, 6, 7, 26, 62, 95, 99, 115, 190, 204, 218–25, 266

Dead Sea Scrolls (Qumran), 12, 33, 40, 41, 48, 134, 181, 188, 193–94, 200, 217–18, 221, 231–32, 243, 264, 268, 269

death, 23, 37, 42, 45, 46, 65–66, 75, 76, 102–3, 105, 106–7, 121, 128, 131, 141, 143, 149, 154, 155, 157, 159, 181, 192, 194, 195, 203, 205, 214, 221, 244, 260. *See also* martyrdom; resurrection and immortality

demons, 34, 37–38, 43, 49, 52, 162, 173, 176, 185, 188, 197, 240

Deuteronomic theology, 42–46, 98, 221, 227–28, 241

diaspora, 42, 48, 84, 107, 251

Egypt (including Alexandria), 7–12, 23, 28, 34, 38, 43, 47, 82–87, 100, 103, 114, 121, 125, 126, 128–32, 135–58, 176, 198, 230, 234, 255, 259 emotions and interior life, 24–25, 28–31, 85, 99, 102–3, 108, 122, 130, 145, 151, 154–58, 163, 206, 219, 231, 259, 261, 270. *See also* passive protagonist

Ethiopic, 4–7, 9, 12, 17–18, 24, 62, 70, 88, 90, 116–21, 177, 191, 192, 201, 235, 253

gender and sexuality, 14, 21, 24–26, 27–34, 43, 52–73, 79, 83, 106, 107, 114–15, 124–25, 131–34, 159, 167, 184, 196, 204, 209, 228, 231, 237–43, 244, 246, 255, 265, 267; eunuchs, 56, 133–34, 144–48, 259

gentiles, 32, 83–84, 86, 94–100, 104, 109, 129, 135–36, 145, 171, 186, 189, 201–4, 209, 214, 242, 256, 261, 268; in Jubilees, 99, 104, 115, 194–95, 199–201, 230

Georgian, 201

God, 28, 55–60, 69, 73–86, 90, 92–93, 99, 117, 194–99, 203–14, 218–22, 234, 255, 256, 257; and creation, 30, 129–32; intervening in human affairs, 12, 26, 31–33, 37, 39, 42–45, 54, 66, 75, 79–86, 101–9, 112, 120, 121–23, 147–52, 155–57, 161–71, 172, 224, 227–30, 247, 259, 261; knowledge of, 9, 125–26, 136–44, 172, 174, 176–79, 181, 184–89; power and sovereignty of, 39, 53, 183–91, 244, 265

heroes, 22, 31, 39–51, 52–64, 67–69, 130, 131, 135, 148–50, 158–59, 170, 178, 183, 195, 218, 219, 228–29, 231, 233, 252, 260, 265, 269; Ezra as, 112, 115, 202; Maccabees as, 93–94, 99, 101, 106, 154–55

historicist versus biblicist approaches, 38, 55–56, 66, 159, 245

history writing, 4, 18, 37, 88–123, 127, 130–31, 148–52, 171, 173, 185–87, 201–4, 208, 213, 218, 221–26, 233, 235, 244, 269; and Greek history, 9, 78, 154, 168, 175, 197–99, 215, 249–51, 262; and novellas, 21, 22, 29, 44, 48, 51, 62, 82–84, 102, 246; post-biblical Judaism and, 33, 116–18, 134–36; and rewritten scripture, 90–91, 111–12, 179, 192–94

idolatry, 28, 30, 78–79, 81, 83, 118–20, 150–52, 166–69, 195–96, 218–19, 259

immortality. *See* resurrection and immortality

Isis, 75, 125, 130, 147, 257–59

Jerusalem, 6–8, 16, 36, 39, 47–48, 53–55, 82–86, 92, 94, 98, 103, 107, 115, 117, 120, 122, 123, 128, 129, 131, 160, 162, 164, 165, 167, 170–71, 180, 181, 184, 186, 194, 197, 200, 201–2, 206–15, 223, 224–225, 239, 254, 265, 268

Jew (*Yehudi/Yehudiyah*) as identity term, 26–27, 32–33, 68, 81, 85–87, 104–6, 116, 231–32, 271

King James Version, 16

Latin, 9, 11, 14, 26, 49, 76, 111, 117, 158, 201, 208, 237, 267; Old Latin, 237

law (including Torah), 13, 32, 33, 46, 65, 66, 94, 98, 99, 112–15, 118–20, 142, 147, 179–80, 184, 186, 192–201, 202, 205, 207, 230, 237, 240–41, 265; and commitment to God, 24, 28, 39, 41–43, 86, 90, 103–7, 209, 212–15; and wisdom, 126–33, 140, 154–56, 162, 189, 255, 257, 261

Luther, Martin, 15, 51–52, 70, 222, 246

martyrdom, 74–77, 101–2, 106–10, 119, 120,
    153–58. *See also* death
messiah, 78, 159, 190, 204, 224–26, 266
Moses, 4–10, 26, 39, 41, 55, 65, 83, 90–91,
    98, 111–13, 130, 140, 142, 148, 149,
    156, 159, 170, 177–80, 186, 192,
    194–97, 207, 212, 228–29, 241, 257
Muratorian fragment, 13, 135, 153

Noah, 76, 177, 178, 183, 185, 188, 195, 246
novellas, 18, 21–87, 88, 91, 97–98, 105, 116,
    124, 132, 196, 199, 219, 229, 231,
    236–37, 239, 241. *See also* history
    writing

Odes, 76, 139, 216, 217–26, 235, 258
Old Greek, 65–69, 78–81
Old Latin. *See* Latin
Old Testament as term, 1–2
Orthodox Church (Greek and Eastern),
    4–5, 16–17, 76–77, 87, 134

passive protagonist, 31, 33, 43, 55, 61,
    137–39, 143–44, 149–50, 152, 231,
    258. *See also* emotions and interior
    life
penitential theology, 160, 221–22, 228, 270
Pentateuch, 4–5, 8–10, 32, 42, 90–91, 178,
    192, 194, 197
Peshitta. *See* Syriac
Pharisees, 70, 121, 215, 223–25, 270
philosophy, 7, 9, 14, 57, 79, 85–86, 104,
    106–7, 132, 135–47, 151, 153–58, 168,
    187, 220, 249, 252, 255–62, 265, 270.
    See also history writing: and Greek
    history; protreptic
Photios, Patriarch, 16
postcolonial theory. *See* colonial
    universalism
prayer, 17–19, 21, 25–30, 37, 49, 55, 57, 59,
    65, 66, 73–77, 79, 81–86, 93, 99,
    103, 108, 112, 127, 140, 146, 160–61,

164, 196, 208, 212, 217–26, 228, 231,
    237–39, 247, 252, 253, 262, 269
prophets and prophecy, 74, 84, 158, 160,
    167, 188, 192, 216, 222, 239, 253,
    254; and apocalypticism, 12, 39,
    126–27, 176–78, 184, 196; and
    biblical prophets, 4, 12–14, 18, 32,
    81–82, 94, 115, 120, 123, 133, 134,
    146, 165, 172, 176–78, 208–13
Protestants and Apocrypha, 1–3, 5, 12,
    15–16, 51–52, 62, 64, 108
protreptic, 138–39, 149–50, 155, 187–88,
    257, 261, 265. *See also* history
    writing: and Greek history;
    philosophy
psalms, 12, 17, 19–20, 30, 74–76, 127, 150,
    163, 200, 217–26, 235, 258, 261,
    269–70
pseudepigrapha as term, 3, 12–13, 15, 169,
    233
purity (including impurity), 30, 167, 198,
    232, 236–37

Qumran. *See* Dead Sea Scrolls

rabbinic Judaism, 22–23, 32, 33, 68, 113,
    131, 176–77, 181, 184, 204, 234, 238,
    246, 267; and writings of Apocry-
    pha, 3–4, 10, 12, 49, 62, 77, 82,
    108–9, 117, 134, 153, 158, 192, 199,
    200, 215–16, 222, 224, 239, 251,
    252
resurrection and immortality, 82, 102,
    118–21, 127, 131, 136–46, 154, 169,
    181, 187, 203, 214–15, 224, 229, 258,
    261. *See also* death
rewritten scripture, 90–91, 111–12, 159, 179,
    192–99

scribalism. *See* writing and scribalism
Septuagint, 8–10, 48, 223, 234, 235
sexuality. *See* gender and sexuality

sin, 65–68, 102, 107, 120, 123, 151, 154–55,
        170, 176, 178, 181, 182–84, 189–90,
        195–96, 202–4, 215, 221, 224–25,
        229, 230, 245, 263, 265, 267, 270;
        confession of, 30, 74, 160–65
Sinaiticus, 10–11, 19–20, 41, 218, 242, 248
Sixtus of Siena, 1, 16
son of man, 190, 266
Synods of Jerusalem and Constantinople
        (1672), 16
Syriac (Peshitta), 4, 9, 17, 87, 88, 122–23,
        201, 211–16, 220–26, 235

Temple, 6, 39, 49, 53, 55, 75–78, 82, 84, 97,
        102, 103, 108, 109, 112, 115, 116, 122,
        123, 138, 145, 160, 164, 167, 170–71,
        181, 186, 193–94, 200, 201–10,
        211–15, 223–25, 232, 264
Theodotionic Text, 65–69, 78–80
time. See calendar
torah. See law
Trent, Council of, 16, 111, 222

Vaticanus, 10–11, 19–20, 41, 164, 218, 242,
        253
Venetus, 41, 108, 242, 248
Vulgate, 10–11, 14–15, 27, 41, 48–49, 67,
        111, 128, 164, 201, 222, 242, 248,
        252

Wisdom, 18, 23, 41, 42, 61, 69, 114, 121,
        124–71, 173–75, 178–82, 187–90,
        196–97, 204–5, 207, 208, 213–14,
        223–25, 228–29, 254–61, 263, 268.
        See also law: and wisdom
writing and scribalism, 3, 4, 9–10, 14–15,
        22, 32, 33, 44, 64, 83, 84, 103, 106,
        111, 164–65, 170, 188, 191, 193, 212,
        214; and apocalypses, 173–75,
        178–82, 196–201, 207, 228–29;
        and wisdom, 124–71, 234,
        255

Yehudi and Yehudiyah as identity terms.
        See Jew as identity term

Index of Modern Authors

Aarne, Antti, 245
Adams, Sean A., 261, 263
Adelman, Rachel, 238, 266
Adler, William, 266, 267
Alexander, Loveday, 87, 248, 251
Alexander, Philip, 87
Allison, Dale C., 171
Alonso-Schökel, Luis, 57, 244, 245
Anderson, Gary A., 240, 241, 243
Argall, Randal A., 255
Asale, Bruk A., 253
Atkinson, Kenneth, 270
Attridge, Harold W., 249, 251, 269
Aune, David C., 260

Baden, Joel S., 258
Baker, Cynthia M., 237, 240
Bakker, Arjen, 254
Bal, Mieke, 244, 247
Ball, C. J., 166, 262
Balla, Ibolya, 133, 255
Barclay, John, 152
Bartlett, John R., 93, 96–97, 249, 250
Barton, John, 4–5
Baukham, Richard, 48, 238
Bausi, Alessandro, 118, 253
Beckwith, Roger T., 234
Bellman, Simon, 237
Bennema, Cornelis, 254
Bergmann, Claudia, 247
Bergren, Theodore, 268
Berlin, Andrea, 271
Berquist, Jon L., 133
Berthelot, Katell, 271

Bhabha, Homi, 271
Bickart, Noah, 239, 243, 247, 251, 252
Bickerman, Elias, 237
Binyam, Yonatan, 253
Boccaccini, Gabriele, 190, 255, 264, 266
Boin, Douglas, 251
Bolle, Helena M., 255
Bolyki, János, 46, 242
Bonfil, Reuben, 117
Börner-Klein, Dagmar, 253
Bow, Beverly, 241
Bowman, Steven, 117–18, 252
Boyd-Taylor, Cameron, 29, 237, 238, 244
Brand, Miryam, 271
Burkes, Shannon, 213–14, 258

Camp, Claudia V., 133, 255
Caponigro, Mark Stephen, 56, 244
Carruthers, Jo, 238
Certeau, Michel de, 89, 248–49
Chatterjee, Partha, 271
Cheon, Samuel, 258
Chesnutt, Randall D., 217
Ciletti, Elena, 245
Clanton, Dan W., Jr., 246
Clifford, Richard J., 254, 256, 257
Clines, David J. A., 29, 237
Cohen, Shaye J. D., 105, 237, 250, 251
Collins, John J., 16, 39–42, 75–76, 131, 140,
    145–47, 152, 175, 179, 191, 235, 239,
    245, 247, 248, 250, 254, 255, 257,
    258, 259, 260, 263, 264, 266, 271
Conant, Jonathan, 234
Constantelos, Demetrios J., 235

Conzelmann, Hans, 255
Corley, Jeremy, 163–64
Cornelius, Sakkie, 259
Cousland, J. R. C., 83, 241, 248
Cowley, Roger, 235
Craven, Toni, 57–58, 244, 245
Crawford, Sidnie White, 28, 237, 244,
    266
Croy, N. Clayton, 85, 248
Curtin, D. P., 253

Dalley, Stephanie, 236
Davenport, Gene L., 267
Davies, Philip R., 234
Day, Linda, 31, 237, 238
De Lange, Nicholas, 234, 235
Dell, Katharine, 260
Deselaers, Paul, 239, 240
deSilva, David, 2–3, 86, 100, 129, 132, 145,
    155, 223, 227, 234, 235, 248, 249,
    250, 254, 255, 256, 258, 260, 261,
    271
De Wet, Chris L., 246
Di Lella, Alexander, 129, 238, 241, 247,
    254, 255
Dimant, Devorah, 48, 242, 243, 266
DiTommaso, Lorenzo, 65, 245
Docherty, Susan, 214, 266, 269, 270
Dönitz, Saskia, 117, 235, 248, 253
Doran, Robert, 93, 249, 250, 251
Drake, Susanna, 246
Dubarle, A. M., 244

Eddy, S. K., 176, 264
Edwards, Suzanne M., 244, 255
Ego, Beate, 239
Eisenbaum, Pamela, 259
Ellis, Teresa Ann, 255
Engel, Helmut, 239, 243, 246
Enns, Peter, 259
Erho, Ted, 253
Eskenazi, Tamara Cohn, 252

Fitzmyer, Joseph, 239, 243
Flint, Peter W., 269–70
Flusser, David, 252
Focke, Friedrich, 257
Fox, Michael V., 29, 237
Fried, Lisbeth S., 205, 252
Fusillo, Massimo, 61, 245

Gabba, Emilio, 249
Gallager, Edmon L., 234, 235
Gamberoni, Johann, 235
Garrard, Mary D., 247
Genette, Gérard, 240
Georgi, Dieter, 254, 256, 257
Gera, Deborah Levine, 243, 244, 259
Gerould, Gordon Hall, 238–39
Gese, Hartmut, 254
Gilbert, Maurice, 125, 254
Gill, Christopher, 236
Glancy, Jennifer, 247
Glicksman, Andrew T., 259
Goering, Greg Schmidt, 129–30, 254, 260,
    267–68
Goff, Matthew, 166, 196–97, 200, 215, 262,
    267, 269
Goldman, Shalom, 242
Goldstein, Jonathan A., 200, 249, 250, 251,
    267
Goodman, Martin, 88–91
Goswell, Greg, 20
Grillo, Jennifer, 68, 245, 247
Grossman, Maxine, 237
Gruen, Erich, 104, 241–42, 248, 250, 251,
    260, 271

Haag, Ernst, 244
Hacham, Noah, 247, 248
Hadas, Moses, 248
Halbwachs, Maurice, 248–49
Halpern-Amaru, Betsy, 267
Halverson-Taylor, Martien, 237
Hanhart, Robert, 10

Hanneken, Todd R., 267
Hansen, William F., 236
Harland, Philip A., 251
Harrington, Daniel, 1–3, 223, 269
Hart, Trevor, 242
Hartman, Louis F., 247
Hayes, Christine, 239, 243, 247, 251, 252
Hengel, Martin, 132, 232, 234, 250, 255
Henten, Jan Willem van, 244, 251
Henze, Matthias, 190, 214–15, 266, 267,
    268, 269
Herrmann, John J., Jr., 246
Herzer, Jens, 171, 263
Hicks-Keeton, Jill, 239
Hiebert, Robert J. V., 155, 246, 260, 261
Himmelfarb, Martha, 245, 248, 251, 253,
    263, 264, 266
Hogan, Karina Martin, 201, 205–6, 214,
    257, 258, 269
Holm, Tawny L., 236
Holzberg, Niklas, 236
Honigman, Sylvie, 9, 234, 249, 271
Horbury, W., 270
Horsley, Richard, 264

Isaac, Ephraim, 177, 253, 264

Jacobs, Naomi S., 239, 240, 242
Jacobus, Mary, 58, 244
Japhet, Sara, 245
Jellicoe, Sidney, 252
Jensen, Hans J. Ludiger, 43–45, 55, 240–41,
    244
Ji, C. C., 242
Johnson, Sara Raup, 87, 164–65, 237, 248,
    252, 262
Johnson, Vivian L., 269
Joslyn-Siemiatkoski, Daniel, 251, 261
Jouanno, Corinne, 236

Kaiser, Otto, 223, 225, 257, 260, 270
Kamil, Murad, 252

Klauck, Hans-Josef, 260
Klawans, Jonathan, 115, 131, 233, 234, 250,
    252, 255, 271
Kloppenborg, John, 254, 255, 259
Kolarcik, Michael, 143, 257
Koltun-Fromm, Naomi, 235
Konstan, David, 235, 238
Kosmin, Paul, 198, 250, 267
Kraft, Robert, 263, 266
Kraus, Matthew, 140, 256, 257, 260
Kugel, James L., 193, 266
Kvanvig, Helge S., 266
Kynes, Will J., 254

Labendz, Jennie, 256
LaCocque, André, 31, 237
Lahey, Lawrence, 66, 245, 246, 247
Lambert, David, 221–22, 247, 270
Lang, Bernhard, 125, 254
Lemos, T. M., 238
Levenson, Jon D., 144, 242
Levine, Amy-Jill, 242, 244, 246
Levine, Lee I., 251
Lied, Liv Ingeborg, 213, 268, 269
Llewelyn, Stephen R., 255
Loader, William R. G., 114, 252

Macatangay, Francis M., 242
MacDonald, Dennis R., 240
Machiela, Daniel A., 238, 243
Mack, Burton, 257
Mattila, Sharon Lea, 132, 255
Mazar, B., 242
McDonald, Lee Martin, 234
Meade, John D., 235
Menn, Esther, 237
Michael, Tony S. L., 261
Miles, Margaret R., 247
Milik, J. T., 236, 242
Miller, Jeffrey David, 242
Mobley, Gregory, 249, 269
Montgomery, James A., 78, 247

Moore, Carey A., 46, 237, 239, 242, 243, 245, 246, 262
Morgan, J. R., 236
Moscicke, Hans, 156, 261
Moss, Candida R., 258
Mroczek, Eva, 196, 217, 233, 234, 235, 267, 268
Mukenge, André Kabasele, 163, 262
Murphy, Frederick J., 269
Myers, Eric, 252

Najman, Hindy, 90, 159, 197, 206–7, 249, 267, 268
Newman, Judith H., 159, 217, 221–22, 255, 256, 261, 262, 270
Newsom, Carol, 175, 264
Nickelsburg, George W. E., 37, 95, 114, 162, 190, 224–25, 238, 239, 240, 241, 248, 252, 254, 256, 257, 258, 260, 261, 262, 264, 265, 266, 269, 270
Nicklas, Tobias, 243
Niditch, Susan, 247
Novick, Tzvi, 238
Nowell, Irene, 45, 241

Olyan, Saul M., 236–37, 254, 256, 270
Orlove, Andrei A., 266
Otzen, Benedikt, 41–44, 238, 240–41, 243, 244

Panken, Aaron D., 252
Patte, Daniel, 233
Pentiuc, Eugen, 233, 235
Perrin, Andrew B., 238, 243
Pevarello, Daniele, 270
Philonenko, Marc, 263
Philpot, Elizabeth, 242
Poehlman, William Riehl, 254
Portier-Young, Anathea, 179, 242, 256, 263, 264, 271
Pouchelle, Patrick, 265, 270

Propp, Vladimir, 238, 240
Purinton, Ann-Elizabeth, 263

Rabenau, Merten, 239, 242
Rad, Gerhard von, 130, 173, 254
Rahlfs, Alfred, 9–10, 223, 234
Rajak, Tessa, 4, 167, 219, 233, 234, 251, 260, 261, 262, 269
Rakel, Claudia, 244
Redditt, Paul L., 260
Reed, Annette Yoshiko, 4, 178, 233, 264, 265, 266
Reese, James M., 138, 147, 257, 259
Reeves, John C., 266
Regev, Eyal, 250
Reymond, Eric D., 270
Rindge, Matthew, 271
Rosen-Zvi, Ishay, 134, 256
Rowland, Christopher, 174, 263, 265
Ryan, Daniel, 262

Sacchi, Paolo, 263
Saldarini, Anthony, 159, 164, 261, 262
Sanders, Jack T., 254
Sanders, James A., 220, 270
Satlow, Michael, 129, 233, 234, 242, 252, 254
Schellenberg, Ryan S., 242
Schmitz, Barbara, 242, 243, 244
Schöpflin, Karin, 235, 246
Schorch, Stefan, 237
Schuller, Eileen, 269
Schwartz, Daniel R., 95, 99–100, 106, 109, 249, 250, 251, 252
Schwartz, Seth, 233–34, 251, 263
Seidman, Naomi, 271
Siegert, Folker, 233
Simkovich, Malka, 239, 250, 270
Skehan, Patrick, 129
Skemp, Vincent T. M., 235
Smith, Mark S., 270

Soll, William, 42–43, 239, 240, 242

Spolsky, Ellen, 246

Steck, Odil Hannes, 163, 261, 262

Stephens, Susan A., 236

Steussy, Marti J., 245

Stocker, Margarita, 243, 244

Stone, Meredith J., 237

Stone, Michael E., 181, 206, 247, 257, 259, 263, 264, 265, 266, 267, 268, 269

Stoneman, Richard, 236

Stroup, Christopher, 263

Stuckenbruck, Loren, 176, 184, 243, 264, 265

Talshir, Zipora, 113, 252

Tamási, Balázs, 212, 269

Testuz, Michel, 198–99, 267

Thomas, Samuel I., 254, 271

Thompson, Stith, 245

Tiller, Patrick A., 265

Tomes, Roger, 262

Torrey, Charles C., 235

Trafton, Joseph L., 270

Turner, Victor, 236

Ullendorff, Edward, 120, 253

Van den Heever, Gerardus, 240

Van den Hoek, Annewies, 246

Van der Horst, Pieter, 222, 247

VanderKam, James, 180, 187, 200, 264, 265, 266

van der Toorn, Karel, 40, 239

Van Gennep, Arnold, 236

Van Seters, John, 90, 249

Voigt, Edwin, 235

Warren, Meredith J. C., 206, 267

Wasserman, Emma, 151, 176, 184, 260

Wasserstein, Abraham, 234

Wasserstein, David J., 234

Weeks, Stuart, 43–44, 241

Weitzman, Steven, 42, 157, 227, 240, 241, 247, 261, 265

Werline, Rodney Alan, 247, 270

Weststeijn, Johan, 244

White, Sidnie Anne. *See* Crawford, Sidnie White

Williams, David S., 97–98, 248, 250

Wills, Lawrence M., 236, 237, 238, 239, 242, 244, 245, 246, 247, 248, 249, 250, 251, 252, 253, 254, 255, 257, 259, 260, 262, 263, 267, 268, 269, 270, 271

Winkler, John J., 236

Winninge, Mikael, 270

Winston, David, 137–38, 255, 256, 257, 258, 259, 261

Wintermute, O. S., 267

Wiseman, T. P., 236

Witakowski, Witold, 252

Wojciechowski, Michael, 260

Wolter, Michael, 174, 263

Wright, Benjamin G., 85–86, 234, 244, 248, 254, 255, 256, 262–63, 264, 265, 271

Wright, Jacob, 252

Wright, J. Edward, 269

Yerushalmi, Yosef, 116, 252–53

Zsengellér, József, 239, 243

Zuber, Beat, 253

Zurawski, Jason, 201, 256, 260, 267

Hebrew Bible

Genesis	43, 193–95, 200–201
1:2	172
2:16–17	263
3:22	263
4:25	177
5:24	177
6	183–85
6:4	265
6:5	267
15:6	36
18:9	36
22	38, 157
24	38, 42–43
29	42
34	42, 55, 195, 200
37–50	23, 27, 42, 231, 258
41:39	124
Exodus	149, 150, 193, 195, 208, 259
12:2	200
15	240
15:3	55
18:21	95
18:25	95
20–23	188
24:1–7	234
34:6–7	217, 221
Leviticus	
15	237
16:8	188
17–26	196
18–20	188
19	265
20:10	68
Numbers	
5	68
25:1–9	94
27	46
Deuteronomy	42–46, 90, 98, 138, 188, 200, 221, 227, 229, 241, 265
4	129
4:30	221
5:26	247
6:4–7	103
13:6–7	270
13:12–15	94
15:11	262
17	85
17–18	138
20:1–9	95
23:1	146
23:2–3	184
26:14	242
28–33	163
29–30	168
30	129, 160
32	129
32:17–18	163
33:29	163
Joshua	93
17:3–6	46
24	150

Judges	54, 90, 93, 94, 249
3	55
3:11	39
3:30	39
4–5	55
5:31	39
8:28	39
1 Samuel	14, 90, 96, 111
2	247
5:5	79
2 Samuel	14, 90, 96, 111
22	247
1 Kings	14, 90, 96, 111
3:5–15	146
4:32	223
18	79
22:16	252
2 Kings	14, 90, 96, 111
13:21	228
21	221
Isaiah	178, 200, 222
6:3	217
11:2–5	224
40–66	160, 162
40:4	163
40:18–41:7	259
44:9–20	166, 259
45:1–7	78
45:21	55
47	162
52–53	139, 190, 231, 258
54:1	145
56	145
56:3–5	146
57:6	242
60:2–3	163
61	215
65:4	242

Jeremiah	158, 160, 161, 164–66, 178, 212
3	245
10:3–8	259
10:10	247
11:18–12:6	261
15:10–21	261
16:5	242
17:14–18	261
18:18–23	261
20:7–18	261
27–33	163
29	164
33:11	238
38:7	170
51	79
51:44	247
Ezekiel	178, 207, 229
7:19–20	237
20	150
23	245
Amos	
6:10	242
Jonah	22, 60, 76, 246
2	247
Nahum	
1:7	238
Habakkuk	81–82
Psalms	200, 217, 223, 269
1	127
3	269
7	269
8	30
14	258
18	269
19	30
21	30
34	127, 269

Psalms (*continued*)

37	127
42–72	269
44	74
51	269, 270
52	269
54	269
56	269
57	269
59	269
60	269
63	269
74	74
78	150
79	74
80	74
96	75
97	75
100:5	238
105	150
106	150
106:1	238
112	127
135	150
136	75
142	269
148	75
151	12, 17, 218–20
151–155	17, 217, 220–21

Proverbs	42, 124, 127–34, 188, 227, 255
1–9	126
8	125
8–9	130, 228
10–30	126
16:1–22:16	124

Job	40, 45, 114, 126, 127, 135, 205–7, 212, 240, 258
28	160–61
38	263

Song of Songs	3
Ruth	43, 93
Lamentations	164, 223
1:17	237
Ecclesiastes	3, 126, 127, 134, 135, 140

Daniel	18, 21–27, 31, 40, 43, 53, 54, 56, 58, 64–82, 99, 115, 124, 126, 127, 139, 146, 173, 174, 177–79, 207, 217, 228, 230, 235, 246, 264
1:8	32
1:17	175
1:20	124
1–4	55
1–6	23, 36, 42, 87, 126, 141
2	113
3	84, 119, 258
4	113
4:13	184
4:17	184
4:23	184
5	83, 113, 259
6	84, 258
7	190
7–12	11, 127, 141, 229
7:9	190
7:11	175
7:13–14	190
7:27	141
8–12	11
9	160, 164, 221, 228, 262
10	230
10–12	186
11–12	203, 229

11:40	173		205, 208, 221, 228,
12	141, 229, 230		229, 235, 260, 261,
12:3	141		262
		1:15–3:8	74
Ezra	93, 96, 109, 111–13,	3–4	126, 189
	115–16, 142, 160,		
	171, 173, 177, 194,	2 Baruch	17, 18, 127, 181, 187,
	195, 199, 207, 221,		202–4, 211–16, 228,
	229, 231, 249, 252,		229, 230, 268
	264	2:1	269
1–6	115	5:5	269
4:7	164	9:1	269
4:11	164	10:2	269
8	234	46:1–3	269
8–10	160	48	229
9	74, 160, 228	48:42–47	267
9:3	115	50	229
		50–51	258
Nehemiah	93, 96, 103, 109,	51	141
	111–13, 116, 146,	51:10	141
	160, 170, 171, 194,	54:15–22	267
	195, 199, 201, 208,	56:5–7	267
	242, 249, 252, 267	59	263
2:7	164	77:13–16	269
2:10	47	85:1–5	269
7–8	111		
9	74, 150, 160, 221,	4 Baruch	17, 66, 158, 169–71
	228		
		Bel and the	
1 and 2 Chron-		Dragon	18, 23, 27, 65, 77–82,
icles	90, 93, 109, 111–13,		87, 117, 120, 151,
	192, 221		166, 231, 259
2 Chr 7:1–3	103		
33:10–13	222	Ben Sira	4, 11, 12, 13, 17, 25, 42,
33:12–13	221		56, 67, 114, 124,
35:1–36:21	111		125, 127, 128–35,
			140, 144, 146, 148,
			153, 159, 175, 192,
Books of the Apocrypha			205, 207, 223, 224,
			227, 228, 229, 231,
Apocalypse of			254, 255, 256
Weeks	*See* 1 Enoch	1:10	254
		5:11	234
(1) Baruch	14, 17, 66, 124, 129,	9:1–9	255
	130, 140, 158–69,		

Ben Sira (*continued*)

15:11–12	234		203, 207, 214–16,
15:11–17	141, 230		228–30, 255, 262,
15:11–20	203		264, 265
16:1–4	255	1:1	264
19:2–3	252, 255	1:7–8	264
22:3–6	255	1:9	12, 192
23:22–27	255	5:5–10	264
24	126, 160, 162, 164,	6–11	184
	189	8	184
24:9–11	16	9:8–9	184
24:33	254	10:4	238
25:16–26	255	10:9	184
25:22	241	10:21	264
26:1–18	255	12:2–3	184
30:18	242	20	230
31:25	255	37–71	141
31:26–31	252	42	130, 228
33:10–15	141	62–63	141
34:1–8	255	72–82	194
36:21–25	255	92–105	141
37:27–31	255	102:5	141, 187
41:5–9	255	102:6–103:15	141
42:9–14	255	103:3–4	141, 187
43	247	104:2	141
43:6–7	194	104:6	141, 187
44–50	138, 150		
44:16	191, 255	Epistle of	
49:13	252	Enoch	*See* 1 Enoch
49:14	191		
50	248	Epistle of	
		Jeremiah	*See* Letter of
Book of the			Jeremiah
Luminaries	*See* 1 Enoch		
		1 Esdras	17, 40, 88, 90–92,
Book of the			109–15, 192, 201,
Watchers	*See* 1 Enoch		252, 267
		1:33	90
Ecclesiasticus	*See* Ben Sira	1:42	90
		3:1–5:6	21, 23, 27, 113, 117,
1 Enoch	4–5, 11, 12, 14, 17, 116,		124, 218
	127, 131, 142, 173,	8:68–9:36	115
	174, 175, 177–93,	9:37–55	112
	196, 197, 199, 200,	2 Esdras	*See* 4 Ezra

3 Esdras	17	Josippon	5, 18, 33, 70, 77, 79, 82, 88, 92, 108, 116–23, 158, 170
Esther (Greek)	3, 10, 14, 18, 21–35, 36, 40–41, 44, 48, 53, 54, 60, 62, 67, 74, 83, 84, 85, 86, 87, 106, 113, 124, 127, 139, 146, 219, 228, 229, 230, 231, 235, 237–38, 244, 246, 258, 268	Jubilees	4, 5, 12, 17, 90, 99, 104, 116, 131, 151, 159, 178, 179, 181, 189, 191, 192–201, 204, 228, 229, 230, 264
6	113	5:2	267
6:13	25	12:2–5	259
8:5	164	20:8–9	259
9:26	164	22:16–23	115
14	74	23	102, 186
14:1–15:5	25	23:13–18	240
14:11–19	247	23:16	245
16:3–6	248	23:31	141
16:10–16	248	Judith	10, 13, 14, 15, 17, 18, 21–24, 26, 29, 33, 36, 39, 40, 42, 43, 44, 48, 49, 51, 52–64, 67, 70, 80, 83, 84, 85, 86, 93, 97, 98, 99, 100, 108, 117, 121, 124, 133, 135, 139, 146, 176, 228, 229, 231, 235, 241, 244, 246, 248
4 Ezra	12, 13, 17, 127, 141, 170, 181, 183, 201–14, 228–30, 252, 268–69		
3:7	267		
3:28–36	268		
4:5–9	263		
5:36–37	263		
6:18–28	229		
7:21–24	267		
7:83–84	158		
7:102–5	228	1:7–11	62
7:105–11	150	6:2	55
7:113–114	229	8–10	237
7:118	267	8:29	124
14:45–46	12	9	25, 148
5 Ezra	118, 120, 169, 208–11, 268	12:1–4	32
		13:18–20	16
		15:9	16
6 Ezra	118, 208–11	16	247
15.43–16:1	268	16:23–25	228

Letter of
Jeremiah   12, 18, 66, 69, 79,
                   124, 151, 158–61,
                   164–69, 186, 187,
                   235, 250, 259, 262

1 Maccabees   10, 11, 17, 18, 92–105,
                   109, 117, 228

1   252
2:37   246
2:60   246
2:51–60   150
6:34   82
7:26–50   243
10:24   262
13:47–48   250

2 Maccabees   17, 18, 26, 56, 82,
                   83–84, 88–93,
                   98–100, 101–9, 154,
                   169, 176, 181, 214,
                   228, 229, 231–32,
                   250, 252

1:13   170
2   252
2:1–4   263
2:21   251
2:24   90
2:24–32   129
2:30   90
2:32   90
6–7   153
7   74, 119, 120, 258,
                   260
7:7–14   261
7:24   250, 262
7:37–38   155
10:4   251
12:43–44   16
13:9   251
15   158
15:1–36   243

15:11   250, 262
15:14–16   228
15:28–36   55
15:37–39   91

3 Maccabees   17, 21, 24, 27, 82–87,
                   88–89, 106, 120,
                   230, 248, 258

4 Maccabees   7, 17, 88, 102, 118,
                   122, 135, 140,
                   153–58, 181, 187,
                   214, 229, 231, 261

2:23   261
3:19   90
5:24   261
5:34   261
7:19   141
9:22   260
9:26–10:21   261
13:9   77
13:17   141
14:5–6   260
16:13   260
16:25   141
17:7   90
17:12   260
18:23   260

Meqabyan   17, 18, 88, 92, 108,
                   116, 118–21, 123,
                   170, 181, 214, 229,
                   253

Odes (biblical
collection)   76, 217, 222
7   76
8   76

Parables of
Enoch   See 1 Enoch

Paralipomena
of Jeremiah   See 4 Baruch

Prayer of
Azariah and
Song of the
Three   65, 73–77, 79, 82,
                           217, 220, 222, 228

Prayer of
Manasseh   17, 112, 217, 221–22,
                           228

3:5   103

Psalms of
Solomon   19–20, 163, 217,
                           223–26, 235, 261

Similitudes of
Enoch   *See* 1 Enoch

Sirach   *See* Ben Sira

Susanna   18, 22, 23, 26, 27, 31,
                           33, 44, 48, 49, 61,
                           62, 65–73, 76, 78,
                           80, 82, 115, 117,
                           135, 218, 229, 231,
                           245, 246, 258

Tobit   11, 12, 14, 15, 17,
                           21–27, 34–52, 53,
                           55, 117, 119, 124,
                           135, 181, 199, 229,
                           230, 231, 238, 239,
                           240, 241, 242, 243,
                           246

Wisdom of
Solomon   13, 14, 17, 79, 120,
                           124–27, 131, 134,
                           135–53, 154–56,
                           181, 187, 192, 214,
                           223, 227, 228, 229,
                           230, 261
1:1   246
2   121

2–5   23, 169, 189, 203,
                           214–15, 231, 238
2:24   13
3:1   16
4:10–11   191
7:17–18   244
7:17–21   257, 263
9:15   234
10   259
12:12   13, 234
12:20   234
13–15   166
13:5   12–13
13:8   12–13
14:24   12–13
14:27   12–13

New Testament

Matthew   40, 41, 215
6   49
16:14   228
27:43   153

Mark   40, 139
13   210

Luke   40, 41
1:19   230
4:18–19   215
6:24–26   187
10   234

John   60, 125, 127, 139, 191,
                           213, 258
2   150
4:22–23   256
18:38   252

Acts   249, 250, 263
8   258
13:13–41   250, 262
15   196

Romans   138, 187

1   260

1:19–32   153

1:20–29   12–13

3:25   158

5   267

5:10   158

7   156

9:20–23   234

1 Corinthians

15   267

2 Corinthians

5:1–4   234

Galatians

4:21–31   209

Hebrews   150

11   150

11:5   192

11:35–36   108

13:22   250, 262

James   187, 188

1:13   234

1:15   267

1:19   234

1 Peter

1:19   158

2 Peter

2:4   192

3:6   192

1 John

1:7   158

Jude

14–15   12, 192, 234

Revelation

14:8   268

16:19–19:3   268

Other Jewish Sources

4QBerakhot   247

4QInstruction   205, 268

4QWords of the
Luminaries   247

Alphabet of
Ben Sira   135

Apocalypse of
Sedrach   211

Apocryphon of
Jeremiah   158

Aramaic Levi
Document   48

Aristeas,
Letter of   8–10, 138, 234

135–38   259

Aristobulus   270

Artapanus,
On Moses   21, 83

3 Baruch   158

Cleodemus
Malchus   92

Community
Rule   188

Demetrius the
Chronographer   92, 198

Derek Eretz
Zuta

1   192

2 Enoch   191

3 Enoch   191

Eupolemus   88, 92

Ezra, Expansions of 211

Ezra, Greek Apocalypse of 211

Ezra, Questions of 211

Ezra, Revelation of the Blessed 211

Genesis Apocryphon 48, 90, 179, 192

Genesis Rabbah
1:2 126
26:6 192
38:13 77
68:14 79

Jason of Cyrene 92, 101

Jerahmeel, Chronicles of 18, 70, 82, 116

Joseph and Aseneth 21, 26, 29, 53, 60, 139, 140, 222
10:9–17 25
14:14–15 25

Josephus 12, 26, 33, 81, 98, 100, 113, 116, 117, 134, 225, 238, 271–72

—*Against Apion*
—1.37 12
—1.201–203 27, 80
—2.51–55 82

—*Antiquities*
—10.70–83 116
—11.1–157 116
—11.239–253 238

—12 21
—12.9 174
—12.154–236 47
—12.412 107
—20 21

—*Jewish War*
—2.152–53 158

—Book 6 17, 88, 92, 120, 122–23, 170

(Pseudo-) Jubilees 200

Justus of Tiberias 92

Lamentations Rabbah
1:16 108
1:50 108, 158

Lives of the Prophets
1:1 222

Maimonides
—*Mishneh Torah Megillah veHanukkah*
—2:18 32

Mekhilta de-Rabbi Ishmael
Bo'1 216

Midrash Rabbah
—5.9 234

Midras Tadshe (Book of Asaph) 200

Mishnah
—*Avot* 2:10 270

Mishnah (*continued*)
—4:1   267

—*Berakhot 9:5*   267

—*Hagigah* 2:1   176–77

—*Sanhedrin*
10:1   12

—*Sotah* 1:5   68

—*Yadayim* 4:5   3–4

—*Yevamot* 4:13   184

Nachmanides,
153

Nicolaus of
Damascus   92, 101

Pesikta Rabbati
—43:180   108

Philo   9, 26, 81, 134, 139,
                                  140, 154, 156, 256,
                                  258, 259, 271

—*Life of Moses*   9

—*On Drunken-*
ness 146–148   268

—*On Flight* 63   257

—*On Joseph*   257

—*On the Deca-*
logue 46–47   234

—*On the*
Giants   191

—*Special Laws*
3.72   257
—3.125–136   242

—*That the*
Worse 83   257

(Pseudo-)
Philo, *Biblical*
Antiquities   90, 267

Prayer of
Joseph   127, 140

Prayer of
Nabonidus   21, 27, 74, 231, 253

Psalms Scroll   218

Reworked
Pentateuch   90, 192

Royal Family
of Adiabene
(Josephus,
Antiquities
Book 20)   21

Seder Olam
Rabbah
28–29   22–23
30   176

Sefer
Hazikhronot   62, 82, 108

Songs of the
Sabbath
Sacrifice   217

Tales of the
Persian Court   21, 27, 29, 48, 231,
                                  253, 258

Talmud,
Babylonian
—*Baba Batra*
16a   267

—*Gittin* 57b   108

—*Megillah* 7b   3–4
—14b   216

—*Sanhedrin* 21b   113

—*Shabbat* 21b   251

Temple Scroll   90, 138, 181–82, 192, 194

Testament of Abraham   21, 45, 230

Testament of Job   21

Testament of Joseph   258

Testament of Moses   102

Testament of Qahat   48

Thallus   92

Theophilus   92

Tobiad Romance (Josephus, *Antiquities* Book 12)   21, 47, 250

Tosefta
—*Hullin* 2:24   158

—*Yadayim* 2:13   4

Visions of Amram   48

Zohar   153

Other Christian Sources

Acts of Paul and Thecla
32–35   83

Ambrose   70, 211

Apostolic Constitutions   222

Aquinas, Thomas
—*Summa Theologica* 3.4.4   169

Athanasius
—*Festal Letter* 39   235

Athenagoras
—*Legatio pro Christianis* 9   169

Augustine
—*City of God*
—18.43   235

—*Epistle*
—28   235

—*On Christian Doctrine*
2.8.12–13   235
—2.22   235

Barnabas, *Epistle of*   187, 188
4:2   192
8:2   246
11:9   216
12:1   13
12:2   211
17:1   246

Benedicite   76

Birck, Sixt   70

Chrysostom, John   108

—*On the Maccabees*   251

1 Clement   150, 223, 262
3:4   13
27:5   13, 153

1 Clement (*continued*)
55:4–6   13, 22, 62
60.2   246

Clement of
Alexandria   14, 113, 116

—*Protreptic*   257

—*Stromateis*
3:16   211

Cyprian, 108

—*On Fortune* 11   251

Cyril of
Jerusalem
—*Catechetical*
Lectures
4.33–36   235

Didache   187

Didaskalia
Apostolorum   222

Epiphanius
—*Panarion*
8.6.1–4   13

Gospel of Mary   139

Gregory of
Nazianzus   70, 108

—*Homily 15,*
On the
Maccabees   251

(Pseudo-)
Hegesippus   117

Hippolytus   70

Irenaeus
—*Against*
Heresies
1.20.1   235

—Jerome   48–49

—*Commentary*
on Daniel 1:3   146

—*Commentary*
on Jeremiah,
praef.   169

—*Helmeted*
Preface
(*Prologus*
Galeatus)   14

Justin Martyr
—*Apology* 1.46   76

Melito of Sardis   234

Odes of
Solomon   139, 216, 217, 222,
                    235

Origen   13, 100, 108,
                    234–35, 250

—*Commentary*
on Matthew
10.18   234
13.57   234

—*Exhortation*
to Martyrdom   76, 158
22–27   251

—*Letter to*
Africanus 7   66

—*Prologue to*
Song of Songs   234

Passio Sanc-
torum Macha-
baeorum   158

Questions of St.
Gregory about
the Souls of Men 211

Rufinus
—*Exposition of the Creed* 30   234

Tertullian   14, 169

—*Adversus Iudaeos* 4.10   107

—*On Female Fashion* 1.3   192, 235

—*On Prayer* 29   76

Theodoret of Cyrus   76, 169

Greek, Roman, and Ancient Near Eastern Sources

Achilles Tatius
—*Leucippe and Clitophon*   24

Aesop, Life of   24, 252

Ahikar, Story of   21, 23, 24, 27, 36, 39, 42, 67, 81, 102, 146, 253, 258

Alexander Romance   21, 24, 102

Apuleius
—*Golden Ass* (or *Metamorphoses*)   24, 147, 254

—Book 11   147, 257

Aristotle   22

—*Poetics*
1450a–51b   89
1459a   89

—*Protreptic*   257, 261

Berossus   198

Chaldean Oracles   125

Cicero
—*On Duties* 2.2–8   257

—*On Invention* 1.19.27   236

—*On the Nature of the Gods* 2.12–15   260

—*Tusculan Disputations* 5.5–11   257

(Pseudo-)Cicero, *To Herrennius*
—1.8.12–13   236

Ctesias, *Persica*   29, 56, 89, 114, 146, 252

Duris   250

Galen, *Protreptic*   257

Euripides, *Antiope*   89

Heliodorus, *An Ephesian Story*   24
8.9   237

(Pseudo-)Heraclitus *Epistle* 4   151

Hermetica   125

Herodotus, *Histories*   29, 56, 83, 85, 89, 90, 91, 114, 249
1.136   252
1.138   252
1.183   78

Herodotus, *Histories* (*continued*)

2.121	80
7.101	252
7.101–4	56

Homer, *Odyssey*   240

| 2.10–11 | 240 |

Horace
Satire 1.8   260

Isocrates, *To
Nicocles*   257

Longus, *Daph-
nis and Chloe*   24

Ninus Romance   24
A.IV.20–V.4   31

Orphic texts   147–48, 220

*Papyrus
Insinger*   129

Petronius,
Satyricon   24

Phylarchus   250

Plato	22, 60, 85, 137,
	139–41, 147–48,
	154, 156, 261, 265

—*Clitophon*   257

—*Euthydemus*
278e–282d   257

—*Menexenus*
236d–248e   262

—*Phaedo* 81c   148, 257
—93–94   261

—*Symposium*   114, 151

—*Theaetetus*

| 176b | 257 |
| —176e–177a | 258 |

Polybius   89

2.56.7–12	250
3.31.13	250
12.23.7	250
12.24.5	250
16.14.1	250
29.12.1–3	250
29.12.8	250

Quintilian
2.4.2   236

*Satire on the
Trades*   129

*Sayings of the
Seven Sages*   129

Seneca, *Letter
to Lucilius*   257

Sophocles,
Antigone   240

Thucydides   89, 96, 262

Xenophon of
Athens   56, 114

—*Anabasis*   89

—*Cyropaedia*   29, 89

—*Hellenica*   89

Xenophon of
Ephesus, *An
Ephesian Story*   24

1.6	44
4.2	75
4.6	81